Strategic
Database
Marketing

For Helena

Also by Arthur Middleton Hughes

Successful E-Mail Marketing Strategies
  By Arthur Middleton Hughes and Arthur Sweetser
  RACOM 2009

Customer Churn Reduction and Retention for Telecoms
  RACOM 2008

The Complete Database Marketer
  McGraw-Hill Publishing Company 1991

The Complete Database Marketer, 2nd Edition
  McGraw-Hill Publishing Company 1996

Strategic Database Marketing
  McGraw-Hill Publishing Company 1994

Strategic Database Marketing, 2nd Edition
  McGraw Hill Publishing Company 2000

Strategic Database Marketing, 3rd Edition
  McGraw Hill Publishing Company 2006

The Customer Loyalty Solution
  McGraw-Hill Publishing Company 2003

Don't Blame Little Arthur; Blame the Damned Fool
Who Entrusted Him with the Eggs
  Database Marketing Institute 1998

The American Economy
  Norvec Publishing Company 1968

The American Economy, 2nd Edition
  Norvec Publishing Company 1969

Strategic Database Marketing

FOURTH EDITION

ARTHUR M. HUGHES

New York   Chicago   San Francisco   Lisbon   London
Madrid   Mexico City   Milan   New Delhi   San Juan
Seoul   Singapore   Sydney   Toronto

Contents

Contents

Acknowledgments

Virtually all the ideas that you will read in this book have occurred to me as a result of stimulating contact with the many master database and Internet marketers quoted in these pages. If you find useful concepts in this book, it comes about because in writing it, "I stood on the shoulders of giants." I particularly want to acknowledge my gratitude to several who helped me in special ways:

Paul Wang, Associate Professor of Marketing, Northwestern University. Paul and I gave 20 two-day seminars together to more than 1,200 database marketers over a five-year period. Paul, more than anyone except Helena, is responsible for the success I have had in this field.

Frederick Reichheld, author of *The Loyalty Effect*. This amazing book, filled with wonderfully insightful ideas has been an inspiration to me.

Brian Woolf, President of the Retail Strategy Center and author of *Customer Specific Marketing*. Brian understands supermarket marketing better than anyone in the United States. His helpful comments on the draft first edition of this book were largely responsible for its success.

Bob James, formerly with Centura Bank. Bob was the first to teach me the science of bank profitability analysis. He is an excellent marketer and a good teacher.

Randall Grossman, Senior Vice President of Bank One in Columbus, Ohio. Randall, formerly with Fleet Bank, pioneered in linking profitability analysis with lifetime value and potential lifetime value to create a super bank customer marketing system.

Bruce Clarkson of Sears Canada. Bruce is one of those people who can see the forest when he is walking among the trees. He explained the principles involved in Sears Canada's marketing reorganization in a way that universalizes the general principles involved.

Paula Hart, former Marketing Director at Dayton Hudson and creator of their *Regards Program*. Paula is an extremely creative marketer who knows how to win customer loyalty.

Arthur Sweetser, former COO of e-Dialog, now CMO of 89 Degrees, who gave me a chance to start in the e-mail marketing world and coauthored with me *Successful E-mail Marketing Strategies* (RACOM 2009). Arthur is a born leader who was primarily responsible for the creation and expansion of e-Dialog to a $100 million company.

1

How Database Marketing Has Changed

But it's not just the stores. It's the social life. The Internet lets us sort ourselves into interest groups and communities that have no relation to geography. I know dozens of married couples that met through online villages of one sort or another. Only a few of them met through dating or matchmaking services. Most of them were posting on forums. It was as if they had all been invited to an online party, and, liking each other's public conversation, they went off into a corner and had a long, private chat.

—ORSON SCOTT CARD

The purpose of database marketing is the same today as it has always been: to create and maintain a bond of loyalty between you and your customers that will last a lifetime. The goal has not changed, but the methods have. We still maintain information about our customers in a database and use it as a basis for our communications with them. In the past we used direct mail, catalogs, and phone calls to communicate. Today we use these plus e-mails, Web sites, cell phone text, voice messages, and social media. These new developments make communications much less expensive and more frequent, but they are also much more complex. Most companies have found it useful to hire a service bureau to maintain their database, and an e-mail service provider (ESP) to send their e-mails and cell phone messages.

1

The process begins with a marketing database that keeps all sorts of information about customers: not only what they buy, but their demographics, families, responses, and preferences. Information storage has become much more sophisticated—using relational databases—and much less expensive. Moore's law describes a long-term trend in the history of computing hardware. The number of transistors that can be placed inexpensively on an integrated circuit doubles approximately every two years. The trend has continued for more than half a century and is not expected to stop until 2020 or later. This same trend has affected disk storage and transmission speed and capacity. The result is that you can afford to retain and use all the information you can collect about a customer in your marketing programs. The only limitation is human creative ability and the willingness to devise methods for using the data. This is the problem that we address in this book.

The biggest change in database marketing in the last decade has been the arrival of Web sites, e-mail, and mobile marketing. At first these seemed like a godsend. The main problem with database marketing was the high cost of communications with customers—$600 per thousand messages. You had all this wonderful information in your database that you could use to build relationships, but you were limited, in most cases, to about one letter a month because of the cost. In the last 10 years, with Web sites including social media, e-mail, and the iPhone, you can send messages to your subscribers and customers for less than $6.00 per thousand—a cost so low that the delivery cost is inconsequential.

E-mail has become the primary way for companies to communicate with their customers. Direct mail is still alive and well, but e-mail is gaining on it. But there is a third communication method that is also growing: one-third of consumers in both the United States and the United Kingdom are viewing their e-mails on their iPhone or similar mobile devices. The use of mobile e-mail is most prevalent among younger consumers, with over half of them spending a significant part of every day glued to their phones. Mobile use is exploding in all directions. All these new communications methods can make use of the information in a customer marketing database. Here, at last, is a way to use your database to build really close relationships with each customer using the data you have collected. What we had not figured on was that the low cost of e-mail and mobile messages has become a curse because marketers have discovered that e-mails are so inexpensive that you can afford to send messages to your customers every week or even every day. The more you send, the more revenue you gain. More and more major corporations in the United States and elsewhere have been sending e-mails, and sometimes mobile messages, to all their subscribers all the time.

Subscriber inboxes are overflowing. The big problem is that the messages, while they can be and sometimes are personalized, are seldom filled with dynamic content based on what we know about each customer. We have these rich databases, but we do not use the rich data that they hold. To use it requires many creative staff members who dream up the dynamic content. The thought is, "Subscribers who are over 65 have certain interests, while other subscribers are college students who have different interests. We will vary our messages based on this knowledge, and also do that for about a half-dozen other subscriber segments to make our relationships richer for them and more profitable for us." This makes a lot of sense, but few marketers today are doing anything like that. They are blasting identical content to every subscriber or customer whose e-mail or address they can get their hands on.

Using the data to target specific customer groups sounds great, doesn't it? That has always been the promise of database marketing. We could send dynamic content when we were sending one message a month. We cannot afford to do this today if we are sending one message to each person every day. The problem boils down to one simple fact: *The lift we get from dynamic content does not seem to be as great as the lift we get from frequent communications.* You can't afford to do both, so you go with the most profitable.

In the pages of this book, we deal with the ramifications of this trade-off between frequency and dynamic content. There are many solutions, and we point them out. To help you understand what is going on today, we present the actual results of 80 large marketers who together send more than 1.2 billion e-mail and mobile messages to their 174 million subscribers every month. There are graphs that show how these 80 companies are generating more than $5.4 billion in annual sales *resulting from these electronic messages.* This $5.4 billion probably represents about only 5 to 7 percent of their total annual sales in all channels. The companies in these charts include major airlines, car rental companies, sports associations, and scores of major familiar retailers. You will learn what is going on in the real electronic marketing world in a way that is available nowhere else. You will learn how your company can use similar methods to yield comparable results.

Take a good look at Figure 1.1. It tells a story that is spelled out in detail in this book. It explains a lot about what has happened to strategic database marketing.

ROI Comparison	Direct Mail	E-mail
Pieces mailed	1,000	1,000
Cost of mailing	$600	$6.00
Conversion rate	2.67%	0.11%
Sales	26.70	1.10
Revenue per sale	$100	$100
Revenue	$2,670	$110
Return on investment	$4.45	$18.33

Figure 1.1 ROI Comparison

The Old Corner Grocer

In my seven previous books on database marketing, I described the customer relationships of the Old Corner Grocer and how his loyalty-building methods are carried out today by modern database marketing. The analogy is still true.

Back in the days before there were supermarkets, all the groceries in the United States were sold in small corner grocery stores. In many cases, the proprietor could be seen at the entrance to his store, greeting the customers by name. "Hello Mrs. Hughes. Are your son and his family coming for Thanksgiving again this year?"

These guys built the loyalty of their customers by recognizing them by name, by greeting them, by knowing them, by doing favors for them. They helped by carrying heavy packages out to customers' cars (there were no shopping carts in those days). These veterans no longer exist.

The supermarkets put them out of business. Prices came down. Quality went up. The corner grocer had 800 stock-keeping units (SKUs) in his store. Supermarkets today have more than 30,000 SKUs. He had a few hundred customers. Supermarkets today have thousands of customers.

As a result, the familiarity of the Old Corner Grocer that established loyalty in the old days has become much more difficult to create and sustain—until database marketing came along. Using the techniques in this book, it is now possible for a large corporation with a marketing database to build a relationship with customers that re-creates the recognition and loyalty of the Old Corner Grocer. We do this over the phone (using caller ID, voice, text, and e-mails), through creative use of a Web site and e-mails, and by providing our employees in marketing, sales, customer service, or at retail counters and teller windows with the kind of information about their customers that the corner grocer used to keep in his head. We are returning today to methods that worked wonderfully in the old days. They work today. They build loyalty, repeat sales, cross sales, and profits. This book explains the principles and provides scores of examples.

Customers have become dominant. There are today in most parts of the United States, the UK and scores of other countries, lots of different stores selling similar products. Most families and businesses today have PCs and advanced smart cell phones—both equipped with Google—so they can look up and find any product or service they want to buy, with comparative prices and customer reviews. You can't fool them anymore. What do they want?

What Customers Want

Companies are discovering what their customers want and selling them that. It is customer-based marketing. But it is really more than that. What customers want today can be summed up in a few general concepts:

- *Recognition:* People want to be recognized as individuals, with individual desires and preferences. They like being called by name.
- *Service:* Customers want thoughtful service provided by knowledgeable people who have access to the database and therefore know whom they are talking to and what they are are interested in.
- *Convenience:* People are very busy. They don't have time to drive a couple of miles to do business. They want to do business from where they are by cell or landline phone or by using the Web with companies that remember their names, addresses, credit card numbers, and purchase history.
- *Helpfulness:* Anything that you can do to make customers' lives simpler is appreciated. Merchants have to think every day, "How can I be more helpful to my customers?" Only those who come up with good answers will survive.
- *Information:* Customers are more literate today than ever before. They use the Internet. Technical information is as important to many of them as the product itself.
- *Identification:* People like to identify themselves with their products (like their cars) and their suppliers (like their cell phones). Companies can build on that need for identification by providing customers with a warm, friendly, helpful institution to identify with.

Whom Do They Listen To?

Increasingly today, customers listen to other customers. They participate in blogs. They read product reviews written by other customers. Young people participate in Facebook and Twitter, exchanging information that suppliers of products and services cannot control.

From 1985 to today, most large modern corporations have built customer marketing databases filled with personal information about their customers. Modern computer technology has been used to create relational databases that store a great deal of information on each household (or company, in the case of a business-to-business product). Not just the name and address are retained. Also kept are:

- E-mail address, plus the cookies that keep track of their Web visits
- Complete purchase history
- Customer service calls, complaints, returns, inquiries
- Outgoing marketing promotions and responses
- Results of customer surveys
- Household (or business) demographics: income, age, number of children, home value and type, and so on
- The profitability, RFM (Recency, Frequency, Monetary Analysis) code, and lifetime value of every customers in the database

What changed, however, is the method of using the database to communicate with customers. Before 2000, we had direct mail and telephone. Now, we have the Web, e-mail, and mobile devices which have changed everything:

- Every company has a Web site filled with information—most with shopping carts.
- Many companies send both catalogs and promotional e-mails to prospective customer.
- Most companies also send triggered messages to individual customers (described later in this book) that make it possible to send each of a million customers a different message based on the information in the database.

- Most companies send transaction messages ("Your product was shipped today.") which was impossible to do before (too slow and expensive). They use these transactions messages not only to keep customers informed but also to sell them additional products and services.

- Most e-mail and mobile communications today are filled with *links* which mean that every message can be an adventure: a gateway to every product and piece of information that the company has available. By using links you can do research, read reviews, print specifications, compare prices, and buy whatever interests you.

Two Kinds of Databases

There are really two different kinds of databases in any company that is engaged in direct marketing of products and services. One is an operational database and the other is a marketing database (see Figure 1.2).

An *operational database* is used to process transactions and get out the monthly statements:

- For a cataloger, this database is used to process the orders, charge the credit cards, arrange shipment, and handle returns and credits.

- For a bank, the operational database processes checks and deposits, maintains balances, and creates the monthly statements.

- For a telephone company, the operational database keeps track of the telephone calls made and arranges the billing for them.

A *marketing database* gets its data from the operational database, if there is one. This data consists of a summary of monthly transactions. But the marketing data also includes much more. It gets data from:

- Preferences and profiles provided by the customers.

- Promotion and response history from direct mail and e-mail marketing campaigns.

- Appended data from external sources such as KnowledgeBase Marketing, Donnelly, Claritas, and so on.

- Lifetime value and RFM analysis, leading to creation of customer segments.

- Modeling for churn and next-best product.

The marketing database passes data back to the operational database. It may tell the operational database:

- Which segment each customer has been placed in, which may lead to operational decisions. Gold customers, for example, may get different operational treatment from silver customers.
- Expressed customer preferences leading to different operational treatment: for hotels, smoking or nonsmoking rooms assigned automatically.

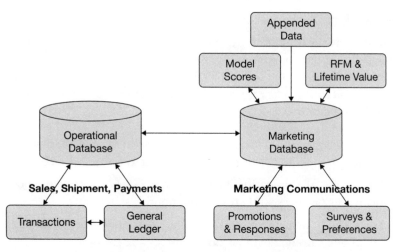

Figure 1.2 Operational and Marketing Databases

The operational database is run by Information Technology (IT). It is run on accounting principles and balances to the penny, since there are legal and tax aspects to its data. It is audited by external auditors. It contains only current data on customers. Old data is archived. There is no data on prospects until a sale is made.

In many companies, there are several marketing databases. For various reasons the database of catalog customers is often separate from the retail store customer database. The Web site and e-mail customer database may also often be kept separately. From the outside it seems like a simple matter to bring all these databases together to get a "360 degree" picture of each customer. But, in fact, this combination is often difficult to achieve. Why should this be so? The reasons are varied, but they often relate to internal company politics. In a typical bank, there are vice presidents for each major product: credit cards, home equity loans, retail (checking and savings accounts), insurance, and the like. The credit card manager receives no bonus or special recognition if some of his credit card customers sign up for a checking account. The retail vice president gets no special reward if some of her customers apply for a credit card. Yet any analysis of bank customers will show that the more different bank products the average customer has, the higher that customer's loyalty is to the bank, which translates to profits for the bank. The organization and compensation system does not reflect the theory of customer relationship management.

Relationship Buyers and Transaction Buyers

Professor Paul Wang described the difference between relationship buyers and transaction buyers.

Transaction buyers represent a major segment of any market. These customers try to engage in comparison shopping for every transaction. They read the ads, consult Google, make phone calls, and get comparative bids. For them, the past has no meaning. They have absolutely no loyalty. Never mind what the supplier did for you in the past. The question is what is your price today? They will shift suppliers of any product for a few pennies difference in price.

Transaction buyers usually get little service. Service is not important to them. Price is everything. There is not much point in trying to win their loyalty since they have none to give. Database marketing may be ineffective here—only discounting will work. They are seldom profitable customers, even though they may buy a lot of products, and they represent an important segment of any market. The best thing that could happen to these transaction buyers would be for them to shift over to buying from your competition. Give them the competitions' catalogs and phone numbers and hope they take the hint.

Relationship buyers are the customers for whom database marketing was invented. They are looking for a dependable supplier:

- Someone who cares about their needs, and who looks out for them.
- Someone who remembers what they bought in the past and gives them special services as a reward.
- Someone who takes an interest in their business and treats them as individuals.

Relationship buyers know that they could save a few dollars by shopping around. But they also recognize that if they do switch suppliers, they would lose something that they value very highly—the relationship they have built up with a dependable supplier that recognizes them and takes good care of them. Many of them also realize that there is an emotional and monetary cost to shopping around for every purchase. They want to concentrate on their success in life, not on their purchasing prowess.

By classifying your customers into these two types of buyers, you can focus your marketing efforts on the one segment that is really profitable: relationship buyers. Your database is used to record the purchases of these buyers and to give them personal recognition and special services. You recognize your gold customers. You communicate with them. You partner with them.

Sears Canada Shows How It's Done

For historical reasons, Sears Canada had separate operations for its catalog and retail stores. One day the company decided to build a combined customer marketing database. Once the database was built, Sears was able to measure the performance of catalog customers versus retail customers. The data was very revealing. Sears found that at that time the average catalog customer spent $492 dollars per year. The average retail customer spent $1,102 dollars per year. Customers shopping both channels were spending $1,883 per year with Sears.

This discovery led to a fundamental reorganization of the whole company. A central Executive Vice President (EVP) for marketing was set up who worked across all channels. Bruce Clarkson, general manager of relationship marketing for Sears Canada didn't stop at integrating catalogs with retail. Using the new database, he focused on retention, acquisition, and purchase stimulation. He proved that the strongest predictive variable for not shopping the catalog was exposure to bad service: out of stock, or merchandise that was not satisfactory. Sears could prove that money spent on improved service would increase customer retention.

Sears set up an RFM system with 189 cells, tracking recency on a quarter by quarter basis. Clarkson's analysis showed that in each quarter between 20,000 and 30,000 new customers acquired a Sears card, bought once, and never bought again. Sears spent a lot of money trying to get the card into people's hands but was not doing enough to get them to use the card. The new database showed that 14 percent of Sears customers were $2,500 plus buyers who contributed 50 percent of Sears total corporate merchandise revenues. Using its database to see what Web site customer did, the company found that 97 percent of sales volume was from people who had the paper catalog in front of them.

Sears used and continues to use its database to understand its customers. Then it took that crucial step to change its organization to make use of what it had learned. It became customer focused. It is a tremendous lesson for the rest of us.

E-mail Marketing Needs to Catch Up

Building a central marketing database is only a first step. In most companies today, e-mail marketing—the most powerful tool available—is not used productively. Direct mail is used carefully because it is expensive. E-mails are so inexpensive that most marketers send millions of identical messages on a daily basis to subscribers who are overwhelmed and annoyed by their overflowing inboxes. Database marketing is not being used effectively by most e-mail marketers—which means most major corporations today. This is a message that you will learn from this book. You will learn how to determine the lifetime value of your customers and of your e-mail subscribers. You will learn how to use that value to direct and manage your marketing program through all communication channels.

Looked at from the customers' point of view, database marketing through all channels is a way of making customers happy; of providing them with recognition, service, friendship, and information for which, in return, they will reward you with loyalty, retention, and increased sales. Genuine customer satisfaction is the goal and hallmark of satisfactory database marketing. If you are doing things right, your customers will be glad that you have a database and that they are on it. They will want to subscribe to and read your e-mails. They will come happily to your Web site and your retail stores. They will want to receive your catalogs. They will appreciate the things that you do for them. If you can develop and carry out strategies that bring this situation about, you are a master marketer. You will keep your customers for life, and you will be happy in your work. You will have made the world a better place to live in.

Take-Away Thoughts

- The purpose of database marketing is to create and maintain a bond of loyalty between you and your customers that will last a lifetime.

- Modern database marketing is trying to re-create for large companies the loyalty enjoyed by the Old Corner Grocers who knew their customers by sight and name.

- Database marketing has changed significantly because of Web sites, e-mail, and mobile marketing. These have reduced the cost of communication, but they have presented a serious problem: there are too many messages.

- Sending dynamically different messages to each customer is the goal, but the lift from customized content is less than the lift from frequent messages: frequency beats customization.

- Electronic links within messages permit customers to do research and discover every product you have for sale as well as a tremendous amount of previously unobtainable data.

- There are two types of database: operational and marketing. Companies must have both.

- Customers today want recognition, service, friendship, and information. They listen, often, more to other customers than to what you are saying to them.

A quiz on this chapter and all figures can be found at www.dbmarket ing.com/STM4. Those taking all the quizzes can receive a Successful Completion Certificate from the Database Marketing Institute which can be used in their résumé.

2

The "Vision Thing"

*It is not from the benevolence of the butcher, the brewer,
or the baker, that we expect our dinner, but from their
regard to their own interest. ... Every individual,
therefore, neither intends to promote the public interest,
nor knows how much he is promoting it. ... He intends
only his own security; and by directing that industry in
such a manner as its produce may be of the greatest
value, he intends only his own gain, and he is in this
... led by an invisible hand to promote an end which
was no part of his intention. ... Consumption is the
sole end and purpose of all production; and the interest
of the producer ought to be attended to only so far as it
may be necessary for promoting that of the consumer.
... The benefits of the division of labor must always be
limited ... by the extent of the market.*

—Adam Smith
The Wealth of Nations 1776

What is database marketing, and how does database marketing work?
How does it relate to direct mail, e-mail, social media, iPhones, and Web
sites? This chapter is aimed at answering these questions. We take a
broad look at the customer's situation today in contrast to the situation
in earlier times—decades and centuries. We attempt to place database
marketing and e-commerce in their historical perspectives as evolutionary forward steps. This chapter is what the first President George Bush
would have called "the vision thing."

Let's settle back, therefore, and see ourselves as painted figures on a grand historical canvas from the earliest Sumerian traders of 5000 BC, up through the industrial revolution, past the electric age, the automobile age, the nuclear age, the jet age, the computer age, the Internet age, and on into thetwenty-first century.

What Drives Industry?

Let's begin with a basic question. What drives industry? Production or marketing? In general, are products manufactured first and then marketed? Or are they marketed first and then manufactured to meet the needs of the market?

This is an important question for economists and marketers. It goes to the heart of the whole philosophy of marketing and particularly of database marketing and e-commerce. To answer it, let's go back to the industrial revolution—an epoch that changed the production system and led to our present affluence. Let's examine the role of marketing in this revolution.

The Industrial Revolution

For thousands of years before 1760, productivity in industry and agriculture was stagnant. Roughly the same number of bushels of grain per acre or bolts of cloth per worker per year were produced in 1700 AD as were produced in 1700 BC. Things stayed the same from year to year and from century to century.

In the period after 1760 in England, however, an unusual series of events occurred that changed the world forever. For the first time, entrepreneurs began to combine significant amounts of capital—machinery and raw materials—with labor in large factories devoted to the mass production of goods. By 1800, thousands of people were organized into enterprises which mass produced cotton thread, pottery, iron products, and other items. For the first time in the history of humanity, mass production, making extensive use of capital, increased productivity, and brought the price of consumer goods down dramatically. It led to England's dominance of world trade for a century. Because of the system developed in the industrial revolution, the average person in developed countries today can expect to live a longer and much more satisfying life than the average person has been able to do since the world began.

The Central Role of Marketing

Why have we become so wealthy in the last two centuries? Is it our production methods or our marketing skills? Most writers have concentrated on the factories and the financial system as the producers of the wealth. In concentrating on these forces alone, however, they have overlooked the main reason that the industrial revolution was possible: the expansion of the market system and trade.

Adam Smith pointed out in 1776 that mass production was the product of the division of labor: many people working together successfully in a common enterprise, producing much more than the same people could produce working independently. But Adam Smith said something else: "The division of labor is limited by the extent of the market." Where the market is small, the gains from the division of labor are correspondingly small. The larger the market, the more efficiencies are possible, the greater productivity, the greater profits, and the greater affluence.

Marketing is the key. Producing a million pounds of cotton thread would not have been possible if marketers had not found a way to sell a million pounds of cotton thread. Marketing is not something that happens after the goods are produced. Marketing is the reason the goods are produced in the first place.

The reason why cell phones, DVDs, and personal computers have been manufactured in the hundreds of millions is not primarily because of the activity of inventors and investors—although they are essential to the process—but primarily because of the activities of the marketers that have made the public aware of the products, created the demand for them, and set up the distribution channels.

New and unknown products—plus new versions of old ones—have to be introduced to the public in a way that creates the orders. Marketing comes first.

The American Market

From 1900 to the present time, the United States has had the largest single market on earth. Everywhere else cultural restrictions, political systems, or physical boundaries combined with poor transportation to limit most markets to comparatively small areas. The United States has spent the last 200 years breaking down barriers, building waterways, railroads, telegraph, telephone and electronic communications systems, super-highways, airports, and massive delivery systems which link all parts of our market together in a freely competitive way.

The result has been the greatest outpouring of production, affluence, and personal freedom ever known. The process has not been directed or controlled by government. Instead the driving force has been free competitive market activity—each entrepreneur trying to satisfy the public best so as to realize his or her own personal dream.

Marketing has been the means by which the division of labor has expanded. Individual marketing heroes have provided the leadership. From 1812 to 1860, Frederic Tudor, one of our first mass marketers, built his fortune by shipping blocks of ice from Boston to the south and to the outside world. He taught the middle class how to store ice and to preserve food. He changed the way people ate and drank. A hundred years later, another hero, Frank Perdue taught us that, "It takes a tough man to make a tender chicken.≤ His chicken empire was not so much a triumph of production—which was superb—but of marketing, which was even better. Jeff Bezos, the creator of Amazon, figured out how to sell books and scores of other things on the Web before most people even knew what the Web was. Americans as a people are master marketers. Our marketers have educated the public and provided the means by which fantastic new products can be developed, mass produced, and delivered at lower and lower prices. To these we can add credit cards, Federal Express, Microsoft, Amazon, and Google as examples of marketing successes that have brightened our lives and extended our affluence.

The Growth of Mass Marketing

From 1950 to 1980, mass marketing predominated. The growth of television built on the solid foundation of national print ads and radio to create mass audiences for national advertising. National brands, sold in supermarkets, department stores, fast food restaurants, and franchised outlets everywhere, homogenized the content of the American home. Mass marketing makes mass production possible. This combination resulted in a constant reduction in the cost and an improvement in the quality of most products as well as a vast increase in the real income of the average American consumer.

Despite the temporary downturn which began in 2008, the American consumer has steadily become more and more affluent. The market has been changing, and our marketing methods have to adapt. The growth in real income conceals another trend which is hard to display in graphic form: the products that Americans are buying with their income have become a lot more efficient and sophisticated.

One result of this productive system is that the middle class has grown from being about 15 percent of the population in 1920 to being 86 percent of the population in 2011. While some of the population always seem to live at the poverty line, the vast majority of Americans today are affluent compared to their grandparents. They have the money to buy the products produced by American industry. In the process, the definition of poverty has changed. The majority of Americans who are classified by the government as living at the poverty level have indoor plumbing, color television sets, cell phones, air-conditioning, washers and dryers, microwaves, automobiles, and access to free health care. They are also a significant buying group.

We have arrived at a point where more than 85 percent of American households have discretionary income. Not all their take-home pay is needed to pay for food, clothing, rent, and transportation. In 1950, the average American family was spending 31 percent of its household income on food. Today that family is spending about 9.8 percent on food, and the food it's getting with that 9.8 percent is better in quality and quantity than what it was spending 31 percent for in 1950. We have all gained. Our basic needs are met. We want something more.

What the Market Consists of Today

We are not at the end of a long evolutionary process. Instead, we are today right in the middle of a vast program of change that is leading us to new levels of wealth and affluence. Our market is still expanding. Look at how our marketing methods have changed:

- *Consumers became owners of the economy.* An amazing development took place in the late 1990s. The average household acquired mutual funds. Twenty years later, 49.9 percent of American households owned stocks, either directly or indirectly. Consumers began to look on American industry from the standpoint of being owners of it rather than as just employees. This changed their attitude as shoppers. They were not tied down to their neighborhood. They began to use the Internet to see what was available.

- *New products were created at an accelerating rate.* If you look at the U.S. market in the last two centuries there was a steady acceleration in innovation. A graph of patents issued during the past 200 years shows a staggering increase during the past decade. There were more patents issued in the 20 years from 1991 to 2011 than in the first 200 years of our nation.

The pace of new product introduction and expansion is amazing. It is not possible for anyone to keep on top of even a small percentage of the new developments today. As a result of this constant innovation, the market is much more complex for the consumer than it once was.

Why the U.S. Economy Is So Successful

Despite the 2009 recession, if we look at the past fifty years, the United States has been going through an unprecedented boom that never seems to stop, while most of the rest of the world does not do as well. Why is that?

Freedom to Produce. We are successful primarily because of freedom. Unlike most of the rest of the world which is burdened with high taxes, heavy governmental regulation, and a culture that frowns on personal advancement at all levels, American business is freer to innovate, to hire and fire, and to produce. We've learned to understand the customer and to design products and services not only to meet the customer's needs, but continually to delight the customer with new products and services that the customer hadn't even imagined.

Freedom to Market. In a trip to Germany, I was astonished at the governmental restrictions on the marketing of products and services there. Stores are closed on Sundays and holidays and at 8:00 p.m. every evening *by law!* In the United States our biggest sales come on weekends and holidays. Every evening billions of dollars change hands when American shoppers visit shopping malls. Why were the German stores closed during these peak shopping days and hours? *Because of the workers!* German stores are not run for the customers. They are run for the workers in the stores. American stores are run for the customers. We keep the stores open at all hours and all days to make our customers happy. By having two or three shifts, we provide more jobs and money for our workers and convenience for the customers. In Germany, keeping the stores closed means fewer jobs and for their workers and great inconvenience for the customers. Marketing freedom is central to our prosperity. Anyone can manufacture products. Only Americans know how to market them. We let the Chinese and other Asians make our products. We design and sell them.

Low Inflation Resulting from Our Trade Deficit with the Rest of the World. The trade deficit came about because Americans bought more every year from abroad than foreigners bought from us. The result: prosperity for the United States. It is a wonderful system! We give China, Taiwan, Singapore, and many other countries dollars which are created by our banking system and really cost us almost nothing. They give us millions of valuable products which they have to work very hard to produce and ship. How did this system result in American prosperity? The flood of inexpensive foreign goods was why we have been able to hold inflation in check here for many years. Low inflation is central to our success. Some American workers were displaced by the flood of imports, of course, but, until the 2008–2011 recession, most of them soon found jobs in an economy that keeps growing and growing.

High Investment. There was a second benefit from the foreign trade deficit—*dollars owned by foreigners in New York banks*. The foreigners were not content to let the dollars just sit there. From the outset, they wanted them earning interest. So the dollars were invested in American business: stocks, government bonds, corporate bonds, mutual funds, and other investments. These were not temporary investments. The trade deficits went on for decade after decade. Those dollars fueled the boom in the Dow Jones and the U.S. industry.

Meanwhile, American consumers, benefiting from this prosperity, became affluent and changed their buying habits.

Customers Buy Products to Reduce Uneasiness. Why, after all, does anyone buy anything? There is one basic reason that is always true: people purchase products because they think that their life will be better with the products than without them. This is true of both consumer and business customers. They don't *know* that their life will be better with the products. They just make that assumption. Sometimes they are wrong.

The Value of Products Is Subjective. The market value of products and services is determined primarily by the customers. A computer, for example, has no value at all unless someone wants it. The money that went into its production is totally irrelevant to potential customers. They simply see the computer as a way to relieve uneasiness. If it will not relieve their uneasiness more than some competing product of which they are aware, they will not buy it, and it will have, essentially, no value at all for them. Obsolescence is an ever-present worry for any business that holds inventory. Constant obsolescence is the result of constant innovation.

In Free Market Exchanges, Both Parties Make a Profit. It is often overlooked that the consumer makes a profit as well as the supplier. Each party to a trade gives up less than he or she gets. If this weren't the case, why trade? Money has exchange value. Purchased products seldom do. If you sell a consumer a computer for $1,000, it must be worth more to consumers than $1,000, or they would never buy it. By making the purchase, consumers give up $1,000, which they could use to buy anything they want, for a (now used) computer which would be hard to trade for anything. For you as a retailer, the computer must be worth less than $1,000, or why would you sell it? The fact that both parties must always make a profit is essential to understanding the market and particularly to the strategy for database marketing.

Purchase Decisions Cause Internal Conflicts in Potential Customers' Minds. All customers are torn between their desire for a product or service on the one hand and their desire to retain their money supply on the other. Acquiring a product tends to reduce uneasiness; dissipation of one's personal money supply tends to increase uneasiness. Life is a balancing act between the two.

The Internal Struggle Affects Different Sides of the Brain. Research on the hemispheres of the brain has made us aware that we possess two different and complementary ways of processing information—a linear, step-by-step style that analyzes the parts that make up a pattern (the left hemisphere) and a spatial, relational style that seeks and constructs patterns (in the right hemisphere). See figure 2.1. It is the left hemisphere that controls our language. It is here that we do our mathematics and calculate prices and bank account balances.

The right brain constructs patterns and recognizes relationships. It is most efficient at visual and spatial processing. It is here that we visualize

Right Hemisphere

Patterns, and
relationships. Visual
and spacial processing.
Imagination and desire.

"If I had that product, I
would be handsome,
cultured, sophisticated,
and popular. I must
have it."

Left Hemisphere

Language, linear
thinking. Mathematics,
accounting, and logic

"I have only $X in my
bank account as a result
of yesterday's
extravagance. I must
resist the right side's
customary exuberance."

Figure 2.1 The Purchase Decision Process

what our life would be like if we were to acquire a new product. It is the source of our imagination and our *desire*.

It is the complementary functions of both sides of the brain that give the mind its power and flexibility. We do not think with one hemisphere or the other; both are involved in the decision-making process. Any significant decision is often preceded by a good deal of logical, linear thinking as a person defines and redefines a problem. This linear verbalized thinking goes on in the left hemisphere. Then there comes a moment of insight when an answer presents itself. This answer occurs when the right side puts all the pieces together into an image of the solution to the problem. Finally the mind tackles the difficult job of evaluating the insight and putting it into a form that can be communicated and applied to the problem.

Advertising Can Appeal to Either Side of the Brain. It is well known in retailing that "*buy one, get one free!*" out-pulls "*50 percent off.*" Why is that? There seem to be several reasons:

1. You can get the 50 percent reduction by buying only one, instead of two, so purchases could prove to be less revenue.

2. Even today, many people are insecure about the meaning and method of computation of percentages. Everyone, however, understands the meaning of *free.* It's a wonderful word.

3. This is basic to database marketing. Wanting products is a right-brain function. Calculating money is a left-brain function; *50 percent off* requires a left-brain calculation plus a right-brain stimulus, which is a

complicated mental maneurver, and hard to process. *Buy one, get one free* is pure right brain. You not only do you get what you want, but you get two of them.

Marketers are faced with a dilemma on the approach. Should they base their message on the price (a left-brain argument) or on the benefits of the product (which appeals to the right brain)?

Products Tend to Become Commodities

There is a problem with both marketing approaches today. Prices tend to become similar as each airline, TV, mobile phone, PC, and automobile manufacturer rushes to match every price move of the competition. The consumer knows that price changes are temporary and and will be corrected soon by competition. Many consumers, moreover, being relatively affluent, are less interested in price than in quality and service.

Product quality also tends to be uniform. Avis, Hertz, National, Budget, Dollar, and Alamo all rent brand-new cars. Detergents, yogurt, canned goods, tires, televisions, phones, and toilet paper are all getting better and better and more similar to one another: each manufacturer produces equally good, high-quality products that do the same thing. Every improvement is immediately matched by the competition.

The Importance of Time

Price and quality have been the staples of marketing for years. Today there is a new dimension entering into consumer decision making, which is of equal importance. It is *time*. People have less and less time available for shopping (or for anything).

Products that can be purchased for $100 but that require a one-hour round trip to the supermarket or the mall are perceived to cost more than the same products that can be purchased for $120 and a telephone call or an Internet click. Our leisure time has acquired a monetary value that it never had before.

To the monetary cost of any transaction, therefore, we must add the cost of the time involved in completing the transaction.

If we can make a purchase more convenient and less time consuming for customers, we make the product more attractive to them, and they are more likely to buy it. In many cases, making this purchase more convenient costs us less than the increased value to the consumer, so both of us make a profit by the change in delivery methods. That is one reason why Amazon has been so successful.

What we marketers are selling today, therefore, is more than the product. It is the product, plus the delivery method. Convenience and service are part of what we are selling. The real decision-making process required for a purchase (from the customer's point of view) looks something like this:

$$\text{Customer profit} = a(\text{utility of product}) + b(\text{value of brand}) - c(\text{money cost}) - d(\text{time})$$

The letters a, b, c, and d represent **weights** which vary with each customer. Lower-income customers place a higher value on c, and a lower value on d (since money is worth more to them, and time is worth less). Busy people place the highest value on d. This was illustrated in the 1970s during the energy crisis. Gasoline prices were controlled at low levels by the government. As a result there were regional gasoline shortages and long lines at the gasoline stations. Across the Texas border in Mexico, gasoline cost much more, but there were no lines and unlimited supplies. For a number of months, Texans drove south of the border to fill up their gas tanks at high prices, while Mexicans came north across the border to wait in lines for the cheap gas.

Providing Information

The fact that the market today is filled with change, uncertainty, lack of information, and ignorance is a wonderful opportunity for marketers. Millions are refinancing their homes at lower and lower interest rates. Interest rates used to be a mystery. Today thanks to Google you can find them out with a click of a mouse. We live in a world in which customers have as much information about products as the suppliers do. This is a result of the Internet.

The American market is not just huge; it is gigantic. It is filled with millions of businesses and hundreds of millions of consumers, each looking out for themselves and pursuing subjective goals of their own. Before the Web came along, no one could possibly know of all the commodities and services that were available, their respective benefits and features, and the prices at which they could be obtained. Now much of that information is at your fingertips.

Database Marketing Arrives

Some time around 1985, database marketing grew out of direct mail marketing when marketers began to realize that they could bring back some of the loyalty and relationships with customers that had been lost when the Old Corner Grocers disappeared from the American scene. These friendly merchants knew all their customers by name. They knew what each person liked and disliked. They knew about their families, their homes, and their jobs. By experimentation, marketers learned that they could build a database of their customers, storing information about their purchases and their lives, which enabled the retailers to send relevant, personal messages that built loyalty and repeat sales.

To support database marketing, a few firms created complied databases of every household in the United States. The data was copied from property records, credit data, census data, and from registration, application, and survey data filled in by American consumers and businesses. Marketers learned to buy lists and data from many sources to the point where there are today more than 40,000 lists of American consumers and businesses that can be purchased ethically and legally for a few cents per name. It became fairly easy to build a comprehensive database of every customer who purchased any product from any merchant. Selling customer data became almost as profitable as selling products.

As the sophistication of the data grew, the techniques for manipulating it grew. Merge/purge software permitted service bureaus to consolidate more than 100 lists of several million rented names in a day or two. At first databases were of a fixed length such as 200 bytes with fixed fields. As the marketing industry grew, relational databases were invented, which made it possible to store an unlimited amount of data about any individual. Disk space got cheaper, and computers became faster and more versatile. By the mid 1990s, it became possible for any marketer to send personal communications to customers with each letter or postcard worded especially for the recipient.

Database marketing worked. It built loyalty. Airlines and supermarkets pioneered in the creation of loyalty programs which enabled customers to earn points toward future travel or purchased products, or to get discounts on current purchases. Today all companies in the travel industry and more than half of all other consumer retailers have some sort of loyalty program built around a marketing database.

Prior to 1998, the only drawback to database marketing was the cost of communication. For the database to be profitable, it was necessary to write personal letters or make phone calls based on the database. It still cost $600 or more to send 1,000 bulk rate letters to any group of customers. With an overall response rate of about 2.67 percent, most marketers could not justify more than one or two letters per customer per month, but, in general, these messages were profitable. They produced loyalty and repeat sales.

After 1998, Web sites with shopping carts and e-mail marketing were born. All households and businesses gradually acquired PCs. Internet Web sites began to list all the products available, so any visitor to the sites could buy almost any product with a credit card and a mouse. Web sites began to greet return visitors by name—just as the corner grocers used to do. The Internet exploded. Over the next dozen years, marketers gradually realized that it was possible to communicate with the customers on their database using e-mails for as low as $6 per thousand messages. What a wonderful opportunity to expand relationships with customers! The cost was so low that it became possible, economically, to send customers an e-mail seven days a week.

Because it was possible, hundreds of companies did just that. Even though filters eliminated most of the unwanted spam e-mails, most consumers found that there were more legitimate communications from reputable companies than they could possibly open and read in a busy day. In a few years, we have gone from sending only a few messages, because they cost too much, to having them so cheap to send that we are sending far too many. Management of companies soon realized that if they increased their e-mails from one a week, to two a week, revenue increased. From two to four per week, revenue grew again. Most companies do not think of the long run; they think of short-term revenue this quarter. The pressure to send more e-mails, in many companies, is intense.

So what has happened to database marketing in the age of the e-mail as a result of this? As the costs of communications go down and the number of messages goes up, the ability to build lasting relationships has been going down because there are just too many messages. In the past, consumers shopped at only a few local stores. Today, with the Internet, there are, in most cases, scores of stores available to any consumer in any location of the United States and throughout much of the world.

How Database Marketing Solves Customers' Problems

Database marketing and Web sites came along just when they were needed. They solved the information problem; they provided recognition, personal service, and a profit to the customer. The Web can be an extension of the database, providing recognition and helpful information.

Database marketing is possible, of course, because of the development of computers with advanced software. We can store scores of facts about every customer and retrieve them in seconds when we need them to provide information and services to each customer. We can use this customer information to create personalized communications that customers like and respond to. Let's take a concrete example. Read the following letter (originally created by Thomas Lix):

Ridgeway Fashions
404 Main Street
Leesburg, VA 22090

Dear Mr. Hughes:

I would like to remind you that your wife Helena's birthday is coming up in two weeks on November 5th. We have the perfect gift for her in stock.

As you know, she loves Liz Claiborne clothing. We have an absolutely beautiful new suit in blue, her favorite color, in a fourteen, her size, priced at $232.

If you like, I can gift wrap the suit at no extra charge and deliver it to you next week so that you will have it in plenty of time for her birthday, or, if you like, I can put it aside so that you can come in to pick it up. Please give me a call at (703)-555-4470 within the next 48 hours to let me know which you'd prefer.

Sincerely yours

Robin Baumgartner, Store Manager

What's my reaction to this letter? Halleluiah! Helena is a Catholic. She has two birthdays a year: her saint's day is August 18, and her birthday is November 5th. I have to buy her something for both days. What should I get for her? She is a very stylish, fashion conscious businesswoman who always wears the latest clothes. I, on the other hand, am color blind and hate to shop. I wander around the malls, "What? What? What?" These people know. "Liz Claiborne"—what is that? I don't know, but Helena does, and she likes it. If the database has the correct information in it (about Helena's tastes and my pocketbook),

I will snap at this opportunity to remove my uneasiness, and save myself time.

This letter can also be quite effective as an e-mail. Scores of stores and catalogers are now encouraging consumers to record their important events. They provide reminders, like this one, in time to help the consumer make up his or her mind before the event. This is classic one-to-one marketing. This is strategic database marketing. This is what it is all about.

Database marketing and Web sites are designed to reduce ignorance and lack of information; bringing a very particular buyer with unique subjective goals together with a specialized solution to the customer's problem.

Database marketing and Web sites, of course, are not universal solutions. They will be effective only in situations in which a continuing relationship between a seller and a buyer is *profitable for both parties*. If one or the other finds that he or she can do better without the relationship, the database or Web project will fail—and it should.

Collecting Information

How would Ridgeway Fashions get the information necessary to send me such a personal letter or an e-mail? It should not be from analyzing purchases. That is too much like the CIA snooping through personal files. It would be an invasion of privacy. To collect this information, when Helena was shopping, a Ridgeway clerk should ask her, "Would you like to be in the Birthday Club?"

"What is the birthday club?"

"Well, you tell us your birthday, your preferences and sizes, and your husband's business address or e-mail. Then a couple of weeks before your birthday, we will write to him and give him some hints on what to buy."

"Hints? He needs hints. OK. Where do I sign up?"

Additionally, Ridgeway could collect the same information by listing its birthday club on its Web site. The information can be stored in the customer's database file. The data goes to the merchandise buyers who have to buy clothing that the customers want. Then, once a month, the computer scans the file for people who have a birthday coming up. They check the warehouse to see if what the customers want is in stock. Then they can write these one-to-one powerful, personal letters or e-mails.

Event-Driven Personal Communications

To create personal letters, Web sites, and e-mails, you need to store a lot of information about your customers and their preferences in your database. The database software will:

- Sweep the database daily to determine relevant targets for communications.

- Determine which product type each consumer is most likely to want to buy.

- Calculate the expected value of each target, recipient, merchandise, and occasion combination.

- Select the winning possibility.

- Generate personalized promotions.

- Monitor the results of each communication and update the database with the results.

Lifetime Value

To know if a birthday club or something similar is going to be profitable for your retail chain, you have to compute the lifetime value of each customer. Lifetime value can be calculated. See Chapter 3. You can figure out the amount of money that is practical to spend on maintaining your relationships with your customers.

Building the database necessary to send that letter to Arthur Hughes was not cheap. The store had to collect a lot of information about Helena and me: sizes, styles, birthdays, budgets, ages, fashions, interests, and preferences. The software had to use all that information to match this data with the products that Helena has already bought at the store and the thousands of products currently available so as to produce the perfect letter at the right time to the right person.

Capturing the information has a cost. Maintaining the database and producing the monthly output has a cost. Mailing the letters has a cost. E-mail is much cheaper. Most of the letters or e-mails sent will not result in a sale. Balancing all these costs are the potential profits that will come from the actual sales (less the returns) that the system produces.

The way to know whether you have built a successful database marketing system is to compute the lifetime value of the Hughes family and all of the other families on your database. Each time you introduce another innovation (sending out a gift suggestion before a wedding anniversary or child's college graduation, for example), you recompute the lifetime value. If the value goes up, you should do it. If it goes down, you should not.

In the next chapter, we build a lifetime value table for Ridgeway Fashions to show how you would go about costing out the Birthday Club to determine whether it will be worth the investment.

Do Database Marketing and Web Commerce Always Work?

If you're wondering whether database marketing and Web commerce always work, the answer is no, they definitely do not. There are tens of thousands of products, particularly packaged goods, for which database marketing or the Web will never work. Too many articles have been written suggesting that database marketing or Web sites are panaceas and that those who fail to use them are blockheads. Don't be fooled. Work out the economics. The next chapter, on lifetime value, will give you a solid tool to determine whether database marketing and a customer Web site will work in your situation.

Is Mass Marketing Ending?

Mass marketing is alive and well. Smart mass marketers will include the URL of their Web site in their ads so that customers can get more information, locate dealers, or buy products directly. Mass marketing will always be essential to make the public aware of new products and of old products for which database marketing and the Internet will not work well. Will toothpaste ever be sold by database or e-mail marketing? Never. Manufacturers of packaged goods will be using mass marketing plus retailers' shelf space long after the people reading this book have been shipped off to a nursing home, located through Google.

Summary

The United States is unique and fortunate. Working in a land of freedom and opportunity, a nation of immigrants built a continental market with few political and economic restrictions. For the last century we have had the largest and freest market on earth.

In this free market, entrepreneurs and marketers seek better and better ways of making customers happy. Customer happiness means purchases, and purchases mean profits for both the buyer and the seller. The size of our market has resulted in economies of scale from mass marketing, mass production, constantly lower prices, and constantly increasing per capita income.

Database marketing and Web sites are aimed at the customer's right brain. Instead of being bombarded with discounts, the customer is showered with attention, recognition, friendship, and service. Why these things? Because that is what customers want. Furthermore, database marketing and Web sites are the only way to start a two-way dialogue in which customers are able to tell you what is on their mind, and you are able to react to their thoughts by varying your services and product mix.

Database marketing and the Internet work for some products because they are uniquely qualified to meet today's customer's requirements, just as mass marketing was the ideal marketing solution for these same products in previous decades. Companies that recognize this shift and take advantage of it will prosper. The others may be consigned to the dustbin of history.

We Americans do have a "vision" that directs our market and our economy. The vision is freedom for and control by consumers. It works.

Take-Away Thoughts

- Marketing is more important than production. Successful marketing is the reason that goods are produced in the first place.

- Better output per acre or per hour stayed the same for 2,000 years. It began to improve with the industrial revolution in 1760 in England.

- Because of capitalism, the average person in a developed country can expect to live a longer and much more satisfying life than has ever been possible since the world began.

- Gains from the division of labor are limited by the extent of the market.

- Mass marketing predominated from 1950 to 1980. It is still alive and well.

- The middle class has grown from 15 to 86 percent of the population.
- More than 85 percent of American households have discretionary income today.
- Customers have become owners of the American economy.
- New products are being invented at an accelerating rate.
- The United States is successful because of freedom to produce and market—low inflation and high investment.
- Customers buy products to reduce their uneasiness.
- In free market exchanges both parties always make a profit.
- There are two sides to the human brain: logical and imagination. Both sides are used to buy products.
- Advertising can appeal to both sides of the brain.
- Time has become an important part of marketing. People will sacrifice money to save time.
- The fact that the market is filled with change, uncertainty, lack of information, and ignorance is a wonderful opportunity for marketers.
- Database marketing aims at bringing back today for large firms the methods that worked well in the past for the Old Corner Grocers.
- Direct mail is limited only by the cost of communication. Database marketing boosts profits by avoiding mailing to those who are unlikely to respond.
- E-mail marketing has eliminated the cost of communication but created another problem: too many e-mails filling up in-boxes.
- To create personal letters, Web sites, and personal e-mails, you need to store a lot of information about your customers and their preferences in your database.
- Database marketing and Web sites are the only way to start a two-way dialogue in which customers are able to tell you what is on their mind and where you are able to react to their thoughts by varying your services and product mix.

A quiz on this chapter and all figures can be found at www.dbmarketing.com/STM4. Those taking all the quizzes can receive a Successful Completion Certificate from the Database Marketing Institute which can be used in their résumé.

3

Lifetime Value: The Way to Measure Marketing Programs

*That loyal customers are a good thing is self-evident to
every business person. Yet the vast majority of
companies don't know the cash value of customer
loyalty, and most don't know they don't know. They
look at their sales figures or at average customer
tenure, and they draw a series of inappropriate or
inaccurate conclusions. ... In most businesses,
accountants treat investment in customer acquisition
as one more current expense, instead of assigning it to
specific customer accounts and amortizing it over the
life of the customer relationship.*

—FREDERICK REICHHELD
The Loyalty Effect, Bain and Company 1996

In this chapter you will learn how to calculate the lifetime value of your
customers and of your e-mail and mobile subscribers. You will learn what
to do with these values once you have computed them. These values are
used to analyze the success of your marketing strategies and to justify
your marketing budget. They will make you a much more proficient
database marketer.

We start with e-mail subscriber lifetime value (LTV), then move on to
customer lifetime value, and finally to mobile customer LTV. They are
different and are calculated in different ways. But you must know how to
handle all three because today almost all customers can be reached by
phone, by e-mail, and by postal mail.

Definition of Customer Lifetime Value

First, a definition: Customer lifetime value is the net present value of the *profit* that you will realize on the average customer during a given number of years—typically three years. Lifetime value can be used in the development of marketing strategy and tactics. Most numbers that make up LTV can be derived from responses and sales resulting from your retail, direct mail, catalog, mobile, or e-mail programs. Some of the numbers have to be estimated. LTV is calculated for groups or segments of groups of customers or subscribers. It can be attributed to individual members of each segment. There are many different things that cause lifetime value to change, some of which are under your control and many of which are not.

Lifetime value is widely used in the marketing industry today to determine the value of a customer or the value of an e-mail or mobile subscriber. How do these measurements differ?

- For *e-mail or mobile subscribers,* LTV tells you the profit you will receive over three years from each of your current subscribers. Knowing that value, you can calculate how much you should spend to acquire new subscribers. You can figure out how much you lose every time a current subscriber unsubscribes. It gives the members of the e-mail and mobile marketing staff within an organization a way of quantifying what they are able to accomplish. It helps them get their annual budget approved. Some e-mail subscribers may have never bought anything and may *never* buy anything. They are people who have signed up to receive your e-mail or mobile promotions. In fact, for most e-mail marketers today, less than 12 percent of their subscribers open their e-mails and less than that ever buy anything. So why do we keep sending them e-mails? Because the cost of delivering e-mails is so trifling ($4–$6 per thousand), we keep on sending them out in the hope of an eventual sale. Many e-mail marketers today do not maintain a database as defined in this book. Instead, they keep a *mailing list.* The list may have only an e-mail or cell phone number on it—not even a name. They do not keep track of what the people on the mailing list do—even though the data is available.

- For *customers,* LTV tells you how much you can afford to pay for maintaining and updating your customer database. It enables you to predict the value of new marketing programs such as loyalty programs, birthday programs, or lapsed member programs. Customers, by definition, have all bought something. They may buy again. Customers today are often multi-channel. They buy in retail stores, from catalogs, from e-mails, on the Web, and by using their iPhones. In our database, we keep track of who they are, what they buy, when they buy, and how much they spend. A customer database almost always has identifying information such as name, postal address, e-mail address, what was bought and when, how much was spent, and often extensive demographics such as age, income, children, housing, and so on. It may have RFM and analytics scores, LTV, and the like.

Because they are so different, we discuss them separately.

E-mail Subscriber Lifetime Value

The best way to start is to show an e-mail subscriber LTV table. Then we can explain the meaning of each row in the table. Figure 3.1 shows a sample of

Row	E-mail Clothes Retailer		Current Year	Next Year	Third Year
1	Subscribers		1,036,113	846,055	690,861
2	Unsubscribers	13.34%	138,252	112,892	92,184
3	Undelivers	5.00%	51,806	42,303	34,543
4	End of Year Subs		846,055	690,861	564,134
5	E-mails Delivered	156	161,633,628	131,984,635	107,774,255
6	Opens	12.65%	20,446,654	16,696,056	13,633,443
7	Unique Clicks	18.75%	3,833,748	3,130,511	2,556,271
8	Sales per Unique Click	2.14%	82,042	66,993	54,704
9	Off-e-mail Sales Multiplier	1.61	132,088	107,859	88,074
10	Total sales due to E-mails		214,130	174,852	142,778
11	Revenue due to E-mails	$160.12	$34,286,518	$27,997,228	$22,861,603
12	**Costs**	30%	$10,285,955	$8,399,168	$6,858,481
13	Subscriber Acquisition Costs	$0.30	$310,834	0	0
14	E-mail Delivery Costs	$2.60	$420,247	$343,160	$280,213
15	E-mail Creation Costs	$0.93	$150,000	$122,485	$100,017
16	Database Maintenance	$0.50	$518,057	$518,057	$518,057
17	Total Costs		$11,685,093	$9,382,870	$7,756,768
18	**Profit**		$22,601,425	$18,614,358	$15,104,836
19	Discount Rate		1	1.11	1.15
20	Net Present Value		$22,601,425	$16,769,692	$13,134,640
21	Cumulative NPV		$22,601,425	$39,371,117	$52,505,756
22	**E-mail Subscriber Value**		$21.81	$38.00	$50.68

Figure 3.1 E-mail Subscriber Lifetime Value Table

an actual company that sells only on the Web and through e-mails. It has no catalog or retail stores.

This is a typical Internet retailer that has a Web site and sends e-mails mainly to women. The e-mails are sent three times a week featuring dozens of clothing products. There is a shopping cart within the e-mail. A subscriber can click on a product and move it to her shopping cart. When she's finished shopping, she can check out the products she wants to buy and pay using a credit card.

While the e-mail itself lists only a few products, it contains a search box and many links so that the shopper can look for any product that the retailer carries. The search box and the links, when clicked on, will transport the subscriber to areas of the retailer's Web site where extensive information on the particular product or service is available. In this way, an interactive e-mail—though very short in itself—makes it possible for the reader to see, get information on, and place an order for any product or service offered by the retailer.

This retailer sells high-priced women's clothing. The average shopping cart value is $160.12. It sells about $34 million worth of clothing a year. Following are discussions of the rows in the table:

1. *Subscribers:* There are currently 1,036,113 subscribers who are sent an e-mail three times a week. The purpose of the LTV table is to determine the value of every one of those 1,036,113 subscribers. There will be new subscribers arriving in subsequent months and years, but this table measures only the value of these original 1,036,113 subscribers. As you can see, many of them disappear this year and in subsequent years.

2. *Unsubscribers:* One reason that people leave, is that they *unsubscribe.* The e-mail and the Web site databases have links where subscribers can say, "No more" and stop getting e-mails. As you can see, 13.34 percent of them will unsubscribe this year, and we are assuming that an equal percentage will unsubscribe in future years.

3. *Undelivers:* The other reason why people disappear is that they become *undeliverable.* Between 5 and 15 percent of all e-mail addresses become undeliverable in any given year. This happens because people change their jobs (and their e-mail may have been provided by their employer) or because they have decided to use another e-mail provider. Only 5 percent will become undeliverable this year.

4. *End-of-year subscribers:* As a result of unsubs and undelivers, the number of deliverable subscribers goes down every year.

5. *E-mails delivered:* This retailer mails three times a week. Some similar retailers mail much more often. They send e-mails to their subscribers more than 365 times a year. These e-mail marketers have much higher unsubscribe or undeliver rates, but they get more revenue from these frequent e-mails.

6. *Opens:* When an e-mail arrives in a subscriber's inbox, she can click on it to open and read it, or she can simply delete it without reading it. Today, the vast majority of promotional e-mails are never opened. This retailers' open rate (12.65 percent) is the HTML open rate. HTML stands for hypertext markup language, which is the predominant markup language for Web pages. It provides the color and graphics of modern e-mails including headings, paragraphs, and links. There are two ways that e-mails are sent out. HTML e-mails send back a signal through the Internet to say that they have been opened, when, and by whom. Text e-mails do not send a signal back that they have been opened, so opens can be measured only for HTML e-mails. This rate is very good. Open rates have come down every year since e-mail marketing began. Some retailers have open rates of less than 5 percent which means that 95 percent of their HTML e-mails never get read by anybody.

Figure 3.2 shows how a sample of 213 large e-mail marketing companies did in their open rates. From this figure, you can see that if your open rates are less than 12 percent, you need to do something about it. You are below average.

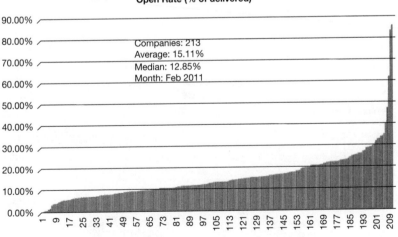

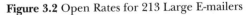

Figure 3.2 Open Rates for 213 Large E-mailers

7. *Unique clicks:* A click occurs when a subscriber clicks her mouse on a link in her e-mail. She may click on several links within any given e-mail. A unique click occurs the first time she clicks on a link. We are not counting here the other links she may click. Figure 3.3 shows how 201 test companies did on unique clicks per open.

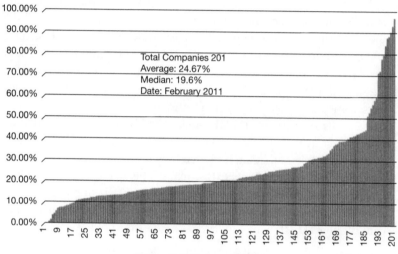

Figure 3.3 Unique Clicks

8. *Sales per unique click:* This shows that 2.14 percent of those subscribers who clicked on a link bought something. This is the basic purpose of the e-mail. This retailer's sales are better than average. Figure 3.4 shows how 83 test companies did on conversions per click:

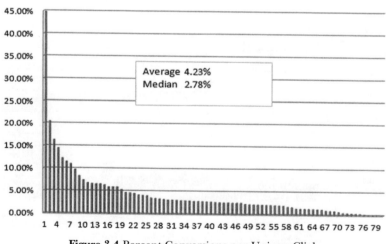

Figure 3.4 Percent Conversions per Unique Click

9. *Off-e-mail sales multiplier:* Here is what happens when a subscriber opens and clicks on an e-mail containing a promotion. She may:

    a. Buy something within the e-mail.

    b. Think about it and buy later from the Web site.

      The second possibility occurs *because she got the e-mail,* and therefore we give the e-mail credit. In most cases, the sales *resulting from e-mails* are bigger in volume than the sales *made in the e-mail.* This is measured by the *off-e-mail multiplier,* which is explained later in this chapter. What the number 1.61 means is that for every sale made in the e-mail, there are 1.61 later sales in the Web site that are the result of the e-mails.

10. *Total sales due to e-mails:* Here we add rows 8 and 9.

11. *Revenue due to e-mails:* We multiply the average order size by the number of e-mail induced sales. The annual total is $34 million, or about $2.8 million per month. Figure 3.5 shows how 78 of our test companies did in generating monthly revenue on- and off-line from e-mails:

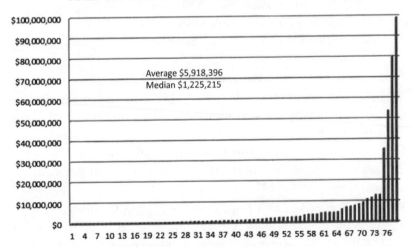

Total On- and Off-line Revenue from E-mails

Average $5,918,396
Median $1,225,215

Figure 3.5 Monthly On- and Off-line Revenue due to e-mails for 78 Companies

Our $2.8 million monthly average compares well with the others.

12. *Costs:* This row refers to the cost of supplying the products or services to the customers. In retail stores, the mark up is typically 100 percent, which means that they buy a dress for $50 and sell it for

$100. In the case of Web site and e-mail retailers, however, the costs are often much lower. They do not have to maintain stores with heat, air-conditioning, parking, employees, marketing, and so on. All they need is a warehouse that has UPS and FedEx trucks backed up to their loading docks. So the costs are much lower than 50 percent. In this case we are assuming that the costs are 30 percent.

13. *Subscriber acquisition costs:* It usually costs something to get people to sign up for promotional e-mails. Retailers can use Google, banners, contests, in-product cards (all described in Chapter 4). Whatever methods are used, they can be boiled down to a per-subscriber number, which is part of the cost of sending e-mails.

14. *E-mail delivery costs:* Most companies today use an ESP (e-mail service provider)—a company that specializes in sending e-mails for other companies (just as companies use a direct mail printing shop to print and mail their direct mail pieces). This row lists the annual cost charged to deliver the 161.3 million e-mails that are delivered this year, which comes to about $2.60 per thousand delivered e-mails.

15. *E-mail creation costs:* Besides delivering the e-mails, someone has to write them, create the colorful pictures, select the segments to be mailed to, and manage the whole e-mail marketing operation. These numbers assume that to create three e-mails per week for a year occupies the time of three people with a total annual salary of $150,000.

16. *Database maintenance:* The company maintains a database that keeps track of what the subscriber does: opens, clicks (on what?), purchases, preferences, e-mail address, postal address (if available), and other data so that the e-mails can be segmented and relevant.

17. *Total costs:* This row says that to acquire subscribers, to pay for the cost of the goods sold, to create and deliver 161 million e-mails in a year costs a total of $11.6 million.

18. *Profit:* The gross profit from e-mail marketing for this company is $22.6 million. Looking to the next two columns in this row, we see that the 846,055 people who are left in the second year out of the original 1,036,113 subscribers from the previous year generate a profit of $18.61 million in the second year. The 690,891 of the original group who are still left in the third year generate profits of $15.6 million.

19. *Discount rate:* We are projecting profits over three years. Money that will be coming in one and two years from now is not worth as much

as money that we have in hand right now. We are going to add together this year's profits with next year's and the year after that. To do that, we must discount the profits that we are counting on from future years. There is a neat formula for calculating the discount rate: $D = (1 (rf \times i))^n$ where i = the rate of interest, rf = the risk factor (in this case 2), and n = the number of years you have to wait to receive the money.

20. *The net present value (NPV):* The NPV is determined by dividing the profits in any given year by the discount rate for that year.

21. *The cumulative NPV:* Cumulative NPV of profits are determined by adding the profits from previous years to any given year's profits.

22. *E-mail subscriber value:* This number is determined by dividing the cumulative NPV profits in each year by the original 1,036,113 subscribers. This tells us that in the third year, each of our original 1,036,113 subscribers is worth *today*: $50.68. This is true even though most of these subscribers never opened their e-mails, clicked on them, or bought anything. It is true even though thousands of them unsubscribed or became undeliverable. This is the crux of the LTV exercise that we have been going through. Figure 3.6 shows how 69 of our test companies computed their lifetime value. Our company is in the mainstream.

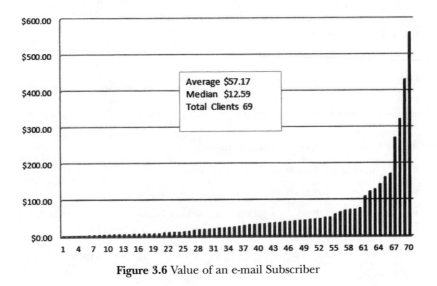

Figure 3.6 Value of an e-mail Subscriber

More on the Off-E-mail Multiplier

Why is the off-e-mail multiplier needed? Lifetime value calculation always involves estimates of the sales resulting from e-mails. Even in the simple case where a company sells only on the Web, there are always non-e-mail related sales from the Web site (resulting from their discovering the Web site through Google, for example) when the e-mail may or may not have led to the sale. The most difficult things to estimate are the off-e-mail sales, which are caused by e-mails. The off-e-mail multiplier helps us estimate these sales.

The off-e-mail multiplier differs from client to client and from product to product. If a store is nearby, many people want to go to see and buy the product, rather than waiting for shipping. For large purchases (air travel, car rental, computers, large appliances, television sets, etc.) many subscribers see the e-mail, are stimulated by it, discuss it with their spouse, and end up buying the product on the phone, from the Web site, or at a store—but not by clicking on the e-mail that started the whole process. In this way, the e-mail is like a TV advertisement, with this exception: the e-mail is better than a TV ad because customers can do research right in the e-mail, seeing what colors and sizes are available, reading reviews, comparing prices, reading specifications, and checking other brands. All this goes on in the e-mail, but the purchase may take place in some other channel with the e-mail not getting the credit. This is why we need an off-e-mail multiplier if we are to estimate correctly the impact of e-mails on the purchase process so we can accurately estimate the LTV of e-mail subscribers.

What Happens When an E-mail Is Opened?

When a subscriber opens her e-mail, she may do any of the following:

- Click on the e-mail and buy something.
- Pick up her phone and order something.
- Check her catalog to see what else is on sale.
- Print out a coupon and take it to a store.
- Get in the car and go see the product.
- Do research on Google for better prices of similar products.

- Discuss it with her spouse or a friend, leading to a possible purchase.
- Remember what she saw and buy it later.

Subscribers do all of the above. The ideal way to learn what subscribers are doing is to have a comprehensive loyalty marketing database (described in Chapter 7) where all purchases in all channels are recorded. Then you will know exactly what is happening when you send e-mails to subscribers. If such a database is not available, you will have to do the best you can in estimating subscriber behavior. Let's start with clicks and conversions.

The Relationship between Clicks and Conversions

There is a relationship between clicks in an e-mail and conversions in e-mails. This relationship is a key method for estimating online and off-e-mail sales. From Figure 3.7 we can see that the average percentage of conversions per unique click is 0.56 percent and that the median is 0.34 percent.

If you study this figure, you can see that some percentages are very high, and many are quite low. One company that has a high percentage sells ink for printers. Everyone with a printer needs ink at some point. It is a nuisance to go to a store for ink—it may be out of your brand. If this e-mail presents a good price for the ink for your particular printer, you

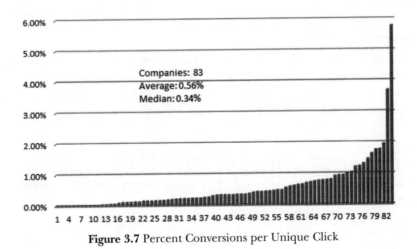

Figure 3.7 Percent Conversions per Unique Click

will click on the e-mail and get it. Rental cars are somewhat similar. If you are going on a trip, you may need a rental car. The e-mail with an offer, arriving at the right time, is the perfect opportunity to reserve a car—particularly since you do not have to pay for the car if you do not use it. High-priced items have their own reasons for their lower conversion percentages. To buy a computer or furniture takes serious money leading to some thought and discussion. You may not be in a position to buy either of them right away when an e-mail arrives. But the e-mail may start you thinking, which may lead eventually to a purchase.

From these numbers we can use the average to estimate a click-to-conversion percentage: an *average* of 0.56 percent of unique clicks produce a conversion *in that e-mail.* For the rest of the e-mail recipients, the message in the e-mail may lead to an eventual Web site or offline purchase, which is why we have an off-e-mail multiplier.

How Can We Estimate the Off-E-mail Multiplier?

There are no "industry averages" for such an off-e-mail multiplier. Many studies have been made that help to throw some light on how to estimate this number. Here are some studies that may help us in our search for the correct number (see figure 3.9). Throughout this discussion we use the number 0.56 percent which is the average conversions per click shown by our 83 companies in Figure 3.7. One company with 900 stores selling children's clothing computed its off-e-mail multiplier based on direct mail and e-mail marketing. It produced some interesting results for different segments. Its off-e-mail multiplier for e-mail marketing was 3.76. The way this was developed is very interesting. The company did an extensive test over three months that looked like the information provided in Figure 3.8.

From the last two columns in the third row, you see that 79 percent of the sales resulting from e-mails were in the store; 21 percent were online

Grand Total	Count	Response Rate	Average Order Value	Dollars per Name Mailed	% Sales in Store	% Sales Online
Direct Mail and E-mail	35,000	25%	$71.71	$17.67	79%	21%
Direct Mail Only	35,000	24%	$68.62	$16.39	83%	17%
E-mail Only	35,000	23%	$67.82	$15.71	79%	21%

Figure 3.8 Test of the Off-e-mail Multiplier

(which were largely, but not exclusively) in the e-mails. Dividing 21 percent into 79 percent gives you an off-e-mail multiplier of 3.76. In reality, the multiplier was more than that. Why? Because some of those online sales were made by some of those 35,000 people after the e-mail had arrived and been deleted. The e-mail, like a TV ad, made them think about that company and its products. Later that day, or that week, they thought, "Hey, that's right. I do need a new dress for the baby. I will go to the Web site and see if the company has our size." That is the type of thought that goes through millions of minds of people who get e-mails but *do not buy right away* in the e-mail shopping cart. This test is a beautiful example of many of the things discussed in this chapter.

- Direct mail produced more direct sales than the e-mail did.
- Direct mail and e-mail together produce more sales than either one alone.
- Not shown are the ROI from each method. E-mail is 100 times cheaper than direct mail, so the profit from those 35,000 that got the e-mails was much higher than that from the 35,000 who got the direct mail and bought more.

Other cases include:

- In 2007, eMarketer estimated that store sales *influenced by online research* totaled $471 billion. Comparatively, retail e-commerce sales were $136 billion. Another way to look at it is that for every $1 in online sales, the Internet influenced $3.45 of store sales. The off-e-mail multiplier could be 3.45 ($471/$136 = 3.45).
- Scotts Miracle-Gro Company does not sell products directly through its e-mails. It sends out e-mails and has found that e-mail-newsletter subscribers buy on average 1.5 times more per year than other offline customers who do not receive e-mails. This could translate into an off-e-mail multiplier of 1.5 (150/100 =1.5).
- Miles Kimball did a study sending catalogs without e-mails and catalogs with e-mails saying, "Look in your mailbox." Those catalogs with the e-mails sold 18 percent more than those without. The off-e-mail multiplier of these e-mails could be 1.18 (118/100).
- Borders offered in-store coupons to its e-mail subscribers. Result: those who used the coupons had 38 percent higher average transaction values than other in-store buyers. The off-e-mail multiplier could be 1.38 (138 percent/100 = 1.38).
- From the statistics available, we find that the surveys show the information provided in Figure 3.9.

Source	Off-e-mail Multiplier
Scotts	1.50
Borders	1.38
Miles Kimball	1.18
Children Clothing	3.76
eMarketer	3.45
Average	2.25

Figure 3.9 Various Off-e-mail Multipliers

- Which is the best number to use? It really depends on the situation. It is certainly possible that the off-e-mail multiplier could be zero— meaning that the e-mails produce no sales beyond themselves. This seems very unlikely. It could be "1" meaning that for every sale in the e-mail, there is one sale on the Web site or a store prompted by the e-mail. A number this low flies in the face of TV experience.

- comScore and DunnHumby conducted a study on the effects of online advertising compared with television advertising across 200,000 consumers, recording their behavior through the use of supermarket loyalty cards. Their research showed that the boost given by online advertising such as e-mails to offline sales was not only higher but also faster than the boost provided by TV advertising.

- A comparative study showed that the percentage of sales lift achieved through TV ads was 36 percent and that through online ads such as e-mails was 80 percent.

- The research carried out by Lightspeed Research for e-Dialog indicated that almost six out of ten people worldwide would be more likely to make an in-store purchase after receiving a marketing e-mail.

Looking at all the numbers, without other information, the children's clothing number of 3.76 seems about right as an average off-e-mail multiplier number.

Multiplier Math

There are many ways of calculating the multiplier. If the e-mails contain a shopping cart, then the multiplier can reflect the additional sales that are prompted by an e-mail campaign:

- Catalog sales
- Retail sales
- Web site sales

In such cases, you create a number which is multiplied by the e-mail conversions (see Figure 3.10). Here the multiplier used is 3.76.

	Rate	Numbers
Unique Clicks	18.73%	1,982,160
Conversion Rate	0.47%	9,316
Sales within E-mails	$98.96	$921,926
Non-e-mail Sales Due to E-mails	3.76	$3,466,443
Total Sales Due to E-mails		$4,388,370

Figure 3.10 Off-e-mail Multiplier Example

There are many cases in which there are no sales in the e-mails—no shopping cart. But there are off-e-mail sales resulting from the e-mail. There we can create the multiplier as an estimated percentage of the unique clicks (see Figure 3.11).

	Rate	Numbers
Unique Clicks	18.73%	1,982,160
Estimated E-mail Induced Sales	2.25%	44,599
Total Sales due to E-mails	$98.96	$4,388,370

Figure 3.11 Off-e-mail Multiplier Where There Are No Sales in the E-mails

Here we multiply arbitrarily by 2.25 percent. You will note that in both cases, the total revenue is approximately the same. We created a percentage that produced the same revenue from the same number of unique clicks.

LTV for a Web Retailer with a Catalog and Retail Stores

Figure 3.12 presents an LTV table for an e-mail retailer who now has retail stores.

We have changed only a few lines, but they tell an interesting story:

1. Because this chain has many retail stores and a catalog, it accumulates many more e-mail subscribers.

5. It is sending only two e-mails per week because it has learned that too many e-mails turn their regular customers off.

Row	Web Retailer with Catalog and Retail Stores		Current Year	Next Year	Third Year
1	Subscribers		2,456,998	2,137,097	1,858,847
2	Unsubscribers	6.98%	171,498	149,169	129,748
3	Undelivers	6.04%	148,403	129,081	112,274
4	End of Year Subscribers		2,137,097	1,858,847	1,616,825
5	E-mails Delivered	104	255,527,792	222,258,073	193,320,072
6	Opens	15.47%	39,530,149	34,383,324	29,906,615
7	Unique Clicks	20.40%	8,064,150	7,014,198	6,100,949
8	Sales per Unique Click	2.15%	173,379	150,805	131,170
9	E-mails Delivered	3.76	651,906	567,028	493,201
10	Total Sales due to E-mails		825,285	717,833	624,371
11	Revenue due to E-mails	$144.67	$119,394,004	$103,848,905	$90,327,777
12	Marginal Costs	40%	$47,757,602	$41,539,562	$36,131,111
13	Subscriber Acquisition Costs	$0.64	$1,572,479		
14	E-mail Delivery Costs	$2.73	$697,591	$606,765	$527,764
15	E-mail Creation Costs	$0.64	$163,538	$142,245	$123,725
16	Database Maintenance	$0.60	$1,474,199	$1,474,199	$1,474,199
17	Total Costs		$51,665,408	$43,762,770	$38,256,798
18	Gross Profit		$67,728,596	$60,086,134	$52,070,979
19	Discount Rate		1	1.11	1.21
20	Net Present Value		$67,728,596	$54,131,653	$43,033,867
21	Cumulative NPV		$67,728,596	$121,860,249	$164,894,116
22	E-mail Subscriber Value		$27.57	$49.60	$67.11

Figure 3.12 E-mail Retailer with Retail Stores

9. The off-e-mail sales multiplier is much higher because the e-mails are driving e-mail subscribers to visit the stores and call the catalog desk.

By way of reference, Figure 3.13 provides the off-e-mail multipliers for our 80 companies. This figure should be taken with a large grain of salt. It is not like the others, which are derived from actual results of e-mail campaigns. This chart is simply guesswork—estimates of how many e-mail–induced sales there are for each e-mail purchase. There is a real number, of course, but few of the companies involved know what it is. These numbers are guesses and may be wrong. The only way to get a real number is to have a loyalty program that tracks every single one of a customer's purchases through any channel.

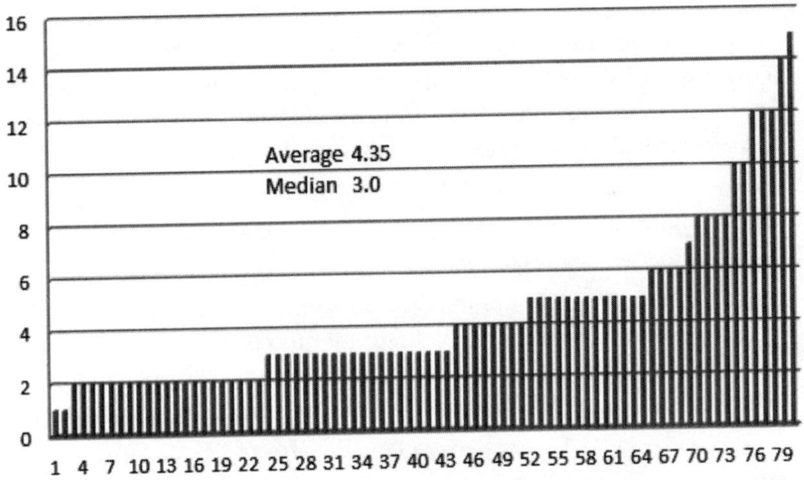

Figure 3.13 Off-e-mail Multipliers for 80 Companies

11. Average order size is lower because retail stores attract lower-income people in addition to the upper-income people typical of e-mail-only shoppers.

12. You will note that the costs of goods sold have increased to 40 percent because the store sales are more expensive than the online sales (they have to keep stores open, employ sales clerks, have air-conditioning, heat, a parking lot, etc.) which are not necessary for online operations.

How You Use the Lifetime Value Number

There are dozens of ways to use the LTV number. Now that you have developed this vital number, you should start using it immediately. Let's start off by listing six methods:

1. *Get your e-mail budget increased and approved:* Now that you have estimated the off-e-mail multiplier, you can show just what revenue your e-mails are bringing in, compared to TV, Print, and Direct Mail. Add to this the fact that your costs are a small fraction of these other methods, and you can make a pitch to get your e-mail budget at least doubled.

2. *Think up new tactics, and cost them out using LTV.* For example, see what a loyalty program would do for revenue, and estimate what it would cost using LTV. Without actually creating this program, you can provide a great estimate of what it will cost and gain. LTV permits you to do your calculations without actually spending any money.

3. *Segment your subscribers by their personal LTV.* Dream up programs to retain the best ones and show, using LTV, how much this segmentation will benefit your company.

4. *Find out the LTV of your unsubscribers.* In some cases, companies are losing their best customers by mailing them too often. Find out if this is true for you. If so, make major efforts to give valuable customers choices on e-mail frequency, adjusting it to what they actually want.

5. *Determine using LTV what you can afford to offer to Web site visitors* to get them to sign up for e-mails. You are probably not giving them enough. If you can boost your offer, you may gain thousands more, and make millions of dollars more.

6. *Use LTV to create an acquisition plan.* Chapter 4 explains how to create a subscriber acquisition plan, based on LTV. This could be the most profitable use of LTV that you could possibly make. Jump ahead, and do it.

Return on Investment

Return on Investment is a performance measure used to evaluate the efficiency of an investment. To calculate ROI, the benefit (return) of an investment is divided by the cost of the investment; the result can be a percentage or a ratio, or more often the dollars produced per \$1 invested. The return on investment from e-mail marketing formula is:

$$\text{ROI} = [(\text{Profit from the sales}) - (\text{dollars invested in marketing})] / (\text{dollars invested in marketing})$$

In the above formula "profit from the sales," refers to the profit after expenses gained from selling the product or service involved. ROI is very useful because of its versatility and simplicity. That is, if an investment does not have a positive ROI, or if there are other opportunities with a higher ROI, then the investment should be not be undertaken.

We will look at two types of e-mail marketing returns on investment:

1. ROI from a single e-mail campaign.

2. ROI from a marketing program involving a series of campaigns.

ROI from a Single E-mail Campaign

A simple ROI comparison would be to compare a direct mail and an e-mail campaign to sell a specific product to a similar group of customers (either consumers or business to business.) Let us assume that a product or service is being sold whose profit (after all the expenses of making and delivering the product) is $100. We are going to send direct mail or e-mail to 1,000 individuals who are on our house file. They have signed up to receive our e-mails. We have their postal address. We are going to determine the ROI of each media used for our campaign.

We have determined from the Direct Marketing Association that the average conversion rate for direct mail to a house file is 2.67 percent. From recent data, we have learned that the average conversion rate for our e-mails is 0.12 percent. This figure is derived from 83 e-mail marketers who together delivered 1,304,632,109 e-mails in February 2011 to 177,502,438 subscribers.

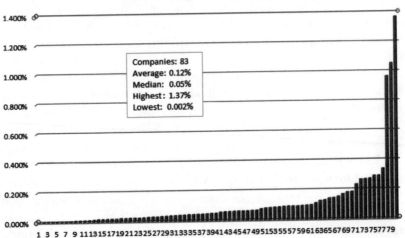

Figure 3.14 Return on Investment

The in-the-mail price of third class (bulk rate) direct mail (including printing, addressing, and postage) is about $600 per thousand. The delivered cost of e-mails is about $6.00 per thousand. This includes the creation of the e-mail and the delivery costs. Comparing the two gives you a ROI for both methods:

ROI Comparison	Direct Mail	E-mail
Pieces Mailed	1,000	1,000
Cost of mailing	$600	$6.00
Conversion Rate	2.67%	0.11%
Sales	26.70	1.10
Revenue per Sale	$100	$100
Revenue	$2,670	$110
Return on Investment	$4.45	$18.33

Figure 3.15 Ridgeway Fashions; No Club, No Web; Just a Good Store

In this example, every dollar invested (cost of mailing) with direct mail produced $4.45 in return on the invested dollar. For e-mail, the ROI was $18.33 for every invested dollar.

ROI from an Ongoing Marketing Program

Few marketing operations consist of a single campaign, like the one shown above. The question naturally arises, "Where did the 1,000 customers that we mailed to come from?" In this simple example, the 1,000 customers appear to be cost free. In fact, that is never the case. Most marketers have to spend a lot of money to rent or acquire these customer names and postal or e-mail addresses, and even more money to maintain them on a database. Most direct and e-mail marketers have a series of campaigns including promotions, welcome messages, triggered messages, and transaction messages. To have a series of campaigns, most marketers maintain a house file: a list or a database of people that they can mail to over a period of time. With direct mail, it is possible to rent the list for each campaign. For e-mails, this is normally not possible. For e-mails, most marketers first have to acquire subscribers through various methods, getting permission from the subscribers to send them periodic e-mails.

In planning an e-mail marketing program, we have to consider many steps, each of which has a cost. For example, the steps might consist of:

a. Acquiring the subscriber with permission to mail to him or her.

b. Maintaining and updating a database or list used for the mailing.

c. Designing individual campaigns such as welcome, promotions, birthday triggers, or transactions ("Thanks for the order" "Your order was shipped today" "Rate the product that you just purchased").

d. Handling preferences, unsubscribes, and undelivers.

e. Managing frequency—some people want fewer e-mails and you may want to honor their preferences.

To illustrate how to compute the ROI from a series of campaigns, let's make some assumptions.

1. We have built up a house file of 1,000,000 subscribers which we acquired by putting an invitation on our Web site. We use search engines to bring people to the Web site, and we incentivize them in various ways to sign up for e-mails. Let's assume that the cost of acquiring a subscriber amounts to $0.18 per subscriber. In total, therefore, we have spent $180,000 to get our one million names.

2. We maintain our subscribers on a database which keeps track of their e-mail address, their first and last names, their date and source of acquisition, their preferences, their purchases, their birthdays, their postal address, their subscribe/unsubscribe status, and their product ratings. It costs us $0.40 per name per year to maintain and update this database. This costs us $400,000 per year.

3. During a year, some of our e-mail subscribers will become undeliverable (their e-mails change and we do not know about it) or will unsubscribe (because they are tired of receiving our e-mails). To maintain our subscriber base at the 1,000,000 level, we will have to acquire new subscribers to replace the lost ones at a cost of $0.18 apiece.

4. We will mail each of these subscribers about 5.64 e-mails per month, consisting of promotional e-mails and other non-promotional e-mails per month (a survey, a preference request, a birthday message, a welcome message, etc.). This frequency (5.64) is similar to what many other e-mail marketers were doing in 2011.

5. The return on investment will look like this (see Figure 3.16).

As you can see, the ROI from e-mail marketing is about $3 for every $1 invested.

Row	ROI From E-mail Marketing	Rate	Year 1
1	Subscribers		1,000,000
2	Unsubs	11.08%	110,800
3	Undelivers	2.85%	28,500
4	Loss during Year		139,300
5	Delivered E-mails	67.68	67,680,000
6	Opens	15.11%	10,226,448
7	Unique Clicks	24.67%	2,522,865
8	Conversions	0.56%	14,128
9	Off-e-mail Multiplier	2	28,256
10	Total Sales due to E-mails		42,384
11	Total Revenue	$171.00	$7,247,686
12	Cost of goods, sales and delivery	$86.00	$3,645,035
13	Investment in E-mail marketing		$1,011,154
14	Profit after investment		$2,633,881
	INVESTMENT IN E-MAIL MARKETING		
15	Subscriber Acquisition	$0.18	$180,000
16	Replacing Lost Subscribers	$0.18	$25,074
17	E-mail Sending CPM	$6.00	$406,080
18	Database Costs per Subscriber	$0.40	$400,000
19	Total Investment		$1,011,154
20	Return per $1 invested		$2.60

Figure 3.16 Return on Investment From E-mail Marketing

Where did These Numbers Come From?

The numbers in this chart are not arbitrary amounts. In fact they come from considerable research data derived from about 214 companies—both large and small—who together sent about 2 billion marketing e-mails per month to about 414 million e-mail subscribers.

The numbers are explained in a series of graphs and data derived from many of these companies in 2011. Following are explanations of the data in this chart using the numbers in the first column of the chart.

1. **Subscribers**. These represent people (consumers or business people) who have provided their e-mails and agreed to have promotional e-mails sent to them. The cost of signing them up averages $0.18

each. Some are free: they came to our Web site using Google or some other search engine, found the Web site so interesting that they signed up for e-mails at no cost to us. For others we paid a search engine for each click. Others came as a result of direct mail, TV ads, print ads, or partners.

2. **Unsubscribers.** We are sending 5.64 e-mails per person per month. This may be more than some people want. As a result, they will unsubscribe. Here is the unsubscribe experience of 197 companies which sent e-mails in 2011:

Annual Unsubscribe Rate for 197 Companies

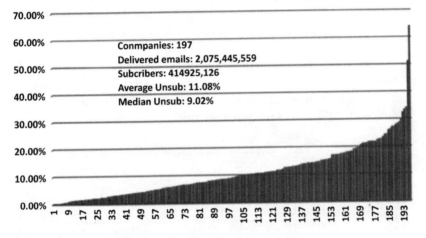

Conmpanies: 197
Delivered emails: 2,075,445,559
Subcribers: 414925,126
Average Unsub: 11.08%
Median Unsub: 9.02%

Figure 3.17 Gain from Birthday Club

3. **Undelivers.** People change their e-mails and do not tell their commercial marketing e-mail senders about it. When the e-mail address is changed, the e-mails "bounce" back to the sender who may try several times to resend the e-mail, and eventually has to give up and count these addresses as undeliverable. It is possible to find some new addresses from various services. Figure 3.18 provides the results of the undelivers from 213 e-mail marketing companies.

4. **Loss during the year.** Adding unsubscribes and undelivers together. To maintain our one million house file, we will have to replace these lost subscribers.

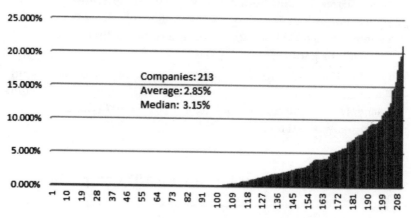

Figure 3.18 Gain from Adding Web Site and E-mails

5. **Delivered E-mails.** Some e-mail marketers send e-mails once a month. Some send more than one per day. Figure 3.19 provides the results of 213 e-mail marketers who together sent two billion e-mails in February 2011 to 414 million subscribers.

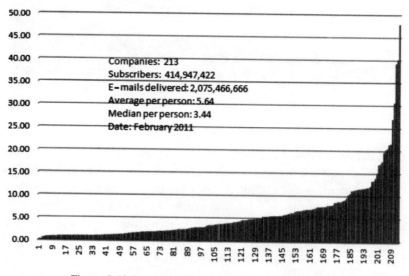

Figure 3.19 E-mails Delivered per Person per Month

6. **Opens.** Less than 20 percent of all commercial e-mails delivered to subscribers ever get opened. From Figure 3.2 we learned that the average open rate was 15.11 percent.

7. **Unique clicks**. Once a subscriber opened his e-mail, if he were interested in it, he would click on a link somewhere in the e-mail. A good e-mail is filled with enticing links. From Figure 3.3 we learned that the average open rate was 24.67 percent.

8. **Conversions** (Sales). Many e-mails contain a shopping cart. Some e-mail subscribers read the e-mail, click on a few links, and buy a product or service. Most do not buy anything. From Figure 3.4 we learned that the average conversion rate of 83 US and UK companies who sent 15,655,585,308 e-mails in a year to 177,502,438 subscribers, and took in a total of $1,645,504,344 in sales within their shopping carts, was 0.56 percent.

9. **Off-e-mail sales multiplier**. When an e-mail arrives, the subscriber may be able to or want to buy a product by putting it in a shopping cart in the e-mail (if there is one). In many other cases, subscribers will, as a result of the e-mail, get in their car and drive to a store to see, and buy advertised products. Others will telephone to order something as a result of the e-mail. Others will think about it, discuss the situation with their spouse or a friend, and a day or two later go to a Web site or store and buy the product. Research shows that there are many more offline, catalog, or Web site sales due to e-mails than as a result of the shopping carts in the e-mails themselves. This is why ROI charts include an off-e-mail multiplier. This is a number which helps to determine the sales that result from the e-mail but are not recorded in the e-mail itself. This number varies from zero up to 12 or even 15, depending on the product and the situation. In fact, some e-mails have no shopping cart at all. For these (football teams, for example) the sales due to the e-mail have to be determined in a slightly different way.

10. **Total sales due to e-mails**. Adding 8 and 9.

11. **Total revenue**. Multiply the average order size by the data in 10.

12. **Marginal costs**. This number represents all costs other than e-mail marketing costs.

13. **Investment in e-mail marketing**. This number is a sum of the data in rows 15 through 19.

14. **Profit after investment**. Revenue (11) less the data in rows 12 and 13.

15. **Subscriber acquisition**. As explained previously, $0.18 per acquired e-mail subscriber.

16. **Replacing lost subscribers**. This is what it costs to replace subscribers lost (4) during the year.

17. **E-mail sending**. This is a combination of the cost per thousand of creating the e-mails, and sending them.

18. **Database costs per subscriber**. Some e-mail marketers just have a list, and do not keep track of any data about their subscribers. Others maintain a database with names, addresses, preferences, sales, etc. The assumption here is that this marketer maintains a reasonably sophisticated database so he can send triggered e-mails.

19. **Total investment**. Sum of rows 15 through 18.

20. **Return per $1 invested**. This is the whole point in the exercise. The ROI of e-mail marketing is $3.39 per $1 invested.

Customer Lifetime Value

Now let's turn our attention to customers rather than subscribers. Customers have bought something from a retailer. We are looking at a store that has developed a method for keeping track of customers by asking for their home phone number. Let us look at a women's dress chain, like our illustrative Ridgeway Fashions, and see how it computes the LTV of its customers. Assume for now that this store has no Web site, no loyalty program, and no e-mail program. Figure 3.20 demonstrates how it can compute its customer LTV.

Row	Ridgeway Fashions LTV Chart		Current Year	Next Year	Third Year
1	Customers		400,000	200,000	100,000
2	Retention Rate	50%	200,000	100,000	50,000
3	Visits Per Year		1.42	1.56	1.65
4	Average Order Size		$97.34	$102.46	$108.67
5	**Total Revenue**		$55,289,120	$31,967,520	$17,930,550
6	Marginal Costs	50%	$27,644,560	$15,983,760	$8,965,275
7	Database & Marketing	12%	$6,634,694	$3,836,102	$2,151,666
8	**Total Costs**		$34,279,254	$19,819,862	$11,116,941
9	Gross Profit		$21,009,866	$12,147,658	$6,813,609
10	Discount Rate		1	1.1	1.21
11	Net Present Value Profit		$21,009,866	$11,043,325	$5,631,082
12	Cumulative NPV Profit		$21,009,866	$32,053,191	$37,684,273
13	**Lifetime Value**		$52.52	$80.13	$94.21

Figure 3.20 Landline Company LTV

Let's explain the rows.

1. *Customers:* We are looking at 400,000 specific customers who shopped there in the first year, giving us their home phone numbers. We are tracking these particular customers over a three-year period. There will be hundreds of other Ridgeway customers who come and go, but this chart is about these 400,000 people and no one else.

2. *Retention rate:* The retention rate of 50 percent tells us that of the original 400,000, only half of them will be shopping at Ridgeway next year. This is typical of some retail stores, many of which have even lower retention rates.

3. *Visits per year:* These tend to go up. Why? Because the remaining customers like Ridgeway for some reason and come back to shop more than the average customer in the previous year. We are winnowing out the disloyal Ridgeway customers.

4. *Average order size:* This tends to go up in later years. In addition to increased visits by more loyal customers, these folks tend to spend more when they shop at Ridgeway.

5. *Total revenue:* This is simply the number of customers multiplied by the average number of visits multiplied by the average order size. This reflects the revenue from these customers that we are tracking, rather than total store revenue which may come from other customers.

6. *Total marginal costs:* These are Ridgeway's *marginal* costs for servicing these 400,000 customers. It includes the cost of the goods sold plus the cost of the utilities, the sales clerks, and all other marginal costs associated with serving customers. It does not include Ridgeway's fixed costs.

7. *Database and marketing costs:* Database costs are to keep track of the customer information. Marketing costs are those costs that were expended to get customers to come into the store.

8. *Total costs:* Equal 6 plus 7.

9. *Gross profit:* Equals 5 minus 8.

10. *Discount rate:* The reason why we need a discount rate in LTV charts is explained in the computation of LTV of e-mail subscribers.

11. *Net present value profit:* This is just the gross profit divided by the discount rate.

12. *Cumulative net present value:* Over the three years, the NPV from the previous years is added to this year to get a cumulative total profit for this and previous years.

13. *Lifetime value:* We get this value by dividing the cumulative NPV profit by the original 400,000 customers. This tells us that the average shopper among these 400,000 is worth $94.21. Of course some buy more than others. This LTV is a valuable number that we will use in our marketing strategy planning.

Ridgeway Introduces the Birthday Club

Assume now that Ridgeway management has bought into Robin Baumgartner's idea of having a birthday club. We will see what this club does to the lifetime value. We are now looking at the LTV of the same 400,000 customers, many of whom have signed up for the birthday club. As we will see, the birthday club improves many aspects of sales for Ridgeway. The retention rate goes up, as do store visits and the average order size.

Row	Ridgeway Fashions With Birthday Club		Current Year	Next Year	Third Year
1	Customers		400,000	220,000	121,000
2	Retention Rate	55%	220,000	121,000	66,550
3	Visits Per Year	15%	1.60	1.84	2.12
4	Average Order Size	12%	$98.21	$110.00	$123.19
5	**Total Revenue**		$62,854,400	$44,526,057	$31,542,259
6	Marginal Costs	50%	$31,427,200	$22,263,028	$15,771,129
7	Database & Marketing	12%	$7,542,528	$5,343,127	$3,785,071
8	Birthday Club Costs	$1.00	$400,000	$400,000	$400,000
9	**Total Costs**		$39,369,728	$28,006,155	$19,956,200
10	Gross Profit		$23,484,672	$16,519,902	$11,586,058
11	Discount Rate		1	1.1	1.21
12	Net Present Value Profit		$23,484,672	$15,018,092	$9,575,255
13	Cumulative NPV Profit		$23,484,672	$38,502,764	$48,078,019
14	**Lifetime Value**		$58.71	$96.26	$120.20

Figure 3.21 Customer LTV of Retailer with Birthday Club

Explanation of Rows

1. *Customers:* The same people, some of whom have signed up for the birthday club.

2. *Retention rate:* The club has improved the overall retention rate because some of the 400,000 who would have defected stayed with Ridgeway because of the benefits of the club.

3. *Store visits:* These are up because the club has brought some husbands of the 400,000 women to make their first visits to the club. Since the husbands have the same phone number as their wives, we do not count these husbands as new customers.

4. *Average order size:* This has grown because the husbands are buying clothes for their wives.

5. *Total revenue:* This has grown due to the Birthday Club.

6. *Direct costs:* These are unchanged.

7. *Marketing costs:* These are the same.

8. *Birthday club costs:* The cost for the birthday club is $400,000. This is made up of paying $5 to each clerk who signs up a woman for the club and the costs of the letters to the husbands. The costs do not go down in the next three years because we keep signing women up, and we don't realize that some of the club members have moved or are not buying, so we keep trying to get in touch with them. This is part of the reason that the retention rate has gone up.

9–14. These lines are computed in the same way as in Figure 3.20.

Figure 3.22 shows that Ridgeway has gained $10.3 million in profit (after expenses) from having the birthday club. This type of analysis is very powerful. It was done by Robin Baumgartner *in advance* to get the approval and funding for the birthday club. She makes these estimates and then works like mad to make them a reality. Lifetime value is always looking ahead, not backward. It is used to estimate or predict the outcome of various marketing strategies rather than to look backward to see what the company did.

Gains from Birthday Club	LTV Current Year	LTV Next Year	LTV Third Year	LTV Gain	With 400,000 Customers
Basic Retail Store	$52.52	$80.13	$94.21		
With Birthday Club	$58.71	$96.21	$120.20	$25.98	$10,392,000

Figure 3.22 Gain from Birthday Club

Why Three Years?

Note that (with few exceptions) in almost all the tables in this book, we are projecting customer activity over three years—not one, or two, or four, or five. Why? For most continuing marketing programs (other than a temporary sale), we are looking at the effect of the program on the customers and subscribers. In our database we want to see if what we are doing is improving the retention rate, the number of visits, or the average order size. These things take time to prove themselves out. Three years is a good number for that. But why not five or six years? We are using LTV to get our budget approved by management. Managers might consider a three-year program. They seldom take seriously any program that takes longer than three years to pay off. They know that most of our companies are in a competitive situation. New products, new companies, and changes in the economy come along. We cannot predict them. Basing any marketing program on what will happen four years into the future is just too much of a stretch. Stick with three years. You can sell that, and it will probably work out.

Adding a Web Site and E-mails

Ridgeway has gotten religion. It sees what everyone else is doing and has decided to invest in a Web site and sending e-mails to customers. It works to get customers to sign up for e-mails. It promotes the URL of its

Row	Ridgeway Fashions Web site & E-mails		Current Year	Next Year	Third Year
1	Customers		400,000	232,000	134,560
2	Retention Rate	58%	232,000	134,560	78,045
3	Store Visits Per Year	2.00	800,000	464,000	269,120
4	Web site Sales per Year	0.2	80,000	46,400	26,912
5	Sales Within E-mails per Year	0.09	36,000	20,880	12,110
6	Total Sales		916,000	531,280	308,142
7	**Total Revenue**	$110.23	$100,970,680	$58,562,994	$33,966,537
8	Marginal Costs	45%	$45,436,806	$26,353,347	$15,284,942
9	Database & Marketing	12%	$12,116,482	$7,027,559	$4,075,984
10	Birthday Club Costs	$1.00	$400,000	$400,000	$400,000
11	Web site & E-mail Costs	$7.50	$3,000,000	$1,740,000	$1,009,200
12	**Total Costs**		$60,953,288	$35,520,907	$20,770,126
13	Gross Profit		$40,017,392	$23,042,088	$13,196,411
14	Discount Rate		1	1.1	1.21
15	Net Present Value Profit		$40,017,392	$20,947,352	$10,906,125
16	Cumulative NPV Profit		$40,017,392	$60,964,745	$71,870,869
17	**Lifetime Value**		$100.04	$152.41	$179.68

Figure 3.23 Ridgeway with Stores Plus Web Site and E-mails

Web site all over its stores and in its advertising. It appends e-mails to its customer records, asking them to sign up. Let's see how Ridgeway predicted that things would work out:

1. *Customers:* Ridgeway signs up for e-mails as many of its customers as possible. It also gets many others to sign up for e-mails, but we do not show these subscribers on this chart. Why not? Because we want to make this a plain apples-to-apples projection. It shows what is likely to happen to these 400,000 customers as a result of the Web site and e-mail program. The fact that the Web site will get many new customers is an additional reason to have it. These customers are not shown on this chart. The purpose of this chart is to respond to the question, "What will happen to our regular customers if we introduce a Web site and start sending e-mails to them?"

2. *Retention rate:* This has gone up from 55 to 58 percent. Why? Because the e-mails we send out about new products and sales will keep some customers from defecting.

3. *Store visits per year:* These are also up because of the e-mails, which include coupons for store visits. We had coupons before, but not as often as we have now with the e-mails.

4. *Web site sales per year:* Some of our retail customers become multichannel customers now that we have a Web site. Multichannel customers spend more than single-channel customers. They tend to be more affluent.

5. *Sales within e-mails per year:* These represent only about 3.6 percent of total sales, but this is a misleading number. E-mails are like advertisements. They permit you to buy right in the e-mail, but they do much more to get people to go to the Web site and buy or get in their cars and drive to the store. It is a mistake to consider just e-mail sales as the total reason for sending e-mails.

6. *Total sales:* These are way up.

7. *Total revenue:* This is up for two reasons: the number of sales is up and the average order size of $110.23 is high because of the number of multichannel people among our 400,000 customers.

8. *Total marginal costs:* These are down from 50 percent to 45 percent. Why? Because some of our sales are on the Web site and in e-mails. Why are these less costly to service? Because a warehouse is much cheaper to maintain than a store. So overall the costs of each order on average are lower than they were when all sales had to be handled by a clerk who works on commission.

9. and 10. are unchanged from the previous Ridgeway LTV table.

11. *Web site and e-mail costs:* These are large costs. They include the warehouse, the Web site, and the e-mail program. They are a lot bigger than the birthday program and produce much more revenue.

12. through 17. These are computed in the same way as before. Lifetime value is way up.

What Has Happened to Our Profits from Going Online?

The numbers given in Figure 3.24 show why all marketers today are adding Web sites and e-mails to their marketing programs. The profits are not just in the e-mails, but also in what e-mails plus a Web site can do for any company that invests in them.

Gains from Marketing Strategies	LTV Current Year	LTV Next Year	LTV Third Year	LTV Gain	With 400,000 Customers
With Birthday Club	$58.71	$96.26	$120.20		
With Web site & E-mails	$100.04	$152.41	$179.68	$59.48	$23,792,000

Figure 3.24 Gains from Web Site and E-mails

LTV for Segments and for Individual Customers

Calculating LTV for all customers is the first step. Your next step is to divide customers into marketable segments. Segments, as we discuss in Chapter 10, can be defined by age, income, lifestyle, products purchased, or any of dozens of different factors. We can compute the LTV of each segment. This will help us to communicate with the members of the segment. We can also use our computers to calculate the LTV of each of our individual customers, and we can store that information in the customer record on our database. We discuss this process in Chapter 10 as well. LTV is the opening of a marketing door that will produce rich profits for those who know how to use it.

LTV for Telephone Landline and Wireless Customers

Before we conclude this chapter, let's look at the way LTV is calculated for telephone customers. For those who are interested in telecom customers,

I have written a whole book on the subject: *Customer Churn Reduction and Retention for Telecoms* (RACOM 2009).

Let's first look at a landline company that also sells broadband to its customers. Refer to Figure 3.25 to see what the LTV looks like.

Row	Landline Customers with Broadband	This Year	Second Year	Third Year
1.	Customers	200,000	183,200	168,178
2.	Churn Rate	0.70%	0.68%	0.66%
3.	Retention Rate	91.60%	91.80%	92.10%
4.	APRU (Average Revenue per Unit)	$76.00	$76.50	$80.00
5.	Revenue	$182,400,000	$168,177,600	$161,450,496
6.	CCPU (Cash Cost per User)	$110,400,000	$101,126,400	$92,874,486
7.	CPGA (Cost per Gross Add)	$50,000,000		
8.	Total Cost	$160,400,000	$101,126,400	$92,874,486
9.	Gross Profit	$22,000,000	$67,051,200	$68,576,010
10.	Discount Rate	1	1.1	1.15
11.	Net Present Value Profit	$22,000,000	$60,955,636	$59,631,313
12.	Cumulative NPV Profit	$22,000,000	$82,955,636	$142,586,949
13.	Lifetime Value	$110	$414.78	$712.93

Figure 3.25 Landline with Broadband LTV

The rows are explained as follows:

1. Customers signed up for landline phone service.

2. Monthly churn is calculated by phone companies since it is a current problem in this highly competitive industry with wireless and cable companies trying to sign up customers.

3. To make it easier to understand, the monthly rate is converted to an annual retention rate.

4. ARPU (Average Revenue per Unit) is telephone talk for phone revenue.

5. Total revenue from the customers in this segment (landline and broadband).

6. CCPU (Cash Costs per User) is also telephone talk for the cost of serving a phone customer.

7. CPGA (Cost Per Gross Addition) is telephone talk for the cost of installing service to a new customer.

8–13. These are computed exactly the same way they were in the previous LTV charts.

LTV for an iPhone Customer

Cell phones, particularly iPhones, are getting to be universal. Soon everyone will have one. Some people are dropping their landline phone. To keep up with the times, Figure 3.26 shows how to compute the LTV of an iPhone customer. The LTV is basically the same for any mobile phone customer.

Row	LTV of iPhone Customers	First Year	Second Year	Third Year	Fourth Year
1	Customers	1,000,000	890,000	213,600	192,240
2	Churn Rate	0.90%	6.30%	0.85%	5.90%
3	Retention Rate	89.00%	24.00%	90.00%	5.90%
4	APRU	$120.34	$130.10	$136.23	$139.86
5	Revenue	$1,444,080,000	$1,389,468,000	$349,184,736	$322,640,237
6	CPGA	$300,000,000			
7	CCPU	$401,400,000	$358,048,800	$87,363,904	$78,452,789
8	Database Cost	$1,100,000	$981,200	$239,413	$214,993
9	Marketing Program	$10,000,000	$8,920,000	$2,176,480	$1,954,479
10	Total Cost	$712,500,000	$367,950,000	$89,779,797	$80,622,261
11	Gross Profit	$731,580,000	$1,021,518,000	$259,404,939	$242,017,976
12	Discount Rate	1	1.1	1.15	1.21
13	Net Present Value Profit	$731,580,000	$928,652,727	$225,569,512	$200,014,856
14	Cumulitive NPV Profit	$731,580,000	$1,660,232,727	$1,885,802,239	$2,085,817,095
15	Lifetime Value	$731.58	$1,660.23	$1,885.80	$2,085.82

Figure 3.26 LTV of iPhone Customers

Why Four Years?

As we said, for LTV three years is standard. For mobile phones four years is standard. Why? Because most phones are on a contract that runs out after one or two years. When the contract expires, users may switch to another company—and many do. So to get an accurate picture of LTV for mobile phones, you have to use four years.

Explanation of Rows

1 Through 7. The same explanation as for landline phones—but the iPhone users usually want many apps and services that run the monthly

cost higher than a regular cell or landline phone. They buy movies, texting, Wi-Fi, and many other features that are not cheap.

8. Companies need a database to keep track of iPhone customers, as they use many features which are additional in cost, such as texting, e-mails, TV, movies, Web sites, product ordering and paying, and so on. These are not simple devices. They include most of the concepts used throughout this book. They represent the future of database marketing.

9–15. Same as previous chart.

Take-Away Thoughts

- Subscriber or customer lifetime value is the standard method of measuring the success of mail or e-mail marketing programs. It is defined as the profit you make from a specific number of people over a three-year period.

- Knowing the lifetime value lets you know how much you can spend to acquire more customers, or how much you have lost when they unsubscribe or go away.

- An LTV table does not include new subscribers or customers. It measures the value of the ones that you already have.

- An average open rate for promotional e-mails is about 10 percent. This means that about 90 percent of all promotional e-mails never get read by anybody.

- HTML stands for hypertext markup language. It provides the color and graphics for modern e-mails.

- Once they have opened an e-mail, readers can click on a link to get more information. That click sends a packet back to the company that sent the e-mail and lets it know who clicked, when, and on what.

- Once opened, about 20 percent of e-mails are clicked on at least once.

- Once clicked on, about 3 to 4 percent of promotional e-mails result in a sale within the e-mail.

- The discount rate permits you to discount future profits to today's value so you can add them to get the net present value of all present and future profits.

- Typically e-mails produce sales within the e-mail shopping cart and also stimulate readers to buy later from a store, a catalog, or a Web site. These subsequent sales are measured by the off-e-mail multiplier.

- Few companies know the value of the off-e-mail multiplier. An average value might be about 3.76, which means that e-mails produce 3.76 sales in other channels for every sale made in the e-mail itself.

- The average return on investment from e-mail marketing is typically about eight times the ROI from direct mail.

- LTV is typically computed over three years. This is because it supports investments leading to future profits; but those providing the funding for marketing activities seldom support projects that last longer than three years.

- LTV can be calculated for market segments, or can even be attributed to individual customers.

A quiz on this chapter and all figures can be found at www.dbmarket ing.com/STM4. Those taking all the quizzes can receive a Successful Completion Certificate from the Database Marketing Institute which can be used in their résumé.

4

Customer and Subscriber Acquisition

It all begins with The List. The possession of a large database of loyal customers and qualified prospects is the foundation upon which successful e-mail programs are built. All elements of sophisticated e-mail marketing—segmentation, personalization, dynamic content, lifestyle marketing and more—depend upon the quantity and quality of the e-mail list. But adding addresses to the company's database continues to be difficult. More than half of all marketers rank the task of developing a qualified e-mail list as their top challenge. E-mail marketers are eager to learn how others are adding to their lists, which tactics work and which are more effort than they're worth.

—SILVERPOP'S LIST GROWTH SURVEY

Subscriber lists cost more money per name and deliver significantly better results because the names are simply qualified at a higher level. In other words, it's a very good bet that a person who subscribes to a home business magazine has a serious interest in working from home. Now if you sell a product or service that benefits a home office professional, you'll find that this list would be a very good choice for your mailing.

—ROBERT IMBRAILE

There are more than 40,000 lists of U.S. consumers and businesses by postal address that you may rent and mail to legally and ethically. A typical consumer name and address will cost you between $0.05 and $1.20 for one time use. You can select the consumers by age, income, housing, previous purchase, or a score of other factors.

On the other hand, your ability to rent e-mail addresses and use them to send commercial messages to people is much more difficult, legally and ethically, because of the Can Spam Act of 2003 and because of general ethical disapproval by the e-mail community of unauthorized e-mail delivery, which is called spam. The value of an opt-in e-mail address varies from about $2.00 to over $200. This chapter is divided into two parts. The first part discusses acquiring direct mail addresses. The second part is about e-mail addresses.

Acquiring Direct Mail Prospect Names

There are two kinds of lists: response lists and compiled names. *Response lists* are names and addresses of people who have bought something from some company. Those who rent out the list often tell you what the purchasers bought and how recently. These lists seldom have demographic data appended. These are the most expensive and valuable of lists. *Compiled lists* are databases of all households in the United States and Canada—usually with complete census and other demographic data. These are wonderful lists, but they are seldom as profitable to use as response lists because half of the households in the United States never buy anything by mail.

People included on response lists may be purchasers from catalogs, subscribers to magazines, people with credit cards, purchasers over the Internet, donors to causes, and so on. The owners of these lists are supposed to have asked their customers whether they object to having their names exchanged with other companies. Most people have no objection. Some unethical companies rent out their responders' names without asking permission. When you rent names, be sure to ask whether specific permission has been granted.

To negotiate your way through the many lists available, it is best to use a list broker. There are scores of these brokers many of whom specialize in particular fields, such as nonprofit or financial services lists. A broker will negotiate on your behalf with list owners or managers to get you the names you want. Response names are usually rented for one time use. You are not allowed to keep the name on your computer after the mailing is over. Anyone who responds to your offer, however, becomes your property. You can expect to pay between \$50 and \$200 per thousand names for a one-time rental.

You can also rent specialized names such as new movers' names. These people have not necessarily responded to anything, but because they have recently moved, they will need to buy a lot of products and services that nonmovers already have. For this reason they are often more responsive than people who have not moved. You can rent a list of expectant mothers, or golf enthusiasts, or dozens of other types of lists.

A Direct Mail Campaign

To see how direct mail customer acquisition works, let's follow a mail campaign from start to finish. Let's assume we are selling some product or service, such as automobile insurance.

We begin with an offer. In this book, we are not going to cover copy writing, which is discussed in excellent books such as *Profitable Direct Marketing* by Jim Kobs, or *Direct Mail Copy that Sells* by Herschell Gordon Lewis, or *2,239 Tested Secrets for Direct Marketing Success* by Denny Hatch and Don Jackson. In general, every database marketing communication should always be a test.

Selecting Lists

Let's say that you want to mail 2 million pieces. You find a list broker and get him to determine the best lists for your offer—these will be people who have responded to some offer in your price range and who have the appropriate age, home ownership, income, and so on. Some lists may have demographics (age, income), but most response lists do not. You may be renting 200 lists with an average of 10,000 names per list. Because there will be many duplicates among the various lists that you rent, to end up with 2 million, you will probably have to rent about 3 million names.

Traditional Merge-Purge

To prepare the names for your mailing, you should use a service bureau such as MBSInsight, KnowledgeBase Marketing, or Merkle Direct Marketing. There are scores of them. Your broker will arrange for name files from the 200 selected lists to arrive at the service bureau on a date that you select. This date needs to be a couple of weeks before the mail drop to give your service bureau time to receive all the names and reformat them for the mailing. You will also provide the service bureau with your customer house file to be used as a suppression file. You may want to mail your house file as well, in some cases, but first you want to make sure you are not paying to rent names that you already own. In renting the names, your broker will have negotiated a "net name" agreement with each list owner that specifies that you do not pay for a name you already own. In addition, if the same name appears on four rented lists, for example, you pay each list owner 25 percent. Most net name arrangements have a minimum net, such as 75 percent, which means that the renters get paid for 75 percent of the names that they send you, regardless of how many are duplicates.

The service bureau will go through a series of steps called "traditional merge-purge" which are described below. In summary, the steps involve:

- Converting all 200 lists plus your house file to a single format—keeping track of the source of each name.
- Running the file through National Change of Address (NCOA^{LINK}) to find out customers' new address if they have moved recently.
- "De-duping" the combined file to consolidate the duplicates and to suppress names on your house file. At this point your 3 million rented names get reduced to 2 million unique names that are not already your customers.
- Dividing the file into segments that permit you to test the effectiveness of each of your 200 lists and of your two offers.
- Running the file through a series of postal software routines to be sure that the names are deliverable and organized to receive the maximum postal service discount.

National Change of Address

When people move, they usually notify their local post office of their new address. The form that people fill out is sent to a central location where it is put into a U.S. Postal Service (USPS) database and sent to service bureaus that are authorized to sell the NCOA^{LINK} service to mailers. NCOA^{LINK} contains approximately 160 million permanent change-of-address (COA) records. Approximately 40 million change-of-address forms are filed annually with the Postal Service. The NCOA^{LINK} database is updated every week with this information.

Service bureaus running NCOA^{LINK} usually charge a few cents per hit. This means that you send them your tape of two million names. They will send the tape back with the new addresses of the folks on the tape who have moved. NCOA^{LINK} changed addresses are kept for four years. About 20 percent of all households move every year, so running your file through NCOA^{LINK} can save you a lot of money. Rented lists often contain obsolete addresses.

Deliverable Software Routines

First-class mail has to be delivered by the USPS, or it will be returned to you. Third-class mail used for most acquisition mailings gets delivered if it is addressed properly, and the recipients are actually living there. It does not get forwarded. If there is some problem with the address, the USPS just discards undeliverable third-class mail—and you will not know about it. Here are some of the routines used by KnowledgeBase Marketing to clean your mail file. Other service bureaus have similar systems:

- *The coding accuracy support system (CASS):* This is a USPS certified system that improves the accuracy of delivery point codes, zip+4 codes, 5-digit zip codes, and carrier route codes on mail pieces.

- *Delivery point validation (DPV):* This contains all delivery point addresses serviced by the U.S. Postal Service.

- *Delivery sequence file (DSF)—second generation:* DSF is an address hygiene tool that provides additional address information about a DPV-verified address to minimize address delivery errors that are not detected by NCOA^{LINK} or CASS-certified processing.

- *Address element correction (AEC):* AEC focuses on inaccurate addresses, specifically those addresses that cannot be matched to the national zip+4 file because of a missing address element.

- *Locatable address conversion system (LACS):* LACS enables companies to update their mailing lists when addresses have been converted by local authorities from a rural to a city style address.

- *Dynamic change of address (DCOA):* Over 30 percent of people who move never submit a change of address with the USPS. In addition, records on the NCOA^{LINK} file are dropped 48 months after the move effective date. The DCOA retains records of address changes for more than seven years, including multiple moves and forwarding addresses.

- *Nixies:* The USPS provides a Nixie elimination service as an addition to NCOA^{LINK}. This service provides footnotes as to why an address match could not be found. This service is very useful for correcting bad addresses.

- *Suppression services:* For acquisition you will want to eliminate your existing customers plus people who do not want to receive mail or who should not receive it. This includes the DMA (Direct Mail Association) Mail and telephone preference files, state "do not call" lists, people in prison, and people who have died.

Why These Software Routines Are Important

Running these routines increases the cost of a mailing. But it also can save you a lot of money. KnowledgeBase Marketing analyzed an acquisition mailing of 3.5 million names that had been done by a nonprofit mailer and processed by an independent service bureau (not KnowledgeBase Marketing). The goal was to see how deliverable the mail was. What it found is shown in Figure 4.1.

Of the pieces actually mailed, 319,662 were either duplicates or undeliverable. At about $0.50 per piece, the nonprofit had wasted $159,831 on the mailing. The mailing produced a net loss of about $50,000. If it had run the proper software routines before it sent out the mailing, it could have turned a $50,000 loss into a $109,000 profit.

Looking at the Type of Address

DSF^2 software produces some interesting reports concerning type of address. Figure 4.2 contains the result of the analysis of a third-class mailing.

By looking closely at the response numbers in the last column, you will see that mail sent to a business address in this consumer mailing had half the response rate of the same mail sent to a residence address. Mail sent to a "drop" had a 30 percent lower response rate than mail sent to nondrop addresses. A "drop" is usually an apartment building where third class mail is dropped in a bundle rather than put into each person's mailbox. In the above situation, suppose that your breakeven rate is 3.09 percent. You could have saved more than $100,000 in the above mailing by not mailing to cells whose response rates were shown in previous mailings to be lower than the breakeven rate.

	Quantity	Percent
Input Quantity:	**3,588,006**	**100.00%**
2 Line Street Address Omits	88	0.00%
Input To AEC Processing (Non-Zip+4 only):	67,659	**1.89%**
Records Matched, Changed (Zip+4 appended)	13,189	0.37%
Input To NCOA/DCOA/DSF Processing:	**3,587,918**	**100.00%**
Nixie Omits	48,397	1.35%
NCOA No Forwarding Address Omits	4,848	0.14%
DCOA No Forwarding Address Omits	26,036	0.73%
Unconfirmed or Invalid Zip Code Omits	650	0.02%
NCOA Moved with Forwarding Addresses (not omitted)	79,979	2.23%
DCOA Moved with Forwarding Addresses (not omitted)	86,430	2.41%
Post NCOA Processing:	**3,507,987**	**97.77%**
APO/FPO Omits	1,076	0.03%
South Pacific Omits	397	0.01%
Prison Omits	294	0.01%
Vulgar Omits	636	0.02%
No Address Omits	88	0.00%
DSF Vacant Address Omits	10,994	0.31%
Input To Merge-Purge Processing:	**3,494,502**	**97.39%**
Internal Duplicate Omits	52,458	1.46%
Mail Preference File Omits	107,953	3.01%
Deceased File Omit	66,747	1.83%
Net Output from Merge-Purge:	**3,268,344**	**91.09%**
Unmailable Addresses Removed:	**319,662**	**8.91%**

Figure 4.1 Deliverable Mail Report

Creating the Mailing Campaign

While the service bureau is running the traditional merge-purge, your marketing staff will be busy creating the campaign. A direct mail campaign often consists of hundreds of different mailing cells, each designed to test something. You typically want to test each list that you rented. You may also be simultaneously testing various offers or packages or copy. Let's say that you have two offers—a standard offer and a deluxe offer. If you have 200 rented lists of about 10,000 names on each, you might split each one in half (called an A/B split) and send half the deluxe offer and half the standard offer. This means that you will have 400 mail segments (200 × 2). You may also be testing other things, such

DSF[2] Summary Report				
ABC Co.–Holiday Initiative				
Total Mailing	**Mail File**		**Response File**	**Response**
ABC Co.–Holiday Initiative	3,126,612		98,288	3.14%
Delivery Type	**Mail File**		**Response File**	**Response**
1 Curb Delivery	1,325,605	42.4%	40,995	41.7%	3.09%
2 NDCBU (Delivery Boxes in Neighborhood)	337,515	10.8%	10,730	10.9%	3.18%
3 Central Delivery	255,539	8.2%	7,829	8.0%	3.06%
4 Door Slot	1,140,432	36.5%	36,970	37.6%	3.24%
U Unknown	67,521	2.2%	1,764	1.8%	2.61%
Address Type	**Mail File**		**Response File**	**Response**
B Business Address	120,677	3.9%	1,983	2.0%	1.64%
R Residence Address	2,938,414	94.0%	94,541	96.2%	3.22%
U Unknown	67,521	2.2%	1,764	1.8%	2.61%
LACS Converted Address	**Mail File**		**Response File**	**Response**
Y Address Has Been Converted to a New Address	361	0.0%	18	0.0%	5.03%
N Address Has Not Been LACS Converted	3,126,251	100.0%	98,270	100.0%	3.14%
Seasonal Indicator	**Mail File**		**Response File**	**Response**
Y Seasonal Address	2,955	0.1%	70	0.1%	2.37%
N Permanent Address	3,056,136	97.7%	96,454	98.1%	3.16%
U Unknown	67,521	2.2%	1,764	1.8%	2.61%
Vacant Indicator	**Mail File**		**Response File**	**Response**
Y Vacant Address	13,185	0.4%	278	0.3%	2.11%
N Occupied Address	3,045,906	97.4%	96,246	97.9%	3.16%
U Unknown	67,521	2.2%	1,764	1.8%	2.61%
Throwback Indicator	**Mail File**		**Response File**	**Response**
Y Throwback	4,000	0.1%	91	0.1%	2.28%
N Not a Throwback	3,055,091	97.7%	96,433	98.1%	3.16%
U Unkown	67,521	2.2%	1,764	1.8%	2.61%
Drop Indicator	**Mail File**		**Response File**	**Response**
Y Drop	22,250	0.7%	482	0.5%	2.17%
N Not a Drop	3,036,841	97.1%	96,042	97.7%	3.16%
U Unknown	67,521	2.2%	1,764	1.8%	2.61%

Figure 4.2 DSF Results of a Mailing

as teaser copy on the envelope, different paper, fonts, and so on. These additional tests will increase the number of your segments.

Caution: don't create too many segments. The cell size will be too small to give valid results, and you probably cannot use all the information generated from the test. A single-variable test is the best policy.

For each test cell you create a mail code: HA322, HA323, HA324, and so on. These codes correspond to the list and the offer being tested. Your mail shop will print these codes on the mail piece that you send out. When customers respond by mail, phone, or via the Internet, you attempt to capture this code from them so that you can see which list and which offer gets the credit for the response. If the mailing is to your existing customers, you may also create a customer number which is printed on the mail piece. If you have built a prospect database (see below), you can check each respondent against the database to find out what they did. This is particularly important today when you give people the option of responding by mail, phone, or on a Web site. Routinely post each response or sale in your database, and you will get accurate information on how each cell in the mailing performed.

The resulting final mail file and the mail codes will be sent to a mail shop that prints your mail pieces. The first step will be to run postal presort routines designed to get the maximum postal discount. Postal discounts come from arranging the mail in USPS required order with USPS codes that help in the sorting of mail and delivering it in trays or bags directly to the post office, or the mail carrier, that will actually deliver each piece. For example, each mail carrier, when he receives a bag of mail finds it sorted for him in the order of his route.

Business-to-Business Customer Acquisition

To be successful in customer acquisition through direct mail to businesses, you need to know what type of business buys your product. A first step is to code your customer database by SIC or NAICS codes. These codes indicate what type of business your customers are: restaurants, law firms, plastic manufacturers, or farmers, to name a few. Dun & Bradstreet or a service bureau can do the code appending process for you. You can learn a lot from this process. One molded wood manufacturer had been mailing to companies with certain SIC codes for years. When it applied the D&B process to its database, it discovered a whole new industry that had been buying its products without their knowing it. A mailing to companies with this SIC code produced outstanding response rates. Figure 4.3 is a chart of U.S. enterprises by SIC code. This chart is taken from Dun & Bradstreet listings. You will note that most businesses are classified as services.

	SIC Range	Number of Businesses	Percent
Agriculture/Forestry/Fishing	01–09	750,070	3.97%
Mining	10–14	43,635	0.23%
Construction	15–17	1,475,050	7.80%
Manufacturing	20–39	815,949	4.31%
Transportation/Communications	40–49	723,649	3.83%
Wholesale	50–51	844,136	4.46%
Retail	52–59	3,046,430	16.11%
Finance,/Insurance/Real Estate	60–67	1,566,304	8.28%
Services	70–89	7,355,026	38.89%
Public Administration	90–97	241,448	1.28%
Non Classified		2,051,173	10.85%
Total		18,912,870	100.00%

Figure 4.3 SIC Codes

A further breakdown of business types can be by number of employees or annual sales. This information is also available from Dun & Bradstreet and its competitors. You can also often obtain the names and titles of the executives in the companies who make or influence the purchasing decisions for your products.

In trying to acquire business customers, therefore, your primary interest is SIC code, annual sales (of the company involved), and the number of each company's employees. Using D&B or other data, you often can know much more about business prospect purchasing plans and needs than you can learn about consumer prospects.

Prospect Databases

Some companies are experimenting with prospect databases. Without them, most mailers learn only two things from their acquisition mailings: which lists work best, and which offers work best. After the mailing, they are required to wipe their systems clean of the addresses that were mailed to. They get to keep information only on the responders.

A prospect database works this way: A mailer negotiates with list suppliers to let the mailer have their names on his or her file for an entire year (or a quarter). The mailer pays the list owner whenever one of its names is used. Since the mailer has the names for a year, he or she can afford to append demographics to the names to learn the age, income, presence of children, home value, dwelling type, own versus rent, length of residence, mail responsiveness, cluster coding, and about 20 other important facts. The mailer could never afford to append this information to a list that is rented for a single use. Armed with this information, after the first mailing he or she can use back-end analysis to see which clusters, age groups, income groups, and so on respond to the offer. Thus subsequent mailing selections can be made not only by list but by demographics and behavior. Those who have done this find that they get much better response rates than they did when they selected by list alone.

The next step, of course, is to develop models that predict the type of person that will respond to each offer. Selecting mailed names using a model enables response rates to go way up. But that is not the end of it.

Compiled Lists

Until now, many mass mailers have seldom used compiled lists. But with your model, a compiled list becomes more valuable. Using the prospect database, the model that is used to select potential buyers from response lists can also be used to select consumers from a compiled list. Since a good compiled list consists of almost every consumer in the country, a good model will select almost exactly the same people from a compiled list that it would from a large group of rented response lists. Compiled lists are cheaper. Figure 4.4 presents some examples of the costs of various types of lists.

Category of List	Price/M
Attendees	$116
Books and CDs	$119
Business Magazines	$140
Consumer Magazines	$108
Donors	$75
Newsletters	$170
Permission Based E-mail Consumers	$170
Permission Based E-mail B2B	$283
Compiled Lists	$55

Figure 4.4 List Costs per Thousand Records

As you can see from the figure, compiled lists can be rented for about half the cost of response lists. Mailers who have been paying between $75 and $120 per thousand names from response lists find that they can get compiled lists for $45 to $55 per thousand. With the model, they can pick the responders from the compiled list. But that is not all: many compiled lists are already coded with all the appended data that is needed for a model. You can buy a compiled list based on an algorithm resulting from a model. There is no need to rent names that your model says are not likely to respond.

Building a prospect database will work for you if you're a high-volume mailer marketing to consumers. You can use a prospect database if you are renting a wide variety of lists with multiple campaigns each year, and if you're willing to negotiate with list managers and owners. One by one these high volume mailers are shifting to building prospect databases.

Acquiring E-mail Subscribers

When e-mail began in the late 1990s, most marketers thought that they could obtain e-mail subscribers in the same way that they acquired direct mail subscribers. By 1998, several companies began to acquire and sell consumer e-mail addresses to other businesses. The whole industry soon ran into a buzz saw of consumer anger and legislative restrictions. Many leading e-mail service companies, such as e-Dialog, were active in helping draft and encourage the passage of this law. Today, most e-mail subscriber names aren't rented in the same way that direct mail subscriber names are.

Why the difference? Several reasons. First, home addresses are public knowledge (collected by governments for tax and property ownership purposes) and can be changed only by the relatively expensive cost of moving. E-mail addresses can be and are created or abandoned at any time with no cost to the user. Scores of Web sites offer free e-mail addresses to anyone who wants them.

Unsolicited direct mail may be a nuisance to some people, but it is kept within manageable limits by costs ($0.50 or more per piece). Marketers are eager to make every mailed piece profitable, so they constantly prune their lists to concentrate on the most likely responders. Unsolicited e-mail, however, is generally a nuisance to everyone. E-mail is so cheap to send that more than 90 percent of all e-mail delivered is still spam, and everyone who uses the Internet pays for it. Spam makes the Internet work harder and slower and uses up disk space in millions of PCs and servers throughout the world. It requires increased network bandwidth to handle the heavy load of unsolicited, unwanted e-mail.

The spam industry has become a criminal enterprise, banned by law in most countries. Some spammers use massive networks of hijacked computers, called botnets, to initiate attacks. They run autonomously and automatically, infecting more than 2.5 million computers worldwide sending about 43 billion spam e-mails each day. Much of it is pharmaceutical spam. Botnets run on groups of hijacked (zombie) computers controlled remotely. Newer bots can automatically scan the Internet and propagate themselves using weak passwords. Botnets today are a significant part of the hidden Internet. At any given time, up to one-quarter of all online personal computers are unwittingly part of one or more botnets.

The CAN-SPAM Act of 2003

Because of widespread consumer reaction to spam, Congress passed the Controlling the Assault of Non-Solicited Pornography and Marketing (CAN-SPAM) Act of 2003, which was further spelled out by the E-mail Sender & Provider Coalition (ESPC) in 2005 and 2008. ESPC rules state that commercial e-mail must not be sent to an individual unless prior "affirmative consent" from the individual has been obtained. According to CAN-SPAM, affirmative consent is the recipient's express consent "to receive the message, either in response to a clear and conspicuous request for such consent or at the recipient's own initiative."

In short: you may not send commercial e-mail to an individual unless you have already received the individual's express permission to do so. This means that all automated methods of e-mail address acquisition are illegal. Some e-mailers use a slightly different intrepretation: you can start sending commercial e-mail without affirmative consent, but must offer and honor any opt-outs.

Few of us meet criminals in our daily offline lives. On the Web, however, we meet them every day. ISPs (Internet service providers) such as AOL or Yahoo! try to screen these spammers out. They are constantly looking for illegal and unethical e-mail communications on behalf of their customers. They design software to ensure these messages don't get through to their customers' in-boxes. In general, they do a good job of it.

As a responsible database marketer, you don't want your e-mails to be considered spam by any ISP. If ISPs think your e-mails could be spam, you won't be able to contact thousands or millions of your subscribers. This is an additional reason why you have to be very certain that you acquire subscriber e-mail addresses in a legal, ethical, and responsible way.

E-mails are very inexpensive to send compared to phone calls or direct mail letters:

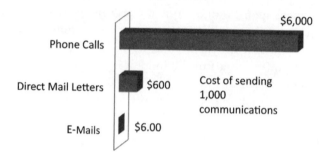

Figure 4.5 Cost of Sending 1,000 Communications by Various Channels

Most e-mail marketers today do not know the value of the e-mail addresses they have acquired. In Chapter 3 we explain the method for determining that value. It is based on the profit you can derive from sending promotional e-mails to your opt-in e-mail subscribers. Typically, the value varies from $2 to $200. An e-mail subscriber for a clothing store may be worth $3.56. That very same subscriber may be worth $242.56 to a car rental company. The person's name and postal address can be rented for $0.10.

Methods of Acquiring E-mail Addresses

There are dozens of legal and ethical ways to acquire the names of e-mail subscribers. In this chapter we cover most of them. The first and most obvious way to acquire subscribers is to get them to sign up on your Web site. It is amazing how many Web sites do not invite registration. What you need, of course, is a prominent box on the top right or left of the Web site screen that invites Web visitors to sign up—giving reasons why it is in their interest to do so. You have to come up with five or six reasons; state them simply and make a compelling case.

I have developed a system for scoring a Web site to determine how good it is at attracting new subscribers. Using this system, you can see in Figure 4.6 how 138 Web sites were scored in July 2010. Figure 4.7 shows an excellent example of a Web site sign up area for e-mail registration.

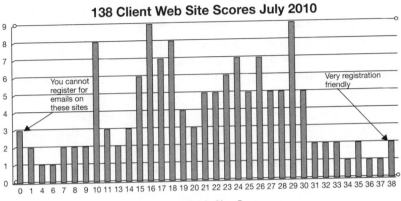

Figure 4.6 Web Site Scores

Sign-up example

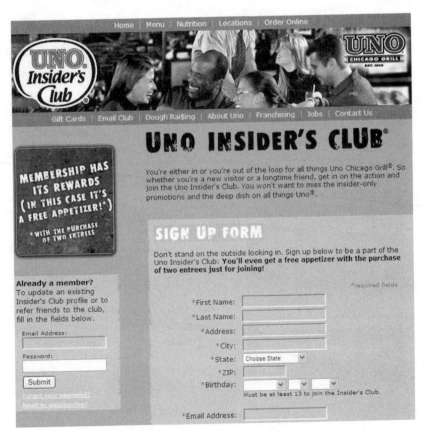

Figure 4.7 E-mail Sign-Up Example

When visitors enter their e-mail in this box, they should immediately see a "thank you" page that asks visitors for their first and last name and their zip code. When they click on a "submit" button, an e-mail should arrive in their in-box within 60 seconds. An ideal welcome e-mail has a place for the subscribers to confirm that they want to get promotional e-mails from you.

One of the best ways to get Web site visitors to sign up is with a popover. An example is shown in Figure 4.8. This is a page that slides over the Web site to invite a sign-up. It appears only once (when visitors first arrive, or as they are leaving) and never appears again. It has proved to be a very powerful sign-up method.

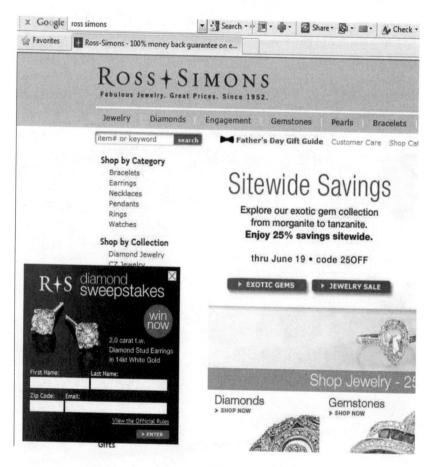

Figure 4.8 Popover

Rewards and Contests

E-mail addresses are so valuable that it is worth your while to give something away to your subscribers as an inducement. Here are some of the methods that work:

1. Reward subscribers for signing up with a discount coupon.
2. Hold contests for subscribers.
3. Provide special prices for subscribers.
4. Reward employees for getting customers to sign up.
5. Have employee contests to boost registration.
6. Train employees to ask for e-mail addresses.
7. Capture customer e-mail addresses at retail locations.
8. Capture e-mails addresses at catalog locations.
9. Offer birthday and anniversary gifts as inducements to register.
10. Sign up subscribers in transaction e-mails.
11. Use mobile as an acquisition channel.

Staff Benefits

Once you know the value of your subscribers, you can determine what you can afford to spend to acquire more. Let's assume that, following the methods discussed in Chapter 3, you have determined that your subscribers are worth $26.45 each. If you have employees with customer contact, you should provide them with approaches for signing up customers for e-mails. A catalog rep, for example, should have a field for customer e-mail in her computer screen. Make sure that she asks for and receives an e-mail address from every caller.

If there is a repeat caller, the existing address will show up on the screen. She can simply say, "Is your e-mail address still Susan88@gmail.com?" If the answer is no, she can enter the new address. You can reward her with $3.00 for doing this—provided that the e-mail is new and that the caller responds to the welcome e-mail by clicking the box that asks if she wants promotional e-mails from your company. The rep gets the same $3.00 if the box is blank and she gets a confirmed e-mail. Suppose the caller gives an erroneous e-mail. The catalog rep gets nothing because the welcome is not delivered, and there is no confirmation.

The same system can be used for other employees such as sales clerks and product installation reps. If the employee has no way of entering the e-mail himself, you can provide all such employees with business cards that can be given to customers, inviting them to sign up. While they are doing this, they can enter the employee's ID number, listed on the card, which is your way of rewarding the right person for the e-mail.

Staff Contests

Even better than a simple cash reward can be a contest in which one employee wins $1,000 every month. Each new confirmed e-mail entered in the system gives the employee one chance to win the $1,000. Every month there's a new winner. You might determine a minimum number of e-mails for someone to win the grand prize.

Subscriber Contests

Here is a really great way to sign up new subscribers. An example is shown in Figure 4.9. In addition to providing an instant reward for subscribing such as free shipping or a one-time X percent off coupon, you should provide all e-mail subscribers with a contest in which they are automatically

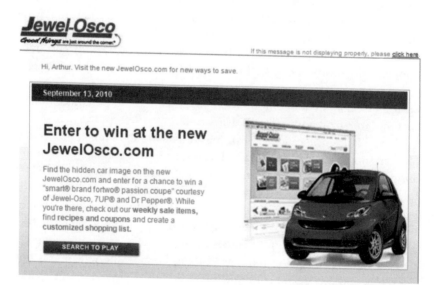

Figure 4.9 Jewl-Osco E-mail Sign Up Contest

entered each time they open one of your e-mails. Suppose that you offer $1,000 worth of your merchandise with the winner to be drawn every month from a pool of all those who opened your e-mail that month. Result: subscribers will stay subscribed. Your open rates will increase, and as a result your click and conversion rates will increase also.

Capture Customer E-mails at Retail Locations

If you have retail stores, then you normally have card reader machines. Put them to a new use. Permit all customers who are wandering around your stores to enter their e-mail addresses on one of these machines. Put signage near the machine listing the benefits of registration (such as the contest). To enter, all customers have to do is to swipe their credit card (which will not be charged) and enter their e-mail address. An example or the machines used is shown in Figure 4.10. One retailer with 900 stores signed up 300,000 subscribers per month with these machines.

Figure 4.10 Verifone MX 870 Used for Entering E-mail Addresses

Birthday Gifts as Inducements to Register

Birthday e-mails have open rates of 62.5 percent higher than promotional e-mails. Click-throughs are 350 percent higher. This is especially the case if the greeting offers some birthday gift. Cold Stone Creamery offers free ice cream on subscribers' birthdays. As a result, in two years, its 1,700 retail stores signed up 2,000,000 subscribers. Its franchises reported "Overwhelmingly positive response … drives people into the stores … people don't come in by themselves."

There are two reasons to ask for a subscriber's birthday:

- Birthday greetings get opened.
- Many people will become subscribers so that they can be on your birthday gift list.

For these reasons you should figure out what you can do for subscribers on their birthday and then advertise that benefit on your Web site and in your e-mails. The customer's birth year may not be important. The month and day are.

Examples of birthday e-mails: Maggiano's Little Italy: $10 off next meal. Dairy Queen: free Blizzard (with purchase of a second Blizzard). Dave & Buster's: $10 worth of free game play. The best gift givers offer something unconditionally. They entice a store visit or online sale experience by offering a real gift. Both Sephora and Victoria's Secret are unconditional birthday gift givers.

The ideal time to ask for a customer's birth date is in the welcome e-mail that comes as soon as a visitor has signed up to be a subscriber. Filling in the birthday should be optional, but the wording should explain why the birthday is asked for and what will happen on that magical day. Of course, it is necessary to set up the appropriate triggers so that the customer's birthday message goes out on time.

If you collect a birth date, of course, you also have to have the customer's first and last names. This provides an excellent opportunity for enhanced personalization. An excellent example is shown in Figure 4.11.

Signing Up Customers in Transaction E-mails

One of the most powerful ways that e-mails can boost the percentage of your e-mails that are opened by your subscribers is to send them transaction e-mails ("Your order was shipped today") in HTML, with promotions of relevant products below the fold, and a request that customers sign up

Figure 4.11 Birthday Greeting

for e-mails if they have not already done so. Transaction e-mails get opened at twice the rate of any other type of e-mail (except for birthday e-mails). In many companies, transaction e-mails are still managed by IT departments. The marketing teams often do not get involved. This is a real missed opportunity for the company, bearing in mind that these e-mails arrive at a crucial time in the customer relationship. You may not be using your e-mail service provider (ESP) to send transactions. This is a big mistake. Here's what you should do:

- Transfer responsibility for transactional e-mails into the marketing department. Use your ESP to send these messages to realize better integration with marketing e-mail, related reporting, personalization, and high delivery rates.
- Use a friendly "from" name, such as your company, brand, newsletter, or department where the transaction took place, such as "SportsBobs Orders."
- Use the subject line to reinforce your brand and convey key transaction-related information: "Your order from SportsBobs shipped on 4/23."
- Because first-time e-mail messages may go to the junk folder rather than the in-box, use strong "from" subject lines to help recipients spot them quickly.

- Position the transactional message content front and center in the message body. Add promotional content below it or to the side. Use HTML to create an attractive message. Transaction information must appear even if the client software blocks the images. Make sure that a recipient can click on all links and view all key information even if images are blocked.

- Invite customers to sign up for your promotional e-mails or newsletters. Explain why it is in their best interest. Invite registered customers to update their personal information with a link in each e-mail.

One of the most successful marketers using this technique is shown in Figure 4.12 from Figis which builds its e-mail database from such transactional e-mails.

Figure 4.12 Transaction E-mail Sign-up Request

Use Mobile as an Acquisition Channel

Mobile can be an attractive channel for data collection for both brands and audiences because:

- The mobile device is always with you and always on so it is a 24/7 response device.

- A mobile call to action can be added to existing media (e.g., poster or off-the-page ad) without incurring extra media cost; it offers additional options (beyond a call center number or URL).

- Mobile can be combined with other channels (e.g., text as a means of collecting opt-in and e-mail as a means of following it up).

- It works. Advertisers have reported 50+ percent of responses to promotions coming from mobile (where a choice is offered) and response rates of 15+ percent for subsequent welcome messages.

- You can get people to sign up using a mobile short code which you can send in a text message. When they enter the code, they are connected to your e-mail sign-up page where they enter their e-mail address.

Figure 4.13 and 4.14 show examples from British Airways and USAir that use mobile effectively for sign-ups.

Appending E-mails to Customer Postal Records

Many companies have thousands or millions of records in their databases of customers who have bought their products. Mailing to them costs between $0.50 and $1.00 each. You can e-mail them for a fraction of a penny. But you do not have their e-mail addresses. There is an easy way to solve this problem. Send all these names and postal addresses to FreshAddress to find the customer's current e-mail, and *get customers' permission* to send promotional e-mails to them.

In general the system finds deliverable e-mail addresses for up to 25+ percent of U.S. postal records. At FreshAddress your customers' names are matched against the FreshAddress database of 525+ million opted-in e-mails and those of several data partners. More than 15 hygiene processes are conducted on the raw matches, removing problematic e-mails. Next FreshAddress sends out a "permission message" to the customers to ensure deliverability and get their permission. The message includes the ECOA (e-mail change of address) link to ensure that your ESP receives

Figure 4.13 British Airways Texting E-mail Sign-up Invitation

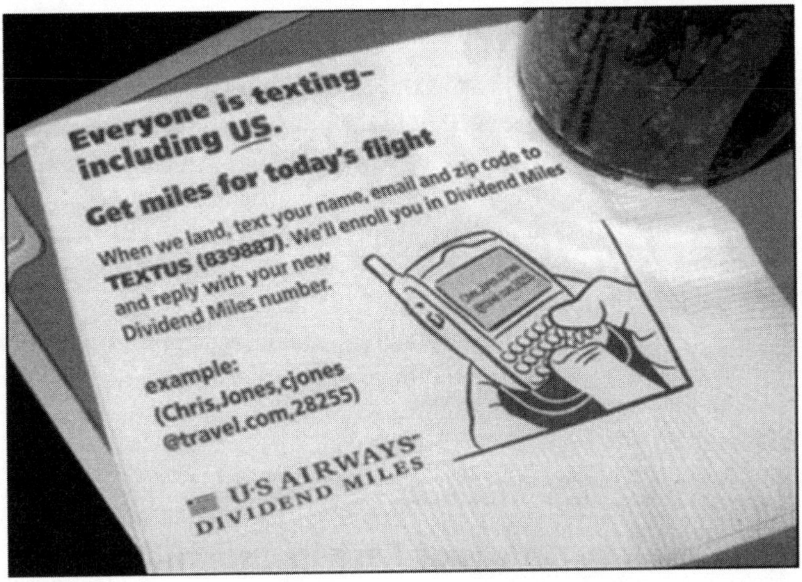

Figure 4.14 US Airways Mobile E-mail Sign-up

the customers' current preferred e-mail address. Your file comes back to you with 25+ percent deliverable, double-scrubbed e-mail addresses.

One company sent 8 million customer names and addresses to FreshAddress. The company received 1,016,454 new e-mail addresses. The cost was about $0.13 per subscriber added.

Ask for E-mail Sign-Ups in TV, Print Ads, and Elsewhere

Television and print advertisements today usually include a toll-free number and a Web site. What they usually lack is a pitch for e-mail sign-up. Getting your ad agency interested in doing this may be difficult, but will be easier once you have calculated the lifetime value of your subscribers. Say that the value of each subscriber is $33.41. The products you are featuring in your TV or print ad may be $30 or $40 each. Think of getting an e-mail subscriber the way you think about selling a product. You pay the ad agency to sell products. Why not pay it for selling subscribers?

The pitch for e-mail subscribers should also be in POP (Point of Purchase) literature in your stores, on your employees' business cards, in all direct mail pieces, on brochures, and on banner ads.

Put E-mail Sign-Ups Inside Product Packaging

Any company that sends products to its customers through the mail or provides them in their stores should include a card inside the product package that invites the purchaser to sign up for e-mails. This is a very inexpensive way to get your message across, particularly if your products are sold by thousands of independent retailers all over the world. A typical manufacturer of clothing, shoes, bedding, or any of thousands of household and business products can use this method.

The card should make it easy to sign up and provide powerful reasons why it is in the customers' interest to go to the Internet and register. The card might also be a prepaid postcard for those who might not go to their PC to register.

Print E-mail Invitations on Cash Register Receipts

What costs only a fraction of a penny to produce and can go with all customers as they depart your business? The answer is a printed cash register receipt. Most cash registers today are linked electronically to the company's database. CVS, for example, has a CVS Rewards program. If you are a member, you do not need to present a card to get rewards points. Just use your registered credit card, and it will look you up, award you points, and deliver a personalized message on your register receipt.

Your goal is to give customers something to take home that will remind them to do what you want—in some cases, to sign up for e-mails when they get home. Of course, if they are already signed up, your intelligent cash register knows that and *does not ask them to do it again.* If they are not signed up, the receipt can give them a message, tell them the benefits, and tell them what to do.

The place to provide the message is the receipt footer. Here you have a lot of options, depending upon your point of sale software. Generally, you have between three and six lines of footer messages that can be programmed. This allows you a great deal of flexibility in getting a message to your customers. With some machines, you can print on both sides.

Buying E-mail Lists

It is possible to rent the e-mail addresses of people who might be interested in hearing about your company and its products. Caution is advised here. It's easy to be scammed in the business of list rentals. Some lists are really nothing more than a huge list of e-mails gleaned from forums and Web sites. It would be spam to send people on these lists e-mails. They are often sold for prices that are too good to be true.

However, if you go about the process carefully, keeping your eyes open, dealing with reputable vendors who can assure you of opt-in names, list rental can be successful.

How successful can you be in acquiring profitable e-mail names by renting them? One company tried a test and discovered some very valuable information. Working with e-mail list brokers, it identified 10 e-mail name vendors that provided 37,500 e-mail addresses of people who were considered potential buyers of the company's products. People who buy these products typically pay about $600 per year, so e-mail name acquisition appeared to be potentially valuable. The test involved sending an e-mail to each of the 37,500 people to get them to buy one of the company's products. As a result of the test, 1,011 people (2.7 percent) made a purchase over the Web and agreed to accept future e-mails from the company. What was particularly interesting was the difference in the performance of the e-mail names from each of the 10 vendors. Figure 4.15 shows them ranked by their conversion rate:

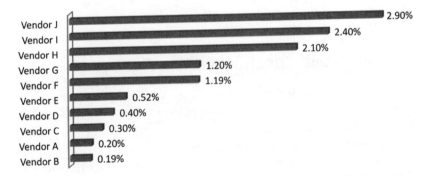

% Conversion from each rented list

Vendor J — 2.90%
Vendor I — 2.40%
Vendor H — 2.10%
Vendor G — 1.20%
Vendor F — 1.19%
Vendor E — 0.52%
Vendor D — 0.40%
Vendor C — 0.30%
Vendor A — 0.20%
Vendor B — 0.19%

Figure 4.15 Percent of Conversions (Sales) from Each of Ten Different Rented Lists

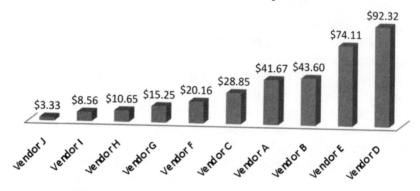

Figure 4.16 Conversion Rate of Rented E-mail Names

As the Figure 4.16 shows, the top two did much better than the others. Vendor I also was the least costly way to acquire a customer. What can you learn from this?

- It is very important to start rental acquisition with a test of several different list vendors.
- The difference in price between various vendors can be as much as 28 to 1.
- Make sure that the vendors you test have plenty more names so that you can use them extensively if they prove to be the winner.
- The total cost of the test (payment for the list rental) was $24,225. Not bad for the knowledge gained from the test.
- The least expensive vendor was also the most productive with results.

Creating a Subscriber Acquisition Plan

Once you have decided on your methods, you should combine a subscriber LTV chart with an acquisition plan. The results look like those shown in Figures 4.17 and 4.18.

You will note that there are six tactics proposed. The cost of your program is $183,000. The profits from acquiring 490,000 more names are $22,965,081. In addition, you can project additional sales through higher open rates resulting from the various tactics.

Typical LTV Chart		This Year	Next Year	Third Year
Subscribers		342,987	303,886	269,243
Annual Unsubscribers	5.30%	18,178	16,106	14,270
Annual Undelivers	6.10%	20,922	18,537	16,424
E-mails Delivered	104	35,670,648	31,604,194	28,001,316
Opens	12.40%	4,423,160	3,918,920	3,472,163
Unique Clicks	23.80%	1,052,712	932,703	826,375
Conversion Rates	2.60%	27,371	24,250	21,486
Store Sales from E-mails	3.20	87,586	77,601	68,754
Total Sales due to E-mails		114,956	101,851	90,240
Revenue	$85.56	$9,835,650	$8,714,386	$7,720,946
Costs	30%	$2,950,695	$2,614,316	$2,316,284
Acquisition Cost Each	$0.10	$34,299		
Sending Costs	$6.00	$214,024	$189,625	$168,008
E-mail Creation	$3.00	$107,012	$94,813	$84,004
Total Costs		$3,306,029	$2,898,753	$2,568,296
Gross Profit		$6,529,620	$5,815,632	$5,152,650
Discount Rate		1	1.1	1.21
NPV Profit		$6,529,620	$5,286,938	$4,258,389
Cumulative NPV Profit		$6,529,620	$11,816,559	$16,074,947
Lifetime Value		$19.04	$34.45	$46.87

Figure 4.17 Subscriber LTV Chart

Plan for Acquiring 490,000 more subscribers over one year	Number of Added Subscribers	Budget for Program	Value of Subscribers Added	LTV for this program
1 Improve Web site	50,000	$10,000	$2,343,376	$46.87
2 Subscriber Contest	200,000	$50,000	$9,373,502	$46.87
3 Terminals in Stores	120,000	$80,000	$5,624,101	$46.87
4 eAppend	30,000	$15,000	$1,406,025	$46.87
5 Transaction E-mails	50,000	$8,000	$2,343,376	$46.87
6 Reward Your Employees	40,000	$20,000	$1,874,700	$46.87
Total	490,000	$183,000	$22,965,081	

Figure 4.18 Acquisition Plan

Where did the estimated added subscriber numbers come from? They are estimates based on your experience with the various tactics. They may not be correct, but having an estimated goal is better than having no goal at all. You can correct them as you go along. Certainly spending $183,000 to generate profits of $22 million is easier to sell to your chief financial officer than a budget of $183,000 with only hope as a goal.

How Many Subscribers Do Commercial E-mail Marketing Companies Have?

The numbers of subscribers to e-mails from our sample companies range from very few—below 50,000—to very many, such as 139,487,097. To put this in perspective, there are about 190,000,000 e-mail subscribers in the United States and more than a billion world-wide as of 2011. If the marketing company is selling a general interest product in the United States—such as a retailer, an airline, hotel, a car rental company, or a sports league—there is really no reason today for a U.S. company to have less than a million. Most should have several million. So the numbers on Figure 4.19 represent, for the most part, a failure to acquire enough subscribers.

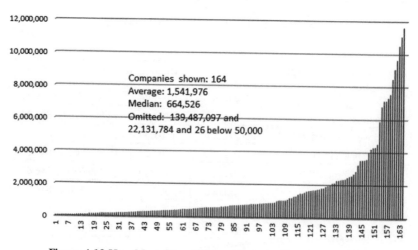

Figure 4.19 How Many E-mail Subscribers do Companies Have

Integrating Your E-mail and Direct Mail Names

Integrating e-mail and direct mail names is a step that far too few marketers take at present. The whole idea of database marketing is to build relationships with your customers that will keep them loyal and buying for years. An important technique is to create personal communications that use their names and recognize their value to your company. In too many companies, e-mail marketing is a separate unit from direct mail marketing. The two units have competing databases, often with hundreds of thousands of identical households. Meanwhile, somewhere else is the catalog database, and finally the loyalty club database. Putting them together does not necessarily save money—it is expensive to do this—but it is a step toward building a 360-degree look at each customer household with the goal of building a lasting relationship.

Take-Away Thoughts

- There are more than 40,000 lists of U.S. consumers and businesses by postal address which you may rent and mail to legally and ethically. A typical consumer name and address will cost you between $0.05 and $1.20 for one-time use.
- There are two kinds of direct mail lists: response lists and compiled names.
- *Response lists* are names and addresses of people who have bought something from some company.
- *Compiled lists* are databases of all households in the United States and Canada—usually with complete census and other demographic data.
- Before you mail any list, first have a service bureau run your list through NCOA^{LINK} This service will find the new address of anyone who has moved.
- There are a series of postal address correction routines that you should use before you mail to large numbers of people. These routines will save you a lot of money.
- Large mailers typically mail many different lists, getting a service bureau to do merge-purge to find the duplicates. Use a list broker to deal with the list owners. You typically rent names for a single use. You may not keep them after one mailing.

> ess to business mailing, use Dun & Bradstreet or InfoUSA to
> the SIC code of your current customers, so you can select
> new prospects that resemble your best customers.

- E-mail subscribers' names can be rented, but most companies recruit subscribers by getting them to come to their Web site where they are offered inducements to subscribe.
- Methods for expanding the number of subscribers you have include subscriber contests, rewards, staff rewards and contests, popovers, birthday gifts, transaction e-mail invitations, mobile ads, appending e-mails to customer postal records, messages on cash register receipts, and co-registration.
- To acquire subscribers, first determine the LTV of your current subscribers. Then use that value to develop an acquisition plan, showing the benefits you will get from acquiring more subscribers.

A quiz on this chapter and all figures can be found at www.dbmarket ing.com/STM4. Those taking all the quizzes can receive a Successful Completion Certificate from the Database Marketing Institute which can be used in their résumé.

5

Building Profits with Recency, Frequency, and Monetary Analysis

Never assume a CHAID program or even a regression model will outperform an old-fashioned RFM analysis if the RFM has been refining the model for more than 20 years.

—David Shepard

RFM helps you define the relationship you have with each subscriber as you can pinpoint where each one is in the customer lifecycle. As subscribers progress through the lifecycle, their needs change until they no longer need you. Using RFM metrics, you can extend the length of time subscribers are engaged with your brand and their overall lifecycle, as well as the value of each subscriber.

—Megan Ouellet
Listrak

Direct marketers have been using recency, frequency, and monetary (RFM) analysis to predict customer behavior for more than 60 years. It is one of the most powerful techniques available to a database marketer. It is the basis for any predictive model of customer behavior, yet differs from traditional modeling in that it requires no knowledge of statistics. It does not require any appending of data. If you have a database of your customers with their purchase history, you can use RFM analysis right now at virtually no cost. You don't need to hire a statistician.

There are two types of facts that you can learn about customers: who they are (demographics) and what they do (behavior). In marketing, we are usually trying to predict behavior. Accurate behavior predictions are important to making profitable marketing decisions. The best predictor of future behavior is past behavior. It beats demographics every time. If you are planning to sell something to your customers, knowing that some of them have bought several items worth $100 by mail or on your Web site recently is worth much more than knowing their age, income, home value, presence of children, or any other demographic information. RFM is pure behavior.

RFM works only with customer files. It cannot be used with prospects, because it requires knowledge of the customers' prior purchase history with you. Prospects, by definition, have no such history. Use of RFM to guide your communications will *always* improve profits more than other method. RFM works with consumer and with business-to-business customer files. It works with any type of industry in which you communicate with your customers for marketing purposes.

Should You Use RFM for E-mail Marketing?

RFM is not as useful for e-mail marketing as it is for direct mail. The key value of RFM is telling you whom *not to mail to* so as to save postage. With e-mail marketing, the delivery cost is so trifling that it can be ignored as a constraint on mailing a list. It is interesting that hundreds of direct marketers who grew up in the direct mail industry are using RFM for e-mail marketing. Why? I am not sure that I know the answer. One answer was provided by Emily Chen at Lyris.com. She said that there are two common misconceptions:

Myth #1: E-mail is cheap, so there's no downside to blasting the message to everyone. There's actually a pretty big downside: list fatigue. Over time, as recipients receive multiple messages they don't find relevant, they become less and less likely to respond, and more and more likely to report your messages as spam. This in turn, lowers your sender-reputation score, the most important factor ISPs use in determining whether to filter your message to the junk folder instead of the inbox. The end result? A damaged brand ("Just what I need, another e-mail from that company") and deliverability issues that can prevent engaged recipients from receiving your messages.

Myth #2: You get a bigger response rate if you send to a bigger list. It seems logical, but it is just not true. Sending to an additional number of warm bodies does not necessarily generate higher click-throughs. In fact, it can actually produce higher spam complaints. You are much more likely to increase response rates when you send relevant, targeted messages to smaller subsets of your lists.

How to Make Money Using RFM with Direct Mail

In this chapter, we cover everything you need to know to make serious money using this technique for direct mail. If you don't already use RFM, you will emerge from this chapter a much more professional marketer who can make your company a lot of money. We begin by describing each of the three components of RFM and then show you how you can increase your profits by segmenting your database into RFM cells and using these cells to direct your customer communications.

How to Code Your Customers by Recency

To code your customer base for recency, you need to store one vital piece of information in every customer's database record—the most recent purchase date. Every time you update your database, be sure that this is updated as well. To create the recency code, you sort your entire database by purchase date, with the most recent at the top. Then you divide the database into five exactly equal parts—quintiles, which you number from 5 (the most recent) down to 1 (the most ancient). The coding process can be seen in Figure 5.1.

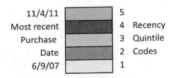

Figure 5.1 Sorting by Recency

Once you have done this, you append a 5 to every record in the top group, a 4 to the records in the next group, and so on. Every record in your database is now coded as a 5, 4, 3, 2, or 1 for recency. This method of creating each of the five divisions is of exactly equal size, 20 percent of the entire database, is called "exact quintiles." There is another way of doing RFM, which has been around for a long time. This method is called "hard coding." Using hard coding, the top quintile is set as being some arbitrary date range, such as 0–3 months. The next is 3–6 months, and so on. That method works, and is in active use in direct marketing operations all over the world. What is being explained here, however, is another more accurate method, also widely used, which produces RFM cells of exactly equal size.

Using exact quintiles creates a certain arbitrary quality in the divisions. The recency dividing line between 5 and 4, for example, may occur on February 12. Because of the sorting process, some customers with a most recent date of February 12 may show up as 5s. Others with the same date can show up as 4s. Don't worry about it. Just do it. We are going to recalculate RFM codes every month, so any arbitrary number assigned this month will be corrected next month. Adjusting the boundaries every month is not worth the effort and ruins the accuracy of the result.

Now that your file is coded for recency, go ahead and do a promotion to your customer base. Not a special test promotion, but some communication that you had planned to do all along which asks customers to respond or make a purchase. Keep track of which quintile every customer is in and which ones respond. If you do, you will have a response picture that will look very much Figure 5.2.

The customers coded with a 5 will respond much better than the 4s, who will be better than the 3s, and so on. The recency code will accurately

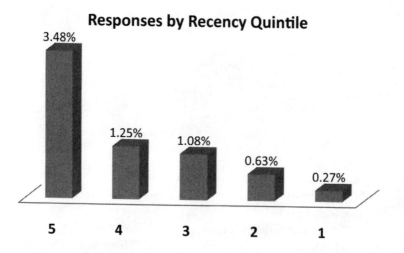

Figure 5.2 Response Rates by Recency

predict who is most likely to respond. These numbers, and all those used in the first part of this chapter, are from an actual promotion conducted by a database marketer who had a customer database of 2.1 million names, going back over a five-year period. They were offering to their customers a video package that cost them about $100 including shipping and handling charges. The graph (Figure 5.2) represent the responses to a test mailing to 30,000 of the 2.1 million names. Each of the five recency quintiles had 6,000 members. Of these, 3.48 percent of the 5s (309) responded; 1.25 percent of the 4s (75) responded. In total only 403 people responded which was 1.34 percent of those mailed.

This means that 98.66 percent of the customers did not respond. This is normal. You will experience the same type of response rates, somewhat better or worse, unless you have a highly unusual offer. What this marketer found, and you also will find, is that recency is a very powerful predictor of response. The 5s responded almost three times better than the 4s.

Why is recency so powerful in predicting behavior? Think about it. I recently bought a new Honda Odyssey—a really great car. I am out on my first day on the road in this wonderful vehicle. I am looking all around. What am I looking for? Another Honda Odyssey! If I see one, I want to honk my horn and wave, "Hey, I've got one too! Aren't they great?"

Most people feel a rush of enthusiasm when they purchase a new car, house, suit, or dress. The feeling lasts for a while. If you were to take out a checking account with the Fleet Bank this week and next week you get a letter from the Fleet Bank, you are going to open that letter. Maybe it is something about your new account. But if you have had an account with Fleet for the past five years and next week you get a letter from Fleet that is obviously not your monthly statement, you may well toss it out assuming that it's just another credit card solicitation. In other words, recent buyers will respond. Ancient buyers may not. Recency works. It is a universal human emotion that we may count on in designing our marketing programs.

If you are a telephone company, recency cannot be the last time the customer made a phone call or the last time customers paid their monthly bill. Everyone would have the same date! Recency is the last time that customers changed their service (added or dropped a line, or signed up for cell phone service). A bank has to count the last time a person opened up a new account or took out a loan. You will have to decide what constitutes recency for your business. You can experiment with different definitions until you get a graph that looks like the one in Figure 5.2. It costs you nothing to experiment and can produce very profitable results when you get the correct answer.

So we have learned how to code our database for recency. Just sort the file by most recent date and divide it into five equal parts. Code the parts as 5, 4, 3, 2, and 1, and check the codes on the responses after any promotion. We have learned something. But before we devote more time to exploring recency, let's explain frequency.

How to Code Your File by Frequency

To code a database for frequency, we need another piece of information in every customer record. It is a number: the total number of times that the customer has made a purchase from you.

948		5	
Purchases		4	Frequency
Per		3	Quintile
Year		2	Codes
1		1	

Figure 5.3 Sorting by Frequency

Figure 5.3 is compiled by sorting the database by the total purchases made by each customer from you. There are many ways of measuring frequency. It could be the average number of purchases per year, the average number of products bought per year, the average number of telephone calls made per month (for a phone company), the total number of checks and deposits made during a month (for a bank). You may experiment to find the best measure for you. What you are looking for is a measure of how important doing business with you is in the minds of your customers, and this is measured by frequency of use of your products or services. Once you have such a code kept in each customer record (and updated on a regular basis), you should sort your database by that number, divide it into five equal parts and put quintile codes into each database record. The process is identical to that for recency.

Then if you do a promotion to your existing customer base and keep track of the frequency quintile that each customer belonged to at the

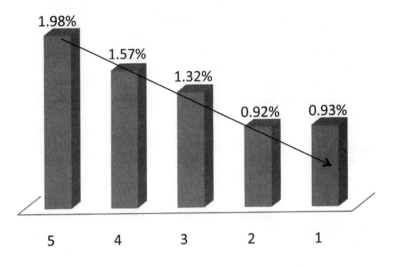

Figure 5.4 Response Rates by Frequency

time of the promotion, you will get a graph of response rates that looks like the chart in Figure 5.4.

This chart shows the same 403 customers whom we graphed by recency in the previous figure, here graphed by frequency quintile. What this illustrates is that frequency is also a good predictor of behavior, but much less so than recency. If you look at Figure 5.2 showing the recency response, you will see how dramatic the response rate of the 5s was (three times the rate of the 4s). Here, the frequency slope from 5 down to 1 is much more gentle. This is generally true of frequency codes. That is why RFM is RFM instead of FRM or FMR. You put the most predictive variable first.

There is something else interesting here, shown by the diagonal line on the graph. There is something wrong with the lowest frequency quintile. The response rate is 0.93 percent. But if it were to follow the trend of the other frequency divisions, the response rate should be less than 0.5 percent. This is not an accident. You will undoubtedly have the same result when you graph your own customer response by frequency. Why do the 1s on a frequency graph respond better than one would suppose?

Because the lowest quintile on a frequency chart contains an abnormal number of recent buyers. A customer who just joined you yesterday is your most recent buyer. So his recency code is 5. Recent buyers are your best responders. But this recent buyer, being brand new, has not had a chance to become a frequent buyer yet, so his frequency code is 1. You probably can't make any money with this universal fact, but it does serve to prove to you that you have done your RFM coding correctly. If your lowest quintile on frequency is not higher than the trend, then you have probably done something wrong.

Response by Monetary Amount

Finally, let's graph these same people by their monetary spending. The method is the same. We keep in everyone's database record a single piece of information: the total amount spent on our products or services, either per month, per year, or in some other way. We are trying to determine the monetary significance of our company to each of our customers, as measured in dollars. We will take this data and sort the entire database by this number, divide it into five equal groups, and assign code numbers 5, 4, 3, 2, and 1.

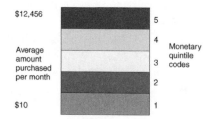

Figure 5.5 Sorting by Monetary Amount

In Figure 5.5 we have sorted the entire file by monetary amount and assigned monetary codes. The left axis represents the amount that each customer has spent per month. The best customer has spent an average of $12,456 per month. The worst customer has spent only $10 per month. These amounts are stored in the customer's database record every time they make a purchase. We sort the entire file by this amount. Let's see what happens when we look at the monetary response rate of these same 403 people who we graphed by recency and frequency.

When you look at Figure 5.6, remember that the 5s represent people who spend a lot of money with your company. The 1s spend very little.

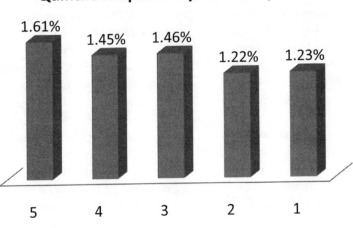

Quintile Response by Monetary Code

Figure 5.6 Response Rates by Monetary Code

Monetary coding is far less predictive of behavior than either recency or frequency. While there is a gentle slope from the 5s down to the 1s, it is not really very dramatic. It is almost flat. What this means is that on small ticket items, monetary is not very predictive. In today's market, a small ticket consumer item would be something that sells for, say, $120 or less. A big ticket item would be something that sells for $1,000 or more. The video in question, which sold for $100, is a small ticket item.

To understand why monetary is not as predictive as recency or frequency, imagine two of your customers: one who spends a million dollars a year on your category of products, and one who spends only a thousand dollars per year. Is there any reason to believe that the million-dollar customer would be more likely to open your envelope containing your promotions than the thousand-dollar customer? No. In fact, I would say that the million-dollar customer would be *less likely* to open the envelope. Why? Because, as a million-dollar customer, she is on everyone's list. Everyone writes to her. She, or her secretary, checks her mail with the wastebasket near at hand. The thousand-dollar customer gets far less mail. He is probably much more likely to open the envelope. So if we go by propensity to open your envelopes (or read your e-mails or take your phone calls) the graph would have exactly the opposite shape, with the 1s having a higher response rate than the 5s.

But once the envelope or the e-mail is opened, the million-dollar customer can write a check for whatever is being sold in that envelope, but the thousand-dollar customer will have to think it over. It may not be within his budget. So, if we are going to go by ability to pay, the 5s will have a very high response rate, and the 1s will be very low. So the final monetary graph is a combination of two opposite human emotions: willingness to open the envelope and ability to pay. That is why the monetary graph, for low-ticket items, tends to be almost flat. The money does not matter.

This is not true for big-ticket items. If you are selling something for $5,000, let us say, then the ability to pay will overwhelm the opening of the envelope and give you a completely different monetary graph. Figure 5.7 shows the response rate for a bank in New York that made a $5,000 certificate of deposit offer to its 250,000 affluent customers.

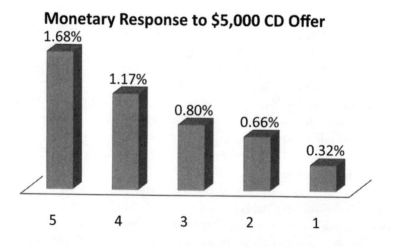

Figure 5.7 Response to Bank CD Offer by Monetary Quintile

In this figure of response rates to a $5,000 certificate of deposit offer, the monetary response rates look almost like recency response rates. You will have the same experience. If you offer customers a commodity or service with a high price, the high monetary quintiles will respond much better than the low ones will.

Putting It All Together

Thus far, we have learned the theory of RFM which is based on three aspects of customer behavior. The theory does not show how we can make money with this knowledge. We are going to show you that right now.

When the coding process is finished, every customer should have in his or her database records three single digits: one for recency, one for frequency, and one for monetary. Every customer is either a 555, 554, 553, 552, 551, 545, 544 ... down to 111. There are 125 RFM cell codes in all. (Later in this chapter, we will learn that you can work with numbers higher or lower than 125.)

When you do promotions to your customers, you keep track of the RFM cell code that each is occupying. The results can be very interesting. Let's see how the company we have been following so far in this chapter coded its database for RFM and did a test of its offer to 30,000 of its 2.1 million customers.

Selecting an Nth

The test group was selected using an Nth. An Nth is a test group that is an exact statistical replica of the full database. For example, if a database had 300,000 customers and we want to select a test group of 30,000 using an Nth, we would divide the 30,000 into the 300,000, with the result of 10. We need to select every tenth record from the master database to create the test group. We will select records 1, 11, 21, 31, 41, 51, and so on taking every tenth record. The resulting test file will have 30,000 members and will exactly mirror the main database. It will have the same percentage of people whose zip code is 22203, whose income is over $100,000, who have two children, and so on as the main database. It does not matter whether the main file is sorted in alphabetical order, in zip code order, or in customer number order. The results will be the same, providing we are dealing with large numbers, such as 30,000.

Results of the Test

When the company mailed the $100 video offer to its 30,000 test group, it got the results shown in Figure 5.8.

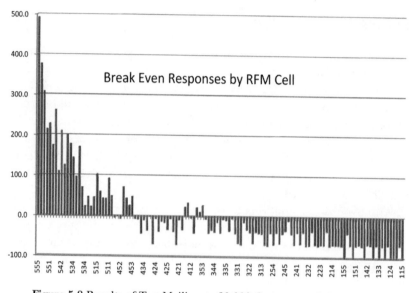

Figure 5.8 Results of Test Mailing to 30,000 Customers   0=Breakeven

On this figure, the bottom (X) axis represents the RFM cell codes of each of the 125 cells mailed in the test. The left (Y) axis represents the breakeven index of each cell. Breakeven is explained in the following paragraph. From this graph we can see that only 34 of the 125 cells did better than breakeven. The remainder lost money. Let's take a moment to explain breakeven.

How Breakeven Is Calculated

Breakeven in direct marketing means that the net profits from sales to a test group exactly equal the cost of promoting to that test group. If, for example, we mail 400 people at a cost of $0.50 each, or $200, and the net profit from that group of 400 people (after credits, returns, cost of goods sold, shipping, etc.) is $200, then we have just broken even. Before we begin a promotion, we can calculate the response rate we will need to get from each cell to break even. There is a neat little formula that tells us this breakeven response rate. It is:

BE = (cost per piece) ÷ (net profit from a single sale)

In the case of the $100 video offer, the company we are studying calculated that it made $40 on each successful sale. The cost per piece of the mailing was $0.55. So the rate it needed for breakeven on each RFM cell was:

$$BE = (\$0.55) \div \$40 = 1.375 \text{ percent}$$

The *breakeven index* is calculated by another neat little formula. It is:

$$BEI = [(r - BE) \div BE)] \times 100$$

In this formula, r equals the actual response rate of the RFM cell. So if the response rate of one cell is 2.5 percent, then the breakeven index is:

$$BEI = [(.025 - .01375) \div (.01375)] \times 100 = 81.82$$

A breakeven index of 0 means that the cell just broke even. A negative number means that the cell lost money.

Results of the Test

In summary, the test mailing to 30,000 had the result shown in Figure 5.9.

	Number	Rate	Dollars
Sales	403	$40	$16,120
Mailing	30,000	$0.55	$16,500
Net Loss			($380)

Figure 5.9 Loss from Test Mailing

The company lost $380 on the test. Was it a failure? Not at all. For a net cost of $380 it learned how 30,000 people, an Nth of its 2.1 million database, would respond to this offer. Since the 30,000 was an Nth, these customers were completely representative of how the entire database would have responded to this same offer. The company then knew which RFM cells would be profitable and which RFM cells would be losers. As a result, it did not mail the offer to the entire database of 2.1 million. Instead, it selected customers from the 34 profitable RFM cells on the rollout. (It also selected a small number of customers from each of the unprofitable cells just to be sure that the coding had been done correctly.)

The selection process is reflected in Figure 5.10. The first column is the test file results. The second column shows what would have happened if

	Test	Full File	RFM Select
Response Rate	1.34%	1.17%	2.76%
Responses	403	23,412	15,295
Average Profit	$40	$40	$40
Net Revenue	$16,120	$936,480	$611,800
No. Mailed	30,000	2,001,056	554,182
Cost per piece	$0.55	$0.55	$0.55
Mailing Cost	$16,500	$1,100,581	$304,800
Profit (Loss)	($380)	($164,101)	$307,000

Figure 5.10 Results of RFM Select Mailing

the company had mailed to the full database of 2.1 million. It would have lost about $164,101. (The appendix to this chapter explains why the response rate to the full file is estimated at only 1.17 percent instead of the 1.34 percent achieved on the test.) The third column shows what the company actually mailed on its rollout. It selected customers out of the 2.1 million who were in the 34 RFM cells that were shown to be profitable on the test. There were 554,182 of these folks. Mailing only to them, the company got an overall response rate of 2.76 percent and a net profit of $307,000. This shows the full power of RFM. You profit by *not promoting* to people who you have learned are unlikely to respond.

What happened when the company mailed to these 544,182 people? This is the most exciting result of this case study. Look at Figure 5.11, which compares the actual response rates of the 30,000 people in the 34 successful RFM cells on the test with the 554,182 people mailed on the RFM selected rollout.

The numbers at the bottom of this graph (the X axis) are the RFM cell code numbers of the 34 cells mailed to which were profitable. The percentages on the left (Y axis) of this graph are the actual response rates of the profitable cells on the test and the corresponding cells mailed to in the rollout. The vertical bars are the response rates of the 34 profitable cells in the test. The lines and dots are response rates of the 544,182 people from those same profitable cells which were mailed to on the selected rollout. It is uncanny how accurately RFM predicted the response of these people. This is why RFM through the years has been selected as the most profitable method for doing direct mail customer promotions. It works. And, it costs almost nothing to use. All the charts and methods explained

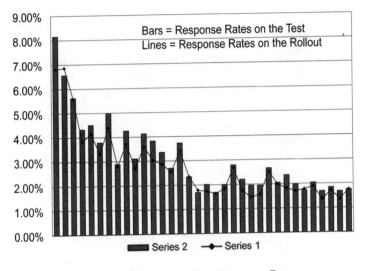

Figure 5.11 Test and Rollout Response Rates

so far in this chapter can be understood by any marketer with no knowledge of statistics. We do, however, have to let you in on a secret that we have been withholding up to this point.

How RFM Sorting Is Done

The RFM sorting is a little more complicated than the earlier sections of this chapter have implied. From the early sections, you got the idea that you would sort your database once for recency, once for frequency, and once for monetary. That is true, and it will work to produce the results shown on the R, F, and M graphs shown in this chapter. But when you come to create the three-digit RFM cells used in the test and rollout shown above, you use a slightly more complicated RFM sorting scheme. You have to sort your database 31 times (see Figure 5.12).

To create RFM cells, you sort the database once by recency, dividing the database into five equal parts. Assign a 5, 4, 3, 2, or 1 to all the members of each of the recency quintiles. Then sort each of these five quintiles by frequency, dividing each into five groups, and assigning the members of each group a 5, 4, 3, 2, or 1. Finally, each of these 25 groups is sorted again by monetary. It seems complicated, and it is. But computers can do this with ease. The result of this process is that every RFM

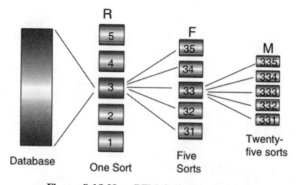

Figure 5.12 How RFM Cells Are Created

cell has exactly the same number of customers in it as every other RFM cell. This becomes very useful for comparing RFM performance and selecting the appropriate customers for promotions.

Paul Wang and I had been teaching database marketing principles, including RFM, in two-day seminars for The Database Marketing Institute for many years. In each seminar, marketers would ask us, "Is there software that does this RFM sorting job?" At first we said, no and told them to ask their IT departments to do the job. But after a while it became obvious that many marketers could not get sufficient help to create RFM cell codes. We decided to create some software to help them out. The result is RFM™ for Windows which is available from the institute (www.dbmarketing.com). Many alumni of the institute and others use this software in their work. They share with us reports of their promotions to customers. From these reports, we have learned a great deal about customer response. The data for all the graphics in this chapter has been obtained from alumni who are users of this software. You can get a free copy of this software on the Internet by clicking on www.dbmarketing.com and downloading it. A few companies per week do this and have been doing so for the past 15 years.

RFM with a Consumable Product

One alumnus worked for a company that sold personalized checks. It had a database of 600,000 customers. The alumnus coded the database for RFM using the methods shown in this chapter. Then he did a promotion to 45,000 customers selected using an Nth. The results were very surprising as shown in Figure 5.13.

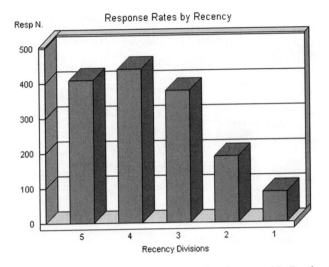

Figure 5.13 Response Rates by Recency for Consumable Product

As you can see in the figure, the response rates for the most recent quintile were lower than those for the second quintile. When I saw that, I wondered if there was something wrong with the theory. How could this be? Then I realized that this company sells a consumable product. The most recent buyers had not yet run low on the product, so they did not order as many. So, I wondered, did the company mail too soon? Should it have waited for these recent buyers to run low? To verify that, I looked at total sales by recency quintile. The graph was gratifying (see Figure 5.14).

These are the same people, arranged differently. The most recent buyers (5s) purchased even more than the next quintile (4s), even though their response rate was lower. What I had not counted on was that recent buyers tend to place larger orders. Since then, I have verified this finding with other alumni. Recent buyers not only have higher response rates, but they tend to buy more per order, and they tend also to buy higher-priced options. Further analysis showed that both frequency and monetary could be used to increase profits for this company. We discovered that this holds in general for most products:

- The highest frequency quintile buys much more than the lower quintiles.
- The highest monetary quintile places much bigger orders than the lower quintiles.

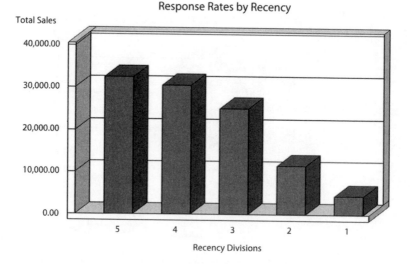

Figure 5.14 Total Sales by Recency for Consumable Product

This customer's breakeven rate by RFM cell was quite different from the company with the video offer. It had 72 profitable cells out of 125 (see Figure 5.15).

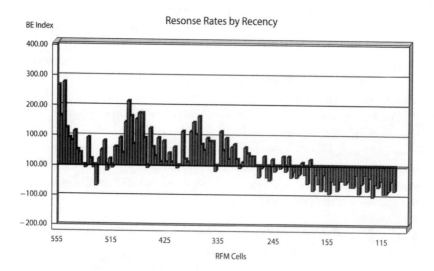

Figure 5.15 Breakeven Index for Consumable Product Test

At this point, you understand the theory behind RFM. It helps you to determine which of your customers will respond and how much they will buy. It is a wonderfully powerful tool.

RFM for Business-to-Business Files

RFM was originally invented primarily for consumer database files. It works well there. It also works with most business-to-business files. Federal Express, for example, has made highly profitable use of RFM in segmenting its business customers. Most business-to-business files are much smaller than consumer files. Many business customer files contain well below 20,000 names. How can such a company make profitable use of RFM? There are two factors to consider.

1. *125 cells are too many for a small file.* The number 125 comes about by multiplying 5 recency divisions by 5 frequency by 5 monetary. Dividing a small business file of 20,000 records by 125 gives you only 160 customers in each cell. This is too small for accurate statistical results. For a business file of 20,000 records, therefore, there probably should not be more than 20 RFM cells, each one having about 1,000 companies in it. To get down to 20 cells, the RFM should be created by reducing the frequency and monetary divisions like this:

   5 recency × 2 frequency × 2 monetary = 20 RFM cells

   If experience shows that monetary is very important in a business's sales (the company sells big ticket items), then the division might be changed to:

   4 recency × 2 frequency × 3 monetary = 24 RFM cells

   There are many ways of doing RFM. Users will have to experiment to see what works best for their situation.

2. *RFM does not beat a sales visit.* RFM is not too useful for those customers being called on by the sales force. The sales force knows far more about the customers than can be learned from RFM analysis. However, most businesses have their sales force calling on only the top 20 percent of their customers, leaving the remaining 80 percent to be dealt with by catalogs, letters, e-mail, and phone calls. If this is the situation in your company, RFM is perfect for helping to manage the 80 percent who do not rate a sales visit. It will tell you which customers are most likely to respond to a phone call, an e-mail, a fax, or a letter.

RFM and Modeling

How does RFM compare with modeling? In this book we have a chapter devoted to analytics. Any good model of customer behavior always includes recency, frequency and monetary amounts. They are the most important available measures of customer performance. Most models, however, go beyond RFM to include demographics, product selection, and other factors. Some of these other factors do help in predicting customer response, so a good model, properly run, can outperform RFM. The problem is that models are usually expensive and difficult for a layperson to run. To run a model you usually have to hire a statistician or outsource your model. You have to buy or obtain demographic data and append it to your file. A good model takes a week or two to run—some companies have spent more than six weeks to get a perfect model run. The cost of the modeling professional, the data appending, and the modeling software, plus the time involved, may run from $5,000 to $200,000, depending on who is doing it and what is involved.

To decide whether to use RFM or a model, you have to consider the economics. The purpose of both modeling and RFM is the same: to increase profits by deciding *not to mail nonresponsive customers.* Modeling is usually expensive. RFM is almost free of charge. Any marketing professional can understand it and use it. The software for creating the RFM cells can be bought for permanent use for as little as $500. You can use it over and over again without paying any fee to anyone. Models quickly become out of date. A $25,000 model needs to be run every six months or more often as the market changes and competition heats up. So to determine whether to use a model, you must accept the idea that the model not only has to be more accurate than RFM (which it probably is) but also that it gives you enough lift in response to pay for the model, plus beating the RFM lift. Except in the case of large databases, this may not be true.

Elsewhere in this book, you will find a number of case studies of companies that make major use of RFM in their marketing program. The studies include Sears Canada and Federal Express. RFM is being used by catalogers, retailers, hotels, airlines, banks, insurance companies, cellular phone companies, and high-tech manufacturers. There are tens of thousands of active users in the United States and Canada. If you have not used it yet, you should look into it because it will definitely improve your response rates and build your profits.

When Not to Use RFM

Using RFM is like taking drugs. It gives you such a high that you want to use it all the time. That would be a mistake. If you use RFM to decide whom to write to or whom to call, some of your customers will never hear from you at all. The more responsive customers may suffer from file fatigue: you will communicate with them too often.

You should develop a customer contact strategy. Figure something valuable that you want to communicate to your less responsive customers once or twice a year just to let them know that you haven't forgotten them. Birthday and holiday cards are useful. Thank you cards are always in season. But don't bother nonresponsive people with continual offers if they do not respond.

Database marketing is meant to be profitable for both the buyer and the seller. If you lose money, it is not profitable for you. If your customers do not respond, you have wasted their time sending them something that they do not want. You have cheapened your reputation your relationship with them, forcing them to reject you. Save your promotional dollars for situations in which both you and your customers are likely to win. It is a favor to both the buyer and the seller.

Also, of course, RFM may not be useful if all you are doing is sending promotional e-mails.

When Should You Use RFM?

Now that you have learned about RFM and have coded your customer base with RFM cell codes, you are in a position to make serious money any time you want to. If management comes to you and asks you to introduce a new product, you know exactly which customers are most likely to respond to your offer, and which are less likely. You can amaze management with your success rates.

Another time for RFM use is during budget season. Once a year, database marketers typically have to justify their marketing program to management for the coming year. One of the best ways to do that is by customer lifetime value analysis described in Chapter 3. Another useful step is to do a customer promotion to high-responding RFM cells a couple of months before your budget comes up for review. You can bring in a lot of sales with very little promotional expense if you just promote to the highest-ranking customers. RFM can open a whole new world for you, at very little cost.

Appendix: Frequently Asked Questions about RFM

How Big Do RFM Test Cells Have to Be to Get Accurate Predictions?

There are two contradictory goals in creating RFM cells. You want them as large as possible so that tests with the cells will be statistically accurate. On the other hand, you want them to be as small as possible to keep the costs of tests down. There is a simple formula that tells you the right size. The formula for the minimum test cell size is:

$$\text{Minimum RFM test cell size} = 4 \div BE$$

Where BE = breakeven response rate. What is the 4? It is a rule of thumb. Use it. It works. If your breakeven rate on a promotion is 1.76 percent, then your minimum test cell size is:

$$\text{Test cell size} = 4 \div .0176 = 231 \text{ customers}$$

Why Use Quintiles for RFM Cells? Why not Deciles?

Deciles (creating 10 recency divisions, 10 frequency divisions, and 10 monetary divisions) are a possible RFM method that some have used. It makes for a very large group of RFM cells ($10 \times 10 \times 10 = 1,000$), which can be used only for the largest consumer files. It has certain obvious drawbacks. Each test is very expensive. If your minimum test size has 231 customers in each cell, as shown above, then each test will require mailing to 231,000 people. That is too expensive a test for anybody. So the answer to the question is that deciles are great for scientific accuracy but useless for practical testing purposes. Stick to something simple that works. Use quintiles or smaller numbers.

For many files quintiles may be too large. As already pointed out, for a business-to-business file of 12,000 names, for example, you would not want to have more than about 20 cells, not 125. You can figure out your distribution by seeing which of the divisions (R, F, or M) turns out to be the most predictive for you. If monetary is very important, then $2 \times 2 \times 5 = 20$ might be the way to go.

I like to use a budget calculation. If you have a large file but management has given you a test budget of only $12,000, then I would figure my RFM cells this way. Suppose your mailing costs are $0.50 each. For $12,000 I can mail only 24,000 pieces. If my minimum test cell size is 240 customers, then I can have only 100 cells ($24,000 \div 240 = 100$). So I would create my RFM divisions as $5 \times 5 \times 4 = 100$.

How Do You Measure Recency with Continuity Products?

Most people use their telephones, electric service, bank accounts, credit cards, and newspapers every day. Most people pay their bills once a month. What constitutes recency in such situations? The answer is different in each case. What we are trying to get at is the last time customers made a business decision concerning your company's services. It could be the last time they opened a new product account, or changed their service, or moved. Keep your eye on the goal: we are trying to predict behavior. You will have to experiment with various events to determine which is the most predictive of response rates.

How Do You Measure Frequency of Purchase?

Frequency is the stepchild. Recency is independent. Monetary is independent. But frequency is closely related both to monetary and recency. It is halfway in between. One customer spent $2,400 two years ago and has not bought since. Another has spent $100 per month for the last 24 months. They have both spent $2,400 with you. Which is the best customer? I would say that the second customer is far better. You are maintaining contact and have hope for future sales and increased sales.

How is frequency measured? What units should be used? There are many possibilities:

- A cataloger or retailer can measure the number of purchases in a year or the number of items ordered.

- A bank can measure the number of checks written and the number of deposits made.

- A hotel can measure the number of visits or the number of nights stayed.

- A telephone company can measure the number of calls or the number of minutes talked.

- An electric utility can measure the number of months in service or the number of kilowatts used per month,

Each of these industries has several possible ways of measuring frequency. *Which is the best frequency measurement?* There is no universal answer, but there is a universal method of finding the answer. The universal method is this: test each of several possible methods and see which of them does the best job of predicting actual response rates. The cost of testing is almost nothing:

- Identify two or more possible measurements of frequency, such as number of purchases or number of items purchased. Use each method to develop separate RFM scores. File both in your customer database.

- Carry out any regularly scheduled promotion to your customer base, but keep track of the frequency quintile that each customer is located in. When the responses come in, append them to the database and draw a graph of the results.

- The correct measurement is the one that produces the most predictive graph. A predictive graph is one in which there is a dramatic difference between the response rates of each quintile. Figure 5.2 is very predictive. Figure 5.6 is not.

You will get some very interesting results. The New York bank, which sold $5,000 certificates of deposit, is described earlier in this chapter. The marketing director tested one measure of frequency and got the graph of the results shown in Figure 5.16.

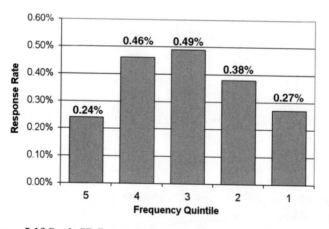

Figure 5.16 Bank CD Response Rates by Frequency with ATM Usage

The chart in Figure 5.16 makes no sense. Why would the best responders be those whose frequency is in the third quintile, and the lowest response rate be from those in the top quintile? When I saw this chart, I called the marketing director at the bank right away and asked her what she had done to create this monstrosity.

"I did just what you told me," she said, "adding together the number of deposits and checks written per month. Then, because the data was available, I added in the number of times that the customer had used the ATM each month. That was how I measured frequency."

At first, her explanation seemed to make sense to me, and I wondered if my understanding of frequency was flawed. But after a while, I figured it out. She was selling a product whose minimum price was $5,000. I asked her "Do people who can afford a $5,000 CD tend to make extensive use of ATMs?"

She pondered this question, and did a little research. What she discovered was that higher income people tend to use ATMs less often than lower income people. By adding ATM usage as a frequency measurement, she was mixing in a contrary factor: a behavior that was the opposite of the desired response purchase of a high-dollar CD. After learning this, we redid her calculations, taking out the ATM usage. We ended up with the chart shown in Figure 5.17.

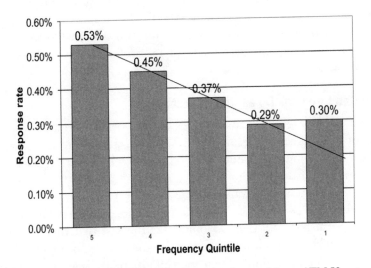

Figure 5.17 Bank CD Frequency Response Rates without ATM Usage

Why is this chart better? Because the measure selected for frequency of use more accurately predict who actually responded to the offer. These response rates are low: the highest is only one-half of 1 percent. But, for the bank, the rates were high enough to make the overall promotion profitable. Its use of the correct frequency measurement enabled it to drop close to 100,000 customers from its next CD promotion, getting almost the same amount of sales but greatly increasing the profits to the bank.

Does RFM measure profitability?

Only very indirectly. There are really two different customer behaviors: responsiveness and profitability (see Figure 5.18).

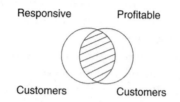

Figure 5.18 ATM Usage Responsive vs. Profitable Customers

Some customers give you thousands of dollars worth of business every year, but they won't respond when you write to them. Other customers who are very unprofitable will answer all your surveys and buy your specials but still won't be profitable. RFM measures responsiveness and not necessarily profitability. Don't confuse the two. However, you can use monetary and frequency as a surrogate for profitability if you have nothing better to use.

Why Don't Rollouts Do as well as Tests?

In the example given in this chapter, the test of 30,000 had a response rate of 1.34 percent. The predicted rollout response rate was only 1.17 percent. Why was the rollout rate expected to be lower? In fact, most marketers find that rollout rates are quite often lower than test rates. There are a number of valid reasons, but the most compelling is that marketers just cannot leave well enough alone. Marketers hate to have unsuccessful tests. So they do things for the test that they could not afford to do for the rollout. They may use the best list, or mail first class, or mail at the ideal time. When the rollout comes, they find that they have to economize, so they get a lower overall response rate.

Because this is so, when you are estimating your response rate after a test, be sure to discount it by a factor, such as 10 percent. If you do that and the rollout is better than you predicted, you will look like a hero. If it is worse, people will think that you are not such a good marketer after all.

How Do You Know the Best Ways to Measure Recency, Frequency, and Monetary Amount?

This problem comes up a lot, and leads many companies to abandon RFM because they feel it will not work in their situation. For example, if you are a magazine with a standard subscription rate, everyone pays the same price. So how do you score monetary? Answer: keep track of other products that subscribers buy from you. These will create differences in monetary amount.

For recency, electric utilities complain that everyone uses electricity all the time so their most recent date for everyone is yesterday. No problem. Use other measures, such as, "When was the last time that the customer changed his service or bought some new product from you?" Use that as the recency date.

The basic rule is to be creative. You are trying to determine how important the products and services of our company are to each customer. If you are debating about using two possible measures, use them both and develop two RFM scores for each customer. Keep them in the customer's record. Then, the next time you run a promotion to your customers, see which RFM system does the best job of predicting behavior. That analysis will tell you which method to use.

Take-Away Thoughts

- RFM has been used for more than 60 years. It is used only for customers, not prospects.
- It tells you which direct mail customers *not to mail to* because their response rates will be below breakeven.
- RFM does not work well for e-mail, because the cost of mailing is so low, you might as well mail them all.
- The formula for the breakeven response rate for a group of direct mail customers is:

$$BE = (\text{cost per piece}) \div (\text{net profit from a single sale})$$

- In recency, the top quintile (5) has response rates very much higher than the next lower quintile (4).
- Every RFM cell has exactly the same number of customers as any other RFM cell.
- RFM is cheap to use. You do not need to know anything about statistics.
- Frequency is not as predictive as recency. The lowest quintile in frequency usually has a surprisingly large response rate because is contains lots of recent buyers.

- For low ticket items (less than $120), frequency is seldom predictive. It is very predictive of responses for big ticket items.

- For typical RFM, you sort the file 31 times and end up with 125 RFM cells from 555 down to 111.

- For an RFM test, you use an Nth which is an exact statistical replica of your main file.

- Once you have done a test mailing, you know which RFM cells were profitable. You mail to only those cells on the rollout.

- There is free software for a trial of RFM. It is located at www.dbmarketing.com.

- For a business-to-business mailing, 125 cells is usually too many. Cut it down by reducing frequency or monetary, such as $5 \times 2 \times 2 = 20$.

- RFM is the basis of any good predictive model.

- Don't use RFM all the time. Use it when you want to make a good impression.

- Frequency is often difficult to quantify.

- RFM does not measure LTV or profitability.

- Rollout response rates do not do as well as test response rates. Why? Because marketers cannot leave well enough alone.

A quiz on this chapter and all figures can be found at www.dbmarketing.com/STM4. Those taking all the quizzes can receive a Successful Completion Certificate from the Database Marketing Institute which can be used in their résumé.

6

From Catalogs to Amazon

The Internet called itself a service, but its effect on our culture has been more like an invasion. We blinked, and suddenly there are these portals in our homes and offices that take us instantly to other people's homes and offices, to stores and libraries, to communities of every kind.

—ORSON SCOTT CARD

Lands' End used to send out simple, promotional e-mails, pitching various clothing items. Then someone there had an unusual idea. Now those e-mails start by telling a story. These are human interest stories, always well-written and always worth reading. In each e-mail, after the story, they feature the clothes they want to sell. The result of this change in approach? Their subscriber list grew from 20,000 to 500,000 in two years. Why? Because their e-mails became interesting and engaging. People opened them and forwarded them to their friends. That's what happens when your e-mails are worth reading.

—NICK USBORNE

This chapter is the story of the role that databases have played in the catalog industry leading to today's Web sites, promotional e-mails, and Amazon.

The Internet and catalog retailing industry in the United States includes 16,000 companies with combined annual revenue of about

$235 billion in 2010. Major companies include Lands' End, L.L. Bean, Miles Kimball, Overstock, and Hanover Direct. The industry is concentrated: the top 50 companies account for about 60 percent of industry revenue. Over time, the bulk of the industry's revenue has shifted from catalog to Internet sales.

Demand is driven by consumers' personal income. Profitability of individual companies depends on effective marketing to build a customer base. Larger firms enjoy central purchasing efficiencies and economies of scale in inventory management, customer service, and telecommunications. Smaller firms compete on outstanding customer service and providing niche products. Average annual revenue per worker for a typical company is nearly $1 million.

Although catalog and Internet retailers sell a variety of products and services, some of the largest product categories are drugs, health and beauty aids; computer hardware and software; and clothing. Many Internet and catalog companies specialize in a single product category, but larger companies are expanding offerings to maintain growth and leverage brand awareness. Amazon has expanded from being an online bookstore to offering more than 29 million products in more than 30 categories.

It All Began with Abacus

The year 1990 marked the founding of the Abacus Alliance, a co-op database designed for catalog marketers. At that time there were only a dozen catalog members of the alliance. Fifteen years later there were 1,800 members and three competing alliances. Instead of one or two monster catalogs like the old Sears Roebuck or Montgomery Ward, today's catalogs average about 64 pages and come out about once a quarter or more often. The way the Alliance works is that catalog members send information to Abacus monthly about the people who bought from their catalogs and what they bought. The Abacus central database contains the names of 90 million households that have purchased from two or more catalog companies in the past 12 months. Any cataloger that has a minimum of 5,000 active buyers can join. Members can receive prospect names of households based on the products that they purchased in the past year.

Members request active prospect names that match the spending behavior of their existing customers. Since Abacus already has the cataloger's existing database, it is able to run a model and score the 90 million households in its prospect database to come up with a million names that work well for the cataloger and that are not already customers of that cataloger. It is a wonderful system that has played a significant role in the success of the catalog industry. If you buy anything from a catalog today, within a couple of weeks you will probably receive a dozen catalogs in the mail from other companies that sell similar or related products. The entire industry depends on the databases maintained by Abacus and its three competitor co-op databases.

Saving Our Trees—Not as Easy as It Sounds

When the Internet arrived in around 2000, many catalogers saw it as a tremendous opportunity. "We can save printing and mailing all those millions of catalogs by creating a Web site with the same information" was the thought in hundreds of minds in the catalog industry. Soon many catalogers were creating Web sites with more and more sophisticated indexing systems so that Web visitors could quickly find what they wanted. Electronic shopping carts were invented and installed so that any product could be purchased from a Web site using a credit card. Over the course of 10 years, Web sites grew from static placeholders to vibrant interactive adventures that contain shopping carts and links to everything that the company has to offer, plus detailed specs, ratings, and reviews. Led by Amazon and Netflix, companies learned to make Web sites personal, greeting visitors by name, and letting them view their accounts and previous purchases.

After the catalog Web sites were built, their builders waited, and waited, and waited. The sales did not come at first. America had not yet become accustomed to the power of Google. Catalogers found that in most cases, to create sales, they would have to continue to mail catalogs. Most of the customers buying from a Web site had the catalog in their hands at the time. That is still true today, although year by year, the members of the public are becoming used to Internet shopping. When they want to buy something, they first go to Google and then go where Google directs them. Even as Internet shopping grows, paper catalogs are alive and well. Why? Because the shelf life of a catalog is about six months. As long as it is kicking around the house, someone is going to see it and be prompted by it to pick up a phone or go to their PC. The shelf life of an e-mail—if it is opened at all—is seldom more than 24 hours.

The Arrival of E-mail Promotions

Depending on Google to supply buyers, however, is a passive marketing strategy. To spur sales requires something active—something like mailing a catalog—which is why the e-mail promotion industry was born. A promotional e-mail is like a catalog. It lists products with prices and specifications. But it is more than a catalog. Done right, it contains scores of links that permit viewers to get more information on each of the featured products. You can see what colors and sizes are available. You can read customer reviews. You can compare prices of similar products. You can use the shopping cart in the e-mail to order your products. Through a search box, you can also reach, read about, and order any of the other products sold by that company, whether they are mentioned in the e-mail or not. These features are contained in e-mails that arrive, like catalogs, in consumers' in-boxes every day.

There are two problems with promotional e-mails: how to get people to sign up for them and how to get people to open and read them once they are delivered. A cataloger can get a profitable consumer name and postal address from Abacus for about $0.07 or less. He can send as many catalogs as he wants. The same is not true of e-mail names. Because of the Can Spam Act of 2003, sending promotional e-mails to people that have not asked for them is against the law. So where do you legally get the e-mail addresses? The answer is that you have to acquire these e-mail addresses through a complex group of procedures that are spelled out in detail in Chapter 4 of this book.

Once you have acquired a customer name and address whether postal or e-mail, you can put the name into a database and use it for promotional mailing. But at that point, the issue of frequency has to be addressed. How often should you send letters, catalogs, and e-mails to people in your database? This is discussed extensively in Chapter 16 of this book.

A bigger problem is what to do about Amazon.

The Amazon Challenge

In 1995, Amazon sold its first book, which was shipped from founder Jeff Bezos's garage in Seattle. During its first four years, Amazon told its investors that it would not make a profit, and it lived up to that promise. What Amazon did was invest in strategic database marketing on a vast scale that is unequaled in the world today. As you read this, Amazon is an e-commerce dream. Jeff Bezos was *Time* magazine's person of the year in 1999. The innovation and business brilliance that sustains Amazon is legendary.

Amazon today sells almost everything including beauty supplies, clothing, jewelry, gourmet food, sporting goods, pet supplies, books, CDs, DVDs, computers, furniture, toys, garden supplies, bedding, and almost anything else you might want to buy. Headquartered in Seattle, Amazon is the world's largest online retailer, with nearly three times the Internet sales revenue of the runner up, Staples, as of January 2010. By 2010, Amazon was attracting more than 65 million customers to its U.S. Web site per month to look at their 29,000,000 products.

Amazon has software developers in centers across the globe. In addition to its headquarters in Seattle, other locations include Slough and Edinburgh (United Kingdom); Dublin (Ireland); Bangalore, Chennai, and Hyderabad (India); Cape Town (South Africa); Iaşi (Romania); Shibuya and Tokyo (Japan); Beijing (China); and San Francisco (United States).

Amazon is based on several concepts of marketing that differ from those of most other Web sites or retail stores. These concepts were and are central to Amazon's success:

1. *Strategic database marketing.* Amazon from the very beginning has been based on a customer marketing database that holds thousands of pieces of information on every visitor to the Amazon Web site: what they clicked on, what they bought, their opinion and ratings of products, and their reviews. The first edition of my book *Strategic Database Marketing* was published in 1993—the year before Jeff Bezos thought up the idea for Amazon. It is almost as if he had read the book and was implementing the ideas contained in it because they are all there.

2. *High-level technology.* The massive technology core that keeps Amazon running is based on Linux. The data warehouse is divided into three functions: query, historical data and ETL (extract, transform and load) which pulls data from one source and integrates it into another. The query servers contain more than 20 terabytes of raw data, as do the click history servers. Amazon's technology architecture handles millions of back-end operations every day as well as queries from more than a million third-party sellers. Amazon has dozens of patents on its methods.

This Amazon concentration on the database is very different from that of retail stores. A retail store is typically run by the product buyers. Stores have limited space. They cannot afford to stock everything so they have intelligent buyers who become knowledgeable about what the new thing is—the trend. They set the fashion by featuring products based on price or quality that will sell the best. Amazon from the beginning has been based on the customer database rather than on professional product buyers. The database tells Amazon what each customer is interested in and how she wants to be served.

3. *Personalization.* From the beginning, Amazon presented its Web site viewers with a particulurly inviting greeting.

Amazon uses cookies on customer PCs so that it can personalize what each repeat visitor sees on the Web site. This permits Amazon to store the personal information from and about customers in its database. While other Web site owners listened to the *privacy advocates* who argued that this personal greeting was offensive to a few customers (which it probably was), Amazon pioneered with personalization as the core principle of the Web site and its whole marketing approach. It stores all credit card numbers in a separate database that's not Internet-accessible, cutting off that possible entry point for hackers. The Amazon goal is pretty straightforward: "To be Earth's most customer-centric company where people can find and discover anything they want to buy online." Its system is complex, massive, and dynamic. Amazon's marketing structure is a lesson in cost-efficiency and brilliant self-promotion.

Using the data it collects on every registered user during every visit to the Web site, Amazon points users to products they might be glad to discover and buy. Amazon recommends products that are:

- Similar to what customers are currently searching for (on-the-fly recommendations that use up massive processing power).

- Related to what they've searched for or clicked on at any time in the past.

- Purchased by other people who are similar in their purchasing habits to the current customer and have searched for what the customer is searching for or have bought what the customer has bought.

- Based on the stuff customers buy for other people.

You can customize the recommendations by giving Amazon more information about your interests and by rating the products you've already bought.

4. *A customer-friendly interface.* Amazon does more than talk about service to its customers. Each product has customer ratings and several consumer reviews. Customers rate products on a hierarchical scale of one to five stars. Amazon members can also comment on other members' reviews. Jeff Bezos explains that customer service is not an addition to their corporate goal—it *is* the corporate goal. He calls Amazon, "The most consumer-centric company." In speeches he tells of technological advances that have enabled customers to find what they want among Amazon's more than 29 million products. Amazon focuses on the customer experience. It wants customers to quickly access their heart's desire and obtain it without hassle. It has spent billions enhancing and developing its Web site interface and customer relations.

There are numerous methods that Amazon uses to assist the customer. All customers may send e-mails to Amazon requesting clarification about making purchases or other information. Amazon employs many people to respond to customer issues by phone and e-mail.

One of the best features, I believe, is "one-click ordering." Next to any product on its Web site is a one-click ordering box as shown in Figure 6.1.

One click and the product is shipped right away to your already stored address, using your already stored credit card. It is about the most customer-friendly system on the Internet.

5. *Partnerships and Web services.* Amazon not only operates many of its own Web sites, but it hosts and manages retail Web sites for a large number of other retailers, including Target, Sears Canada, Bebe Stores, Timex Corporation, and Marks & Spencer. Amazon hosts more than a dozen types of Web services, including e-commerce, database, payment and billing, Web traffic, and computing. These Web services—many of which are free—create a reliable, scalable, and inexpensive computing platform that has revolutionized many small businesses' Web sites. For instance, the Fulfillment by Amazon (FBA) program lets merchants direct inventory to Amazon's fulfillment centers. After the products are purchased, Amazon packs and

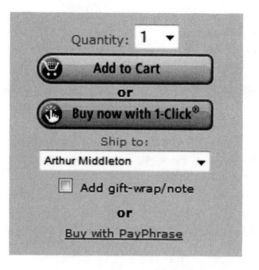

Figure 6.1 One Click Ordering

ships the products for the merchant. Amazon's Fulfillment Web Service (FWS) lets retailers embed FBA capabilities straight into their own sites, thus enhancing the retailer's business.

6. *Affiliates.* Amazon has a Web services program in which independent retailers and third-party sellers (affiliates) agree to place links on their Web sites to Amazon or to specific Amazon products. Nearly 1 million companies have joined Amazon in this program, resulting in approximately 40 percent of Amazon's revenue.

7. *Universal product offering.* Amazon signed up so many different partners that it today sells just about any product in any category that anyone would want. For every product shown, Amazon usually lists scores of new and used options of the same product with prices compared. People have no reason to go anywhere else.

8. *E-mail marketing.* Amazon uses its tremendous customer database to send permission based e-mails suggesting products that it believes that the recipients would be interested in buying. I am one of those recipients. I buy books on physics and history as well as biographies. Because of Amazon e-mails, I purchased five books that I had not known about but proved to be exactly what I wanted.

9. *Ratings and reviews.* Just about every product listed has a customer rating and several customer reviews.

10. *The long tail.* Chris Anderson, editor-in-chief of *Wired* magazine, coined the term *long tail* to explain that through the Internet, products that are in low demand can be listed on Web sites and can collectively have a total sales volume that exceeds the sales volume of the current bestsellers or blockbusters. (See Figure 6.2.)

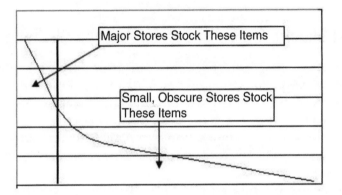

Figure 6.2 The Long Tail

There are two reasons why the long tail is so successful: First is that by using the Internet, a retailer can have one warehouse for the entire country instead of the hundreds of warehouses that are required by brick-and-mortar stores. The central warehouse can maintain thousands of less popular items that would be impossible to stock in the traditional retailing system. Second, through links in Web sites and e-mails, it is possible to have access to goods stocked in partner companies, with the partner company fulfilling the orders coming to it from the central Web site.

Examples of Web sites that benefit from the long tail include eBay, Yahoo!, Google, Amazon, Netflix, and iTunes. According to Anderson, "The future of business is selling less of more." A significant portion of Amazon's sales, for example, come from obscure books that aren't available in brick-and-mortar stores. The total volume of low-popularity items that it sells exceeds the total volume of high-popularity items.

The key reason the long tail works is that the Internet has dramatically reduced the search costs for products and services. EBay was the first to discover this, followed by Amazon. Google capitalized on it to become the powerhouse it is today. Before the Internet, consumers spent far more time hunting for things than they have to nowadays. So the long tail benefits consumers. But it also benefits business because before the Internet it was very difficult for vendors of obscure items to find customers.

Before Netflix, video rental stores like Blockbuster could stock only a few thousand titles in their stores. Netflix can stock more than 100,000 titles in a few warehouses. Consumers get a wider choice, and less well-known movies get a wider audience.

What Should You Do about the Amazon Challenge?

Those who are reading this book cannot hope to beat Amazon at its marketing game. Why not? Because Amazon has a 15-year head start. It is now the biggest Web retailer in the world. Most other competitors today are controlled by managers who are looking only at next quarter's revenue and profits. Few, if any, investors today are willing to accept four years with no profit so that you can build the perfect customer marketing database system.

Competing with Amazon is not like Avis trying to beat Hertz. It is more like humans trying to compete with God. So what should you do?

If you can't beat them, join them. This universal adage really applies today. Even if you are Walmart, AT&T, or Sears, you cannot hope to create a strategic database marketing program that can compete with Amazon. It is too late for you. But there are still ways to succeed. You can do what Target and other large companies have done: join Amazon as an affiliate partner. Amazon is amazingly willing to talk to potential partners and make them a deal that will be profitable for both. If you do decide to be an affiliate partner, you will be able to do all of the things in this book that you would like to do but are unable do in your current situation. You will be able to profit from strategic database marketing.

The Importance of Ratings and Reviews

One important part of Amazon marketing is ratings and reviews. Reviews are the most read parts of most promotional e-mails. Seventy-seven percent of online shoppers employ user-generated reviews and ratings when making purchase decisions according to Jupiter.

Shoppers who find user-generated reviews and ratings useful tend to spend more heavily online than other online buyers do. Moreover, they are more likely to say they are highly loyal to, buy more frequently from, and return their purchases less frequently to stores that feature user-generated product reviews. These positive results from reviews and ratings show the overall value of such programs in terms of profitability and customer retention. (See Figure 6.3.) Lightspeed reported that of 1,000 people in the United Kingdom, 72 percent had read a review for a product or service on the Internet in the last 30 days; 37 percent had read a review in the last week.

Younger people (ages 18–24) at 63 percent were less likely to read reviews than those over 25 (75 percent), and men were slightly more likely to read them (75 percent) than women (69 percent). Adding ratings and reviews to a Web site or an e-mail improves the conversion rate by as much as 4 points according to some studies. This, in many cases, means doubling the sales. It also improves click and open rates. Ratings and reviews are considered by marketers to have multiple benefits for their marketing program.

Power Reviews surveyed 1,200 consumers who shopped online at least four times a year and spent $500 or more annually. It found that the vast majority placed high value on ratings and reviews.

Time Spent on Online Research by 1,200 Consumers

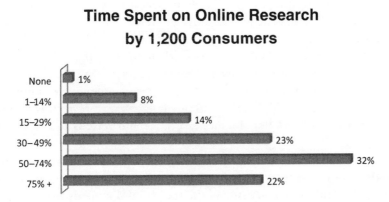

Figure 6.3 Consumer Report by Power Review's 2007

Customers who write reviews report that they write more product reviews than the number of purchases they make in a year. Whatever the reason, many of these customers are engaged with a retailer in this fashion and may be driven to purchase more actively if more retailers presented reviews in a manner that is appealing to these shoppers' needs, such as via quick-read aggregated ratings.

Petco's vice president of e-commerce, John Lazarchic, discussed the raw value of reviews, stating, "No matter how many reviews they receive, customers continue to add their voice. A product may already have a rating of 4.9/5, but someone will still write another positive review."

Negative reviews have real value. Oriental Traders chief Taylor reported that the company received several negative reviews on a particular package of bulk candy. The reviews said that the product didn't look at all like the picture. It turns out that the reviews were right. The picture was updated and information about the ratio of hard to soft candy was added to the product description. Oriental Trading also added a comment inside of the reviews to let new customers know that the photo had been changed.

One company that places special attention on reviews is Dell. When it was able to put reviews on a product, it found that conversions averaged 4 percent higher than the normal conversion rate and that the average order value increased by 18 percent.

Amazon has been providing reviews for years. Many sites have copied the idea. It turns out that when you have them, customers read them more than anything else on a promotional e-mail or Web site. People like to read what others say and often trust consumer reviews—particularly when the reviews include some negative content. They like to read consumer reviews more than anything that they read which is written by the promoters of the product. Some marketers report that 4.5 star rated products sell better than 5 star rated products. Why? Because consumers think that less than perfect ratings suggest that the rating is more honest. For this reason, getting some negative reviews is a high priority for any marketers including ratings and reviews in their Web site or e-mail.

Amazon profits from negative reviews by offering alternatives to the product. Amazon has a section called, "Items mentioned in these reviews" on the right hand side of the reviews. If somebody writes a negative review and suggests another item, Amazon shows it to the readers. This is something that is easy for Amazon to do because it sells just about any product sold by anyone. It is a great cross-sell opportunity.

Negative reviews are often spotted by search engines like Google. This means that with negative reviews, you are more likely to show up in a search. A site with 90 positive and 2 negative reviews on a product is more likely to show up on a search than one with all positive reviews. When visitors come to the site, they will read many reviews and purchase the product after reading all the reviews.

However, 75 percent of respondents say that they would be deterred from buying after reading three bad reviews. Forrester reported that after reading a negative review:

- 47 percent search for an alternative product.
- 37 percent read professional/editor-written reviews of the product.
- 26 percent continue to shop for the product regardless of the negative ratings/reviews.
- 18 percent look for a retailer/manufacturer that offers a money-back guarantee.
- 7 percent contact the retailer for clarification of the issues raised in the negative review.
- 7 percent contact the manufacturer for clarification of the issues raised in the negative review.
- 6 percent post a follow-up question for the author of the negative review.

Getting Customers to Provide Reviews

The hard part is getting people to write reviews. Some marketers suggest that rather than sending follow-up e-mails after the product has been delivered, they solicit reviews with a simple "Review this" button positioned on the Web site in a space near the presentation of the product or service. Making it convenient encourages those who lack enough motivation to contribute.

To make sure that you get some negative reviews, some marketers allow users to select from a predetermined list of "good" and "bad" qualities. They also allow users to preview what they write before posting a review to check for errors and mistakes. This builds user confidence. Dell and others find reviews so powerful that it often includes a contest. Dell reads all negative reviews and often responds to the reviewer making suggestions. It has some rules for reviewers:

1. Make it short and sweet.
2. Provide examples.
3. Make a point that Dell could use to improve the product.
4. Make sure the points you are making are relevant to others reading the review.
5. Always have a contest (see Figure 6.4).

Figure 6.4 Dell Product Review Contest

6. Let the brand managers know about the rejected products (see Figure 6.5).

Most Rejected Reviews All Products
The following products have the greatest number of rejected reviews:
980 rejections out of 4790 reviews submitted–XPS M1530
617 rejections out of 2384 reviews submitted–XPS M1330
454 rejections out of 1472 reviews submitted–Inspiron 530
433 rejections out of 1704 reviews submitted–Inspiron 1720
340 rejections out of 956 reviews submitted–Inspiron 1525
337 rejections out of 1254 reviews submitted–XPS 420
331 rejections out of 1253 reviews submitted–Inspiron 1501

Figure 6.5 Reviews that Reject Products

Rejection Codes and Trends

Dell digs deeply into all reviews. It:

- Sets up rejection codes so it can track common problems.

- Hunts for trends or recurrences in key words.

- Determines if Dell should stop selling the product.

- Makes sure to take care of the customer and their needs.

- Summarizes information in reviews in side bars or provides the ability to sort reviews by selected information.

- Lets readers know how much the reviewers paid for the products being reviewed.

Burpee's Seeds

Burpee launched a feature on its Web site that allowed customers to post pictures of plants and vegetables they had grown using Burpee products. In the first week alone, with no promotion, Burpee received between 200 and 300 e-mails with pictures. The company understood that it had a highly engaged customer base that was willing to share their experiences because hobbyists typically love to share their creations. Burpee wanted to create more opportunities to engage its customers online as well as see if it could use this customer trait to drive more sales. Based on this success, Burpee launched a customer reviews and ratings feature on its site with the help of experts from Bazaarvoice. Burpee developed the reviews and ratings structure based on the few key elements buyers care about with respect to plants in general and vegetables in particular. Over time it narrowed the ratings and reviews down to factors such as taste and yield for vegetables and plant performance for plants. The company displays reviews and ratings at the bottom of the product detail page with links to read and write just below the product picture at the top of the screen.

The bottom line is that the use of product reviews in marketing e-mails produced a 20 percent lift in conversion over e-mails without product reviews.

Netflix Success with Reviews

Netflix is the world's largest movie rental company. More than 85 percent of Netflix members join because of personal recommendations. The company solicits feedback from customers in the e-mail that acknowledges that the customer has returned a movie. Netflix collects the reviews and ratings and posts all except the profane and irrelevant on the site. Then this content is used to feed the recommendation engine.

Netflix has a small, dedicated team manually examining all reviews submitted; this step is critical to keeping reviews and ratings a valued service. Through focus groups and surveys, Netflix has found that users gain more enjoyment from and have more ownership of their rental experience because the reviews and ratings are present. Members feel that they are getting movies targeted to them. Netflix customers rate an average of 120 movies. At this writing, I have reviewed 980 Netflix movies.

Netflix's internal research and usage logs show that customer reviews are more relevant to its users than professional movie reviewers are, so the company discontinued the use of professional reviews. It uses trackable clicks, such as voting on the usefulness of a review, to determine the likelihood that someone will rent. Netflix uses this information for forecasting and analysis. For example, new theatrical releases get reviews on Netflix even though they are not yet available on video. Members see a review for a popular release and put it in their queue now. This helps predict a film's rental pattern. More than 70 percent of Netflix's 100,000 titles are older films that are suggested to members based on the millions of recommendations generated from user reviews and ratings.

The Value of Database Marketing

The shift from the catalog industry to promotional Web sites to promotional e-mails and Amazon within the past 20 years has shown the value of database marketing in an entirely new light from where we were when the first edition of this book came out. The concept (customer marketing database) was correct. The modern use of the concept is quite different and far more profitable.

Costing Out Ratings and Reviews

Let's see how ratings and reviews can improve profits for a typical marketer. We pick a marketer who sells on the Web and in stores. He sends promotional e-mails displaying his products. In Figure 6.6 he has no ratings and reviews. The figure shows how the LTV of his 500,000 subscribers might look.

You will note that he acquires 500,000 subscribers in various ways, including PPC (pay per click) from Google. His average order value is $146. He sends out e-mails every week with an open rate of 12 percent.

He reads this book and realizes that ratings and reviews will substantially improve his sales and profits. It costs him $300,000 per year to manage an R&R program. This includes a staff of three to manage the program and a contest for customers who review their purchases. What happens to his profits as a result?

Sales before Ratings and Reviews		This Year	Next Year	Third Year
Subscribers		500,000	380,000	288,800
Unsubs	14%	70,000	53,200	40,432
Undelivers	10%	50,000	38,000	28,880
Delivered	52	26,000,000	19,760,000	15,017,600
Opens	12%	3,120,000	2,371,200	1,802,112
Unique Clicks	22%	686,400	521,664	396,465
E-mail Conversions	2%	13,728	10,433	7,929
Other Sales due to E-mails	2.10	28,829	21,910	16,652
Total Sales		42,557	32,343	24,581
Total Revenue	$146	$6,213,293	$4,722,103	$3,588,798
Costs of Goods Sold	45%	$2,795,982	$2,124,946	$1,614,959
Google PPC	$0.25	$125,000		
Ratings and Reviews	$0.00	$0.00	$0.00	$0.00
E-mail Costs	$4.00	$104,000	$79,040	$60,070
Web site Costs	$0.60	$300,000	$228,000	$173,280
Database Costs	$0.50	$250,000	$250,000	$250,000
Total Costs		$3,574,982	$2,681,986	$2,098,309
Gross Profit		$2,638,311	$2,040,116	$1,490,488
Discount Rate		1	1.1	1.15
NPV Profit		$2,638,311	$1,854,651	$1,296,077
Cumulative NPV		$2,638,311	$4,492,962	$5,789,039
Lifetime Value		$5.28	$8.99	$11.58

Figure 6.6 LTV before Ratings and Reviews

As you can see in Figure 6.7, R&R boosts his open rate, his click rate, and his conversion rate. These minor improvements boost his profits by $3.4 million, with an ROI of $8.70 per $1 spent (see Figure 6.8).

Take-Away Thoughts

- The U.S. catalog industry had 16,000 companies selling more than $235 billion worth of goods and services in 2010.
- It got started with Abacus in 1990—a co-op catalog database.

Sales with Ratings and Reviews		This Year	Next Year	Third Year
Subscribers		500,000	390,000	304,200
Unsubs	12%	60,000	46,800	36,504
Undelivers	10%	50,000	39,000	30420
Delivered	52	26,000,000	20,280,000	15,818,400
Opens	15%	3,900,000	3,042,000	2,372,760
Unique Clicks	23%	897,000	699,660	545,735
E-mail Conversions	3%	26,910	20,990	16,372
Other Sales due to E-mails	2.30	61,893	48,277	37,656
Total Sales		88,803	69,266	54,028
Total Revenue	$148	$13,142,844	$10,251,418	$7,996,106
Costs of Goods Sold	45%	$5,914,280	$4,613,138	$3,598,248
Google PPC	$0.25	$125,000		
Ratings and Reviews		$300,000	$300,000	$300,000
E-mail costs	$4.00	$104,000	$81,120	$63,274
Web site Costs	$0.60	$300,000	$234,000	$182,520
Database Costs	$0.50	$250,000	$250,000	$250,000
Total Costs		$6,993,280	$5,478,258	$4,394,041
Gross Profit		$6,149,564	$4,773,160	$3,602,065
Discount Rate		1	1.1	1.15
NPV Profit		$6,149,564	$4,339,236	$3,132,230
Cumulative NPV		$6,149,564	$10,488,801	$13,621,031
Lifetime Value		$12.30	$20.98	$27.24

Figure 6.7 LTV with Ratings and Reviews

	This Year	Next Year	Third Year
Without R&R	$5.28	$8.99	$11.58
With R&R	$12.30	$20.98	$27.24
Gain			$15.66
Times 500,000 Subscribers			$7,831,992
Three Year Investment			$900,000
Return on $1 Invested			$8.70

Figure 6.8 LTV with Ratings and Reviews

- By 2000, companies began to build catalog Web sites with shopping carts. Customers found them using Google—a good, but passive way to attract customers.

- Companies began to send e-mail promotions to get visitors to come back to their catalog Web sites. The e-mails became catalogs themselves, with shopping carts and links to any product that the supplier sold.

- The big gorilla in the living room is Amazon, which has become the largest retailer on the Web, with 29,000,000 products and 1 million affiliates.

- Amazon practices all the strategic database marketing concepts discussed in this book.

- Amazon makes the long tail a reality—selling more obscure items than mainstream items.

- Ratings and reviews have become essential to successful database marketing on the Web.

- Ratings and reviews are intensely read by customers, and they boost the open, click, and conversion rates.

A quiz on this chapter and all figures can be found at www.dbmarketing.com/STM4. Those taking all the quizzes can receive a Successful Completion Certificate from the Database Marketing Institute which can be used in their résumé.

7

Loyalty and Retention

*Loyalty is the result of our marketing efforts. It's an
indicator of how successful we have been with our total
marketing effort. We must never forget that loyalty is
not the obligation of the customer. Rather, it's the result
of us providing such a continuous set of positive
shopping experiences for the customer that she chooses
to keep returning to do business with us.*

—Brian Woolf
Loyalty Marketing—The Second Act

*The first step in managing a loyalty-based business system
is finding and acquiring the right customers: customers
who will provide steady cash flows and a profitable return
on the firm's investment for years to come, customers
whose loyalty can be won and kept. Loyalty-based
companies should remember three rules of thumb:*

- *Some customers are inherently predictable and loyal,
  no matter what company they're doing business with.
  They simply prefer stable, long-term relationships.*

- *Some customers are more profitable than others.
  They spend more money, pay their bills more
  promptly, and require less service.*

- *Some customers will find your products and services
  more valuable than those of your competitors.
  No company can be all things to all people. Your
  particular strengths will simply fit better with certain
  customer's needs and opportunities.*

—Frederick Reichheld
The Loyalty Effect

149

What constitutes customer loyalty? Is it a series of actions, such as repeat purchases, or an emotional bond, such as recommending your company to a friend? I think that true customer loyalty is something like a successful marriage. It is a relationship in which both parties are satisfied with their relations with each other. They are not worried every day that their partner will stop loving them or run off with somebody else. They will come through misunderstandings and arguments with their relationship still intact, or even stronger. Developing a bond of loyalty between you and your customers is what database marketing is all about.

Easier and More Complex

Building and maintaining customer loyalty has become both easier and more complex because of the Internet:

- *It is easier* because you can send your customers as many e-mail messages as you want for a trifling cost. You can set up your Web site with cookies so that it recognizes customers by name when they arrive. You can empower your customer contact personnel—sales clerks, customer service, catalog reps, and so on—with detailed information about what each customer is doing in all channels. That was not possible before the Internet.

- *It is more complex* because customers today expect that you will maintain a complete picture of their behavior: on the Web, in e-mails, in retail stores, and through your catalog. For this you need a complex database that is fed by all these sources. In this way your clerk in the store can say, "How is your new TV working out?" referring to something the customer bought on the Web. Or the clerk can tell her that the sweater she ordered from the store catalog is now back in stock and will be shipped today. "Wow!" is the reaction of the customer to these two pieces of information from a store clerk who is selling perfume. Who can use this system? Banks, insurance companies, retailers—any company that wants to build an unbreakable bond with its customers.

It takes a lot of work and some expense to set a system like this up. Is it worth it? You can determine whether it is or not by lifetime value. We do some computation on LTV at the end of this chapter. In the meantime, let's review the meaning of customer loyalty.

Loyal customers are more valuable than the average customer. They tend to:

- Have higher retention rates
- Have higher spending rates
- Have higher referral rates
- Have a higher lifetime value
- Be less expensive to serve
- Buy higher-priced products or services

There is one key measurement for loyalty. It is retention rate (sometimes measured as the repurchase rate, or the renewal rate). Retention is more important than the spending rate or the frequency of spending. Why? Because when customers are gone, they're gone. It is hard to get them back. As long as you have them, there is always a possibility of working out any problems and getting them to spend more or trade up to higher options.

The link between loyalty and database marketing is communication. Loyalty is built and maintained by two-way communications between you and your customer. Customers make purchases. You thank them for their patronage. You ask your customer for their preferences. They respond. You store their preferences in your database. Then you modify your services to make sure that their preferences are honored. Acting on these preferences involves a lot of little perks and services that show customers that you really are loyal to them. When they see the *Wall Street Journal,* instead of *USA Today* on the doorstep of their hotel room door in the morning in some new city without having to ask for it the night before, they realize that you listened to them and are being loyal to their preferences. The database is central to the process: this is where the customer preferences and other data are stored. You use the database to create the personalized services and messages that build loyalty.

Customer Preferences

One of the most inexpensive but powerful customer marketing techniques is to get customers to provide you with their preferences for services. This can be done in writing or over the phone, but today increasingly is done on the Web. The advantages of creating a customer profile with preferences are twofold. You learn more about the customer, and the customer feels that he or she has played a role in the services received and has been listened to by your company. Tests and controls can show that customers who complete a profile with preferences are more loyal than other customers. (Were they already loyal, or did the preference creation process make them so?) For preferences to work, of course, you will have to modify your services or communications to customers based on their expressed preferences. This is where the database becomes important. With an automated system you can have a means of using the database stored preferences on a daily basis to provide personalized services and communications.

Employees throughout your company, all over the world, have to have access to the database so that they know about these preferences and act on them day after day. Your Web site will have to reflect what is in the database. Will the cost of collecting customer profiles and preferences and acting on them be justified by increased retention and increased revenue? This can be determined by setting up control groups that are not asked to complete preference forms.

The Importance of Caller ID and Cookies

When a guest calls room service today in most modern U.S. hotels, the operator says, "What can I do for you, Mr. Adams?" Referring to the customer by name is superior customer service and has become standard in hotels. What many companies have not realized is that the same principle that applies within a hotel can also apply to customers calling your customer service from their home or office. When a repeat customer calls your customer service, caller ID permits you to know who is calling before you answer the phone. The customer's entire record, from the database, should automatically show on the customer service rep's (CSR's) screen.

The customer can be greeted by name with some personal information included in the conversation to make it clear to the customer that your CSR knows who the customer is and knows how important that customer's patronage is to your business. Because you're using caller ID, it is not necessary for customers to give their customer number, name, address, and so on. To build loyalty, you set up an automated system that re-creates the personal relationships that the Old Corner Grocer used to maintain with his customers.

The same benefits of caller ID on the Web are created by cookies. When customers come back to your Web site, the screen says,

"Welcome back, Susan," and you add the customer's name and address to any forms that the she has to fill out to order products or services. The costs of caller ID and cookies today are very low. The cost of the software to provide the database information to the customer service reps and the Web site is also comparatively low. Is this personalization worth it? Does it make a difference in terms of customer retention and spending? This should be tested using control groups. However, I can state definitively that your Web site must use the customer's name and have dynamic content that reflects what you have learned about the customer if you want to build and maintain customer loyalty.

Event-Driven Relationship Messages

There are lots of ways to build loyalty with event-driven communications. (Chapter 11 is devoted to this important loyalty building method.) These are not sales pitches. They are expressions of friendship. Some companies send birthday or holiday cards. Do such cards do any good? With a database, you can test this by not sending the cards to 20 percent of the customers. After a year, you measure the spending and retention rates of the two groups. You can see right away if there is a difference and how much. You can see your expressions of friendship are paying for themselves in terms of retention and sales.

Some companies use their database for trawling. They look for events. National Change of Address (NCOA^{LINK}) should be run on any database four times a year. About 20 percent of Americans move every year. When NCOA^{LINK} is run, you will know the identity of the 5 percent of your customer base that has just moved. You will have to decide what to say to the movers. "How do you like your new home in Cleveland? Maybe with a new home, you should upgrade your iPhone?"

Other trawling results can be based on behavior. Did they just make a big purchase? Have they reached an anniversary with your company? "Congratulations on ten years of loyalty! We want you to know that we value your business, Mr. Hughes. Ever since your purchase of a Kenmore dishwasher ten years ago, we have been happy to have you as a customer. We are delighted that our relationship is continuing into another decade!"

Is this just a neat thing to do, or are there solid economic benefits to be derived from it? Your database holds the answers.

You Need a Universal Customer ID Number

Here is where many loyalty programs fail. Do not create a special number that has no meaning for the customer. Make the number something that is easy to remember. The best two are:

- The customer's telephone number (landline or mobile)
- The customer's e-mail

When the customer is interacting with you anywhere (at a teller's window, at the checkout counter in a store, on the Web, on the phone), make sure you know who she is instantly with her complete record visible on the screen of whomever she is talking to. Use her name. Put things like, "Member since 1982," on the Web site or in all e-mails. Tell clerks to say, "Wow. You have been shopping with us since 1982, Mrs. Adams." Why? It builds and maintains loyalty. To do this, you absolutely must use cookies on your Web site. It is amazing how many Web sites today still do not greet their customers by name. Using the name is the heart of loyalty building in any situation. Keep saying to yourself: "What did the Old Corner Grocer do when a customer came into his store?"

You must have caller ID on any phone that customers might call. You must have lookup tables from any document that the customer may produce that will enable you to put the customer's data into the database where it belongs.

Would You Recommend Me?

Frederick Reichheld has one of the best ways to measure customer loyalty. He recommends that companies ask their customers one question: would you recommend me to your friends? The answer is much more indicative of loyalty than satisfaction scores. With automobiles, for example, most satisfaction scores are between 80 and 90 percent, but the repurchase rate of the same brand is about 35 percent. Using his basic question, Reichheld developed a net promoter score. To get the score, subtract the number of people who wouldn't recommend you from those who would. The score is often negative. Many companies have used this score to determine how well they are doing and, if the score is negative, to decide what to do about their situation.

The question can easily be asked in an e-mail. SmartBargains does a good job of this. It sends out an e-mail to buyers following a purchase as a means of gauging customers' shopping experiences (see Figure 7.1).

Thank you for your recent order from SmartBargains.com. We hope you are enjoying your latest bargain!

As a followup to your order, we'd like you to answer a few quick questions. They should take you less than one minute to complete, but they are extremely important and allow us to identify ways to continually exceed your expectations.

On a scale of 0 to 10, how likely would you be to recommend SmartBargains.com to a friend or colleague? (0 = Extremely Unlikely, 10 = Extremely Likely)

☹ 0 = Extremely Unlikely   ☺ 10 = Extremely Likely

○ 0 ○ 1 ○ 2 ○ 3 ○ 4 ○ 5 ○ 6 ○ 7 ○ 8 ○ 9 ○ 10

What is the primary reason for the score you gave us?

Figure 7.1 SmartBargains.com Recommendation E-mail

Loyalty Programs

Finally, of course, you can build and maintain loyalty with formal loyalty programs. By a loyalty program I mean a system in which a customer has specifically signed up for a program. He receives a plastic card with his name on it. He uses the card whenever he shops in a retail store, on the phone, or on the Web. The card does two things: it provides the customer with some benefit he could not get without the card, and it provides you with valuable information that you can use to understand the customer and build his loyalty. Before you begin a loyalty program, you have to decide what you expect to get out of it and what role it will play in your total marketing program.

In some cases, the card is not essential. There may be no opportunity to display the card if the loyalty program membership is completely electronic. Do not waste money on a plastic card if it is not needed. But make sure that your members know that they are loyalty program members.

Brian Woolf made a detailed study of customer loyalty programs and customer behavior. He started out by asking, "What customer behavior do you want to reward?"

- Do we want *better* or *more* customers?
- Do we want *high-* or *low-*spending customers?
- What is more important: increased sales or increased profitability?

- What changes in behavior are required to hold onto more of our good customers and lengthen their average stay with us?

- Of the behaviors we have chosen as our goals, which are the most profitable ones we should be rewarding?

These are important questions to ask before you launch any program designed to maintain or increase loyalty. Loyalty programs require resources. They are not free. Money can be wasted unless you know what you are doing. As Brian notes: "We must water what we want to grow. But first we must decide what we want to grow.... All customers are not equal. Behavior usually follows rewards."

Customer Registration

The loyalty program for a retailer, bank, or other service provider begins with a customer application or registration form. The idea is to capture not just the name and address, but also some information about the customer that is relevant to her purchasing decisions concerning your products or services. Be sure to get her e-mail address with her permission to contact her through e-mail. You will also want to find out age, income, home ownership, and length of residence. To get the customers to register, there has to be something in it for them. If they ask, "Why should I register?" your answer could be, "Because we want to reward our regular customers more." What are the rewards? You must determine that. They could be lower prices for card holders, access to information not available to others, or points toward achievable rewards. The rewards must be so compelling that most customers will want to register.

If you have the customer's postal address, you can obtain all the demographic information you want by paying a compiled database company, like KnowledgeBase Marketing, for the information for a few cents per name. This may be better than turning off some potential members who resent providing all the information that you want.

Instant Discount Rewards

Reward programs that offer instant discounts were pioneered by supermarkets. They offer members a discount when purchasing certain products—discounts that nonmembers can't get. While they are open to everyone, they particularly appeal to lower-income customers. People join to get the instant rewards these programs offer.

For the retailer, the instant discount programs provide a wealth of information about what each member is spending day by day. Members' purchases can be directed to desired areas. A member who buys a lot but has never bought at the deli, for example, can be offered e-mail coupons good only at the deli, leading him to start buying in a new category.

Some retailers use straddle pricing: cardholders get lower prices on your competitors' advertised specials, while you retain margins on other products. When a regular customer stops shopping with you, you know instantly because she isn't using her card. You can send e-mails to her to win her back before her alternate retailer becomes a habit. Thus, one by one, you can individually target members to retain their loyalty.

Points Accumulation

Programs featuring points accumulation were pioneered by airlines. Instead of discounts, members accumulate points toward future purchases, such as travel, hotel rooms, and automobile rentals. Such programs also offer perks for members who have accumulated lots of points. These members are given the label gold or platinum. These programs are used mainly by participants with higher incomes. People join to get rewards that are more important to them than discounts.

There is no question today that loyalty can be created or increased by awarding points or some similar reward. The basic idea behind points is to avoid discounting your product. Points represent a gift or reward that cannot easily be related to the price of the product or service. Millions of Americans' loyalty to an airline is molded by frequent flyer programs. These airline points programs work. Do loyalty programs work for other products and services? The answer seems to be yes, but not as well. There are scores of other programs run by restaurants, retail stores, banks, hotels, credit cards, long-distance services, and others who reward customers with points. Many companies have been able to prove, using control groups, that these programs do build loyalty.

Benefits to customer in point accumulation programs include:

- A sense of belonging
- Being treated better, such as service upgrades, club floors, club lounges
- Recognition of their status as members
- Pride in building up equity in points toward future purchases

Marketing messages—usually e-mails—sent to points accumulation program members cover such subjects as:

- How many points the member has accumulated and what she can do with them.
- What she has to do to achieve a higher status level (e.g., move from gold to platinum).
- Benefits from encouraging friends and family members to buy from the program sponsor.
- Why she should join a related club.
- Asking her to provide her profile and preference information so she can receive perks and rewards that appeal to her.
- Invitation to post information on a blog.
- Invitation to a viral marketing program.
- Ability to buy T-shirts, luggage tags, hats, and other brand-identifying products.
- Information on company and brand history going back to the founding of the company and including details on how the products are made or developed.

The Membership Application

All loyalty programs start with a membership application in the store or on a Web site. The customer answers a few questions, such as providing his name, address, and e-mail address. You let him read the fine print about the benefits and regulations of your loyalty program. You capture his home and e-mail addresses and then you send him a welcoming letter or e-mail, in which he confirms his willingness to continue to receive e-mail communications from you about the program.

Companies with both types of loyalty programs (discounts and points) have found that starting with the application form they are able to compile a wealth of data on consumer behavior leading to modification in prices, products, and services that improve sales and customer retention. In addition, using the data, the program managers can create e-mail marketing programs that help build loyalty, increase sales and retention, and reactivate inactive customers. Brian Woolf said, "The primary purpose of a business is to acquire, satisfy, and retain customers, profitably. The primary purpose of a loyalty card program is information, which then helps achieve the goals of the business. Customer information is used to help a business retain its customers (i.e., build loyalty). But it is also used to help accomplish the other business goals of customer acquisition; satisfying customers with the right location, product assortment, quality, service and friendliness; and doing so cost-effectively, by helping identify inefficient and wasteful areas of spending, particularly expenditure on low yield customers."

Brian gave as an example this quote from Steve Burrows, director of retail operations of the Hale-Halsell Company, based in Tulsa, Oklahoma: "Some time after the card launch in our Super-H stores, we utilized our zip code report to more efficiently reach our customers. We were able to cut 25 percent of our ad copies. We requested a name and address report for five area zip codes where we were sending 20,000 ads—and where we are now sending only 750 ads directly to our card customers in those areas. We will save $250,000 this year in our 14 stores—all previously wasted. This is just the tip of the iceberg. We had been sending out ads weekly, equal to three times our customer count. I am using 50 percent of this to finish paying off my program expense and the other 50 percent goes straight to my bottom line. After one year, advertising expense has been cut dramatically."

Loyalty programs, thus, are a win-win situation for consumers and for the companies that offer them. Most of today's loyalty programs, like frequent flyer programs, were started before the advent of the Internet and e-mail marketing. Many of the program managers haven't yet caught up with the possibilities that e-mail marketing offers for their loyalty programs.

How Loyalty Programs Affect Attitudes toward Financial Institutions

Carlson Marketing did a study[1] of more than 2,000 people who statistically represented 2 million financial institution customers. The study showed that:

- Tailored benefits and awards (65 percent) and communications and offers (59 percent) that met their personal needs were important factors in choosing a loyalty program.

- Having friendly (73 percent) and professional (75 percent) staff was a major factor in determining a customer's primary financial services institution.

---

[1] *Carlson Relationship Builder 2007* (Minneapolis: Carlson Marketing, April 2, 2007) http:// www.carlson.com/media/article.cfm?id=427&group=marketing&subhilite=0&terhilite=0.

- 23 percent called their primary financial services institution with questions in the last three months, but nearly double that percentage (45 percent) used the institution's Web site for transactions.

- E-mail and the Internet were preferred over face-to-face interactions when obtaining information (39 percent vs. 25 percent) and when accessing customer services (44 percent vs. 31 percent).

- 51 percent would sign up for e-mails from their primary financial services institution if they were offered.

Loyalty and Affluence

Wealthy consumers are more loyal than other consumers. A nationwide survey by Parago (www.parago.com) showed that high-income households exhibit greater loyalty and are influenced more by loyalty programs than are average-income households. Even more influential than age, gender, or geography, household income proved to be most indicative of the strength and impact of customer loyalty. In total, 94 percent of high-income households said that their membership in a loyalty, rewards, or frequent customer program had a strong to moderate influence on their purchasing decisions compared to 78 percent for all consumers.

As income increases, so do the importance and impact of loyalty programs on consumers. Among loyalty program members, 92 percent of high-income households ($125K+) are actively enrolled in an airline frequent flyer program, compared to 51 percent of all respondents. Hotel program membership showed similar income-dependent results, with 78 percent of high-income households enrolled in a hotel reward program, compared to only 35 percent of the general population.

High-income households also differed in the types of rewards they preferred to receive from loyalty programs. Compared to the general population, high-income households were less interested in price discounts and more interested in receiving both rewards and recognition for their loyalty. In the Parago study, 39 percent of high-income households named the "special treatment" they received from loyalty programs as one of their favorite things. Particularly among male travelers, first-class upgrades, perks, and faster check-in and boarding were more important to them than the free miles.

The loyalty programs affected consumer behavior. According to the survey, 93 percent of U.S. consumers were willing to depart one hour earlier than needed for a flight—if it meant they could fly on their preferred frequent flyer airline. Of frequent flyers, 67 percent said they would be willing to pay $25 more (or 5 percent more) for a ticket on their frequent flyer airline rather than fly with a competitor.

How to Use Your Customer Database to Promote Loyalty

Once customers are registered and on your database, you can create periodic reports that will enable you to direct your loyalty program in profitable directions. There are dozens of things that can be done. In fact, just about all the loyalty promoting steps described in this book are available to you now that you have a database rich with transaction history derived from customers' use of their membership cards.

I should note that, depending on your situation, you may not require customers to use their cards when they make a purchase. As a result of their registration for the card, you have their telephone number. You should have at least one credit card (Mastercard, Visa, Amex, or your own proprietary card) registered with you with the card numbers in the database. Every night (or more often) when all your point-of-sale (POS) systems are polled to provide data for your database, you can run all the credit cards used and telephone numbers provided against lookup tables in your database, so you can record transactions in your customers' files even though they have not used their membership card or provided their card number when they made a purchase. Of course, with a good POS system connected with your database, just the entering of the phone number at the POS station will bring up a customer transaction history on a screen at the station so that the clerk can talk to the customer as if he knew her.

With this data, you can create lifetime value tables as described in Chapter 3, or triggered communications as described in Chapter 11. You can do segmentation, as described in Chapter 10. You can set up tests and controls as described in Chapter 14. The registration, therefore, is the entrance to the world of loyalty marketing.

What Reward Should You Offer?

When you're considering what reward to offer, consider this case study related by Chris Moloney of Parago: "A large, national paint company wanted to develop a loyalty rewards program for their most valuable customers. Most of these customers were professional or semi-pro painting contractors. The program was designed to reward them for their paint purchases. Despite my strong recommendations to the contrary, the company insisted that the only reward would be more free paint and some paint-related products. The program launched rather poorly. Why? Our research indicated two main issues. First, painters were simply not motivated by free paint. It was far less interesting for them than a free airline ticket or a TV. Second, most of these painters passed through the cost of paint and materials, showing the receipts for the costs to customers. Free paint, therefore, provided almost no financial value to the contractors. As a result, with no financial or personal motivation surrounding the rewards, the program did not modify customer behavior. In a short time we changed the program to offer items like portable CD/radios designed for "on the job" usage and leather portfolios for contractors to use in writing bids. Within three months, the company saw exponential growth in program enrollment and activity. The return on investment was significant."

Be careful with points, however. If you are a supermarket or discount retailer with a very low profit margin, the points can eat you alive. A better strategy would be to provide card holders with reduced prices on certain featured items, rather than awarding points at all. Many stores set up their POS systems to record the savings on selected items at the bottom of the cash register receipt, "Today you saved $6.71 by using your Wynn Dixie card." This, you can afford. It is a form of communication. It builds loyalty. It is much less complex than a points program which requires monthly statements and redemptions.

Is Loyalty Inherent in the Customer, or Can You Create It by Your Actions?

Frederick Reichheld's book, *The Loyalty Effect,* burst onto the database marketing industry like a welcome rainstorm. When I read it several years ago, I learned a lot. Reichheld's ideas are so important that they permeate every chapter of this book. If you haven't already read it, you should run out right now and buy a copy yourself.

As you can see by the quote at the beginning of this chapter, Reichheld identified loyal customers as central to the success of any enterprise. To be successful, therefore, you have to recruit the right kind of customers (loyal ones) to begin with and then develop programs to foster and maintain that loyalty by the way you treat them. Loyalty is a two way situation: if you want customers to be loyal to you, you must be loyal to them.

How Customers Are Recruited

Reichheld pointed out that your method of attracting and supporting customers may be the most important factor in maintaining customer loyalty. Customers acquired through discounts tend to be less loyal than those acquired through the promise of excellent service. As I have already pointed out, discounts do not foster loyalty. They make customers think about what they are paying instead of what they are getting.

The Importance of Loyal Employees

Another key contribution of Frederick Reichheld is recognition of the importance to customer loyalty of employee loyalty. He pointed out that many, if not most, customers are loyal not to the brand or the firm but to the people who serve them at the firm. When you lose employees, you often lose customers as well. Any marketing program aimed at customer retention must begin with looking at employee satisfaction and retention. This is not normally an issue dealt with in marketing books. It should be. The problem is that employee retention throughout a company is seldom something that the marketing department can influence directly. It they want to retain customers, however, marketers must recognize that customer loyalty and employee loyalty are usually tightly linked.

Acquiring the Right Customers

Given that loyal customers are better to have and more profitable than others, what can you do about it? Until Reichheld's book came along, there was one universal answer: figure out who the loyal customers are and treat them well. Provide the things we have discussed in this book: gold cards, president's clubs, advisory panels, member nights, special toll-free phone lines, and hundreds of special services that will encourage these loyal people to stick around for a long time.

There is nothing in Reichheld's book that disagrees with these recommendations. But there is little to support them either. Reichheld simply changed the subject. The route to loyalty, he explained, is to recruit loyal customers to begin with. "Some customers are inherently predictable and loyal, no matter what company they're doing business with. They simply prefer stable, long-term relationships."

His book provides dozens of examples of companies that have figured out the characteristics of their loyal customers. They have developed simple rules that aid them in attracting the right kind of customer and avoid the wrong kind. Some of his examples include:

- An insurance company discovered that, for it, married people were more loyal than singles. Midwesterners were more loyal than Easterners. Homeowners were more loyal than renters. Once the company found these things out, it used the knowledge to guide its acquisition strategy.

- MBNA discovered that people reached through an affinity group— such as doctors, dentists, nurses, teachers and engineers—were more loyal credit card holders than people reached through general direct mail campaigns.

- Many companies used their databases to learn that customers attracted by low-ball discount offers were more likely to disappear than were customers attracted by non-discounted offers. They tended to leave as soon as the competition made them an even lower offer. Were they different people, or had the offer made them think of the company's products in terms of price rather than value? Who knows? It really doesn't matter. Discounting is not a profitable long-range strategy.

Treating Loyal Customers Better

The 80/20 rule applies in all industries. The top 20 percent of your customers give you 80 percent of your total revenue. Banks compute this by measuring profitability on a monthly basis. Figure 7.2 is a chart showing how one bank divided its customers into five segments with this result:

In this example, the top two segments totaling 16 percent of the customer households produced 105 percent of the profits. The bottom 28 percent of the customer households were losers. Many companies have an idea that their customer value looks something like this, but few have taken the time to actually do the analysis and figure out who their

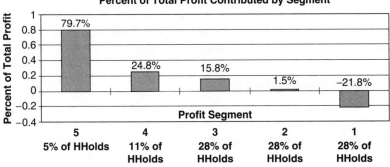

Figure 7.2 Profit Contributed by Household Segments

loyalists are and who the others are. As noted earlier, Best Buy found that 20 percent of its customers were unprofitable.

Once you have determined customer profitability segments, however, there are many things that you could and should do to retain your best customers. Here is what some people do:

- Have special customer service lines, Web sites, and phone numbers for gold customers, putting their best agents on these lines.
- Create advisory panels made up of their best customers.
- Have special members-only nights for gold customers.
- Have special seminars or reports.
- In business-to-business situation, host an annual retreat at a resort for the CEOs of their best customers.

Dropping the Losers

In addition to keeping your loyal customers, you should do something about the losers. If these customers are actually costing you money and eating up profits that other customers are creating, you must do something about it.

The first step is to identify these people. Once you know who they are, you can re-price their services or move them toward the door. One bank lets all its employees know which segment each customer falls into. For those customers at the bottom—those who are losing money for the bank—the employee screens suggest re-pricing of products. Their loans are renewed at a higher rate. Waivers are not granted. Even more interesting, by using caller ID, the call center software makes losing callers wait for five or six rings before anyone from customer service picks up. Gold customers are answered by a special gold team on the first ring.

Does Price Cutting Create Loyalty?

Brian Woolf, in his insightful book, *Customer Loyalty—the Second Act*, explains that, "Sales always grow when prices are cut. Unfortunately, we now know that new customers attracted by such promotions typically exhibit low loyalty and require constant 'price feeding' to keep returning which means continued lower gross margins. Heavy promotional pricing is not a recommended tactic for building loyalty. Offers to existing customers that reward frequency and spending are far more effective in achieving that goal. . . . Several years ago one major U.S. retailer was suffering from the sales doldrums. To address the problem, it reduced prices in its weekly circulars from previous levels. As expected, this triggered higher sales and transactions—but also less customer loyalty. Its best customer numbers, already down 10 percent from the previous year, continued to fall during the promotional period despite the increased foot traffic. The promotion simply resulted in gaining low margin sales rather than building customer loyalty."

Interviewing the Defectors

Probably the most important names on your customer database are those of loyal people who have recently deserted you. These people are valuable. They provide important clues as to what you are doing right and doing wrong. You should set up an ongoing program to interview them to determine why they left. To make the most of the situation, you should determine the lifetime value of each customer and keep it in the customer's database record. When you lose customers, therefore, find out if their lifetime value is higher or lower than the LTV of your existing customer base.

Increasing the Number of Loyal Customers

There are four basic means of increasing customer loyalty:

- Have high-quality products and services
- Offer excellent customer service and support

- Have a friendly and loyal staff
- Provide excellent, highly personalized, relevant, and rapid communications

If you don't have the first three items, your database communications won't save you. But if you do have them, then communications—particularly e-mail communications—become a very high priority for building loyalty and profits.

Loyalty-Building Communications

Your Web site, direct mail, and your e-mails are the lifeline of your customer loyalty program. To create loyalty-building communications:

- Create personalized e-mail transaction messages in HTML, and send them out quickly
- Acknowledge all customer input within a few seconds, and fulfill requests within a few hours
- Ask for customer preferences and modify your communications and services based on these preferences
- Develop trigger messages that treat each customer as an individual rather than as a member of a large herd
- Thank customers for their business, personalizing the e-mails with such comments as how long they have been your customers

As you develop your loyalty-building communications, keep in mind how our Old Corner Grocer built customer loyalty. When customers came to his store, he greeted them by name. He started his conversations with topics he believed were of interest to them, based on previous conversations. The grocer remembered where his customers lived and how far they had to travel to get to his store. He remembered what they said to him and used it in future conversations. He would point out where the products they wanted could be found in the store, put things aside for them, replaced defective products, helped them carry heavy packages, and so on. He congratulated them on birthdays and anniversaries. He remembered how long they had been customers and how much they spent with him. He knew each customer's family members and used that knowledge to suggest products and services.

As you can see from this listing, there are many things that one help-ful, intelligent, and caring human being can do for another human being that result in friendship and—in commercial terms—loyalty. Our database can store a lot of customer data, though not as much as the cor-ner grocer kept in his head, but our goal should be to get as close to what he stored there as possible. Let's see how direct mail and e-mail messages can be used to build loyalty.

Log On as a Customer

An important step in achieving customer loyalty is to have a number of your staff members log on to your Web site, make purchases, and receive direct mail and e-mails to be sure you know what your output looks like at the receiving end. Those who log on should be given a list of things to test, starting with the categories listed in Figure 7.3, to see just how well your company is responding.

Have them search each e-mail received to see if they can get all the information they require. Can they reach customer service through text chat or on the phone? Can they return a product without a hassle? Are their e-mails correctly personalized? Are their preferences honored? Is there a feedback e-mail link clearly visible in every e-mail? Does some-one check the sending e-mail address daily to read and respond to all feedback received?

Building Loyalty in Older Customers

Of Internet users ages 55 to 83, 72 percent regularly make Internet pur-chases according to PEW research. How do you appeal to these folks? Recognize their needs. Shop PBS added icons to its site that let visitors increase the font size on product pages. Elderluxe moved much of the detail about featured items to the main product page to make it easier to find.

Address the concerns of older users. The PEW study suggested that finding ways to reduce concern about providing personal or payment information online would increase the percentage of online adults who shop via the Web.

FirstStreetOnline puts the HackerSafe and VeriSign security certifica-tion symbols on every page and provides easy access to the company's pri-vacy policy, mission statement, and management profiles. Despite these steps, about 25 percent of customers aged 65 and older use the phone to place orders, rather than entering credit card information online.

American Airlines, for example, provides many sources of information for members of its frequent flyer program, including:

- E-mails with the flyer's AAdvantage account balance showing which miles were posted.

- Personalized e-mails featuring American Airlines product and service news, current promotions, exclusive discount codes, fare sales, travel tips, and special offers—customized for the member.

- Special travel savings bulletins, including discounted weekend fares, special mileage offers, fare sale news, cruises, and vacations.

- AAdvantage partner promotions, partner information, and offers.

The Hallmark Gold Crown Loyalty Program

Several years ago, there were 5,000 independently owned Hallmark Gold Crown stores. Few people buy cards only at these stores. People are busy. They buy where it is convenient. To protect these Gold Crown stores, the Hallmark marketing staff created a special loyalty program. At the inception of the program the Gold Crown stores did not think of themselves as a network. They thought of the Hallmark Card store down the street as their competition. The Hallmark marketing staff had to teach them that their competition was the mass markets.

How the Program Was Developed

Laurie Broderick of The Carlson Marketing Group in Minneapolis developed the initial plan working with Cindy Jeffreys of Hallmark Cards in Kansas City. The test was not difficult to sell, but the rollout required that thousands of individual store owners had to agree to the program, fund it, participate, and carry out all the rules of the program.

The test was done in 16 stores in two cities, Kansas City and Denver. These stores were chosen because they had the point of sale technology that made it possible to track behavior at the consumer level—what products were purchased in detail. In the test, the consumers enrolled in the stores and immediately got a sequentially numbered temporary card. Customers earned 10 points for every dollar they spent, with a reward certificate for every 100 points. Hallmark issued a permanent card after each consumer had earned 500 points. Reward certificates were issued quarterly as they were earned. The test was measured based by comparing total store sales, transactions, and the individual average transaction of each customer, with similar statistics from the national average.

Lessons Learned in the Test

The test resulted in increased call volumes that exceeded anything that had been anticipated. There was a backlog. The service center couldn't call customers back fast enough. There was a backlog in the enrollment process and in getting out the permanent plastic cards. Another problem was in creation of control groups. Hallmark marketers soon realized that to prove that what they were doing was working, or not working, they had to set up a control group for every single program: every bonus offer, every customer segment.

For the rollout, Cindy and Laurie revised the base reward structure to 200 points for a $1 reward. This lowered the payout to 5 basis points. They added points for cards and bonus offers. They offered 25 points for every greeting card purchased—the key behavior they wanted to drive. They added unique seasonal bonus offers and ornament offers, and they still had the flexibility to give special offers and stay within a profitable financial reward structure.

They lowered the hurdle rate to get a permanent card to 200 points. They learned that once you have a consumer who has raised her hand and who wants to be included, you should not keep her waiting too long. The sooner you get that plastic card in her hands, the sooner you get her actively engaged in the program and get her using it. They capped the quarterly reward certificate at $20. If the consumer earned more points, they just banked them to the next quarter.

After consumers earned 200 points, they were sent a welcome kit including a 100-point bonus, a plastic card, and a description of the system. Every letter was personalized with their transaction balance and the stores where they shopped. The letter included a product brochure announcing all the new Hallmark product lines for the season.

The result: after three years, there were 13 million members in the program. It became the largest active member database loyalty program in the world. Ten million customers used the card every year. The Hallmark Gold Crown stores became very successful. The dollars per transaction, the number of trips customers made, total store sales, and total store transactions were all up, compared to controls. The program grew to the point where a quarter of all the transactions and a third of all card shop dollars were on the card.

Challenges

As the program matured, Hallmark accumulated greater point liabilities and therefore dollar liabilities. It had to combat "loyalty fatigue" by trying to make the program seem fresh and new to customers, illustrating to them the benefits of being in the program so that they didn't tire of it. New members were excited at first with a lot of activity which then tapered off. Hallmark had to be constantly working on coming up with new creative ideas and making fresh new offers to keep member interest.

Hallmark soon learned to create customer segments based on behavior. Some members came in once a week to buy one card. There were lots of little transactions. Others came in once a year, at Christmas, spent a lot, and didn't come back for a year. It was important to understand customer behavior and treat each segment differently. If you are someone who comes in just once a year at Christmas, there is no economic sense in mailing you a Valentine's Day, Mother's Day, and summer mailing.

Increased LTV Resulting from Loyalty Programs

Loyalty programs increase the lifetime value of customers. Here is an illustration of what happens when we introduce a loyalty program (see Figure 7.3). Let's look at the LTV from a retailer who has everything except a loyalty program.

Row	Retail Store with Web Site & E-mails		Current Year	Next Year	Third Year
1	Customers		400,000	232,000	134,560
2	Retention Rate	58.00%	168,000	97,440	56,515
6	Total Sales (Visits per Year)	2.29	916,000	531,280	308,142
7	**Total Revenue (Average Order Value)**	$110.23	$100,970,680	$58,562,994	$33,966,493
8	Total Direct Costs	45.00%	$45,436,806	$26,353,347.48	$15,284,921.70
9	Marketing Costs (TV, Print, DM) Radio	12.00%	$12,116,482	$7,027,559	$4,075,979
10	Birthday Club Costs	$1.00	$400,000	$400,000	$400,000
11	Database, Web Site & E-mail Costs	$7.50	$3,000,000	$1,740,000	$1,009,200
12	Total Costs		$60,953,288	$35,520,907	$20,770,101
13	**Profit**		$40,017,392	$23,042,088	$13,196,392
14	Discount Rate		1	1.1	1.21
15	Net Present Value		$40,017,392	$20,947,352	$10,906,109
16	Cumulative NPV		$40,017,392	$60,964,745	$71,870,854
17	**Retail Shopper Lifetime Value**		$100.04	$152.41	$179.68

Figure 7.3 LTV of Store Without Loyalty Program

Next we show the effect of adding a loyalty program to this chain of stores, as shown in Figure 7.4.

You will note the changes: The retention rate has gone up, the total sales, and the average revenue per sale. The cost of the program was about $5 per customer per year. (See Figure 7.5.)

Row	Retail Store with Loyalty Program		Current Year	Next Year	Third Year
1	Customers		400,000	244,000	148,840
2	Retention Rate	61.00%	156,000	95,160	58,048
3	Total Sales (Visits per Year)	2.74	1,096,000	668,560	407,822
4	**Total Revenue (Average Order Value)**	$115.21	$126,270,160	$77,024,798	$46,985,127
5	Total Direct Costs	45.00%	$56,821,572	$34,661,158.92	$21,143,306.94
6	Marketing Costs (TV, Radio Print, DM)	12.00%	$15,152,419	$9,242,976	$5,638,215
7	Birthday Club Costs	$1.00	$400,000	$400,000	$400,000
8	Loyalty Program Costs	$5.00	$2,000,000	$1,220,000	$744,200
9	Database, Web Site & E-mail Costs	$7.50	$3,000,000	$1,830,000	$1,116,300
10	Total Costs		$77,373,991	$47,354,135	$29,042,022
11	**Profit**		$48,896,169	$29,670,663	$17,943,104
12	Discount Rate		1	1.1	1.21
13	Net Present Value		$48,896,169	$26,973,330	$14,829,012
14	Cumulative NPV		$48,896,169	$75,869,499	$90,698,511
15	**Retail Shopper Lifetime Value**		$122.24	$189.67	$226.75

Figure 7.4 LTV of store that has added a loyalty program

Retail Store with Loyalty Program	Current Year	Next Year	Third Year	Gain
Before Loyalty Program	$100.04	$152.41	$179.68	
With Loyalty Program	$122.24	$189.67	$226.75	$47.07
With 400,000 Customers				$18,827,657

Figure 7.5 Effect of a loyalty program

Take-Away Thoughts

- Building and maintaining loyalty today is easier than it used to be because of e-mails and cell phones, and more complex because customers expect that you will maintain a 360 degree knowledge of their purchases from you.

- Loyal customers are more profitable for you than other customers.

- Calling customers by name on the phone, on Web sites, and in e-mails is essential to maintaining loyalty.

- You need a universal ID number like phone numbers or e-mail addresses for all customers.

- Reichheld suggested that, "Would you recommend me?" is a good way to measure loyalty.

- There are two types of loyalty programs: instant discounts (for lower-income customers) and points (for higher-income customers).

- The primary purpose of a loyalty program is obtaining information which helps achieve the goals of the business.

- Your actions toward customers can determine their loyalty.

- Acquiring the right customers is a way to build loyalty.

- In a typical customer segmentation scheme, the lowest segment is unprofitable. Your profits come from the top two segments.

A quiz on this chapter and all figures can be found at www.dbmarketing.com/STM4. Those taking all the quizzes can receive a Successful Completion Certificate from the Database Marketing Institute which can be used in their résumé.

8

Making Each Communication an Adventure

In face-to-face conversation, you can see if you're holding someone's attention. Is your audience rolling their eyes or glancing at their watches? Or are they smiling and nodding enthusiastically? E-mail interaction gives you the same kind of insight. That sort of trackability is what makes it very different from a postcard or television. Best of all, with e-mail, your constituents can talk back to you. It's as easy as hitting the reply button. When was the last time you were able to talk back to a commercial and have your voice heard? Exactly. You can even take e-mail interaction to the next level by adding forms and surveys.

—CHRIS BAGGOTT
E-Mail Marketing by the Numbers

The thing about interactive media is that it's just that: interactive. That is, the media is designed and built to allow people to do things and to get results from those actions. I used to work with a phenomenal creative director who, back in 1998, said: "Every click is a wish." What an amazing line. It reminds us that every time someone presses down on that mouse button, she's expecting something great to happen, and the best sites are the ones that deliver on that wish.

—GARY STEIN
Director of Strategy, Ammo Marketing

A direct mail piece just lies there. It is what it is. Print ads also just lie there. Television ads are colorful and filled with music, but they are one-way blasts. E-mails and Web sites are the only advertising media that can be really interactive, where the reader gets to do something besides read, watch, and listen. If the e-mail is good, the reader can explore, do research, get answers, make purchases, vote, respond to questions, and ask questions of her own. In short, a good e-mail is an adventure for the reader. Few companies are exploiting the full potential of Web sites and e-mail marketing. This chapter tells you how to do this.

One way to describe interactivity is: "How to make your e-mails seem short," because that is a distinguishing feature of a really good interactive e-mail. In direct mail copy, nonprofits have found that they got more donations from a six- or twelve-page letter than from a one-page letter. The opposite seems to be true with e-mails, with this exception. To be convincing to a reader, you do need a lot of content, but most of it should be available through links which lead to a Web site or landing page. When a reader first opens the e-mails, he thinks, "Oh, this is short and easy to read. I'll see what it says." While reading the short e-mail, if he has questions or wants to know more, he clicks on a link, which takes him to a Web page with additional content. In a good interactive e-mail, 90 percent of the total content is accessed by a link rather than appearing in the e-mail. Links are the secret to interactivity. They are a wonderful way to get the user actively involved in your e-mail. Instead of just reading it, the reader is clicking on links.

An effective Web site is not like a brochure, it is more like a conversation. And in a conversation, if one person does all the talking, the other quickly becomes bored. If your Web site provides no opportunity for your visitors to interact with it, they'll feel uninvolved and leave. What can you do on your Web site or e-mail to keep people interested? Include:

- Their name
- Dynamic personalized content from the database
- Product ratings and reviews
- Feedback forms to gather information
- Surveys and polls
- Automatic subscribe and unsubscribe to your mailing list
- Bulletin boards and discussion forums

- A search box that leads wherever the reader wants to go
- Interactive games and puzzles
- The ability to forward to a friend
- Multiple-choice tests
- Detailed specifications about any product
- Research into the history of any subject

How E-mails and Web Sites Work

E-mails were the first use of the Internet back in 1971, long before Web sites existed. The Internet was created by connecting many computers to wired networks so that each computer could receive information from other computers digitally. The networks rely on switches (routers) that direct the little boats (digital packets) on their way through the Internet to their destinations. Packets hold the information contained in e-mails, Web sites, video, or telephone conversations. A packet can leave one computer and travel halfway around the world through many different networks and arrive at another computer in a second or two.

To create an Internet packet, for example, the packet software (called a "client") breaks up the message into packets of about 200 bytes. A byte consists of eight bits (a bit is a zero or a one). Each packet is put into a frame that contains extra bits with the information necessary for routing the packet from one computer to another. The main advantage of packet-switching is that it allows millions of computers or mobile phones to use the same network of communication lines. Sharing allows for very efficient use of the worldwide network.

With the Internet, computers aren't connected directly to other computers. Instead, each packet is independently routed over common lines to its destination. When a packet is ready, the host computer sends it over a telephone line or cable to a router. The router examines the destination address in the frame and passes the packet along to another router, chosen by a route-finding system. A packet may go through a few or thousands of routers in its travels from one computer to another. When the packets reach their final destination, they are reassembled in the correct numerical order at the destination computer.

Figure 8.1 illustrates one of the billions of electronic packets that travel every minute of the day all over the world on the Internet. The packet begins and ends with an electronic flag so that the routers can know where

Flag: Packet Ends Here	Packet # & Controls	Payload: Webpage, TV, VoIP or Email	Address: To where?	Flag: Packet Starts Here

Figure 8.1 A Packet in Its Frame with Its Address and Control Bits

each packet begins and ends. It has an electronic address of the destination computer and a packet number with control bits to ensure that the data in the packet is not corrupted. The payload is a group of bits that contain the information that the packet is transporting from the source to the destination computer. This information may be a little section of a Web page, of a TV picture and sound, of a VoIP voice conversation, or of an e-mail.

All packets travel at close to the speed of light: 186,000 miles per second. Because of the various lines and routers involved, a packet may take a few seconds to get where it is going.

How HTML Works

HTML (hypertext markup language) is the language used to create the colorful e-mails and Web sites we are all familiar with. The images shown in a typical HTML e-mail or Web site as they appear on your PC or mobile device may not actually be in the e-mail itself. They may be located on the server of the company sending the e-mail or Web site images. Each image has its own particular internet address called a URL (**uniform resource locator**). When you open an e-mail or a Web site, your computer sends a packet to the URL asking for certain images in the e-mail or Web site. Each packet has information that says, in effect, "Arthur Hughes has just opened the e-mail we sent him and wants to see this image." The packet races through the Internet to the location (the URL) where the image is stored. The sending company's server sends the image back to Arthur in one or more packets and also notes that "Arthur Hughes has just opened his e-mail." When the packets with the images arrive at your PC, the HTML code converts them into a picture or drawing which you see on your screen.

As you can see, two things happen at once: the delivery of the images and the knowledge of what the e-mail or Web site viewers are doing. The packets sent back to the company contain the address of your computer or mobile device. The address is essential so that the image can be sent back to the PC that is requesting the image. Because of this address, every time a user opens an HTML e-mail or Web site, the sender knows the e-mail or Web site has been opened, who opened it, and when. When you click on a link in an HTML or text e-mail (e.g., to see a different page or section of the e-mail), you see new information because a packet has been sent to the server asking for the new page. The server sends it and records the fact that you clicked on a link. Packets sent back may also include your input (such as your name, a product order, or your response to a survey question).

Many times the recipient's messaging client (such as Outlook) is set up to protect the recipient's privacy. If this is the case, the user may see a yellow line at the top of the e-mail that lets the user know that the images have been blocked. When you click on that notice to unblock the images, you are also sending a message to the e-mail sending company that you have done something with the e-mail (opened, clicked, downloaded, etc.).

The messaging client (such as Outlook) puts the *subject* and *from* line of each e-mail in an in-box—a list of all messages that have arrived for you. The in-box displays the message headers: who sent the mail and the subject of the mail. It may also tell you the time, date, and size of the messages. You can use the header to select the messages you want to read, to skip, to delete, or to mark as "junk" or spam.

Think of how different all of this is from direct mail. With direct mail letters, postcards or catalogs, you have no idea of what your customers are doing with them. They may have read them or chucked them out. Or the postal carrier may not have even delivered them! With e-mail you know that your message has been received and opened (if it was) and that the links were clicked on (if they were)—by whom and when.

Outlook (and other "clients") also show e-mail recipients a reading (preview) pane (see Figure 8.2). The reading pane shows a part of the message text, either to the right of or below the message header. Many

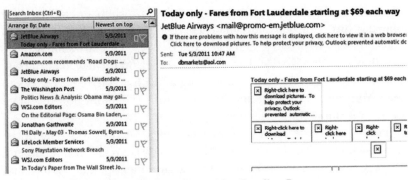

Figure 8.2 An Inbox with a Reading Pane

e-mail receivers go through a series of steps before they actually read or delete an e-mail. They look at the sender and the subject lines. If they are interested in knowing more, they look at the reading pane to get an idea of what is inside. Only if that view piques their interest will they actually open the e-mail.

Many e-mails are sent and received as just text, with no HTML. In the case of text e-mails, the sender doesn't know whether you have opened the e-mail, since text e-mails don't send packets to the sender. There is no way to track whether text e-mails have been opened. You can, however, check the links in a text e-mail. When you click on a link in a typical text e-mail, the sending company can't know that it was the text e-mail that led the viewer to its site unless it has put codes in the links that identify the subscriber.

The Effect of Having Lots of Links

E-mails and Web sites with lots of links get more reader interest than e-mails with fewer links, according to MailerMailer. Analyzing 300 million e-mails sent in 3,200 campaigns in 2007, it found that e-mails with more than 20 links were clicked on many more times than e-mails with few links.

Putting a lot of links in an e-mail or on a Web site takes time. But it pays off in terms of reader interest. And that, after all, is what we are trying to accomplish in database marketing.

How do you let readers know that there is a valuable link present? There are many ways. If you see a product displayed, under it you see a row of stars that shows how customers have rated the product. Then you see a link to reviews. With a good product, you can spend an hour reading the reviews if you want to.

On a good product page, you can click on the video and hear a description of the product. You can click on Live Help and talk to a live operator directly from your e-mail. There are reviews that you can read. You can rate the product yourself if you own it. There are similar products that you can take a look at. When you click on them, you get a page similar to the one that you are looking at, with a video and reviews to read. You can click on the specifications and read about how this large product is shipped.

Putting all these links into an e-mail is a lot of work. Why do it? Because interactivity boosts sales. There is a direct relationship between clicks and sales. The more time that a customer spends reading and doing research in your e-mails (and Web sites), the more likely she is to buy something. It is like having a conversation with your customers. Why did the Old Corner Grocers chat with their customers? Because the grocers knew that chats build loyalty, which builds sales. This is still true today. So fill your e-mails with interesting links to encourage clicking.

Why do links work? There are several reasons. First, of course, links permit readers to get answers that help them to make up their minds about buying a product. But second is the fact that by clicking on interesting links, the reader is spending more time on the Web site or e-mail. The links are increasing the "dwell time" a concept pioneered by MediaMind (formerly Eyeblaster). Marketing campaigns that actively engage consumers online for longer periods of time—by enticing them to "dwell"— are more likely to generate high conversion rates and are three times more effective at driving brand-related Web searches, according to an Eyeblaster study. Dwell rate measures how successfully a digital ad captures user attention by quantifying the proportion of users who physically touch the ad. Dwell time measures the length of user engagement with ads and various other characteristics of interactivity.

The Eyeblaster study showed that digital ads with high dwell levels were more effective in generating conversions. An analysis of more than 13 billion rich-media impressions served in 2009 found that increasing dwell from 5 to 15 percent increased conversion rates 45 percent on average, from 0.4 to 0.6 percent.

So how do you increase the dwell time? By having a lot of interactivity, which can be measured by links. The MailerMailer study found that there is a relationship between the number of links and the number of clicks. See Figure 8.3.

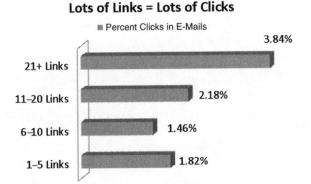

Lots of Links = Lots of Clicks

■ Percent Clicks in E-Mails

- 21+ Links: 3.84%
- 11–20 Links: 2.18%
- 6–10 Links: 1.46%
- 1–5 Links: 1.82%

Figure 8.3 Relationship between Links and Clicks (MailerMailer 2007)

Using Cookies to Boost Interactivity

A good interactive Web site is very personalized. If the reader is someone already on your customer database, what he sees when he opens the Web site derives some of its content from his database record. With the use of cookies, it is possible to welcome the reader to the e-mail by the use of his name wherever appropriate—and not just in the initial greeting.

A cookie is simply a piece of text. It isn't a program. It can't do anything. It is placed on your PC by a Web site and is designed so that only that Web site can retrieve it. A Web site can't make use of any other Web site's cookies to learn any information about you, because it doesn't have a lookup table that would correspond to any other Web site storage system.

A Web site can use cookies in many different ways. For example, it can greet you by name when you return. It can accurately determine how many people actually visit the site. It can find out how many unique visitors arrived, how many were new rather than repeat visitors, and how often a particular visitor comes to the site.

The first time a visitor goes to a Web site, the site creates a new ID in its database and puts the ID in a cookie, which it places on the visitor's computer. The next time the user visits the site, the site looks for its cookie and updates the counter associated with that ID in the database. It now knows how many times the visitor has returned. Sites can store also user preferences in the lookup table accessed by the cookie so it can customize the page appearance for each visitor. In the blink of an eye, it goes to its internal lookup table, realizes who you are, and says, "Welcome back, Arthur."

Cookies make it possible to keep track of what you are doing while you add items to your shopping cart. Each item you add to your shopping cart is stored in the site's database along with your ID. When you check out, the site knows what's in your cart by retrieving all your selections from the database. It would be impossible to set up a convenient shopping system on Web sites without cookies.

When a repeat visitor receives one of your e-mails and clicks on a preference or order form, she will find much of the form's data, such as name, address, phone number, and e-mail address, are already in the appropriate fields. Why? Because she filled out that data on a previous visit to your site, and you were smart enough to use cookies. Because of cookies, if your reader starts to fill out a form but gets distracted and surfs to another Web site, when she returns to the form, she will find that her previous entries are still there. How can it do that? By saving all entries in a database record as soon as the visitor enters them and by putting a cookie on her PC.

The Importance of Cookies

You will read a lot of criticism about cookies by privacy advocates. The privacy aspects are, in my opinion, overblown. If you can say, "Welcome back, Arthur," you will get more repeat visitors, and boost your sales. It is as simple as that. Don't just have a link that says, "My Account" and make visitors click there, entering their e-mail address and password. This means that you really have the information, but you are not using it properly. Why did the Old Corner Grocer greet people using their names when they came into his shop? Because he understood that this made them feel more at home. They came back and shopped more. You can do the same thing. It costs nothing to do this—while the programmers are creating your Web site, they can add greetings based on cookies with a dozen or more lines of code. As you set a cookie, you can have a box that says, "Remember me when I come back" which is already checked. The privacy extremists can uncheck that. I suppose that privacy addicted visitors to the Old Corner Grocer could say, "Please do not use my name when you welcome me back to your store," which is really the same thing—but I doubt that anyone would actually say that. My strong recommendation: greet repeat visitors by name. You will profit from it.

Interactivity Involves Remembering What People Do

Amazon and Netflix are perhaps the world's experts at interactive e-mails. On either site, if you click on a movie or a product, the site immediately suggests other movies or products triggered by what you clicked on. A good interactive e-mail or Web site remembers everything you clicked on.

When you come back to the e-mail or the corresponding Web site later, the e-mail hasn't forgotten your expressed interest. Very few database marketers, however, have mastered this.

Recalling recent conversations isn't really all that unusual in real life. If you have a conversation with a friend about a movie you saw, you would be shocked if the friend couldn't remember this conversation five minutes later. Yet that is the case with 95 percent of the Web sites and e-mails today. Their short-term and long-term memories are usually nonexistent. Having a memory is an important feature of successful interactive e-mails and Web sites.

Planning an Interactive E-mail or Web Site

When you plan an interactive e-mail, ask yourself what you want the reader to do when he looks at your e-mail or Web site:

- Buy a product
- See something he will want to forward to a friend, thereby adding to your subscriber base
- Complete a survey
- Register for a newsletter
- Learn more about your products, brand, company, services, and so on
- Download a white paper or program
- Do research that leads him in a certain direction
- Share an opinion on the product or service

Once you have a plan for where you are going, the e-mail or Web site has to be designed with this plan in mind. When you have completed the e-mail design, read it as you expect your readers will—to see if the finished product actually produces the results you want.

Basically, each e-mail or Web site should be an adventure, an experience that will make the reader think, "Wow! I'm glad I read that!" That is a hard standard to achieve every time, but that should be your goal. If that isn't your goal, you shouldn't be in the database marketing business in the first place.

Does Animation Pay Off?

Fashion retailer Bluefly Inc. conducted an e-mail marketing test on what the effect of animated text within a marketing e-mail was on e-mail recipients' behavior. The text in question was "Shhhhh," which scrolled across the message. It was a light-hearted approach to promoting a private sale for select Bluefly customers who made up 35 percent of the e-retailer's e-mail list.[1] Using Web analytics from Coremetrics, Bluefly saw a 5 percent increase in CTR (Click Through Rate) for recipients of the animated version (25 percent of the 35 percent sample) over recipients of the nonanimated version. But more important, shoppers who received the animated e-mail and clicked through generated a 12 percent increase in dollars spent per thousand e-mails compared with shoppers who received the non-animated version and clicked through.

As a result of this success, Joellen Nicholson, director of marketing at Bluefly, decided to use the animation in many more e-mails. Nicholson planned to, "Change the percentage, giving more people the animation. We will use our analytics to see how the metrics play out to a larger group. We want to see if it still holds true, to see if this animation is a clear and distinct winner.... We use Web analytics extensively, looking at daily, weekly, monthly, and quarterly reports to track e-mail performance."

Maintaining Linked Data

Paper catalogs can lie around a consumer's home for months. It isn't unusual for a consumer to order something from a six-month old catalog. Marketing e-mails, on the other hand, have a shelf life of only a couple of days. Our in-boxes fill quickly with old messages. We delete them and get on with life. That is no excuse, however, for an e-mail marketer to delete linked content from a Web site unless it is clearly obsolete (e.g., prices that are no longer valid). E-mail readers are encouraged to send interesting content to their friends and relatives. An interesting video, photo, or white paper may crop up in someone's in-box days, weeks, or months after its first use. Don't delete this content. What does it cost you to keep old articles, white papers, or videos? If you do some research, you will find that you can keep most of your old content on a Web site for years for $0.05 per month or less. Why is this important? Let's look at an example.

Suppose you run an annual conference. After the conference, you post 50 white papers linked to the conference Web site and send the links to your e-mail list. Scores of attendees and others download these papers. A year later, you are preparing for a new conference. In cleaning up your Web site, you delete all those links to last year's conference white papers.

---

[1] http://www.internetretailer.com, March 12, 2008

What a mistake! Without your lifting a finger, search engines like Google have indexed the materials from last year's conference. A Web visitor a year from now will enter a query in Google and find a reference to one of these white papers—except that the paper no longer exists on the Web. Or your e-mail has made the rounds and a recipient clicks on a link to read the white paper. Either person might have read the paper, given that it came from your old conference, and decided to register for the new conference. With conference registrations of $1,500 or more, what is the ROI of keeping old data available? Perhaps $150 per dollar.

Video in E-mails and on Web Sites

Video in e-mails can increase sales. There is a huge audience for Internet video: 116 million U.S. consumers watched Web videos in the first half of 2010. And video isn't just for a young audience. YouTube attracts all age groups for its video content: 18 percent are under age 18; 20 percent are 18–34; 19 percent are 35–44; 21 percent are 45–54; and 21 percent are 55 or older.[2]

FirstStreetOnline sells gifts, gadgets, and household products aimed at older consumers. The retailer introduced a weekly video called FirstStreetReports in which a mature man provides nontechnical explanations of the products. Sales and conversion rates on those products went up by double-digit percentages.[3]

HavenHolidays conducted a highly successful test of video in its promotional e-mails for its amusement park. After scrubbing the subscriber list to get rid of bounced addresses, online marketing executive Carolyn Jacquest produced a five-minute video showing the park's features. To discover the optimal length, she sent clip sizes to the in-house accounts for its U.K.-based audience's 10 most-popular Web mail providers or receivers. From the test results, she learned that 20-second clips were optimal for deliverability. The copy at the top of the HTML design was, "Fun Filled Easter at Haven!" A 320 × 180 pixel video box automatically started rolling when the message was opened. If the subscriber's system didn't let her see the video in the e-mail, she saw a link to a microsite.

---

[2] http://www.screenandtvwriter.com/phpBB/viewtopic.php?=&p=33160.
[3] Mark Gordon, president and CEO. www.FirstStreetOnline.com, http://www.internetretailer.com/article.asp?id=26243&ref=ya.

Embedding the video e-mails worked. The Easter campaign had a 3.38 percent conversion rate—50.2 percent higher than previous non-video campaigns, which were 2 to 2.5 percent. The 20-second clip had a deliverability rate of 96 percent, with a CTR of 27 percent. Including the word "video" in the subject line produced a 14.6 percent boost for opens.

Unfortunately, a large number of subscribers couldn't view the video because their client (something other than Outlook) didn't show the video in a satisfactory manner. Those subscribers clicked on the Haven microsite to see the video. Despite this failure, the conversion rate improvement was impressive.

Make Your Messages Conversations

The most successful e-mails are written like a conversation between two people, one on one. An excellent way to learn to do this is to read *The Art of Plain Talk* by Rudolph Flesch (out of print, but available through Amazon and Alibris). Here's a quick summary:

- Use short sentences; the shorter the better.
- Use lots of personal references, such as people's names; personal pronouns; and human interest words, such as *man, woman, child, father, mother, son, daughter, brother,* and *sister.*
- Avoid affixes, such as *para-, pseudo-, infra-, meta-, ultra-, hypo-,* and *circum-.* Use root words instead.
- Use a familiar word rather than rare words, concrete terms rather than abstract ones, short words rather than long ones, and single words rather than several ones.
- Use verbs; they give life to a sentence. Use the active voice rather than the passive voice or subjunctive.
- Be careful with adjectives; adjectives are the enemy of the noun. This is because, very often, if we use the precise noun, we don't need an adjective. For example, instead of saying "a large, impressive house" we could simply say "a mansion."

Create the E-mail's Author

One of the first questions readers ask is, "Who is writing to me?" Who are you? Are you a company? A mysterious someone hiding behind a bunch of colorful images? You can use yourself as the e-mail author or create a persona. The writer should be a person, such as the director of customer service, a product manager, or the CEO. Sign the e-mail and, if possible, add a friendly photo of the sender. When Safeway first started its customer newsletter, it was signed by Bill McDown, a division manager whose picture was featured on the newsletter's first page. When he went to the stores, people often recognized him and came to shake his hand. The first year of the program, he got 3,000 Christmas cards from Safeway customers. If you can equal that, you have a great e-mail or direct mail piece.

Also try to give your reader a sense of who you are as a person, what your work involves, and how you know so much about the products or services featured in the e-mail. Don't talk like a know-it-all; talk like a user or a developer. Tell readers that you have tried the product or service yourself and found that it works for you. Or tell them what you did to develop the product so people would find it useful.

Most e-mails should be conversational. Even for a business audience, don't be too formal. How you speak should reflect your brand personality. For an entertaining consumer product, use a fun tone that's reflected in the vocabulary.

While you are deciding who you are, research the best e-mails. Get your office buddies to forward you the best ones they regularly receive. Make a library of great e-mail ideas. We call these "nuggets." To write this book, I reviewed our library of more than 200 nuggets and have provided the best of them in this book.

Once you have written your copy, read it out loud to yourself. Many times you will find that what seemed good on paper doesn't read well out loud. It should, so change it.

Get the Reader Involved

The best e-mails are two-way conversations. You can't have a conversation in direct mail. You can have one over the telephone, but phone calls are expensive and too intrusive. Marketing phone calls often make recipients angry. With e-mail, you can have the interaction of a phone call without the annoyance. After all, subscribers don't have to open the e-mails. They can look at the subject line and say, "Let's skip that one." But once they have opened your e-mail, you should somehow make the experience fun and interactive. Look what an enthusiastic subscriber, Dan McCarthy said:

I love the daily e-mails from steepandcheap.com. It's a Web site that's focused specifically on outdoor gear. The thing that's great about the e-mails is that they aren't at all focused on the product—they are instead focused on making me laugh or telling me a story, which makes me read the e-mail. As a result, I click on the product link almost every day. There is no other e-mail that gets this much of my attention each day. The bottom line is that they seem to really understand their target audience and know what I'm interested in. The stories are off the wall, and worth reading even if you aren't into outdoor gear!

One way to create interest is to invite the reader to send in articles, questions, or comments to be included in future e-mails. Lots of people like to see their name published, whether online or off. You can make it possible and generate interest in your e-mails at the same time. To do this, give readers a subject to write about. For instance, if there was recently a conference or industry event, ask readers to write a session summary and send it to you.

Another way to stir up interest is to include a poll or survey in every newsletter, using multiple-choice questions. The topic could be anything of interest to your readers. Provide the results in the next e-mail. Subscribers will want to read the next e-mail to see how their responses compared to everyone else's.

Make E-mails Interesting

REI's e-mails are filled with outdoor adventures, such as an interview with Peter Potterfield, who shared his experience in hiking New Zealand, and one with Lauren Reynolds, who shared her advice on running right. Each e-mail features one particular experience plus access to 400 other similar stories. While the reader is scanning one of these adventures, she can check out the deal of the day, the deal of the week, the top sellers, the deals under $20, the Just Added, and a search box that brings up thousands of outdoor gear products. What the reader is getting is adventure. What REI gets in return are opens, clicks, and conversions.

PETCO has another interesting idea: it e-mails letters from a pet to the pet's owner. A typical e-mail might read, "Jennifer: Louie wrote you a letter. Check it out." Clicking on the link leads the subscriber to a page with a cute letter "written" by Jennifer's pet. He tells Jennifer about all the products he would like to have—all sold by PETCO. Jennifer can buy any of them by clicking on links in the e-mail.

Create Dynamic, Personal Content

The best e-mails are filled with dynamic, database-driven customer preferences. They contain customized subject lines, greetings, offers, or special images. They strike a responsive chord in readers that helps them realize that you are speaking directly to them as individuals, not to the world in general.

To create dynamic content, you need demographic information from your database about your subscribers, such as zip code, occupation, hobbies, age, household income, or spending habits, and you need to use that information to provide content that speaks to the reader's particular interests. Subscribers like being addressed as individuals:

> Dynamic content builds brand loyalty. It can improve a reader's attitudes toward your company. It builds clicks and conversions. To create dynamic content, you need to do most of the things recommended in this book, such as building a marketing database with demographic data about each subscriber. Use that information to create segments with dynamic content related to the interests of subscribers in that segment. Give subscribers choices on the information they receive. This reduces the number of subscribers turned off because they receive non-relevant e-mails. And include lines like, "Thank you, Arthur, for subscribing on 08/04/2011." Such wording is personal and adds credibility to your e-mails. It helps ISPs identify your message as legitimate, not spam.

Offer Wish Lists and Gift Registries

Net-a-porter created a series of four e-mails. The first e-mail began, "A Show-Stopping Dress for Every Occasion—Create a wish list and send all your must-have ideas to your loved one." Below this was a "<u>start now</u>" button that took subscribers to a landing page titled. "A Party Dress for Every Occasion." The e-mail concluded with, "This e-mail is part of a series of four daily e-mails. If you would prefer not to receive the rest in the series, please <u>click here</u>."

This series is a version of the "birthday club" in which women provide a retailer with their preferences in clothing—sizes, colors, and brands—their birthday, and their husband's or boyfriend's e-mail address (see Chapter 2). The results are e-mails from the retailer to the men reminding them of their loved one's birthday and suggesting gifts the men could purchase through a link in the e-mail. The brilliance of this technique plays on the fact that most men hate to shop, particularly for women's clothing. Most women love to shop but find it difficult to hint to their significant others what they would really like to receive as a gift.

If you have a series of newsletters that is planned in advance, such as a Christmas schedule, try listing the schedule in each newsletter so subscribers can see what is coming and go back to see what they missed. See Figure 8.4 for an example of how Miles Kimball does this. Readers can click on the underlined issues to read something they missed. It helps readers understand how the holiday messages are organized. It is more reader-friendly than just sending e-mails one after the other because readers may think they are getting too many.

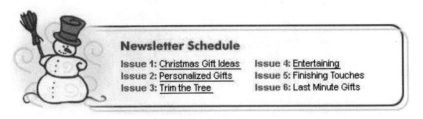

Figure 8.4 Miles Kimball's Christmas E-mail Schedule

Make Web Sites and E-mails Interactive Adventures

SmartBargains is one of the most creative, interactive, and successful e-mail marketers on the Internet. Subscribers receive its e-mails every day of the year. Figure 8.5 is a sample e-mail that starts off with a treasure hunt. It's hard not to click on the X. Price reductions are for today only! Clicking on the button takes you to the retailer's home page, shown in Figure 8.6.

The reader is not aware that by clicking on the links in the e-mail, she is actually viewing the home page. It seems to her as if the e-mail she is reading is loaded with links. There are more than 50 links on this page alone. Scroll over one of the tabs in the top navigation bar, and a drop-down list appears with additional links.

In the upper right-hand corner of the home page is an invitation to sign up for "hot deals and exclusive offers." Few Web sites give such a prominent place to the e-mail sign-up box. And the search box is just below the top navigation bar. Search boxes are essential for any Web site. They should be as easy to find as this one is.

Figure 8.5 A SmartBargains.com Treasure Hunt E-mail

Figure 8.6 SmartBargains.com Home Page

Now look at the sorting feature below the "One Day Clearance" head-line. Visitors have five options to sort by: best sellers, new arrivals, low to high price, high to low price, and greatest percentage off. How handy and interactive!

Each link is an invitation to a new adventure. Just above the "Free Shipping" headline, the visitor has three options. When she clicks on "Clearance," she lands on the Clearance page, as pictured in Figure 8.7.

Figure 8.7 SmartBargains.com Clearance

The entire e-mail appears to its readers as a treasure hunt of links. Yet the e-mail itself is small and opens very quickly, since the links are really located elsewhere. This is an extremely sophisticated linkage of an e-mail with a Web site.

Write Text Specifically for Mobile Devices

Writing text for a mobile version of your e-mail is very different from writing text for the regular version of your e-mail. A mobile device's screen is tiny—between 2 and 4 inches. When you write the mobile version of your message, visualize your readers. What will they be doing while they read your text? Riding in a cab, waiting for a plane, eating on a train, or being stuck at the wheel of their car in traffic? They are probably operating with one hand, and their attention is somewhere else. They will scan their in-box rapidly and skip most of its contents.

If you use tracking URLs, you will have to compress them to fit them on the small screen. The messages must be short. Any message over 12 kilobytes may be cut off halfway through. Long sentences force readers to scroll a lot, which can be frustrating. Despite the obstacles, however, many subscribers will want to view your important e-mails on their mobile devices.

To get subscribers to sign up for mobile messages, include a mobile option on your Web site and in the admin center in all your e-mails. Before you launch any text e-mail for mobile, send it to yourself to make sure it works on regular cell phones, not just on a smartphone. American Airlines, for example, really plays up, mobile e-mail messages, as can be seen in Figure 8.8.

Figure 8.8 American Airlines Cell Phone Invitation

Take-Away Thoughts

How does your Web site or e-mail measure up when compared with the following interactive metrics? Give yourself a rating from 0 to 10 for each of the following:

- *Is there personally relevant content?* Does it use the subscriber's first name in the message body and on the Web site?

- *Do you have a meaningful reference to the brand?* Web sites and e-mails are advertisements. How clear is the brand to the reader?

- *How obvious and easy is your navigation and search?* How easy is it to get around in your Web site or e-mail? Are your search boxes or menus easy to find? Are the links obvious to the readers? Give yourself a low score if they are so fancy that the reader is unsure of how to activate what he is looking for.

- *How many links do you have?* And how many do the average readers click on?

- *How does your message help the reader identify with her lifestyle?* Visualize the reader. What images can you show her that will help her identify personally with your message?

- *Do you have a switchable template?* On a good e-mail or Web site you should be able to easily interchange the e-mail's content based on the reader's or product's dynamics. For example, if you sell bathing suits and you send e-mail to both men and women, in the section where the suits are shown, it should be easy to switch copy and images based on the reader's gender.

- *How appealing is your overall design?* Look at the e-mail or Web site as a whole. Have you created a Michelangelo or thrown together a bunch of unrelated images and fonts?

- *How interesting and exciting is your Web site or e-mail?* Like publishing a daily newspaper, every issue has to be good. Will your readers say, "Wow! Am I glad I read that!"?

A quiz on this chapter and all figures can be found at www.dbmarket ing.com/STM4. Those taking all the quizzes can receive a Successful Completion Certificate from the Database Marketing Institute which can be used in their résumé.

9

Listening to Customers

I've found that many companies have a tendency to focus so much on selling their product or service that they forget to listen to what their customers are telling them. The goal for any business is to make money, but that goal is more easily attained when you listen to your customers and know and understand what their needs are. The best way to do that is by listening to what they tell you. More often than not, in the course of a conversation, a customer will divulge information that is vital to your overall success.

—ALAN HALL

Watching the launch of Apple's iPad, I was struck by the fact that Steve Jobs famously doesn't pay too much attention to customer research. ("We do no market research. We don't hire consultants," he said recently.) And yet—or should that be because of—this refusal to pay much attention to what customers say they want, Apple has become the ultimate game changer. Customers want to be surprised and delighted. And to surprise and delight someone, you don't ask them "What can we do to surprise and delight you?"

—SHAUN SMITH

Last week, while speaking at an e-mail conference, I asked a room full of e-mail marketers how many of them listened to customers, either through tools from companies like Radian6, Nielsen Buzz Metrics, StrongMail, or within their own communities and loyalty programs. Only about six hands shot up. I then asked, of those companies that listened, how many edited or changed their campaign content based on what they heard. Only one hand remained in the air. Out of a room of 40-plus e-mail marketers, only one was listening to consumer sentiments and trends on the social Web and adapting the content of their e-mail based on that knowledge. The best part was that it wasn't a retailer or travel firm, but a financial services business! Who would have guessed?

—Ryan Deutsch

The three very different quotations above are all correct. Alan Hall is talking about how to retain your existing customers. Shaun Smith is talking about designing a new product. Ryan Deutsch is talking about listening to customers. As database marketers we have to do all three. Let's start with retaining customers.

Retention is built and maintained by two-way communications between you and your customer. Customers make purchases. You thank them for their patronage. You ask your customers for their preferences. They respond. You store their preferences in your database. Then you modify your services to make sure that their preferences are respected. Acting on these preferences involves a lot of little perks and services that show customers that you really are loyal to them.

The database is central to the process: this is where the customer preferences and other data are stored. You use the database to create the personalized services and messages that build loyalty.

Sears obtains essential customer preferences on its excellent Web site. At www.sears.com you can look up any product through a neat preference cascade. I bought a new clothes washer on the Sears site. My purchase cascade started with Appliances. On this page I clicked on Front Load Washers (31 results). I clicked on several options: Maytag, White color, and Capacity (2+ cu ft). This brought up a white Maytag 2.4 capacity front loader with complete product specs (several pages) with an "add to cart" button, which I clicked on.

The "add to cart" button brought me to cross sale suggestions. This screen suggested a next-best product: a matching dryer which mounts on top of the washer. I already had a dryer, but I was worried about the mounting. So I bit and bought the dryer at the same time (I am a sucker for convenience).

But that was not the end of it. Sears brought me to a profile screen where it asked me several important questions.

How I feel about brands:

- I typically buy top-of-the-line name brand products.
- I buy name brand products at a moderate price.
- I am always looking for a bargain. I will try any brand if the price is right.

How I feel about technology:

- I buy products with the latest features and innovations.
- I buy products with mainstream features and technology.
- I am not interested in technology, keep it simple for me.

Home status:

- Home owner
- Renter
- Lived in my home for less than 6 months
- Plan to move in the next 6 months
- Plan to remodel in the next 6 months

Presence of children:

- Baby (age 0–age 1)
- Kids (age 1–age 12)
- Teenagers (age 13–age 18)
- None

Look at these questions. They are wonderful! They can be used by Sears to market to me by reflecting and respecting my preferences. I am a home owner who buys the latest features and buys top-of-the-line products. Does your company have a similar system to learn what your customers want? The result of the Sears questionnaire should be that the company does not contact me when its products are on sale, but does so when there is some new innovation that does a better job. I want the best, not the cheapest. I am not everyone. I want to be marketed to as the person that I am.

Using the Preferences Information

Now that you have information about customers, their transactions, and their preferences stored in your customer marketing database updated frequently, a set of special programs that carry out a function called "trawling" can begin. Trawling implements a large number of marketing business rules. Trawling software looks at every record in the database that has been changed since the last update and applies business rules to the data it finds. For example, trawling will determine if the customer:

- Is about to have a birthday or anniversary
- Filled out or changed a preference profile
- Had an unusually large transaction
- Reached a milestone with the company in terms of total sales, years with the company, and so on

Each hit during trawling has a programmed marketing response. Depending on the situation and the customer's preferences, the customer may be sent an e-mail or a direct mail message, she may be called by customer service, a sales person may visit her, or the Web site may have a special message for her if and when she logs on. These are automated communications. Once set up and programmed, they will take place automatically.

The National Australia Bank (NAB) serves more than 8.3 million customers. Its "national leads" system prioritizes events and alerts the appropriate bankers each morning so that they can take appropriate action. The goal is to ensure that customers are contacted with meaningful opportunities at the right times through the right channels. The system works this way:

- The warehouse is updated with an average of more than 3.5 million transactions per day.
- Every night, queries trawl the warehouse to search for any unusual changes in customer behavior or preferences.

- Once a month, each customer is scored using a model that predicts the customer's propensity to purchase various products and a propensity to respond to product offers. The best leads are selected and sent to the bankers.

- Every night 250 communication vectors are run combining the events detected plus the preferences and the propensity predictions. The software recommends the action to be taken via ATM, e-mail, mail, or leads to call centers, branches, or business bankers who follow up with a phone call or personal mail.

Trawling Results

What were the results of the trawling exercise at the bank? Here are five successes:

- During the first year of this system more than 1 million leads and $4 billion in growth opportunities were sent to NAB bankers for action.

- During the next six months, 570,000 new leads were sent which resulted in the closing of $4.4 billion worth of new loans.

- During the second year of the system, premium sales of banking products increased by 25 percent over the previous year, while sales of wealth management products increased by 40 percent.

- The close rate for leads increased by five times over the close rate before the new system began.

- The bank achieved a $391 million return on investment on one campaign.

So, How Do You Get Started?

To get started, create a preference profile on your Web site. Study the Sears example. Do not ask too many questions. Think, "Why would anyone want to fill out this profile?" Come up with some good answers. In the Sears example, I was buying an appliance. I wanted to be sure that Sears knew what I wanted.

How soon after the profile is filled out should you act on the expressed preferences? The answer is right away. The person most likely to buy another German chocolate cheese cake from you is a person who has a mouthful of it right now. If Arthur just bought a washer and a dryer, he may need a dishwasher or a new refrigerator. He may be making his decision in the next 24 hours. You will need to develop business rules that spell out what to do when a customer has filled out preferences on a profile form. Too many companies do nothing at all when a customer fills out a profile. That is like leaving money on the table.

Getting the Information

It used to be very difficult and expensive to get information from customers. If you had a survey you wanted them to fill out, you had to get the form to them. Then they had to fill out the form and mail it to a processing center, where clerks keyed the results into a computer, which entered the results into a database. It was very slow, and you were lucky to get as much as 7 percent of your customers to complete the forms. By the time you got the information into your database, the customer may have forgotten all about you.

Today, with Web sites, the process is infinitely simpler, cheaper, and more comprehensive. You put a bunch of questions on your Web site, in your e-mails, or in a text message to customers' iPhone. The subscriber answers the questions and hits "submit." The data is quality-checked by your software (which will ask the subscriber to fill in any missing data) and then put directly into your subscriber database. After the subscriber enters her answers, the data isn't touched by human hands again. You have the data available the same day it is entered, and the cost is almost nothing if you have the supporting software. You start by immediately sending an e-mail thanking the subscriber for participating. You begin what may be a long and profitable relationship.

The trick, however, is to get the subscribers to give you the information you want.

Why Would Subscribers Provide You with Information?

We all know that people do what is in their own best interest, but do we act as if we knew it? For subscribers to spend their time giving you the information you want, they have to get something out of it. Before you design a survey, therefore, think through the subscriber-motivation process. Create something you can give to subscribers electronically that they consider valuable, such as:

- Downloadable information
- Newsletters

- E-mails about products and sales
- Membership in a club
- Coupons
- Free shipping for products they are ordering

Sample Subscriber Benefits

Chase Bank has paperless statements that provide "a convenient and environmentally friendly way to access your credit card statements." Chase will make a $5 donation to the World Wildlife Fund for every card member who goes paperless by a fixed date. What's in it for the card member? "Switch to Paperless Statements and you'll also be entered in our sweepstakes for a Natural Habitat Adventures Classic Galapagos Cruise for two—a $12,500 value."

What Information Do You Need?

Before you design a subscriber information form, think through exactly how you can and will use the information you get. Make a list of all the possible information and what you can do with each piece. Then prioritize the pieces so those at the top of the list will be items you can use every day. Here are a few ways you can use such subscriber information:

- Create subscriber segments based on their needs or interests so that your direct mail and e-mails will be relevant to them
- Send information related to the retail store closest to them
- Send direct mail and e-mails about the products they are interested in
- E-mail them only as frequently as they want to hear from you

Don't Ask for Too Much at Once

Don't ask for too much information at once because subscribers won't give it. They may become distrustful and unsubscribe. On the Internet, we are accustomed to asking people for their e-mail address; it is the only way we have of communicating with them. On the home page of every Web site—and on any page that links to the home page—marketers must put a box so that visitors can enter their e-mail and postal address. Of course, if you already have their postal or e-mail address, your Web site should be smart enough not to ask for it again. This is important! Customers hate redundancy. Right next to the request box, you tell them what they can expect to receive from you. If you will send a newsletter or report, you should have a link next to the box that says, "Click to see a sample."

When subscribers click on the "submit" button, you store the information and immediately send them an e-mail confirming that they really want to receive what they have asked for. How soon should you send this opt-in requesting e-mail? Within a few seconds. Never longer! This is e-mail marketing etiquette.

The confirmation e-mail can ask one or two questions (the top ones on your list) but not too many. It is vital that you get subscribers to confirm their permission for you to correspond with them.

Many marketers cringe when they hear the phrase *double opt-in*. This confirmation method, however, is very important in preserving an e-mail database's quality. It gives an e-mail marketer the best possible chance to develop profitable subscriber relationships. Figure 9.1 is an example of a simple double-opt-in practice that I like from TopButton. Right in the e-mail confirmation page, it asks the new subscriber to validate his e-mail address.

Some e-mail marketers ask for much more. Resort vacation exchange company RCI has five pages of preferences with over 100 questions for its members to fill out. Is this too much? RCI has over 3 million subscribing members living in more than 200 countries. It has over 4,000 affiliated resorts located in 100 countries. For members to decide where they want their vacations among these various resorts, perhaps 100 questions aren't too many. RCI has arranged more than 54 million exchange vacations in the last few years.

Now that you have sent and received an e-mail, you can ask more questions. Your subscribers are in a question-answering mood. Strike while the iron is hot. Get the information you need before it is too late.

What to Ask For

If you study your business and your customers, you may decide you need only a few—usually not more than 10 or 15—pieces of customer information to enable you to create segments so that you can send relevant direct mail and e-mail messages. The data can be broken down into four categories:

Registration Notice:

- We're sorry for the inconvenience, but we want to make sure you spelled your email (ahughes@e-dialog.com) correctly. Please double check below. If you did spell it correctly, please click on the continue button below.

It's Official - YOU'RE IN!

Congratulations! You've got full-on access to the TOP BUTTON web site and e-mail alerts!

Some of our most exclusive sales are promoted only by mail. So you don't miss a single event or party, fill in the postal information below and you'll also be automatically entered to win an iPod nano.

1. YOUR INFO   2. MEMBER PERKS

E-mail address	ahughes@e-dialog.com	Zip Code	33316
First Name	Arthur	Last Name	Hughes
Address	2100 South Ocean Drive	Address2	
City	Fort Lauderdale	State	FL
Mobile Phone	954-767-4558	Gender	Male

▸▸ CONTINUE

Figure 9.1 Topbutton.com Welcome E-mail

- *Contact information:* Name, e-mail address, street address, phone number
- *Basic demographics:* Gender, age, marital status, income, children, house type
- *Preferences:* Product interest, e-mail frequency
- *Attitudes:* Viewpoints on pricing, levels of service, and so on

Don't ask for too much information or anything that you don't need in developing relevant messages. Some of the necessary information can be gained by appended data (see the next section) so you don't need to ask for it. When asking for anything, be sure to let your subscribers know how you will use the data and that their privacy will be protected. Let them know how they will benefit from giving you the information.

Shop It To Me does a good job of sharing its intentions as part of the sign-up process. See Figure 9.2.

Figure 9.2 Shop It To Me Sign-Up Page

Obtaining Demographic Data

As discussed in Chapter 6, if you have the subscriber's street address, you can get all the demographic data you could want appended to your database file. Since this information is so readily available, you don't need to ask subscribers to provide it.

Is appended data accurate? Not in all cases. Maybe the subscriber just got a promotion last week and his income went up by $15,000. Is that reflected in his personal record in these databases? Of course not. On the whole, these databases' information is probably 80 percent accurate, good enough for you to create customer segments. And it is better in most cases than what you could get from your subscribers. Why? Because much of the information is considered personal and private, so some subscribers will resent or resist providing it. You may lose subscribers by asking for it. They may give you false information. And you may be able to get only a fraction of your subscribers to provide it. By appending data using a compiled database provider, you can get close to a 90 percent match rate, which is really all you need.

In some cases, however, you may have to ask for demographic data directly: if you're legally obligated to do so or if, in the very first interaction, you will use this information in a way that will provide immediate value to your subscriber. For example, Jack Daniel's is legally obligated to prohibit access to its online content to anyone under 21, so it has a good reason to ask for date of birth right from the start. Parents.com asks for some very personal information upfront (see Figure 9.3) with the purpose of making every site visit personalized to an individual member from the get-go.

Figure 9.3 Parents.com Data Request

Continuing the Dialogue

As you begin marketing to your subscribers and customers, you can ask a question or two during the course of transactional and other messages. Before you send a message to any person for any reason, your software should scan the person's database record to see what information is already there. You can compare this information to the list of important pieces of information required for creating marketing segments.

Let's say you sell clothing. The software sees that you are missing the type of clothing this subscriber is most interested in. In your next promotional or transactional message, include a question that will solve this mystery.

Perhaps you are interested in whether this person is keen on seeing low-cost items, top-of-the-line items, or mainstream items. A question in the next marketing message will help you to determine what kind of information to feature in the future.

Don't Lose the Data

Some of your e-mail or Web site subscribers will become distracted while filling out your forms. When they come back to look at the form, their information will have disappeared, and they will have to start over. *Don't ever let that happen.* You will annoy your subscribers and may lose them as a result. Solution: use cookies. Whenever a subscriber begins to fill in a form, save each piece of data and place a cookie on the subscriber's PC. If he has to log off and come back later, he will be delighted to find that the data he entered is still there waiting for him.

Is this hard to arrange? Sure. So are most of the recommendations in this book. But just because it's hard doesn't mean you shouldn't do it. If your e-mail programmers say what you want is too difficult for them, get other programmers. Everything we recommend in this book is doable and should be done. Marketing is too important to be made subservient to the abilities of a few programmers. You can quote me on this.

Don't Be Like IVR

Most subscribers hate interactive voice response (IVR) systems. In most cases, IVR's purpose seems to be to keep the caller from ever talking to a live person. Web sites and e-mails should be just the opposite of IVR. Whatever the subscriber wants to do should be anticipated with links. In every e-mail, include a search box so that the subscriber can search on the site for anything not available in the links, a toll-free number and an e-mail address, and a "live agent" button so the subscriber can have a text chat any time with someone who is knowledgeable and can get things done.

But be warned. Don't put advanced features like text chat on your Web site or in your e-mails if you're not prepared to make the experience a pleasant one for your customers. You really must have someone supporting the customer dialogue around the clock. If you can only cover certain hours, make that clear right next to the input box.

Provide Feedback Functionality in Every E-mail

One of the most frustrating things about a poorly constructed e-mail is the failure of the subscriber to find a way to respond. You read the e-mail (which is supposed to be a two-way conversation), and you may really want to get in touch with the person who sent the message. You hunt high and low, but there is no e-mail address or phone number anywhere in the e-mail.

If you really want to listen to your customers, you have to make it possible for them to say something to you—and you have to read what people say. Rule: put feedback functionality, whether an e-mail address, a toll free number, or a link to a form on your site, in every single e-mail and Web site so that you can have a real conversation with your subscribers. Someone in your company should check the feedback daily. It's a courtesy to subscribers who take the time to compliment, complain, ask for information, or point out a problem.

Make the Data Entry Process Fun

As you have learned by now, e-mail marketing is a lot of fun. It is highly creative. It calls on you to use your imagination and dream up wild ideas that no one has thought of and then try them out. It also calls for keeping up with what is on other Web sites and making use of the many new and great ideas being implemented. When you design your data-gathering forms, think up interesting or amusing ways to ask for the data and to thank your subscribers after they have entered each piece of information.

Here is where e-mail becomes separated from the corporate Web site. Corporate Web sites are often stodgy and bureaucratic. Committees are formed to review each aspect of the site. In many cases, marketers can't introduce new ideas without putting them in front of a sceptical committee. The process takes time and may be a serious impediment to a creative and exciting Web site.

The same isn't true of marketing e-mails. If you are sending e-mails out every week or every day, no committee has time to oversee what you are doing. So you are free to experiment. You can use your imagination and creativity. At the same time, be sure to test each new idea. If you try a new approach to data gathering, use an A/B split. Send half of your e-mail recipients the A approach and the other half the B approach.

Keep track of which version each person got. Get a report *tomorrow* on which got the better response. If the A idea wins, that becomes your control for the future.

Don't Ask for Information You Already Have

Many companies ask for the same data repeatedly. Big mistake. Program your software to check every data request in any outgoing e-mail with the data already stored in your database. If the data is already there, don't ask for it again. If, however, the data is quite old, you may ask if a subscriber's profile or preference has changed. In this case, show the data you already have and let the subscriber decide whether to change it or leave it. Don't show subscribers a blank form and make them work. Each survey question should be carefully selected for that particular subscriber. The Old Corner Grocer didn't ask his customers every day what their phone number was or where they lived. Why would you?

Pre-enter Data on Any Order Form

A subscriber has put something in her shopping cart and is ready to check out. She is confronted with a form with about 12 boxes to fill in. If this is an existing customer, make life easy for her. Fill in every box you have information for (name, mailing address, shipping address, etc.). Let her know that she can change any box she wants.

The first time your subscriber shops, offer to store her credit card number for her convenience. Ask her to provide a personal name for her credit card. Tell her why this is safe. When she makes another purchase with you, list her stored credit card numbers by name. She clicks on a link beside the name of the card she wants to use, and all the credit card information is automatically filled in, except for the three-digit number on the back of her card.

Why should you go to all the trouble to do this? Because you are a professional database marketer. Your goal is to make shopping a pleasure for your customers.

Manage Frequency Preferences

The Kayak travel comparison site does a great job of clearly setting expectations in its first newsletter and throughout its site. Its messages are sent weekly on Wednesdays. The preference center in the e-mail allows subscribers to easily manage what they receive, and it gives them control:

- Get more!
- Get less ...
- Make some changes ...

It also asks for feedback:

- What do you think of Kayak.com?
- Would you recommend Kayak.com to a friend?

E-mail frequency is such an important subject that we have devoted a whole chapter to it (Chapter 16). As you know from this chapter, many marketers want to send more e-mails, and most subscribers want to receive fewer.

Organize Profiles and Preferences Requests

In setting up the area on your Web site or e-mail that asks for subscriber data, there are several links you should have. Most should be triggered by a button on every page of your e-mail or site, not just the home page:

- Make it easy for subscribers to change their e-mail or physical address while they enter the profile information. When they do enter changes, tell them that the changes have been entered into their database record and then send an immediate e-mail confirming the change.

- Make sure that subscribers can unsubscribe from all your e-mails at once or each one separately. That way, if they don't want one newsletter, they can still get the others and you won't have lost them entirely. Let your users change the content they receive as their interests change.

- The unsubscribe link must be easy and functional, with a simple form asking why they are unsubscribing before they click and leave you forever. Easy means, "click here to unsubscribe," not "send us an e-mail with 'remove' in the subject line." That isn't easy. Don't make them enter an ID and password to unsubscribe. That is an outrage.

- Don't wait for more than a few minutes to grant the unsubscribe request. Of course, CAN-SPAM allows you 10 business days to process unsubscribes. That should not be your guide. Don't risk annoying your possibly still very valuable offline customers who simply don't want to receive e-mails from you anymore.

- As soon as they have unsubscribed, send them a confirmation e-mail or send them to a landing page that says, "You have unsubscribed." Let them know: "You can always come back later—or right now by clicking here."

- Be sure there is a viral component in every e-mail. Give all subscribers a chance on every page to forward whatever they are looking at to a friend by entering the friend's e-mail and clicking on a button.

- If you have a partner who wants to send e-mails to your subscribers, make this clear in the subscription form, giving subscribers a chance to say no. Some subscribers will want the partner information, but many won't and will be annoyed that they are sent more than they wanted. Annoyed with whom? With you.

- Provide a link to your privacy policy on the subscription page. They won't bother to read it, but it reassures them that it is there. The Direct Marketing Association (DMA) has instructions for how to write a privacy policy, which can be found at *www.the-dma.org/privacy/creating.shtml#form*. You must be a member to use this info.

- Provide a link to customer service and to the "contact us" page. This is just as important as the privacy policy. There is nothing more annoying than wanting to contact the company about some issue and having to search all over the e-mail or the Web site for the proper link. Give subscribers your toll-free number everywhere in your e-mails that they might look for it. Talking to customers on the phone is one of the costs of being in business.

- Don't ask for a password unless it is absolutely necessary. Why do subscribers need a password if all you do is send newsletters? It is a nuisance for the user (trying to remember all his passwords) and may lose you subscribers who try to come back later and can't remember the password. If you need a password, make sure your response to a subscriber who has forgotten his password arrives in his in-box within a few seconds of his request, or you may lose him forever. Your goal is to make the process easy for subscribers, not difficult.

- Don't ask registrants to invent a nickname for themselves. Always use their e-mail as their ID. People are registered at dozens of sites today. Using their e-mail address makes it much easier than remembering dozens of IDs and passwords.

- Provide a list of e-mails and a sample of any promotional e-mails or white papers that they will receive as a result of registering. Describe the benefits of each item to them with a short paragraph, such as ClickZ does with its subscription page (see Figure 9.4).

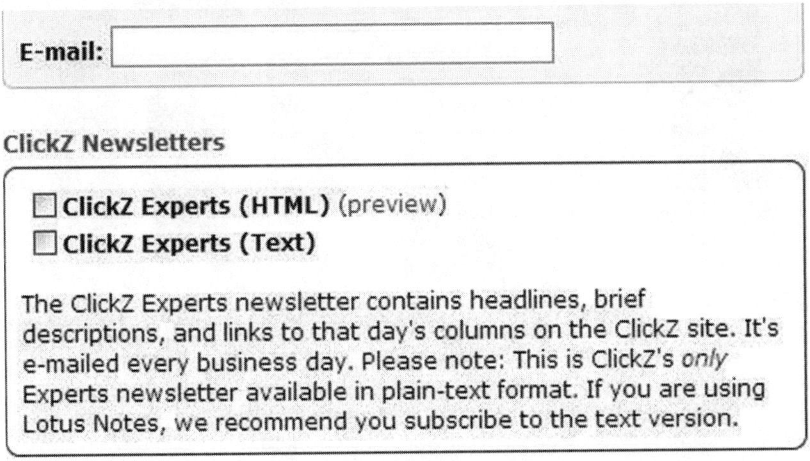

E-mail:

ClickZ Newsletters

☐ **ClickZ Experts (HTML)** (preview)
☐ **ClickZ Experts (Text)**

The ClickZ Experts newsletter contains headlines, brief descriptions, and links to that day's columns on the ClickZ site. It's e-mailed every business day. Please note: This is ClickZ's *only* Experts newsletter available in plain-text format. If you are using Lotus Notes, we recommend you subscribe to the text version.

Figure 9.4 ClickZ Experts Newsletter Subscription Form

Get Customer Preferences

To help to segment customers, you need to know their preferences regarding your products or services. Spiegel for example has a quiz that asks, "What's Your Signature Style? Take Our Quiz & Find Out!" On the Spiegel Web site, you answer a dozen or so entertaining questions. Then Spiegel tells you which of six styles fits you best: Modern Romantic, Natural Sophistication, Simple Chic, Relaxed Glamour, Definitely Dramatic, or Understated Elegance. By clicking on a link, you see a page for each of these six styles, including fabric and outfit recommendations. Spiegel lets the registrant forward the quiz to friends. Once you know your style, you can get Spiegel e-mails with product recommendations based on that style. (See Figure 9.5.)

Caution: once you have determined a subscriber's product preferences, put them in her database record and make sure all subsequent e-mails reflect those preferences. Too many marketers come up with a clever idea like this but forget about it in subsequent e-mails, asking subscribers to tell you their preferences again. It destroys the relationship you are trying to build.

Figure 9.5 Spiegel Signature Styles

The Likert Scale for Responses

The Likert scale, developed by Rensis Likert in 1932, should be the standard method for survey question responses. It comprises five levels:

- Strongly disagree
- Disagree
- Neither agree nor disagree
- Agree
- Strongly agree

Using the Likert scale, you can compare responses on your surveys with responses to similar questions on other surveys. Likert responses can also be converted into bar charts.

Satisfaction Surveys

The best time to conduct an e-mail customer satisfaction survey is when the experience is fresh in subscribers' minds. If you wait to conduct the survey, responses may be less accurate. Your subscriber may have forgotten some of the details or may confuse you with another company.

Using the Likert scale, the basic questions to ask are:

- Are you satisfied with the purchase you made?
- Are you satisfied with the service you received?
- Are you satisfied with our company overall?

You should also ask:

- Are you likely to buy from us again?
- Are you likely to recommend our company to others?
- What did you like about your experience with us?
- What didn't you like about your experience with us?

How to Use Survey Answers

The most important part of a satisfaction survey is what you do with the results. There are five basic things you should always do:

- Set up a system to give you the overall results in graphic form. See if your satisfaction ratings are going up or down.
- Find out those things that the customer doesn't like and fix them.
- Respond to all who said anything at all negative. Thank them for their frankness, telling them what you intend to do as a result of their input. You can convert unhappy customers into staunch advocates if you listen to them, correct the problem, and tell them what you did.
- Store the fact of their answering the survey in the subscribers' database record along with the date. *Don't ask them to respond to similar surveys for the next month.*
- Thank all who completed a survey with a short e-mail saying how pleased you are that they took the time to do this and telling them what you have done with the results of past surveys.

Follow-Up on Survey Response

Here is how a couple of subscribers reacted to a survey question:
- A Netflix member, Shane Sackman, contacted Netflix customer service via phone after not receiving a movie he had ordered. "I chose the satisfied option for my answer, which redirected me to a thank-you

page with links to customer service in case I had any additional questions," said Sackman. "It was a very simple a survey that I appreciated because it showed me as a customer that Netflix cared and that they were constantly looking to improve their service."

- Sackman then received a follow-up e-mail:

Dear Shane:
Thanks for recently contacting Netflix Customer Service by phone. In order to serve you better, we would love to hear how we did.
   I am **satisfied** with my Netflix Customer Service experience
   I am **unsatisfied** with my Netflix Customer Service experience.

Thank you!
The Netflix Team

A Pottery Barn customer, Jillian Bilodeau, experienced amazing customer service from Pottery Barn. She had purchased a few items online. When they arrived, she realized the shipment didn't include a hanging rod to hang the products. She called customer service only to find that the rod was actually a separate item and would cost $20.00. "Although the customer service representative was very friendly, she still had to break the news that I would most likely have to pay for the rod along with another $8.00 shipping fee. So, I ordered two rods to hold the three products I originally purchased, now bringing my second order to $40.00 of unexpected fees plus shipping," she said.

"The next day, I received an e-mail asking me to take a survey to evaluate the customer service experience. I was honest, explaining how the customer service rep was great, but that I should have been made aware of all items I needed to purchase at once. Two days later, I received a call from customer service explaining how the second shipping fee was waived and that I should expect a $20.00 merchandise credit that I could use online or in stores to make up for the inconvenience. I am very impressed with the customer service I received and now have no negative thoughts towards Pottery Barn ... any more. The satisfaction survey was no joke and was taken seriously."

Get Customer Ratings and Product Reviews

Many Web retailers routinely ask customers to rate and review products they buy. Then they put the customer ratings next to their product offerings on the Web site or in any e-mails describing the product. How important are these ratings? Very important.

Bazaarvoice reported that the ability to refine site search results by customer ratings led to 22 percent more sales per unique visitor on a same-session basis and 41 percent more sales per visitor on a multisession basis. It also found that the return rate of products purchased online with 50 or more customer reviews was half the return rate of products with 5 or fewer reviews. In a 2007 study, ForeSee Results reported that reviews drove 21 percent higher purchase satisfaction and 18 percent higher loyalty than product listings without reviews. EMarketer reported that online U.K. retailers found their customer retention and loyalty scores rising by 73 percent once they implemented consumer-generated ratings and reviews. Bath & Body Works found that e-mails with customer reviews had a 10.4 percent higher average order value, a 7.5 percent higher CTR (Click through rate), and 11.5 percent higher sales overall.

In 2007, comScore reported that more than three-quarters of review users in nearly every category said that the review had a significant influence on their purchase with hotels ranking the highest (87 percent). It also reported that 97 percent of those who made a purchase based on an online review said they found the review to have been accurate. The numerical rating by users is important. comScore also found that consumers were willing to pay from 20 to 99 percent more for a five-star–rated product than for a four-star–rated product, depending on the product category.

MarketingExperiments tested product conversion with and without customer product ratings. Conversions more than doubled, going from 0.44 to 1.04 percent, when the five-star rating was displayed with the product.

PETCO found that allowing shoppers to sort products within a category by customer rating led to a sales increase of 41 percent per unique visitor. It also found that shoppers who browsed the site's "Top Rated Products" page, which features products rated most highly by customers, had a 49 percent higher conversion rate than the site average and 63 percent more dollars per order than other site shoppers.

Finally, Forrester Research reported that 71 percent of online shoppers read reviews making them the most widely read consumer-generated content.

Word Survey Questions to Educate Subscribers

You can reach people with a survey by asking them questions that help them notice things they never noticed before. "Do you prefer option

A or option B?" might just be a way of getting people to notice that you even have an option B.

The very act of asking a question may change the experience for the customer. One firm shows subscribers a group of testimonials. The message says, "We hope that when we've completed our job for you, you'll be willing to write one, too." That thought increases the likelihood that people will look for something good to say, which increases the likelihood that they'll enjoy the event.

Be Honest in Your E-mails

- Be honest in your e-mails. Subscribers will notice false statements. Lilia Arsenault received an e-mail from Spiegel that began: "Dear Spiegel Customer, as you prepare to celebrate the season, we would like to thank you, our very special customer, for a wonderful year." Spiegel offered 20 percent off on everything on the site.

- Lilia's reaction: "I wish Spiegel was more honest with me. I appreciate being called their 'very special customer,' but I've never shopped with them and probably don't deserve a thank you, so I know that they don't really mean what they said to me. So why not use this opportunity to learn more about me so I do become their 'special customer'?"

Using Customer Feedback to Design New Products

As I pointed out at the beginning of this chapter, you may be called on to create entirely new products or new ways to deal with customers. For this, you need really creative customers with creative ideas. From time to time, you will probably have customers with nutty ideas. Try to save these customers and respond positively to them. Set up a Web panel for a group of them to give you their ideas. The panel could discuss, "How can we redesign our product or our marketing program to include some new exciting ideas?" An hour spent with such a group could be well worthwhile.

Take-Away Thoughts

- Make it easy for customers to give you their thoughts and opinions. Include an e-mail address and a toll-free number in every communication.

- When you hear from customers, send them an instant e-mail or text message telling them that you have received their message and will get back to them.

- Ask for preferences, and set up your database so that you can honor those preferences.

- Set up a trawling system in your database to look for significant actions that you should send your customers a message about.

- Set up your database to ask for and receive input from iPhones as well as from PCs.

- Make a prioritized list of what you need to know about each customer.

- When they read a message that has a form to fill out, be sure that all the data that you have is already filled out in the form.

- Decide which customers need appended data, and get it.

- Use every outgoing communication as a means of getting another input from your customers.

- Don't ask customers to invent nicknames or passwords. Be sure that you really need these things.

- Get customer ratings and reviews of all your products. Put them in all messages that feature products.

- Periodically, survey customers to ask their opinions. When you get them, thank them and figure out how to use their ideas.

- Use the Likert scale for responses.

A quiz on this chapter and all figures can be found at www.dbmarket ing.com/STM4. Those taking all the quizzes can receive a Successful Completion Certificate from the Database Marketing Institute which can be used in their résumé.

10

Customer Segmentation

Market segments are not neat and tidy. ... The same consumer may enjoy shopping in both Neiman Marcus and Kmart."

—WILLIAM H. DAVIDOW
Marketing High Technology

I'll give you a look at the average inbox in 2011: less segmented and less personal. That totally contradicts everything I was meant to believe! But yes, 2011 will be the first year that the average message in your mailbox will become less relevant via personalization and segmentation. For some five years the experts are saying that each following year would be the year of relevance, adding that segmentation and personalization are the ways to get there. But this year it is not.... The numbers from the DMA show that the volume of e-mail has reached an all time high, but less of these have personalized or segmented content. For instance the e-mail with personalized content has dropped from 38 percent to 22 percent.... Don't get me wrong, the way to get into people's minds, hearts and wallets is still to deliver value. And segmentation and personalization are top tactics to raise that value. Just know that you are in the inbox in between all these e-mailings with average to low value. Takeaway: Know that your e-mailing sits between lots of uninteresting messages. So make a great first impression and use tactics like segmentation to deliver on added value.

—JORDIE VAN RIJN

Let's start off by defining *segmentation*. There are really two kinds of segmentation:

1. Divide a group of people into segments based on some criteria (where they live, what they bought, their age or income or ethnicity, etc.) and send them all the same promotion to see how they react.
2. Do a similar division and create a different message to each segment based on what you think or have learned will appeal to that segment.

The first is easy. We can call it *learning segmentation*. You can learn something from it: which segment responds best to your message. It can be done at almost no cost. You make no money on the first round—you only learn something. You make money later by *not mailing* to those you now know are least likely to respond.

The second is very difficult. We can call it *dynamic segmentation*. You have to figure out what each segment likes, then create copy and images that appeal to each separate segment. It requires research (on what to say) and creativity (thinking up and writing copy that works). You make money by *getting higher response rates* as a result of the better copy you create for each segment.

Successful database marketing's goal is to become profitable through acquiring and retaining customers who, as a result of your efforts, are happy and loyal and buy a lot. As we know by now, for marketing communications to be effective, they must be relevant to each subscriber. Relevance is in the eye of the recipient, not the sender. So how do you find out what your customers consider to be relevant to them? You can use learning segmentation followed by dynamic segmentation.

The Old Corner Grocer had a couple of hundred customers. He could keep their data in his head. His loyalty strategies, if they were any good, were based on what he could learn from the customers by trial and error. Today we have thousands or even millions of customers. To manage them, we cannot create a million different marketing programs. We create a few segments and create a marketing program for each segment. The programs should be personalized, of course. They can say something different to each person (based on what we know about him, his behavior, etc.). "Since you have been a loyal customer since 1992, Mr. Hopkins ..." or "Since you took a cruise with us to Alaska last year ..." To create these communications, you have to have several things: a database with data about the customer that can be used for personalization, the segment that the person is in, a marketing plan for the segment, and an automatic system to produce the communications that uses all the above. Let's take an example:

- **Segment:** Retired couples who visit their children and grandchildren.

- **Strategy:** Get them to register their children's and grandchildren's cities and birthdays. Suggest air packages to the proper destinations a month in advance of each date.

- **Communication:** "We can fly you both from Atlanta to Portland, Maine, next month to visit David and Tracy for Tracy's birthday. The price is only $189 each round trip. If you are interested in learning more, *click here*."

The goal of customer segmentation is to develop database marketing action programs that lead to measurable increases in retention, cross-sales, up sales, and referrals. Wherever possible, these action programs should operate automatically with outgoing messages sent based on dates or transactions. Some of the examples in this chapter are from the travel industry. But segmentation is required for any sort of industry: insurance, retailing, financial services, and so on. As you read this, substitute your industry for the travel and other examples.

Segment Definition

An ideal segment is one that:

- *Has definable characteristics* in terms of behavior and demographics: for example, retired couples, business travelers 30–60, college students, families with young children, and so on. Business customers should be segmented by SIC code (Standard Industrial Code), annual sales, and number of employees.

- *Is large enough* in terms of potential sales to justify a custom marketing strategy with appropriate rewards and budget.

- *Has members who can be motivated* by cost-effective rewards to modify their behavior in ways that are profitable for your company.

- *Makes efficient use of available data* to support segment definition and marketing efforts.

- *Can be measured in performance*, with control groups.

- *Justifies an organization* devoted to it. The managing organization can be a single person or part of a person's time, but there should be someone in your company who "owns" each segment.

Defining the segments requires insight, analytics, and anecdotes:

- *Insight* requires experienced marketing strategists who develop hypotheses about each possible segment including the rewards necessary to modify member behavior.

- *Analytics* involves using statistical analysis that supports or rejects each hypothesis: Does such a segment exist? How much are the people in that segment spending now? What is their income? When do they purchase in our category? How much will it cost to change their behavior?

- *Anecdotes* are success or failure stories that illustrate what your company or other companies have done to modify the behavior of segments like this one. They offer a clue as to what is likely to work in terms of an actionable strategy. You start with an anecdote and then develop a hypothesis which can be tested before any rollout.

Dynamic Segment Strategy

Each dynamic segment requires a custom marketing strategy. One size may not fit all. Some people are motivated by premiums or discounts; others by perks; others by exotic destination packages, and so forth. For example: a businessman whose travel is paid for by his company may not be primarily interested in discounts. He may be interested in perks that give him status or make his travel more relaxing.

A valid strategy for each dynamic segment involves:

- *Communications* to the segment (direct mail, e-mail, mobile, on-location personal attention).
- *Rewards* designed to modify behavior.
- *Controls* to measure the success of the strategy.
- A *budget* for implementation of the strategy.
- *Specific goals* and metrics for engagement: for behavior modification.
- An *organization that accepts responsibility* for the segment.

Infrastructure

Dynamic segment marketing strategy involves a database infrastructure with a user-friendly analytical and campaign management front end which can be accessed by authorized personnel. To support the strategy the infrastructure should be:

- Available to all authorized users 24/7 over the Web.
- Updated frequently to keep it current and fresh with feedback from actions of the segment members.
- Designed to permit the development of automated segment campaigns, event-driven communications, back-end analysis, creation of control groups, and measurement of success.
- Easy for marketers to understand and use in their work.
- Capable of supporting multichannel communications: e-mail, direct mail, mobile, point-of-sale communication, personalized Web, inbound and outbound telephone contact.
- Capable of supporting standardized segmentation applications.
- Able to support automated customer contact strategies without extensive manual intervention.
- Able to support central marketing programs, while assisting decentralized branch initiatives. In other words, you set up a system in which you can run programs centrally, but you let regional managers create their own marketing programs at the same time.
- Able to provide speedy evaluation of campaigns to support continuous improvement.
- Capable of moving from ad hoc analysis to automated marketing programs.
- Designed so that top management can learn, on a regular basis, whether the segment strategy is working—and where it falls short.

Dynamic Segment Action Plan

The dynamic segment action plan should show how we get from here to there. It guides the development and implementation of the segmentation strategy. It includes:

- A road map showing what will happen and when. "Send each policyholder a birthday card and a policy review 45 days before the policy renewal date."
- A budget for the infrastructure and for the segment marketing plans.

- Standard application of segmentation—how to maintain consistency and control while providing flexibility and localization of power.
- An organization chart that shows who is responsible for each segment.
- Specific goals to be achieved with milestones for measurement of success.
- Automatic tests and reports that show how each segment is working out.

Segments and Status Levels

Segments are different from status levels. You can look at a *segment* as a marketer, trying to build loyalty and repeat sales. You can look at a *status level* as a customer trying to earn recognition, increased status, and perks. (See Figure 10.1.)

For an airline customer, for example, silver, gold, or platinum status can have real value. You get preferential treatment in upgrading or choice of seating. You get to go on the plane first. On a recent trip, for example, my flight was cancelled. I rushed to get a seat on another flight. There were only two seats left, and eight people were trying to get on the plane. Since I and another passenger were platinum status, we were the only two who got on the plane. Airline passengers who have achieved these status levels usually like them. Some customers work hard to achieve them. Your literature to them has to refer to their status. But within gold customers, for example, you can still have different segments. Look at these two gold members of an airline:

- Jim Jones (32) successful salesman with a wife and two young children. He flies a lot on business. His travel is paid for by his company.
- Sam Wilson (72) and Janet Wilson (70), retired businessman and wife. They fly a lot to visit grandchildren and take vacations in Europe. They pay for their travel themselves from accumulated savings and their pensions.

Both have the status of gold, but they have very different lifestyles and interests. They should be put in different segments. Marketing offers that will tempt the Wilsons to visit Vienna in October will not tempt Jim Jones who hates being away from his wife and children and could not easily take them to Europe in the middle of the school year.

Your segmentation scheme should not be too complex and expensive. One high-priced consulting team developed an elaborate marketing

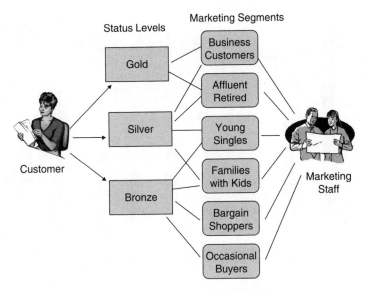

Figure 10.1 Status Levels and Segments

program for a large corporation. The plan, which went from marketing planning through execution and postexecution, involved 35 separate steps, including establishing contact strategies, developing metrics, closed-loop tracking, monitoring progress, and socializing. It was a good plan, but it was cumbersome and expensive. It lacked the close touch with the market that real database marketing involves.

A more successful segmentation scheme was developed by a retailer based on consumer behavior. The retailer looked at not just how much customers spent but at when they bought and what they bought. Some customers bought only once a year—at Christmas. Others bought only necessities. Some bought only items on sale. On the other hand, there were customers who were fiercely loyal to the chain and others who wanted to be the best-dressed people on the planet. In total, the retailer broke its customers down into three large groups: gold, silver and bronze, each divided into three smaller segments. Figure 10.2 makes the segmentation scheme clear.

The segments were developed based on a very sophisticated analysis of the customer's habits. The retailer looked for answers to the following questions:

- Who are my best customers?
- What percent of sales do they generate?

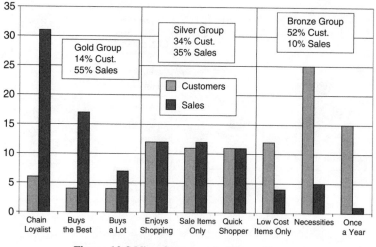

Figure 10.2 Nine Segments in Three Groups

- How big is their clothing budget, and the chain's share of their wallet?
- What are their demographic characteristics?
- When and what do they buy in our category?
- Who buys full price versus only items on sale?
- When and what do they buy from the competition?

Armed with lots of statistics from its marketing database, it went through five steps to create the segments:

1. Determine the behavior that drives each segment.
2. Identify naturally occurring clusters of customers, each with a unique buying pattern based on a 24-month purchasing history.
3. Enhance these clusters with lifestyle data and demographics.
4. Conduct an in-depth survey of each cluster to determine competitive information and fashion attitudes.
5. Emerge with a multidimensional picture of each customer segment.

Once the segments were identified and backed up with statistical analysis, the retailer had to develop a marketing strategy for each segment. In essence, it decided to put its marketing money where it would do the most good. It allocated its marketing budget to each of the major groups:

- For the *gold group* (14 percent of the customers with 55 percent of the sales) the goal was retention. These were the most valuable individuals to the chain. It allocated 60 percent of its marketing budget to programs designed to retain this loyal group. It let members of the group know how valuable they were to the store and provided special services and status perquisites.

- For the *bronze group* (52 percent of the customers and 10 percent of the sales) the chain decided that it should not waste resources. Members of this group did not spend much money in the store. Therefore, $1 spent here would not do anywhere near as much good as $1 spent on the gold customers. So it allocated only 5 percent of its entire marketing program to these bronze customers.

- The *silver group* was right in the middle. Here, the goal was to encourage members of the group to move up to gold status. The chain felt that it could motivate those who enjoyed shopping to spend more time in the store. It could encourage the sale shoppers with sale offers. It experimented with special programs for the quick shoppers so that they could find what they wanted quickly—more quickly than at their competitors' stores. The chain allocated 35 percent of its marketing budget to this 34 percent of the customers.

So how did the retailer measure its success? By measuring retention and migration using control groups. It had specific goals for each group. How could it see whether its programs were working?

- *Attrition and retention*: Were the retention programs working on the gold group?

- *Migration upward and downward*: How many of the silver people could they get to become gold? How many slipped down to bronze status?

- *Incremental sales per program and per season*: The store had regular seasonal programs. It could measure the effect of these programs on each of the nine segments.

- *Frequency of seasonal purchases*: Christmas was always the big season. But what about spring and fall buying? How did each segment respond to those seasons?

- *Dollars spent per trip and per season*: The shopping basket was a key measurement of success.

- *Number of departments shopped per trip and per season*: It was possible to take people who had visited only one or two departments and make them an offer that would get them to go to a new department. The measurement is: did they keep buying in the new department after the promotion was over?

- *Number of items shopped per trip and per season:* Bundling is a technique that will never go out of style. If you buy a dress, you have to buy matching shoes, and perhaps a belt. To make bundling work, you have to start with the buyers to make sure you have something to offer. Next you have to develop POP (Point of Purchase) displays and train the sales force to make the bundling work. The real test is which segment responds to bundling and which does not? Maybe you are motivating the wrong segment.

- *Share of customers' wallet:* Here the retailer conducted a continual review of share of wallet to see how it varied with each segment.

A Direct Mail Case Study Demonstrating Segmentation

This is an interesting case study. It involves all aspects of segmentation and RFM analysis. It was provided by Paul Blaser. First, his results (see Figure 10.3), and second, how he got them.

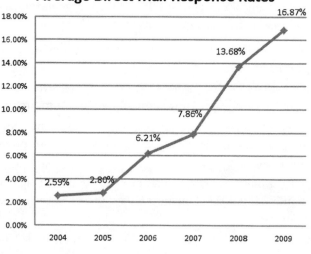

Figure 10.3 Direct Mail Segmentation

As Paul described his methods: "First we built out a new customer relationship management (CRM) database to roll up transactions under individual customers. The subsequent upturns resulted from better and better segmentation made possible by our new CRM app.

"We started with the basics. We mailed only to people near our locations and made sure to include previous redeemers and loyalty program members and we got a spike.

"Then we assigned weighted values to various transaction types based on their relative values and we got another big redemption spike. Next we scored customers with a recency-frequency-monetary (RFM) model, and again got a big spike in redemption rates.

"Then it got challenging. RFM scoring is great for making sure you send to recently active customers. Our best customers, the ones who come most often and spend the most per visit, tend to be the ones who redeem direct mail. So recent direct mail redemption is heavily weighted in our model. But three factors conspired against the success of our segmentation model.

- "First, we mail only three times a year, so the weighted redemption transactions that float a customer to the top of our mail file are four months old at best.

- "Second, we add hundreds of thousands of customers to the CRM database every quarter, and these customers have no significant redemption history.

- "Third, we have 3.5 million customers in our database. But we only have budget to mail to just under a million of them.

"This forced us to choose between potentially valuable new customers and older direct mail redeemers. We wanted to mail to the newest customers, but many of them came into the CRM system with a sweepstakes entry or a 'more-info' signup or another transaction type that's worth much less than a direct mail redemption. We couldn't mail to everyone, so we mailed to the previous redeemers instead of the newer customers. But we knew that some of the new customers would become valuable redeemers given a chance.

"Our challenge became finding a way to pick out the would-be redeemers from the new customer population. Our solution was a data mining algorithm called a 'Naive Bayesian Classifier.' By combining previous years' transaction data with geographically derived psychographic profiles and freely available census demographic data, we can predict who among our newest customers has the most in common with our best direct-mail redeemers from years past. This allowed us to calculate a good classifier score in the new customer population as equal to a previous redemption in the relatively dated customer population. The result of all this was the next spike on the graph."

A Hotel Example of Segmentation

In August 2009, Tjibbe Lambers, director of marketing and analytics for Hershey Entertainment and Resorts, reported that the chain had increased its revenue by 17 percent and room bookings by 10 percent over the previous year as a result of segmenting direct mail to its existing customers.

The mailings were keyed to spending patterns and guest preferences—such as families booking connecting rooms—on file from previous stays at the Pennsylvania attraction. Through digital variable printing techniques, Hershey was able to design and send out several different creative packages.

"If we're speaking to a family segment, we use photography that shows families together or a mother with kids in a bed," said Lambers. "Or if you came to the Hotel Hershey and used the spa, the next time around we'll write to you about spa packages available in the fall season." The strategy was the outcome of a three-year effort to centralize all of Hershey's customer data into one system.

Segmenting by Nielsen PRIZM Segment Codes

The Nielsen Company (www.nielsen.com) has been developing consumer segments since 1974 when the PRIZM lifestyle segmentation system was first introduced. The segments have catchy names and are based on such factors as income, age, lifestyle, and purchasing habits. The current PRIZM version contains 66 segments that can be organized into 14 social groups and 11 lifestage groups.

Figure 10.4 shows some examples of the segment names and descriptions within these groups:

How You Can Use Nielsen's PRIZM Segmentation System

You can send Nielsen or another marketing service provider who has PRIZM coded on its in-house database your customer file and have the provider append segmentation data to it. By doing this, you can determine which segments have a propensity to buy your product and which ones do not.

As a test, a nonprofit mailer that appealed to a certain group of older donors used PRIZM segmentation to generate market research information for a nationwide mail campaign. It applied PRIZM segment codes to a sample of its prospect file and donor base. The results were quite revealing. It discovered that its best donor segments were those shown in Figure 10.5.

15. Pools & Patios - Formed during the postwar Baby Boom, Pools & Patios has evolved from a segment of young suburban families to one for mature, empty-nesting couples. In these stable neighborhoods graced with backyard pools and patios—the highest proportion of homes were built in the 1960s—residents work as white-collar managers and professionals, and are now at the top of their careers.

17. Beltway Boomers - The members of the postwar Baby Boom are all grown up. Today, these Americans are in their forties and fifties, and one segment of this huge cohort—college-educated, upper-middle-class and home-owning—is found in Beltway Boomers. Like many of their peers who married late, these Boomers are still raising children in comfortable suburban subdivisions, and they're pursuing kid-centered lifestyles.

18. Kids & Cul-de-Sacs - Upscale, suburban, married couples with children—that's the skinny on Kids & Cul-de-Sacs, an enviable lifestyle of large families in recently built subdivisions. With a high rate of Hispanic and Asian Americans, this segment is a refuge for college-educated, white-collar professionals with administrative jobs and upper-middle-class incomes. Their nexus of education, affluence and children translates into large outlays for child-centered products and services.

Figure 10.4 PRIZM Segment Examples

PRIZM Segment	Index
55 Golden Ponds	159.8
37 Mayberry-ville	148.5
33 Big Sky Families	146.0
43 Heartlanders	142.9
56 Crossroads Villagers	142.8
57 Old Milltowns	135.7
51 Shotguns & Pickups	134.1
11 God's Country	133.2
21 Gray Power	132.4
50 Kid Country, USA	130.7

Figure 10.5 Best Performing PRIZM Segments

The index was created by comparing the percent of the population in the area being mailed with the percent of the donors. An index of 100 meant that the percent of the donors was exactly equal to the percent of the population mailed. The bottom segments are shown in Figure 10.6.

PRIZM Segment	Index
04 Young Digerati	61.1
16 Bohemian Mix	61.1
29 American Dreams	57.9
54 Multi-Culti Mosaic	57.5
65 Big City Blues	55.8
66 Low-Rise Living	54.5
61 City Roots	54.1
44 New Beginnings	47.8
64 Bedrock America	42.2
35 Boomtown Singles	32.6

Figure 10.6 Lowest Performing PRIZM Segments

These were low-performing segments for this nonprofit. Increased profit for it came from mailing only to profitable or best-performing segments, and not mailing to unprofitable or lowest-performing segments. It mailed about 70 million pieces per year. To do the segment selection, it worked with a marketing service provider that had a database of compiled names which already had the segment codes appended. With the knowledge of which segments would be most profitable, it used the best-performing segments as a selection criterion for direct mail lists. The projected results of using this system were quite remarkable as can be seen in Figure 10.7.

	Mailed	Response Rate	Responders	Average Gift	Total Revenue Or cost
Previous Mailing Plan	70,000,000	5.00%	3,500,000	$10.00	$35,000,000
Top 30 Segment Mailing	70,000,000	5.93%	4,149,894	$10.00	$41,498,940
Additional Gross Revenue					$6,498,941
Segment Selection Cost	70,000,000				$1,400,000
Net Increase Gross Revenue					$5,098,941

Figure 10.7 Revenue Gain from Mailing to Profitable Segments

The previous response rate overall was about 5 percent with an average gift of $10. By mailing only to the top 30 PRIZM segments, the nonprofit increased its response rate to 5.93 percent, thus producing an increase in gross revenue of $6.5 million. From this, it had to subtract the cost of selecting by PRIZM segments, priced at $20 per thousand names (in addition to the other costs of the names and the costs of the mailing). The net increase in gross revenue was $5 million per year. How was the nonprofit able to know that the response rate would increase from 5.0 to 5.93 percent? Because in its previous mailings, that was the response rate of the top 30 PRIZM segments.

Appending Data to Your Segments

To create a customer segment, you need to know something about the members of that segment. You will want to keep track of their spending with you, of course. But you may want other information: what they are spending with other companies and something about them personally and their lifestyle. By this, I mean their age, income, children, type of home ownership, and other aspects of their lifestyle in addition to their cluster.

There is quite a bit of information that you can get appended to your customer and prospect database. You can use the appended data to create your segments and build relationships with your customers. Let's examine this available data.

Start with the Census

Let's begin with the U.S. census. The last census was in 2010. In previous censuses every sixth house was given the "long form" which was 40 pages long. This time the Census Bureau used the *American Community Survey* (ACS)—an ongoing statistical survey, sent to approximately 250,000 addresses monthly (or 3 million per year). Those who receive the survey provide answers to a list of questions about themselves and their households, including their profession, how much money they earn, their source of health insurance, their preferred mode of transportation to and from work, and the amount of money they pay for housing and utilities.

This information, stripped of personal identification, is made available to companies that maintain compiled lists of U.S. households. From statistical analysis it is possible to attribute to any U.S. household a number of demographic facts that are assumed from their propinquity to those households who participated in the American Community Survey. This compiled data may be purchased to be appended to any file of consumers by their postal address.

Quadrant Analysis

One of the most powerful techniques of looking at customers is quadrant analysis. Following is an example from the travel industry. It compares hotel guest spending with guest household income. A sample of such chart is shown in Figure 10.8.

Q1 High Income, High Spend	
Population	5,337
% Total	11%
Income	$132,713
Marital	77%
Average Spend	$4,527
Total Spend	$24,160,599
% Spend	33%

Q2 High Income, Low Spend	
Population	18,270
% Total	36%
Income	$132,330
Marital	80%
Average Spend	$625
Total Spend	$11,418,750
% Spend	15%

Q3 Low Income, Low Spend	
Population	21,687
% Total	43%
Income	$60,375
Marital	55%
Average Spend	$589
Total Spend	$12,773,643
% Spend	17%

Q4 Low Income, High Spend	
Population	5,368
% Total	11%
Income	$59,296
Marital	51%
Average Spend	$4,766
Total Spend	$25,583,888
% Spend	35%

Figure 10.8 Quadrant Analysis for Hotel Guests

Quadrant analysis can be used for a particular property, or for a segment. It enables a hotel chain to determine a different strategy for each quadrant. In the above example, strategy might be to focus marketing efforts in Quadrant 1, who are people with a high income that spend a lot at the hotel. Quadrant 3 might be ignored in marketing because they spend little and have few resources to spend more. Quadrant 4 is a most interesting quadrant. These lower-income guests spend a lot. Why?

It could be that their companies are picking up the tab. Marketing messages to this segment should probably be directed to their employer in addition to the member.

Direct Mail Dynamic Segmentation Profit Gain

You can estimate the profit that will come from dynamic segmentation using direct mail. Let's assume that we have a department store, like the one shown earlier in this chapter that has nine customer segments. Let's assume that the store decides to create the segments and mail to people on a periodic basis with messages based on what it has learned about each of the nine segments. The high-ranking segments will get messages once a week. The low-ranking segments will get messages twice a year. Each segment will get products and offers that are designed for that segment. Some segments respond to low prices; others respond to high fashion or technology. Figure 10.9 shows the store before the segments were used for the mailing.

Members of the store marketing staff have now read this book, and they have decided to divide their customers into nine segments and create dynamic mailing programs to each segment. How might things work out? See Figure 10.10.

Direct Mail No Segmentation		This Year	Next Year	Third Year
Customers		1,000,000	500,000	300,000
Retention Rate		50%	60%	70%
Visits per Year		2.1	2.3	2.5
Sales Per Year	2,100,000	1,150,000	750,000	
Revenue	$110.56	$232,176,000	$127,144,000	$82,920,000
Cost	50%	$116,088,000	$63,572,000	$41,460,000
Marketing	$2.00	$2,000,000	$1,000,000	$600,000
Database	$1.00	$1,000,000	$500,000	$300,000
Total Cost	$119,088,000	$65,072,000	$42,360,000	
Profit		$113,088,000	$62,072,000	$40,560,000

Figure 10.9 Direct Mail No Segmentation

DM Dynamic Segmentation	This Year	Next Year	Third Year	
Customers		1,000,000	600,000	420,000
Retention Rate		60%	70%	80%
Visits per Year		2.52	2.76	3
Sales Per Year		2,520,000	1,656,000	1,260,000
Revenue	$110.56	$278,611,200	$183,087,360	$139,305,600
Cost	50%	$139,305,600	$91,543,680	$69,652,800
Marketing	$3.00	$3,000,000	$1,800,000	$1,260,000
Database	$1.50	$1,500,000	$900,000	$630,000
Total Cost		$143,805,600	$94,243,680	$71,542,800
Profit		$134,805,600	$88,843,680	$67,762,800

Figure 10.10 Direct Mail with Dynamic Segmentation

As a result of the dynamic segmentation messages, the retention rate has gone up. The visits per year have gone up by 20 percent, but the average order size has stayed the same. To get these results, the store increased its marketing budget by 50 percent and increased the amount spent on the database by 50 percent. These are not minor increases. Despite these increased costs, profits have shown a significant gain as can be seen in Figure 10.11.

Profit Gain from Dynamic Segmentation	This Year	Next Year	Third Year
No Segmentation	$113,088,000	$62,072,000	$40,560,000
Dynamic Segmentation	$134,805,600	$88,843,680	$67,762,800
Profit Gain	$21,717,600	$26,771,680	$27,202,800

Figure 10.11 Profit Gain from Dynamic Segmentation

How Many Segments Should You Have?

Some marketers doing segmentation create hundreds of segments. This is a mistake. Limit yourself to numbers that you can manage. For most companies, 10 segments are plenty. Let's conclude this chapter with a few case studies or examples showing how companies have successfully developed and used segmentation.

Case Study: Airline Passenger Segmentation

An international airline decided to develop specialized programs for its frequent flyers with segments based on their travel patterns. The goal was to increase revenue by customized communications. Based on the exploratory work, the airline set up seven major passenger segments (see Figure 10.12).

Segment	Size	2-Yr Round trips + Trip Fragments	Business Round trips	Comments
High Flyers	15%	6 or more	1 + but not all	Heavy business and leisure
Big Business	6%	6 or more	All	Heavy travel, all business
Leisure Life	10%	6 or more	0	Heavy travel, all leisure
Up and Coming	9%	2 to 5	1 or more	Some use, mostly business
Temporary Tourist	23%	2 to 5	0	Some use, all leisure
One-timers	17%	1	0 or 1	Minimal 2-yr flight activity
Lapsed	22%	0	0	Some flights prior to 2 years

Figure 10.12 Airline Passenger Segments

The High Flyers comprised about 15 percent of the file but over 50 percent of the revenue and combined round-trips and trip fragments. Based on the analysis, the airline for the first time had a workable customer segmentation plan that could be used to drive its marketing activities. Since 15 percent of its file represented 50 percent of its revenue, it could concentrate on retaining and expanding this segment. More important, it was able to identify 39 percent of its customer base as having very low revenue potential so this segment could be given minimal marketing resources. The airline was able to create a marketing budget that gave it a much higher return on investment than its previous efforts.

Case Study: Life Stage Segmentation

An international resort company wanted to create customer segments based on their life stage. To do this, with the help of KnowledgeBase Marketing, it:

- Used AmeriLINK demographic data as the basis for segregating the customer base into six predefined life stages.

- Compared group differences to guide the creation of marketing messages tailored to each life stage.

The analysis showed that travel patterns, interests, and spending could be predicted based on two key factors: age and presence of children. Combining these factors with number of resort stays, the company created six segments based on analysis of 91,000 customers:

1. *Gold coaster:* 45+ years, not traveling with children 15 years or under.
2. *Family:* All adults traveling with children.
3. *Older independents:* 35–44, not traveling with children.
4. *Younger independents:* 25–34, not traveling with children.
5. *High school students:* 16–18, not traveling with children.
6. *College/university students:* 19–24, not traveling with children.

The top three segments represented 79 percent of all guests. The bottom three segments contained the remaining 21 percent of the guests.

Individual marketing programs were created for each of the six segments, with the marketing budget allocated based on the importance of the segment to the company. The most valuable 10 percent of customers contributed to 43 percent of total revenue. Lodging and activity passes were most strongly associated to the top 20 percent of high-revenue customers. Using these segments, the company was able to:

- Develop customized marketing programs for each segment.
- Retain and expand the most profitable segments.
- Produce a higher return on investment from marketing than had existed before.

Segmentation Enhancement, Hypothesis, and Analysis

Development of segments begins with dreaming up segment hypotheses. "I think that such a segment exists (retired people who visit their children and grandchildren and who would be willing to register this information with us). I think that the segment spends a significant amount of money each year. I believe that we can come up with some cost-effective marketing strategies that will move the behavior of segment members in directions that are profitable for our company. I want to do the analysis to see if I am right." Typically, you can use analytics to go into your database to determine the characteristics of the segment that you have dreamed up: its size, spending habits, demographics, history, and so on.

The result of the analytics will feed into automated strategy development concepts for each segment. "There are X number of retired people on the database. Some tests were run to see if they would register their travel objectives for the coming year. 12 percent of those approached registered. The 12 percent across our entire database amounts to about 82,000 people."

E-mail Subscriber Segments

E-mail makes segmentation come alive. It is possible through e-mail to communicate with each segment as often as you wish at comparatively little expense. Here are some basic ways that segmentation is conducted with e-mail subscriber segments:

- *Purchase behavior. Easy:* buyer versus nonbuyer; *medium:* one buyer versus multiple buyers versus nonbuyers. Another name for this segmentation method is lifecycle segmentation.

- *E-mail activity. Easy:* active clicker versus nonclicker; *medium:* active clicker/opener versus opener versus inert.

- *Web activity. Easy:* added items to cart versus never visited site; *medium:* no visits versus added items to cart versus browsed multiple categories.

- *Tenure on database. Easy:* new e-mail addresses (within 30 days) versus older addresses; *medium:* new versus 30–90 days old versus more than 90 days on the database.

- *Channel shopped. Easy:* on Web versus at store; *medium:* on Web via e-mail versus on Web not via e-mail versus at store, thanks to e-mail versus at store.

- *Click categorization. Easy:* number of clicks on opened e-mails; *medium:* number of repeated clicks on opened e-mails; *advanced:* audience segmentation based on categories of items clicked on.

To do segmentation of subscribers, first, separate subscribers into buyers and nonbuyers. Many e-mail marketers have a million or more subscribers, but less than 10 percent of them have ever bought anything online. At a minimum, your segmentation scheme should be buyers and nonbuyers. You have little excuse for treating them alike; buyers should be treated better.

You can easily prove this idea's validity by setting up a control group of buyers who get the same blasts nonbuyers get. The remaining buyers get welcome, thank-you, and preferred buyer messages based on what they bought and on what you learned in the online fulfillment process. If you shipped a product, you probably have the buyer's complete name and street address. With this information, you can get appended data and personalize her e-mails. Basic rule: treat buyers better, and they will buy more.

How Many E-mail Marketers Actually Segment Their Subscribers?

Numerous studies have shown that segmentation improves open and click rates. The Marketing Sherpa E-mail Marketing Benchmark Guide 2008 reported that for the mailers studied, open rates for segmented versus non-segmented campaigns are as much as 20 percent higher on average for the first 30 days. This rate drops to 14 percent higher in days 60 to 90. But many marketers do not use segmentation in their e-mail marketing programs. Why not?

The problem is the cost. Despite the fact that every database marketer agrees that segmentation is a good idea which will improve customer response, many marketers do not have the staff to take advantage of dynamic segmentation. For the bulk of e-mail marketers, all subscribers get the same messages: buyers and nonbuyers; clickers and nonclickers; single channel (Web) and multichannel (Web, retail, and catalog). In a study that I did in 2010 of 132 major e-mail marketers, 61 percent did little or no segmentation of their subscribers.

Why does it cost more? It is easy to do learning segmentation, but the hard part is dynamic segmentation: to develop different content to send to each segment. Many marketers today are sending two or more e-mails per week to their subscribers. If they create, for example, four different segments, and send mail to each segment twice a week, then they will have to create the content for eight different e-mails every week to send to their subscriber segments. Most e-mail deployment units in even a major corporation today have only a handful of creative people available. To develop one really good e-mail takes, at a minimum, one person a full day. Few companies have more than two creative staffers available in addition to the other personnel involved in their e-mail programs.

Why Segments Don't Work for Most E-mail Marketing Programs

I have spent 32 years in the database marketing–e-mail marketing business. I have seen it from the beginning. Database marketing grew out of direct mail in 1985 because of the high price of postal mail. At that time it was becoming relatively easy to get names and addresses of consumers and business people to send promotions to. What we discovered was that some people respond and most do not. The database was invented as a means of reducing the cost of mailing by keeping track of the responders so that you could mail mostly to them. Later learning segmentation was developed. Companies with demographic data and analytics experts found it possible to decide from a file of people you had never mailed to who would respond and who was unlikely to respond. You made money by *not mailing* to lower deciles.

After we learned how to do that, we discovered dynamic segmentation. In addition to not mailing to lower deciles, you could improve response by dividing your mailing file into actionable segments: seniors, college students, and families with young children, for example. Each requires different messages and different products. You put someone in charge of each segment, and tell that person to do research and think like a member of the segment, writing copy that resonated with the people in the segment. Response rates went up. Every sophisticated direct mail marketer used segmentation to boost profits.

When e-mail came along, those of us in the database marketing world assumed that this new medium was ideal for building customer relationships. Instead of sending a letter *once a month* for $600 per thousand letters, we could afford to send e-mails *every week* or even *every day* for $6 per thousand e-mails. What a saving. What a wonderful way to maintain contact and boost sales.

So, we thought, let's take the next step and create dynamic segments as we learned to do in database marketing, creating e-mails for each segment. Preliminary tests showed that we were not wrong. I urged e-mail marketing clients to use dynamic segments in their e-mails.

After a couple of years, we did surveys on the use of dynamic segmentation. We found that only about a fifth of the e-mail marketers were creating and using segments in their e-mail promotions. "What is wrong with the others?" we thought. "Don't they want to improve their open rates by 14 percent?"

Actually, after we looked into the situation, we found that those not using segments in e-mail marketing are doing it for quite rational and economic reasons. Following are the reasons why dynamic segmentation often does not work well for e-mail marketing:

It is possible to use learning segmentation, but what can you do with the results? With delivery rates of e-mail down to $6 per thousand, the cost of e-mail delivery is so trifling that other costs become more important. You might as well mail to everyone in your database.

As for dynamic segments, when you are mailing as frequently as once a week or more, the economics are just not there. To do it you have to hire the staff to dream up and write copy for each of your segments.

In the direct mail days, we typically sent one letter—perhaps two letters—a month to each customer. If you had four segments, for example, there was plenty of time for your staff members to dream up and write copy for each of their segments. They had two weeks or more to do it.

With e-mails we soon learned that frequent e-mails are very profitable to send. Go from once a month to once a week, and profits go up. From once a week to twice a week, profits still rise. From twice a week to once a day, still more profits. Of course, by doing this, you may be losing your most valuable customers who unsubscribe because they are sick of so many communications, but management seldom looks beyond this quarter's sales. "Send more" is the watchword; so almost every e-mail marketer has been doing just that.

Result: It is almost impossible to write copy for dynamic segments if you are getting out e-mails on a weekly or daily basis. Creative segment managers are hard to find. They are too expensive. Even more expensive is the appending of demographic data and building a database (rather than a mailing list) that is needed to support dynamic segmentation. A 14 percent rise in open rates (which may mean a 0.2 percent rise in conversions) will not pay the cost of hiring many creative writers and the database needed to support them to develop custom e-mails for your segments.

Conclusion: With e-mail marketing, you may not be able to use the knowledge you gain from learning segmentation to boost your profits. Dynamic segmentation is expensive; the lift you get from dynamic segmentation with e-mail marketing is not as great as the lift you get from frequent mailing. For e-mails, therefore, dynamic segmentation may be economically impractical.

Why Is It Expensive to Create Dynamically Segmented E-mails?

It is expensive to create dynamically segmented e-mails because, in the first place, good e-mails are much more expensive to create than good direct mail pieces. A direct mail piece is what it is: a piece of copy with products, prices, and color. A dynamic e-mail, on the other hand, is much more complicated because it is filled with *links*. You may be showing only eight products, but each product, if done right, contains many links. Figure 10.13 shows a simple example for one product:

Introducing the faster, smarter Intel Core processor family
Help Me Choose ›

Dell recommends Internet Explorer 8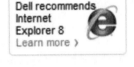
Learn more ›

Inspiron Mini 1012 Netbook

★★★★★ (65 Reviews)

10.1" | 3lbs

Dell Price $449⁹⁹

As low as $15 / month[1]

 Apply | Learn More

View Details ›

Select ›

Figure 10.13 Product with Links

The figure shows just one product in an e-mail that probably contains eight such products. Look at what you can click on: Details, pricing, 65 reviews, the processor, Explorer 8. Each of these has to work, and it has to lead to hundreds of other links. To get this right will take an experienced e-mail creative person at least a full day.

But the dynamic segmentation is much more difficult than this simple example. There are two basic ways to create dynamic segmentation: add creative people or add collaborative filtering software. Collaborative filtering is what Netflix and Amazon use. They divide all e-mail subscribers into "soul mates" who are people with similar tastes. That is how Netflix can suggest movies to you that you have never seen: it has a huge database of millions of people, each of which has rated hundreds of movies. It knows what Arthur Hughes likes. It has built up a group of other Netflix subscribers who have similar tastes to mine. Every time I rate a new movie, my group of soul mates changes a little—a few added or subtracted—so that by knowing what movies my soul mates like (that I have not yet seen), Netflix can make intelligent and profitable suggestions to me.

Collaborative filtering software is expensive. I do not know what it costs, but my guess is that you could not have something similar for less than $2 million per year.

As mentioned earlier, additional creative staff is also expensive. A typical e-mail development staff might consist of three people at about $150,000 per year. One of those people is the creative one. If you want to send two e-mails per week and have eight different segments, you will have to create sixteen different e-mails per week. It takes about a day, on average, to create a dynamically segmented e-mail complete with links like the Dell example shown in Figure 10.13. That is 16 creative worker days per week.

So, to your regular staff of one creative, you will have to add two more creative people at a cost of more than $100,000 per year. That is a lot cheaper than collaborative filtering software, but probably less than half as good. They will have to be backed up by a professional database that holds all the segments and the products that they are likely to be interested in. To do the segmentation, you have to append data to all your e-mail records. This is not cheap. The process for a large marketer costs a minimum of $1.5 million per year. So let us assume that the additional cost of dynamic segmentation is $1,682,000 in the first year.

Look closely at Figures 10.14 and 10.15. I have included the extra costs of segmentation—$1,682,000 in the first year, which consists of building and maintaining a database for $1 million and $682,000 for the additional creative staff and e-mail delivery. I have also shown the benefits:

- Unsubs from 9 percent down to 6 percent
- Opens from 11 percent to 13 percent
- Unique clicks from 16 percent to 17 percent

The result is that profits from e-mail marketing go up. Your ROI is about $3.00 for every extra dollar spent (see Figure 10.16).

E-mail without Dynamic Segmentation		First Year	Second Year	Third Year
Subscribers		1,000,000	830,000	688,900
Unsubs	9%	90,000	74,700	62,001
Undelivers	8%	80,000	66,400	55,112
E-mails Delivered	104	104,000,000	86,320,000	71,645,600
Opens	11%	11,440,000	9,495,200	7,881,016
Unique Clicks	16%	1,830,400	1,519,232	1,260,963
E-mail Sales	1.94%	35,510	29,473	24,463
Sales Generated by E-mails	3.76	133,517	110,819	91,980
Total Sales from E-mails		169,026	140,292	116,442
Revenue	$88.94	$15,033,213	$12,477,567	$10,356,381
Costs	40%	$6,013,285	$4,991,027	$4,142,552
Creation Cost	$1.44	$150,000	$124,500	$103,335
Delivery Cost	$6.00	$624,000	$517,920	$429,874
Database Cost	$0.00	$0	$0	$0
Total Cost		$6,787,285	$5,633,447	$4,675,761
Profit		$8,245,928	$6,844,120	$5,680,620

Figure 10.14 E-mails Without Segmentation

E-mail with Dynamic Segmentation		First Year	Second Year	Third Year
Subscribers		1,000,000	870,000	756,900
Unsubs	6%	60,000	52,200	45,414
Undelivers	7%	70,000	60,900	52,983
E-mails Delivered	104	104,000,000	90,480,000	78,717,600
Opens	13%	13,520,000	11,762,400	10,233,288
Unique Clicks	17%	2,298,400	1,999,608	1,739,659
E-mail Sales	2.78%	63,896	55,589	48,363
Sales Generated by E-mails	3.76	240,247	209,015	181,843
Total Sales from E-mails		304,143	264,604	230,206
Revenue	$88.94	$27,050,450	$23,533,891	$20,474,485
Costs	40%	$10,820,180	$9,413,556	$8,189,794
Creation Cost	$8.00	$832,000	$723,840	$629,741
Delivery Cost	$8.00	$832,000	$723,840	$629,741
Database Cost	$1.00	$1,000,000	$870,000	$756,900
Total Cost		$13,484,180	$11,731,236	$10,206,176
Profit		$13,566,270	$11,802,655	$10,268,310

Figure 10.15 E-mails with Dynamic Segmentation

Effect of Change in Profits	First Year	Second Year	Third Year
Without Dynamic E-mail Content	$8,245,928	$6,844,120	$5,680,620
With Dynamic E-mail Content	$10,268,310	$13,566,270	$11,802,655
Increased Profits from Segmentation	$5,320,342	$4,958,535	$4,587,690
Increased Costs from Dynamic	$1,890,000	$1,675,260	$1,483,173
Return on Investment	$2.81	$2.96	$3.09

Figure 10.16 Results of Dynamic Segmentation of E-mails

So why don't more e-mail marketers do this? There are at least three good reasons:

1. They have not done this type of analysis which is really above the heads of most e-mail marketing staff members. They have never calculated the LTV of their subscribers. They do not have staff with these skills. They probably do not know, at any given time, their costs, their conversion rate, or most of these numbers.

2. E-mail marketing staff members are not paid to do this type of analysis. They are paid to create and get out the e-mails in order to make next quarter's revenue goal.

3. E-mail staff members are operating on a fixed budget. Their goal is to keep the costs per e-mail down, not to increase them. If they wanted to create a database, where would they get the budget? Who would run it?

The lesson: e-mails are expensive to segment dynamically because you send so many of them. You can afford to and should do dynamic segmentation if you are sending direct mail, or if you are a very big e-mailer with collaborative filtering software like Amazon. Otherwise, if you are sending e-mails, you may find that your e-mail marketing staff is not prepared to do this type of analysis. You may have to get the additional resources they need to do dynamic segmentation.

Take-Away Thoughts

- Two kinds of segmentation: *learning segmentation* divides your customers by some criteria and sends them all the same message. See which group responds best and use that info. *Dynamic segmentation:* send each group different offers and text to get a better response.

- An ideal segment: large, well defined, can be motivated, and measured. Justifies a person's time.
- Segmentation requires insight, analytics, and anecdotes.
- Segmentation action plan involves a road map, budget, goals, and tests.
- Segments and status levels (gold, silver) are not the same.
- Response rates can be improved by segmentation and RFM.
- Nielsen PRIZM segment codes can be profitable in deciding whom to promote to.
- Demographic data can be appended to any database that has postal addresses.
- Dynamic segmentation with direct mail is a winner.
- Segmentation does not work for e-mail promotions if you are mailing very frequently. There is not enough time to create dynamic content. The tradeoff: with e-mails the lift from segmentation is not as great as the lift from frequent e-mails. Result: many mass e-mail marketers do not use dynamic segmentation.
- Good e-mails with lots of links are more complicated to create than good print copy.
- There are LTV charts that show the lift from dynamic segmentation. In general, e-mail marketing staff members do not have the budget or the analytic capabilities to get the resources for database marketing.

A quiz on this chapter and all figures can be found at www.dbmarket ing.com/STM4. Those taking all the quizzes can receive a Successful Completion Certificate from the Database Marketing Institute which can be used in their résumé.

11

Transactions, Triggers, and Web Sites

It is easy to forget that the first "killer app" that made it essential to be online was … e-mail. Before there was anything to buy online, we wrote letters, sending them electronically and often getting nearly instant replies. No delay, no envelope, no stamp. E-mail brought huge numbers of people to the Internet, where spammers could reach them and sell them stuff.

—ORSON SCOTT CARD

Marketers are overlooking the potential revenue contribution that transactional messages can provide. The Direct Marketing Association and Shop.org detail that average order value for retailers is approximately $98. Applying this average order value to an average transactional message volume (e.g., order confirmations), and applying an average 3 percent revenue contribution from these transactional messages, results conservatively in approximately $2.9 million dollars annually in additional revenue.

—DAVE DANIELS,

JupiterResearch

The amazing thing about triggered e-mail is that it solves a huge execution problem. Setting up and sending several targeted e-mails takes time and effort. If you automate that process, all you have left to focus on is the actual marketing. Imagine that. By "actual marketing," I'm referring to the testing, content

251

tweaking, and creative effort that goes with driving the
right responses. The idea of triggered e-mail is not to set
up the process, design your e-mails, and then ignore
them. Automating these communications takes the pain
of execution off your shoulders, so you can focus on the
marketing aspects of these communications.

—CHRIS BAGGOTT,
E-Mail Marketing by the Numbers

This chapter is about transactions, triggers, and Web sites. As compared to promotional messages, these transactions and triggers have much higher open and click rates. They are about the most effective messages you will ever send to your customers. They are also often the most neglected. The other neglected area is using your Web site to communicate with your customers. Let's start with transaction messages.

Personalize the Transaction Message

A transaction is always the result of subscriber input: she has asked for something to be sent to her or to be downloaded. She certainly gave you her name. For this reason, you should use her name. The main body of the message should begin with the subscriber's name. Never say "Dear Valued Customer" in a transactional e-mail. In promotional messages you may know only the e-mail address, so you can't personalize the message. But all transactional messages can be, and therefore should be, personalized. If you test, you will find that personalized messages produce more clicks and conversions than non-personalized ones.

Many retailers haven't learned how to do transactional messages properly. Silverpop is a major ESP (E-Mail Service Provider) which often does useful studies of the e-mail marketing scene. Of the transactional e-mails sent by major corporations, 44 percent weren't personalized in any way, according to Silverpop.

When I order something off of Amazon, I know and
expect to receive an e-mail almost immediately
confirming my purchase. You know what, I never open
it. I just need to see it show up, look at the subject, and
mark it as read. Same thing goes for when my order
has shipped.—Natalie Nagele

Higher Open Rates

Despite what Natalie says, there is no question that transactions have higher open rates than promotional messages. This is shown by an Experian report (see Figure 11.1).

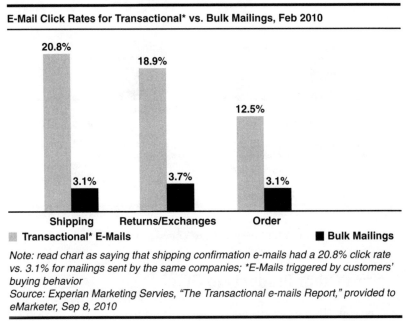

E-Mail Click Rates for Transactional* vs. Bulk Mailings, Feb 2010

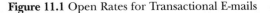

Note: read chart as saying that shipping confirmation e-mails had a 20.8% click rate vs. 3.1% for mailings sent by the same companies; *E-Mails triggered by customers' buying behavior
Source: Experian Marketing Servies, "The Transactional e-mails Report," provided to eMarketer, Sep 8, 2010

119505   www.**eMarketer**.com

Figure 11.1 Open Rates for Transactional E-mails

Not only are transaction messages opened more often, but they generate more revenue (see Figure 11.2).

Send Them Right Away

Transaction messages should be sent within 10 seconds of the event that triggered the message. Timing is very important. Your customer has just made a purchase, and he is sitting at his computer waiting for you to send him something. He is in a buying mood *right now*. He may not be in a similar mood tomorrow after he gets his phone bill. In the Silverpop study, only 38 percent of the transactional e-mails arrived in one minute or less; 23 percent of the e-mails took 10 minutes or more to arrive.

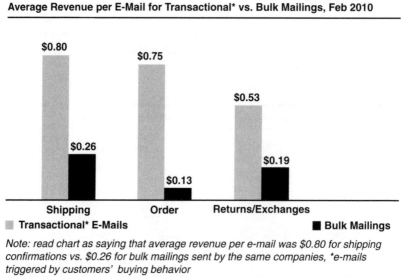

Average Revenue per E-Mail for Transactional* vs. Bulk Mailings, Feb 2010

Note: read chart as saying that average revenue per e-mail was $0.80 for shipping confirmations vs. $0.26 for bulk mailings sent by the same companies, *e-mails triggered by customers' buying behavior

Source: Experian Marketing Services, "The Transactional e-mails Report," provided to eMarketer, Sep 8, 2010

119503   www.eMarketer.com

Figure 11.2 Revenue from Transactional E-mails

Suggest Other Products to Purchase

This is your best opportunity to communicate with your customers. Transactional e-mails have higher open rates. In planning your transactional e-mail program, estimate what might come from doing transactions properly. Intelligent marketers don't do these things out of the goodness of their hearts; they do them to boost sales and customer relationships. Properly designed transactional messages can be highly profitable. They arrive at exactly the right time (when the customer is in a buying mood), they get opened, and they make relevant cross-sale recommendations which make it easy for the customer to buy then and there.

Despite this situation, 79 percent of transactional e-mails from major corporations like Nordstrom, Neiman Marcus, Saks, Target, Toys 'R' Us, and Walmart contained *no offer of additional products or services*, according to Silverpop's *How Top Retailers Use Transactional E-Mail* (2007). Even worse, many transactional e-mails from major corporations included a warning not to respond to the e-mail.

How long should it take you to come up with the complementary products to illustrate at the bottom of your transactional e-mails? No time at all, if you have done your homework and have a template ready (see Figure 11.3).

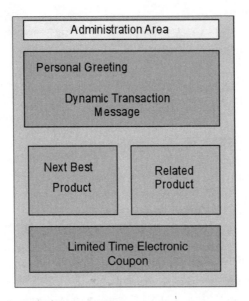

Figure 11.3 Dynamic Transaction E-mail Template

When you assemble the creative that illustrates your cross-sell products, use a template like the one shown in the figure. Products can be assembled by intuition (belt, shoes, and coat to go with a dress) or by something more sophisticated based on an analysis of similar customers' purchasing experiences, if you are set up for this.

However you do it, you need a lookup table that lists the image location for each item that you sell, along with the image location of its complementary products. The images are automatically inserted into the lower half of any transaction message that mentions its complementary product. The template has space for the other images with suitable wording, such as, "Here's what other customers bought who ordered a Yellow Balau Wood Patio Bar Cart. Click on any item to learn more."

For E-mails Always Use HTML Rather Than Text

HTML lets you know that readers have opened your message and clicked on links, which a text e-mail can't do. By using text you throw away a golden opportunity to interact with your customers. A 2007

Silverpop study reported that 42 percent of the transactional e-mails sent by major corporations were sent as text. This is unfortunate for these companies, since HTML transactional messages look better and can be measured.

Text e-mails also can't easily include a logo, which deprives subscribers of the emotional connection to the brand. Jupiter Research estimated that the average online retailer could generate as much as $250,000 annually by improving the delivery and cross-selling functions of its transactional e-mails using HTML.

Link to Relevant Web Site Pages

How many e-mails have you read that suggest you go to the company's home page or, worse, that you copy the URL into your browser? If you take the first route, you will end up on a page that may have nothing to do with the product you just bought. If you copy the URL into your browser, the company will never know if you visited the page or not.

Everything in database marketing should be measured and tested. Don't ask a subscriber to paste something into her browser or to go to a URL. This is a sure sign that you aren't a very good database marker. Instead, use a link.

A Face in the Crowd

Rate this title: ☆☆☆☆☆

Click one of the stars above to rate this movie. Rate movies you've seen to get personalized recommendations based on your ratings.

Recommendations in Classics

Figure 11.4 Examples of Links

In Figure 11.4, if Arthur clicks on the number of stars for the movie "A Face in the Crowd", he is transported to a page where he can learn more from hundreds of related links. Figure 11.5 shows you the "Recommendations in Classics" landing page.

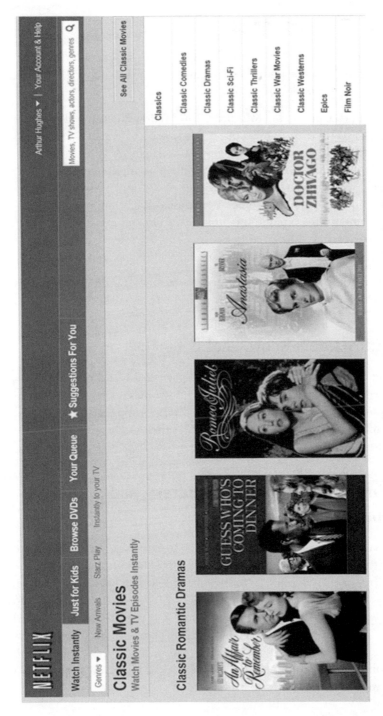

Figure 11.5 Netflix's "Recommendations in Foreign" Landing Page

Include Dynamic Content

In addition to the subscriber's name, the message should use some information from the subscriber's database record to make the content dynamic. For example:

> Thank you, Susan, for your order for a Yellow Balau Wood Patio Bar Cart. We plan to ship your order as soon as possible. We will notify you when it has been shipped.
>
> You may be thinking of other items that might complement your purchase. To help you make up your mind, we have taken the liberty of making some suggestions, based on what other customers who bought this item have also selected. Some of these items are displayed below. You can learn more about and order any one of them by clicking on the images shown below.

This is what Amazon and Netflix do in their transaction messages. Why should they be the only ones to get the cross-sales?

Let Subscribers Know What Is Coming

A good transactional e-mail should be part of a series of messages: a thank-you message, an order shipment information message, a product rating message. Let customers know at the beginning that they will get three messages and what they are. And let them know why you will ask them to rate the product.

Provide a Name, an E-mail Address, and a Phone Number

A transactional message can start a dialogue with a customer, leading to a long-term relationship with repeat sales. It is hard to have a dialogue with a company; it is easier to have a dialogue with a person. If possible, then, your transactional message should be from a person and should list an e-mail address and a phone number. The person can be an actual person, or it can be a persona who is supported by your customer service staff. The main goal is for your customer to feel that she is talking to a person and not a computer—someone she can identify with and get in touch with in case something isn't right.

Use Transactional Messages to Make Your Customers' Life Easier

Before you create a group of transactional e-mails, think about how the messages will affect the customers who receive them. Will they require customers do something difficult? Or will they provide information and reassurance? Consider the transaction e-mail from Microsoft in Figure 11.6.

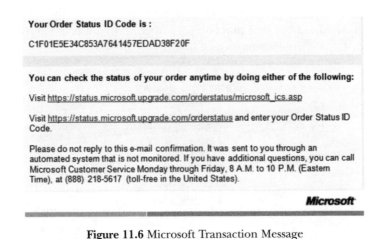

Your Order Status ID Code is :

C1F01E5E34C853A7641457EDAD38F20F

You can check the status of your order anytime by doing either of the following:

Visit https://status.microsoft.upgrade.com/orderstatus/microsoft_ics.asp

Visit https://status.microsoft.upgrade.com/orderstatus and enter your Order Status ID Code.

Please do not reply to this e-mail confirmation. It was sent to you through an automated system that is not monitored. If you have additional questions, you can call Microsoft Customer Service Monday through Friday, 8 A.M. to 10 P.M. (Eastern Time), at (888) 218-5617 (toll-free in the United States).

Microsoft

Figure 11.6 Microsoft Transaction Message

The message shown in the figure is probably one of the worst transaction messages ever sent. Is this message user-friendly? Take a look at what Microsoft asks this customer to do. If he visits either of the links, he will have to enter the really complex order status ID code. That won't be easy for customers who aren't familiar with the copy and paste function. Suppose the customer thinks something is wrong with the order. The only way he can reach anyone from Microsoft is to read that impossible Status ID code over the phone to someone. He isn't allowed to reply to the e-mail.

Send Transactional Messages to Yourself

Transactional e-mails are typically set up as automatic messages based on orders or transactions received. Sometimes the results are unfortunate, such as "With the *0 TrueBlue points you've earned as of June 3, 2011*, you're

on your way to redeeming your next Award Flight." Sending some
e-mails automatically to yourself can help reduce the possibility of
embarrassing transaction communications.

Why Are Many Transactional E-mails Sent as Text?

Talk to any e-mail marketer, and she will agree that HTML messages are
more productive than text messages. So why does her company send
transactional messages as text? The answer is usually that the text messages come about because of a complex organizational problem typical
of many large corporations today.

Figure 11.7 Example of a Transactional E-mail Delivery System

If you study Figure 11.7, you can begin to see the problems. Catalog
telesales' software, for example, is connected directly to the shipping
department, which ships the orders. The shipping department sends a
transactional e-mail, which is usually text and normally can't easily
include cross-sales. The alternative is for the order to go through IT to

the ESP, which can send out an HTML e-mail. But in many cases, IT has database update schedules that result in slow message delivery. IT, typically, updates the data warehouse on a monthly or weekly basis—very seldom daily or more often.

The same type of problem occurs with online orders placed via e-mail or a Web site. These order channels often have to go through IT to the shipping department. This can result in a text message rather than an HTML message and a warning not to respond, since the shipping department isn't set up to receive and respond to e-mails.

Making the changes necessary to get out instant HTML e-mails that include relevant promotional copy (and that can accept customer responses) usually requires cultural and political shifts within the organization. IT has to accept that messages should go out instantly and that all messages will come from the ESP, not from IT or the shipping department. Finally It must accept that the message must be from some person who, when contacted, will be able to provide a meaningful response.

It sounds simple, but in many cases it isn't. To accomplish personalized, dynamic, cross-sale transactional e-mails requires leadership from the marketing department. In many companies, the e-mail function is at such a low level in the organizational structure that getting the various parties, particularly IT, to listen and accept change is almost impossible. The results outlined in this book that some companies achieve with transactional messages can come about only if there is effective leadership in the marketing department.

Fortunately, this situation is changing. Many large corporations have realized the importance of e-mail and mobile marketing and have dedicated senior level resources to oversee these functions. Successful retailers have streamlined this entire process. Shipping departments send electronic messages to the ESPs, which send HTML and can respond to customer inquiries, as depicted in Figure 11.8.

To start with, all transactional messages should be sent by the ESP in HTML or multipurpose Internet mail extensions (MIME) format so that they can be viewed on a PC or on a handheld device. To accomplish, this many companies will have to reorganize their transaction processing procedures similar to the one shown in Figure 11.8. IT will remain in the loop, of course, but not as a delaying factor. The shipping department won't send e-mails to customers but will send electronic notices to the ESP.

To ensure that all transactional messages include a next-best product (NBP), a standard administration section, and other features, marketing will need to set up a transactional e-mail template.

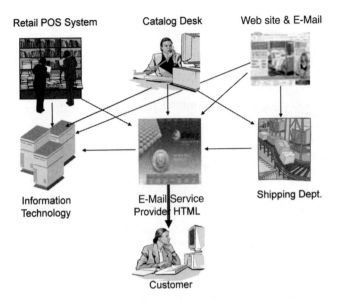

Figure 11.8 An Ideal Transactional Message Delivery System

E-mails from Offline Transactions

Now that you know how profitable transactional messages can be, you should generate as many as you can. If you have offline sales (retail, wholesale, or catalog), try to capture an e-mail address from each transaction. Your stores' POS system should be set up to accept customer e-mail addresses. Store clerks and call center staff should be offered incentives to ask customers for their e-mail addresses, "So we can get in touch with you to let you know if there is any problem with your order," or another valid, helpful reason. If every e-mail address generated from an offline sale is worth $11 to $26 in increased revenue, you can afford to reward any customer contact staff member with at least $5 per e-mail address—or give the reward to the customer.

Danger: IDs and Passwords

One of the most annoying aspects of e-mail marketing is the use of customer IDs and passwords. Many thousands, if not millions of subscribers are lost every year because they can't remember their ID on a Web site that they are revisiting. Even more are lost because of the password problem: subscribers click on the link that asks, "Forgot your ID or Password?" and wait, and wait, and wait for an e-mail to arrive. They get tired of waiting, and you have lost them forever. One problem with such systems is that customers' e-mail client, such as Outlook, is somewhere else on their PC, so they have to leave your Web site to view your responding e-mail. How can you deal with this?

One answer is to find a way to send responses to such calls for help instantaneously. But really you should first ask yourself, "Why do we have to have IDs and passwords? What do we gain from this?" Come up with a good answer, or drop the idea. You already know what you lose from having IDs and passwords—many of your subscribers.

If you have to have an ID, the best ID is the subscriber's e-mail. Use that, and that alone, and you can't go wrong. If you have to have a password, make sure you respond to a forgotten password request within a few seconds of receiving the request. If you wait as long as two minutes, you may lose many subscribers forever. Nothing is more annoying than waiting and waiting for a password that never seems to come.

Change of E-mail Address

E-mail marketers typically lose 10 to 15 percent of their subscribers' e-mail addresses every year. Part of this is due to the result of subscribers often changing their e-mail address and not notifying their commercial correspondents about it. But a lot of it is because of a poor address-change procedure (or no procedure at all). If you don't make it easy for subscribers to change their e-mail addresses, you will lose many of them. You will be throwing away the money you spent to acquire them, plus the revenue you would have gotten from them in the future.

Many, if not most, e-mail newsletters today have no obvious way for subscribers to update their e-mail addresses. Some newsletters simply say, "If you'd rather not receive this newsletter in the future, click here," without any reference to a possible address change.

Include a link in the administrative section on every page of your e-mails that says, "Update your preferences or change your e-mail address." When subscribers click on this link, they see their current e-mail address and their preferences, and they are given the ability to change either or both.

After they hit the "submit" button, they should be sent to a landing page that says their changes have been received and they will receive a confirmation by e-mail. Next, send a confirmation e-mail to the new address within a few seconds to make sure it was entered correctly and to confirm any other details subscribers might have changed. At this time, thank them for making the change and, if possible, reward them with a coupon for a discount or with a download.

How Leading E-mail Marketers Are Using Transactions

In 2008, JupiterResearch did an important study of 200 leading e-mail marketers. One question asked what features of transactional messaging they were using and what they planned to use. The results are summarized in Figure 11.9.

Tactic	Currently	Plan Soon	No Plans
HTML and Images	71%	15%	14%
Cross-Sell, Upsell Offers	53%	31%	16%
Dedicated IP Address	50%	28%	22%
Delivery, Performance Reporting	45%	33%	22%
Dynamic Content	45%	33%	22%
Cart Abandon Triggers	41%	35%	24%
Report on Transactional Messages	39%	36%	25%
A/B Split Testing	36%	37%	27%
Accreditation	36%	31%	33%
Message Authentication	31%	38%	31%
Sponsorship Ads	30%	31%	39%

Question: From this list which transactional e-mail tactics do you use currently, and which do you plan to deploy in the next 12 months? N = 200 e-mail marketers 2008 JupiterResearch Strong Mail E-mail Marketing Executive Survey September 2008

Figure 11.9 Transactional Tactics Used and Planned

The fact that only 36 percent are doing A/B split testing should be a cause for alarm. Such testing really costs nothing to do and can yield very useful results. Only 45 percent are presenting dynamic content. Where have the other marketers been? The answer is that they have been busy shoveling e-mails out the door without having the time or resources to do a good job or measure whether their efforts are working.

Triggered E-mails

The database in database marketing is the foundation for building a relationship with customers. It permits sending customers personalized communications that are unique to the person involved. These personal messages are what distinguish database marketing from direct marketing. In the past, however, time was a problem. If a flight was cancelled, you could not send out a postcard. If something that your customer wanted that was out of stock just arrived, sending a letter would not work. She may have already bought the item somewhere else. If you have empty seats going to Pittsburgh on Friday (where you know your customer wants to go), a direct mail letter just is too slow. This type of message has to go out ASAP. That is where e-mail, mobile and text messages have revolutionized database marketing. We can send out messages with last minute information that not only tells the customer about something important, but also permits the customer to take action on the information *in the message itself.* These are triggered messages that can be sent to customers by e-mail to their PCs or cell phones.

A triggered message is a communication to a subscriber that you send because of something important to his life. It may be about his birthday, an anniversary, a deadline, a cancellation, a long awaited or unexpected event, or an important reminder

Because it is important to him, and to him alone, it gets a high open rate. Since, like transaction messages, it gets opened, it is one of the most important marketing messages that you can send. It should always be in HTML.

Once a customer has opened an HTML e-mail, you can track what he does while he is reading it. Does he open and click? Which topic does he click on? You can set up a system to automatically send an e-mail based on what he does on your site. For instance, if he puts something in his shopping cart and then abandons the cart, you can send an instant e-mail offering to help him make a decision on the items in the cart. E-loan uses automated e-mails to remind prospects to complete their online mortgage applications or their auto loan forms. These two types of automated e-mails produced a 300 percent lift in response over a control group. E-loan recaptured a significant number of loans through this process.

Increasingly, marketers are uniting Web analytics with automatic triggered messages to reach potential buyers while they are thinking about a purchase. In this case, e-mail recipients are choosing when the time is right for them rather than for the company marketers. Other examples of such triggered messages include:

- *Incomplete actions:* When the recipient has clicked through but not bought anything; send a message offering free delivery for this week only.
- *Reactivations:* When registered consumers haven't opened their e-mails for months; send a "have we upset you?" message with an incentive.
- *Cross-selling:* When people have bought within the last day or two; point them toward complementary products

Triggered e-mail marketing isn't that complicated to set up. The important part is to think through, in advance, what follow-up promotions would be relevant and effective. For example, a gift retailer created a follow-up campaign for everyone who had abandoned her cart over a three-day period with some excellent results. It saw a 50 percent open rate of which 50 percent clicked through to the site and of which 53 percent converted. This is an overall sales rate of 13.25 percent for the outgoing e-mails—which is a high level to achieve for any e-mail marketer. The ROI of abandoned shopping cart e-mails makes this marketing method imperative for almost any marketer today.

Advance Delivery Messaging: The Cell Phone Connection

The mobile e-mail market was expected to be $27 billion in 2011, according to the Radicati Group. Of mobile devices 70 percent is estimated to be iPhones or other smartphones in 2011. Mobile network carriers are pushing Internet service heavily to improve revenue. Although Internet use is limited to less than 10 percent of the mobile-device population today, 47 percent of those who have mobile devices use them to access and respond to e-mail.

JupiterResearch estimates that in 2011, 54 percent of European mobile users access the Internet on a regular basis. Internet use among U.S. mobile consumers is still very low, but that gap is expected to close rapidly. Why? Consumers have discovered that e-mails on their cell phones can be really useful when they are on the road. Better to get the message while they are traveling rather than miss it and find out about something important after the trip is over.

Because a cell phone is quite different from a PC, marketers should send messages in MIME format to make sure they work well on both PCs and cell phones. Ask your subscribers if they receive e-mail on their cell phones. Once you know the answer, you can segment and personalize their messages. Design special messages just for mobile users, such as this one:

Dear Miss Williams,
When you're juggling a busy life, it's easy to lose track of where you're meant to be and when. Luckily, our new text message reminder means one thing you don't need to worry about is your Ocado delivery.
A few hours before your groceries are due to arrive, we'll drop you a text message to remind you that we're on our way. We'll also tell you the van registration number and the name of your driver for a little extra peace of mind. And talking of peace, don't worry if you have an early delivery—we'll never send you a text message before 8 a.m.
So we might not be able to help you remember your sister's birthday or when to put the bins out, but we can make sure you never forget your shopping again. Well, it beats tying a knot in your hanky, doesn't it?
Tell us what you think by e-mailing demandmore@mailocado.com.

Be sure to give mobile users control of message frequency, however, to avoid angry backlash.

Once you have set up a mobile e-mail program, you can make it a special feature of your brand. If you do this right, you can gain subscribers who are eager to sign up for triggered messages on their cell phones.

"Brand Is Back" Trigger

Rue La La sells upscale brand-name clothing at a discount to its members. It instituted a "Brand Is Back" trigger which notified members that a brand that they had previously bought was now back in stock. The program's objective was to target active buyers.

Rue La La reminded active members (opens and clicks within a certain number of days) who had either purchased from a returning brand or signed up for a reminder for that brand in the previous 12 months. The trigger emphasized relevance and brand loyalty by reinforcing members' past positive moments of engagement and increases conversion rates.

Figure 11.10 is a beautiful example of using e-mail correctly; it uses the customer's name, it has dynamic content, and it includes a viral reminder in the phrase: "Invite friends, Get $10".

Figure 11.10 Brand Is Back Trigger

Check Trigger Accuracy

E-mail campaigns are always checked for accuracy before they are sent out, but triggers are another story. These individual e-mails are sent out every day, automatically, without anyone reviewing them. Over time, errors can creep in to your triggered e-mails without anyone realizing it. For example, the e-mail may offer a product or service that is no longer available. A link may have become defunct. The copy may mention an out-of-date event.

How can you make sure that millions of triggered e-mails are correct? Create a seed list when triggered e-mails are first set up. Make sure that the seed recipients look in their in-boxes and check the messages for validity. Since triggered e-mails get opened more often than almost any other e-mail, you *must* make sure they are correct.

Trigger Types

There are more than fifteen different type of triggered e-mails that you can send. The idea of a trigger is that some event (past, present or future) is prompting you to get in touch with the subscriber. Following is a list of triggers.

The Transactional Trigger

For your business determine what the typical transactions are that deserve a message. Certainly asking the customer to rate the product and the purchasing experience should come high on your list.

Apple stores in the United Kingdom offered their customers a choice of a paper or an e-mail receipt for their store purchases. What a wonderful way to capture e-mail addresses and send out a triggered message that is sure to be opened! The clerk asked for the customer's e-mail address so he could send the receipt. The receipt is, of course, part of the opt-in process.

The Pre-Event Trigger

Customers bought tickets to a ball game, conference, concert, or Broadway show. The show is three days away. An e-mail reminding them of the event with a map will always be opened. Will the event sponsors be selling T-shirts or CDs at the event? Sell them online in the e-mail to save customers time (and ensure that they get the one they want). If you know that your customer is going on a trip, a "bon voyage" e-mail will often have an 80 percent open rate.

In B2B, conference organizers typically provide a preshow attendee list to sponsors. If the list includes e-mails, you have an ideal business audience you know is traveling to the conference. A message asking if the attendee wants to receive e-mails from you—with an idea of what business services you provide—is ethical and could produce a response.

Messages resulting from a pre-event trigger often remind subscribers of an upcoming flight, a scheduled Webinar, live seminars, or other public events. You can set up a series of messages that are planned in advance.

If you have set up status levels for your customers (e.g., silver, gold, and platinum) with special services and rewards for those at each level, you can always get your triggered e-mails opened by mentioning the customers' status. For example, you can announce when the customer has reached a magic threshold. Harrah's, for instance, tells its customers when they are "only one visit away from our Total Diamond reward level." Airlines can do the same thing for people who come close to becoming gold.

The Post-Transaction/Event Survey Trigger

After any event or purchase, a satisfaction survey will almost always be opened. Find out how customers liked the product and the purchase process. Get a testimonial if you can, and put it on your Web site and in future e-mails. While you have their attention, now is the time for some direct listening and selling (more on that later in this chapter). Your first objective should be to get permission to send additional e-mails, if you don't already have it. The second is to suggest another product that might have a relationship to the one just purchased.

The Operational Trigger

Operational triggers include double opt-in notices, password notifications, profile updates, and software updates. Operational triggers can include credit card expiration notices, shipping notices, and customer service responses. Other functions include welcome messages for new customers. Most of these operational triggers will almost always be opened. Make sure you put some personalized promotion *below the fold*.

Figure 11.11 is a renewal notice for an old membership. Membership triggers can be tied to other kinds of membership status as well, such as a monthly statement, loyalty program messages, and amount of time customer has been a member.

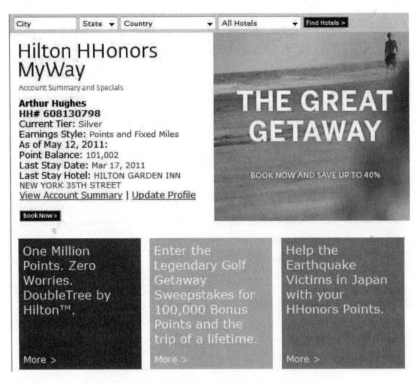

Figure 11.11 Membership Renewal Trigger

The Reminder Trigger

These are event triggers based on a key date on the customer's profile. They include birthday reminders, anniversary reminders, wedding reminders, and notices of friends' birthdays. A birthday is usually an excellent trigger with a very high open rate. Many companies offer something free on the subscriber's birthday, such as a dessert, 25 percent off, or another suitable gift that gets the birthday girl to claim her gift. Baskin Robbins offers ice cream, as does Safeway. Many restaurants offer a free meal if the birthday boy is accompanied by at least one paying guest.

This should be a standard trigger for any retailer, a trigger sure to be opened. Birthday messages can be personal and provide recognition (see Figure 11.12).

amazon.com   Thousands of gifts eligible for FREE Super Saver Shipping

Shop   Your Amazon.com   Find Gifts   Gift Cards

Hi Arthur Hughes. You asked to be reminded about this event.

Lydia McCabe's Birthday – coming up in 7 days
(May 5, 2011)

Gift Recipient: Lydia McCabe
You can view and edit your occasions from Your Gift Organizer page.

See if Lydia McCabe has a Wish List?
Search for Lydia McCabe's Wish List on Amazon.

Looking for a great gift?

Most Wished For	Most Gifted	By Price	By Personality
Books	DVDs	Under $25	Gourmet
Kitchen & Dining	Electronics	Under $50	Geek
› See all 23	› See all 23	› See all 4	› See all 13
› See all Gift Guides			

Figure 11.12 Birthday Triggered E-mail

Birthday triggers don't have to be confined to the subscriber's birthday. Here's one from Woot:

- **Happy Woot Birthday** this month! No, not your regular birthday—the day you signed up for a Woot account. The anniversary is this month. Chances are your so-called friends won't even realize this occasion is happening, much less get you any presents. So here's a gift from your true friends at Wine Woot to ease the pain.

- During this month—and this month only—you may enter the coupon code NEMATIC for $4.98 off shipping on your Woot winery-direct order. It'll only work once, so use it wisely. But don't wait too long. Once we turn the page on our calendar to next month, you won't be able to use it any more.

The Sales-Cycle Trigger

These are event-triggered messages that begin with a customer's interest in a product. Triggers can be follow-up messages, product notifications, or information requests. These e-mails get opened because they are related to the rest of the sales process and customers'_needs. The customer owns product X 4.0, and release 5.0 just became available. You can send a message letting the customer know that 5.0 is available.

The Fare-Tracking Trigger

Many Internet travel sites offer a system that tracks airfares and signals customers when a fare matches their ballpark price. Fare Alert allows users to track an unlimited number of trip itineraries and receive e-mail notification when the fare meets or beats a traveler's specified price. Orbitz, Expedia, Travelocity, and Kayak offer something similar.

Can these alerts replace spending time on multiple Web sites looking for the right trip price? Carol Sottili tested five sites and found that none "could totally replace a few solid hours of self-directed hunting." But they are a great example of triggered e-mails. Whether it is worth using these sites depends on what you think your personal time spent hunting for the right fare is worth.

The Pre-Catalog Trigger

Catalogers have learned that sending a triggered e-mail announcing the imminent arrival of a paper catalog boosts sales by as much as 18 percent over just sending the catalog alone. The e-mail can feature the cover of the catalog and have a subject line like, "Look in your mailbox: Exposures catalog." The effectiveness of pre-catalog e-mails has been public knowledge for the past several years, but less than 5 percent of catalogers use them. Why? We suspect it is because in most companies, catalogs and call centers are in separate departments from Web sites and e-mails. Too bad for them.

The Behavioral Trigger

Your goal is to match behavior, purchases, actions, and subscriber profiles with a series of customized communications. This is complicated but worth the effort in terms of opens and conversions. For example, if the customer just bought a pair of skis, you might send him an e-mail about ski outfits.

The Welcome E-mail

Sending an immediate follow-up to a new subscriber is such an obvious step that you might think I am wasting your time telling you do to this. But many well-known and respected companies do a bad job of responding quickly to their new subscribers. According to the E-mail Experience

Council's "2006 Retail E-Mail Subscription Benchmark Study," 13 percent of retailers hadn't sent their first e-mail within three weeks of the subscription date. These delinquent retailers included iTunes, CDW, Sears, 1–800-Flowers, Walgreens, Drs. Foster & Smith, Snap-on, QVC, Sam's Club, Shop.MLB, NFL Shop, Niketown, and Reebok.

Welcome e-mails are among the most opened e-mails—second only to purchase-related e-mails. Despite this, many companies fail to use them effectively. A 2008 study by Return Path[1] showed that 60 percent of companies studied didn't send welcome e-mails at all to new subscribers. Worse, a third of the companies studied failed to send any e-mails of any kind to new subscribers in the 30 days during which the study was conducted. Because of this failure to communicate, many subscribers may forget they subscribed and don't open the e-mail when it does come, making them more likely to hit the "report spam" button. If you wait too long to contact subscribers, you may miss the boat. Subscribers will forget they signed up or will buy from someone else.

In the same study, Return Path found that though 70 percent of companies asked for more than just an e-mail address at sign-up, three-quarters of those who collected the additional information failed to use it to personalize or customize their e-mail messaging.

"It really damages your brand because you're not living up to the expectations you've set," reported Bonnie Malone-Fry, director of strategic services at Return Path. "You've already stated your intentions of making the program more relevant to the subscriber. By not implementing them, there's a huge disappointment factor."

When they get there, however, welcome e-mails are among the most opened and the most clicked on, as indicated in Figure 11.13.

	Opens	Clicks
Welcome E-mails	58%	18.0%
Acquisition E-mails	20%	6.0%
Newsletters	31%	3.5%
Reactivation E-mails	9%	1.8%
Promotional E-mails	9%	0.5%

Figure 11.13 Opens and Clicks for Various Types of E-mails

---

[1] Research Study: Creating Great Subscriber Experiences by Bonnie Malone Fry Director, Strategic Services Returnpath.com www.returnpath.net/blog/2008/06/research-study-creating-great.php.

Airlines and Triggered E-mails

Have you taken a plane lately? If you look around, you will notice that perhaps half of the passengers arrive with boarding passes that were printed on their home computers. Airlines are sending e-mails to passengers before their flights, encouraging them to do this. Passengers can more quickly check in and frequently pick their seats. They don't have to wait in line for the boarding pass machines. They can directly check their bags or, even better, proceed to security as soon as they get to the airport if they have no bags to check, saving 5 to 15 minutes. It is a great idea that saves passengers and the airline time.

Airlines also save real money, from paper costs to personnel, when their passengers check in online from home. US Airways offered 1,000 bonus miles to anyone who checked in online. The airlines would really like to see everyone start doing this routinely.

Sending travelers e-mails on the day of departure to get them to check in early is an excellent example of a triggered e-mail—a really valuable e-mail service that gets open rates in the high 90s as opposed to the industry's average of 16 percent as explained in Chapter 3. If you can get your subscribers to open your e-mail, that is half the battle.

Boarding Passes on Cell Phones

Continental Airlines passengers in Houston can board flights using just a cell phone or PDA. Instead of a paper pass, Continental and the Transportation Security Administration (TSA) let passengers show a code the airline sends by e-mail to their cell phone or PDA. A TSA screener will confirm the bar code's authenticity with a handheld scanner. The TSA says the electronic pass allows screeners to better detect fraudulent boarding passes.

Air Canada also offers paperless boarding passes on cell phones. The number of flyers using the new procedure doubled each week after Air Canada launched the option. Delta and US Airways soon after developed plans to follow suit.

How Airlines Use Triggered E-mails

A survey of airline triggered e-mails showed how some airlines are using this medium. Delta followed the purchase of a day pass to the Crown

Room with a series of e-mails offering trial membership and ability to apply the price of the day pass to the cost of annual membership. US Airways allowed newly reactivated lapsed flyers to recover miles frozen because of inactivity or to trade up to a higher-priority tier in the frequent-flyer program. American Airlines sends flyers who redeem their miles an offer to purchase additional miles to "reach that next trip."

These triggered e-mails tend to strengthen the personal link between the airline and its members. Each is a message that the travelers recognize as being uniquely targeted to them.

Following is a welcome airline trigger:

Dear Lloyd,
Thank you for flying with JetBlue Airways on flight #1218 from Buffalo on May 06, 2008. We apologize that the DIRECTV was inoperable during your flight.
    As a gesture of apology and goodwill, we have issued each customer on your flight a $15 JetBlue electronic Voucher. The Voucher is for you and is nontransferable. JetBlue Vouchers are valid for one year and can be applied towards airfare on JetBlue Airways reservations.
    When you are ready to use your Voucher, please visit our Web site at www.jetblue.com. You will have the option to apply your Voucher, using the information below, during the payment portion of your reservation. You may also call 1–800-JETBLUE (555–2583) with your confirmation number D1IJCF for this flight. Please visit our Web site's Help section for more information on how to use your Voucher.

This is an excellent example of the power of e-mails to build lasting relationships with customers. It is personal. It recognizes that the service given was not as good as it should have been. It provides a gift that has real value—as opposed to a simple apology. It encourages the customer to come back. And, finally, it is very economical to send, as opposed to direct mail.

The Web Site and the Database

One often overlooked way of communicating with customers is by dynamic content on the company's Web site. Every time someone visits your Web site, you should try to capture that person's name if you do not already have it. Then you do two things: you welcome her back by name when she comes back, and you vary what she sees on the site based on what she told you or did last time she was on the site. I usually buy books from Amazon. Occasionally, however, I buy something else. In one case

I looked at bath towels, but did not buy. The next time I went to the Amazon site, I saw a display of bath towels. For most Web sites, this would be amazing. For Amazon, it is normal.

There are three kinds of Web sites. They are formal, shopping, and welcoming:

- *Formal Web Site:* These sites present themselves as a Shining City on the Hill. They represent the corporation: a large, successful, impersonal business. You cannot do business with such a Web site; you can only respect it and be impressed with it. It is usually run by a committee. Changes in any part of the Web site take weeks. The goal is to be impressive.

  About formal Web sites, the less said the better. These are very old fashioned. Many business-to-business Web sites are formal affairs. These companies want you to know that they are successful, established businesses. They want your respect. Any actual sales are done by members of the sales staff who point to the Web site as showing that they represent a large and well-established outfit.

- *Shopping Web Site:* At these sites, everything is for sale. All the company's products are displayed. You are encouraged to put them in your shopping cart and buy them *now.* The Web site is designed to feature the products that management is eager to sell to any visitor. The Web site is run by the sales department. The goal is to boost sales.

  Shopping Web sites are often quite successful. They rarely use your name. Their content does not vary with the visitors—in fact, long-standing customers see the same Web site as do new visitors. Their buyers fight over which products will be featured today—those that are most profitable for the firm.

- *Welcoming Web Site:* This kind of Web site is designed for the subscribers and customers. Companies want to learn what you are interested in so they can help you. They encourage registration for their newsletters. There are surveys, games, humor, and stories. They want to learn who you are. As soon as they do, they use your name and your preferences throughout the Web site. They want to be your friend and servant. What you want is more important to them than the products they have for sale. Once they know something about you, the Web site changes completely: it seems to be designed just for you. The Web site is based on a marketing database with details about each customer. The goal is to know you and to serve you.

Welcoming Web sites are always personalized—once they learn who you are. The content of the Web site is linked directly to their customer (and subscriber) database. From the beginning, they pick up on little hints in order to personalize their site. For a totally new unknown visitor who lives in Fort Lauderdale, somehow they pick up on this location and show you something about your city that tries to make you feel at home. This is the shop around the corner—even though the Web site location may actually be 2,000 miles away. Once you have clicked on something, they show you lots of similar products. They try to get your name and use it from then on, every time you visit the site. We are describing Amazon—the most successful Web site in the world. But we are also describing Netflix and many others.

Take-Away Thoughts

- Transactional messages should always be personalized. Never say, "Dear Valued Customer."
- Transactional messages have higher open rates than promotional e-mails, and they generate more revenue.
- They should be sent out right away—within a few seconds of the transaction.
- They should be in HTML and always suggest other items to purchase with links to the suggested products.
- Never recommend that readers go to your Web site. Instead, provide a link in the e-mail.
- Transaction e-mails should always include dynamic content related to the interests of the customer.
- Transactional messages should always provide a name, an e-mail address, and a phone number so that customers can get in touch with you.
- Send transactional messages to yourself to make sure the messages are working right.
- You may need to reorganize your message sending system to make sure that all transactions are sent in HTML.
- Try to send e-mail transactional messages from all offline transactions.
- Never require user IDs or passwords unless absolutely necessary. You will lose customers if you do.

- Be sure to make it easy for correspondents to change their e-mail address. Put a link to do this on every page of every message.

- A triggered message is a communication to a subscriber that you send because of something important in his or her life.

- Many triggered messages should be sent to subscribers' cell phones.

- To check trigger accuracy, send all messages to yourself.

- Triggered messages include: pre-events, events, post-transaction surveys, reminders, sales cycle, fare tracking, pre-catalog, and the welcome e-mail.

- Airlines use triggers to get passengers to print their boarding passes in advance.

- There are three types of Web sites: formal, shopping, and welcoming.

A quiz on this chapter and all figures can be found at www.dbmarketing. com/STM4. Those taking all the quizzes can receive a Successful Completion Certificate from the Database Marketing Institute which can be used in their résumé.

12

Campaign Performance Measurement

Business-to-consumer (B-to-C) and business-to-business (B-to-B) marketers alike are failing to use metrics at even a high level to gauge the effectiveness of their mailings. Although B-to-C marketers are slightly more engaged with using the barometer-oriented metrics … than are their B-to-B counterparts, many fail to use these metrics at least once a month. Barometer-oriented metrics are useful, particularly for trending mailing performance over time. Marketers should seek to use aggregate click-through, click-to-conversion, profit-per-mailing, and revenue-per-subscriber information as KPIs [key performance indicators] for each mailing. Additional measures, such as average order value (AOV), will vary based upon the offer, merchandise selection, and even time of year. While valuable, AOV is a variable that should be used via merchandising and creative tactics to affect the primary barometer-oriented KPIs.

—*JupiterResearch*

Campaigns are being created by the marketer, for the marketer. With the pervasiveness of the social Web, e-mail program content should be based on listening and understanding the things surrounding your brand and customers and then adapting program content and cadence accordingly.

E-mail marketing programs cannot base subscriber relationships on the e-mail channel alone. E-mail subscribers are interacting with the community, loyalty program, Facebook page, Twitter streams, and a number of other channels that are hard to identify and even harder to track. Attribution for the e-mail channel remains primarily based on last click, but the reality is that most brands' e-mail subscribers represent their most engaged and profitable customer segments. In order to maintain this, we need to treat subscribers accordingly.

—Ryan Deutsch

This chapter is about measuring campaigns. Campaigns are the way that direct mail and e-mail marketing are conducted. A campaign is typically sent ("dropped") to a selected group of customers, prospects, or subscribers at about the same time and is measured as a group. It could be the "Valentine's day campaign," or the "we miss you" campaign or something that can be defined in a phrase. Typically, a direct marketer defines his work as a series of campaigns, each of which has a starting date, an ending date, a general theme, and a definite group of recipients. Since campaigns follow the way direct marketing is conducted, to see how we are doing, we measure campaigns and compare their results.

There are many types of direct mail and e-mail campaigns described in this book, including newsletters, sales promotions, surveys, viral promotions, triggered mail, and transactional mail. We can sum these up by listing several types of marketing communications:

- Promotional messages
- Newsletters
- Transaction e-mails
- Triggered messages
- Welcome messages
- Reactivation messages
- Thank-you e-mails
- Surveys

You can probably come up with additional types of communications that are useful in your business. Today, every time there is a purchase, there should be a sequence of transaction messages, including a thank-you message, and a "rate your product" message.

In addition, you should have triggered event-driven communications, such as birthday greetings, suggestions for a complementing product to the one just purchased, a thank you, a survey, a white paper requested by the subscriber, and a confirmation of a registration.

You may also have an active reactivation program going on at all times. Most of this must be conducted by direct mail, rather than by e-mail, to avoid being considered spam. As a matter of course, you should send a postcard or other direct mail piece to those registrants whose names and addresses you have in your database but who are undeliverable. After a suitable interval, you may find that sending a direct mail piece to someone who has unsubscribed is productive. Philosophy.com sent a "we've missed you" reactivation trigger e-mail campaign to those who hadn't purchased in the last 90 days. Results: 67 percent opened the e-mail, 55 percent clicked through, and 11.5 percent converted. The reactivation e-mails generated $3.34 for each delivered e-mail.

Direct Mail Campaign Response Rates

With direct mail campaigns, you normally can measure only the number of people that buy the product you are advertising or call your toll-free number as a result of the mail that they have received. The average response rate for the 1,122 industry-specific campaigns that were studied by the Direct Marketing Association in 2010 was 2.61 percent.

Within sectors, nonprofit fundraisers had the highest success rate with direct mail, getting rates of 5.35 percent. Retail stores averaged 3.36 percent, and business-to-business mail response was slightly higher, in general, than mail to consumers.

Personal and repair service mailings averaged 3.07 percent; and travel averaged 2.98 percent. The two sectors at the bottom of the list—computer/electronic products and packaged goods—still got better than a 2 percent response rate.

Mailing to your existing customers always gets a better response than mailing to rented lists of prospects. In general, you should assume that with a good direct mail piece sent to a good list, you should average slightly better than 2 percent. This is far different from the sales rate on e-mails, which, as you will see later in this chapter, averages 0.11 percent. Despite the difference, e-mail may produce a much higher return on investment.

The balance of this chapter is devoted to measuring e-mail campaigns since so much detailed and useful information is available.

What Can You Measure in E-mail Campaigns?

E-mail marketing's measurement potential is almost limitless. There has never been anything like it in the marketing field. Comparing e-mail's measurement possibilities with those of previous marketing forms is like comparing business in 1870 with business today. In 1870, there was no electricity, telephone, radio, television, automobiles, aviation, or fast mail service which would have permitted mass marketing. By 1970, we could measure a direct mail list's pulling power, and the effectiveness of the offer and copy. By 1990, we could measure the response by various demographics or zip codes. Today with e-mail, we can measure all the above and just about anything else that you can imagine. We devote this chapter to e-mail campaigns because that is what we can measure accurately today. What can we measure in an HTML e-mail campaign?

- Effectiveness of the from and subject lines
- Offer, copy, text placement, images, and video
- Opens, clicks, downloads, conversions, deliveries, and unsubscribes
- Demographics and geographics of recipients of all the above
- Success of campaigns by all the above
- Success of our entire e-mail marketing program by all the above
- Value of an opt-in e-mail address
- Cost of a delivered e-mail
- Number of sales produced
- Volume of sales produced
- Profits from conversions resulting from e-mails
- Effect of e-mails on offline sales
- Conversions per campaign
- Effectiveness of reactivation campaigns
- Revenue per delivered e-mail
- E-mails produced by store visits, catalog purchases, and Web site registrations
- Return on investment

Measuring Deliverable Subscribers

In a campaign, we send out a million e-mails to a list of people who have provided us with their e-mail addresses and permission to use the addresses for commercial promotions to them. We have previously verified this permission by sending each person an e-mail to his address, asking him to click on a link that sends a packet back to us, indicating he has received the e-mail (verifying the address's correctness) and wants to hear more from us, thus verifying that this is truly an opt-in situation. This is called the double opt-in system, which I highly recommend. Only about 20 percent of all e-mail marketers today use the double opt-in method. The others send promotional e-mails to people who have provided their e-mail addresses without this important verification step.

Despite this authentication, a percentage (from 2 to 10 percent) of every batch of promotional e-mails you send out, which may even have just been confirmed recently, still fail to be delivered (they bounce). Why?

Most e-mails bounce because the addresses are no longer valid. About 20 percent of all e-mail addresses change every year. This happens because consumers switch to new e-mail providers, create new accounts, or move to new companies. Users seldom notify their commercial e-mail marketers when their e-mail addresses change. In fact, some people actually change their e-mail addresses just to get rid of these marketing messages. Even if an address is valid, a mailbox may be temporarily unavailable because the owner has exceeded the allotted disk space, or a mail server may be temporarily unavailable because it is processing a large volume of mail. If the address doesn't exist anymore, of course, the failure will be permanent.

When you send an e-mail, it goes to a message transfer agent (MTA) at the company that sends your e-mails for you, which transfers messages from one computer to another. Each MTA has a mail queue with a certain number of slots available to process outgoing messages. Each slot holds an outgoing e-mail until that e-mail has been delivered successfully or until the MTA determines that it can't be delivered. If your outgoing list has lots of bad addresses, the rate at which your mail can be delivered will drop, since many slots will be filled with e-mails with bad addresses that the MTA repeatedly tries to deliver.

When an e-mail bounces, it comes back to your MTA's automated bounce handler. The bounce handler sends a series of bounce messages to the addressed domain to test whether the bounce was temporary or permanent. The bounce handler tracks what happens to the messages it sends and responds accordingly. Some companies use a three-strike rule. If there are three or more consecutive soft (temporary) bounces over more than 14 days, they are automatically converted into a hard (permanent) bounce.

Since messages can bounce for many different reasons, the bounce handler doesn't take the subscriber off the list right away. Instead, it waits for about 10 days after the first bounce and then sends a warning message to the subscriber. At the end of every marketing promotion, your e-mail service provider will give you a report on which e-mails were delivered and which had permanent bounces. You will then get a deliverability rate, such as 95.30 percent.

This is much better than what the U.S. Postal Service (USPS) can do for third-class (bulk-rate) mail. If a bulk-rate letter can't be delivered, the local post office just chucks it out without telling you. You can't find out how many letters were delivered or which customers didn't get their mail. Of course, if you want to pay the price, you can send your letters by first-class mail which is always forwarded or returned to you if it can't be delivered. Most marketers can't afford to use first-class mail; it is too expensive for promotional mail. Even USPS bulk-rate mail with all its deliverability problems costs about 100 times more per message than does e-mail.

E-mail Campaigns

For this chapter, I have collected the data on many major e-mail marketers who, collectively, send more than 2 billion e-mails to their subscribers every month. These are not presented as the best or the worst. They are average e-mail marketers. Seeing what they are doing is useful to understanding what the industry is doing today. Figure 12.1 shows how our 191 test companies count their campaigns in a month.

The more campaigns you send out, the more difficult it is to have really creative and different e-mails. When you are sending more than one e-mail a day, it is almost impossible to do segmentation or dynamic content or e-mails that are filled with interesting links. There is a trade-off between quality and quantity. Unless they are a news organization, few commercial marketers that send as many as one e-mail a day to their subscriber base can send really interesting, exciting e-mails.

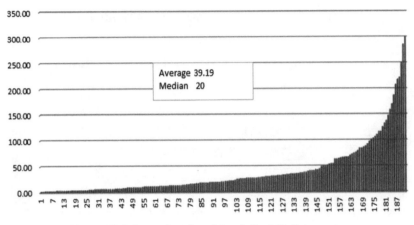

Figure 12.1 Campaigns in a Month for 191 Companies

Mailing to a New Client

Sending e-mails is a very complex business that can easily go wrong unless done by professionals with experience. For one thing, ISPs (Internet service providers such as AOL) could mistake mass e-mails from legitimate mailers for spam. The mistake could cost the mailer thousands of dollars until the situation is corrected.

For example, one ESP handled the first mailing for a new client with 16 million opt-in e-mail addresses. It wanted to warm up the ISPs so they wouldn't be concerned about getting so many e-mails from one source. First, it created a cell for each major ISP. Within each cell it segmented the audience by length of time on the list (6 months, 7–12 months, etc.). It sent e-mails gently to each ISP, keeping the number sent at or below 480,000 per day for the 10 largest ISPs and 240,000 per day for the remaining ISPs. The first e-mails were to those subscribers added to the file most recently. It took approximately 11 days to mail the whole 16 million for the first time.

How Many E-mails Do Large Companies Send Out in a Month?

From Figure 12.2 you can see that some marketers are sending out an awful lot of e-mails. This is why most successful marketers outsource their e-mails to experienced ESPs (e-mail service providers) rather than trying to perform this function in-house.

E-mails delivered per subscriber per month for 192 companies

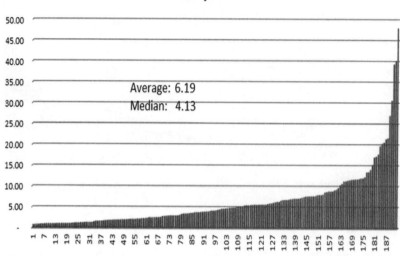

Figure 12.2 E-mails Delivered to the Typical Subscriber per Month

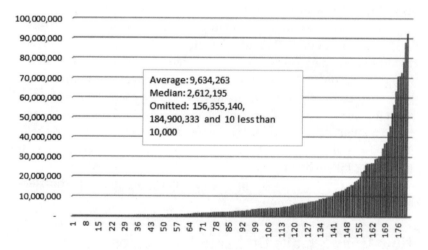

Figure 12.3 E-mails Delivered in a Month by 180 Companies

On the receiving end are the subscribers, many of whom are getting more e-mails than they want.

From Figure 12.2 you can see that the average company of 192 test companies is sending more than six e-mails to their subscribers per month. That is more than one per week. Why so many? Because they have discovered that the more they send, the more revenue they make. Since e-mails are very inexpensive to deliver (compared to direct mail), the only limit is the number of interesting things that you can think up to put in your e-mails. Some are not even limited by that—they send almost the same thing in each e-mail.

Measuring Opens

When an e-mail arrives in your subscribers' in-boxes, your subscribers have several choices: they can open it and look at it, they can open it and unsubscribe, they can delete it, or they can send it to a spam or junk mail folder, where it will eventually be deleted. If it's an HTML e-mail and subscribers open it, your computer sends a packet to your Web service, whether your ESP or your internal e-mail-sending software, saying that the e-mail was opened. HTML stands for hypertext markup language, which is a type of computer code that converts text into the colorful e-mails that we are all familiar with today. A *Web service* is a software system used to send and receive e-mails. It uses Web services description language (WSDL). It is part of the complex software systems that have been developed for the e-mail world so that any computer in any country today can send and receive e-mails from any other computer in the world.

Your Web service tracks the packet (see Chapter 8) which has been received from the e-mail recipient saying that the recipient has opened her e-mail. It will update that subscriber's database record. That is more than you can expect with direct mail. Most consumers today toss out direct mail promotions without even opening them. There is no way you can tell what they did with your letter, postcard, or catalog unless they contact you by mail, phone, or e-mail.

A few hours after each e-mail campaign is sent out, your Web service will begin producing reports on open rates and bounces. These are crucial measures of the success of any e-mail marketing campaign.

Some open rates are as low as 5 or 6 percent. Few are as high as 50 percent. Each company's situation is different, so there is really no such thing as an average open rate. One thing is certain: the overall average open rate for promotional e-mails is falling. Every year it is lower than it was the year before.

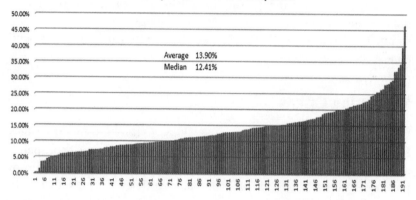

Figure 12.4 Open Rates for 191 Email Marketers

Figure 12.4 shows the open rates for 191 household word companies that we are tracking in this book, who together mail about 2 billion e-mails per month. They can be considered representative of the industry. Note that the average open rate is only 13.9 percent. This means that 86 percent of the e-mails that are delivered never get read by anybody. Actually, the number that is read is probably considerably lower than that because of the reading panes that show an e-mail as being opened when it has not really been opened at all. A reading pane is the space at the right or under your e-mail inbox where a portion of each e-mail is visible when you click on each item in your in-box. You have not really opened the e-mail when the portion of the e-mail shows up, but it is counted as an open by campaign software.

How is an open calculated? Some common ways include:

- Unique opens divided by e-mails delivered—about half of e-mail marketers use this method.

- Total opens divided by e-mails delivered—about 8 percent use this method.

- Unique opens divided by e-mails sent—about 15 percent.

- Four total opens divided by e-mails sent—about 5 percent.

- The rest have another method altogether.

These differences, combined with differences in what is considered "delivered," mean that the open rate for the same mailing can range from 12 to 35 percent. In this book, we calculate the open rate as unique opens divided by e-mails delivered. This is the method most major ESPs use.

Measuring Clicks

If your HTML e-mail is good, it has lots of interesting things for recipients. Each interesting thing is accompanied by a link. There are descriptions of products subscribers can read. There are surveys they can take. There are videos they can watch. There are forms they can fill out, and there are shopping carts they can fill with products.

Each of these things is a link, which is usually blue underlined text or an image they can click on. Hidden behind the link is the URL (uniform resource locator) of the image, form, file, or video. Clicking on the link sends a packet to your site saying, "Send us this image." The site will send the image. Your MTA (message transfer agent) keeps track of it all: "Arthur Hughes just clicked to see the video of the Super Bowl ad." Your database, maintained by the company that sent you the e-mail, will be updated with that information.

Figure 12.5 covers the same marketers as those in Figure 12.1. Since the average open rate is 13.9 percent and the average unique click rate is 23.28 percent, then only 3 percent of the average e-mails delivered by these marketers are clicked on.

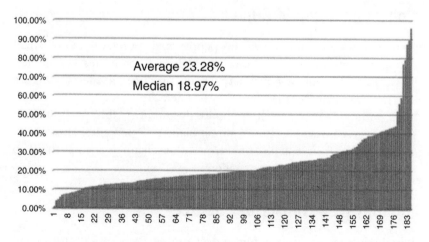

Figure 12.5 Clicks as a Percentage of Opens for 185 Marketers

What does a click mean? It means that your subscriber has clicked on a link in her e-mail. It could be to see a picture of something, to see the sizes or colors, or to do anything at all in your e-mail that you have provided a link for. When she clicks on this link, your computer will send a packet back to the sender of the e-mail saying "Helena Hughes has just clicked on this link and wants you to send the images with the colors of the scarves shown in her e-mail." Your software will send her the requested information and will also post your database with the information that at 7:06 p.m. Helena Hughes clicked on this particular link in her e-mail. So from all the e-mails you send, your database will be filled with detailed information about your subscribers and what they do when they receive your e-mails. There has never been as detailed information available on the effect of marketing communications in the history of the world.

A unique click is the first click by one of your subscribers. She may click more than once, but a unique click is the most important click to measure. It means that not only has she opened her e-mail, but that she has started reading it.

Clicks are a vital measurement of e-mail marketing success. They are way stations on the road to a purchase or a visit to one of your retail stores. The more click-throughs, usually the more interesting your e-mail is to your subscribers and the more likely you are to sell something. The click-through rate (CTR) can be measured as a percentage of opens or a percentage of delivered e-mails. In most cases it is measured based on opens.

Conversions within E-mails

Finally, we want to know how many people made purchases in the e-mail shopping carts. Figure 12.6 shows the results of 61 of our test companies:

We can also look at how many e-mails produced a sale (see Figure 12.7). As you can see, there are very few delivered e-mails that produce a sale within the e-mail itself. Compare this number (0.11 percent) with the average conversion rate for direct mail (2.67 percent). Most of the sales resulting from e-mails come from other channels such as the Web site, the retail stores, and the catalogs.

Monthly New-Subscriber Sources

People are constantly moving and changing their postal and e-mail addresses. About 20 percent of a direct mail and 20 percent of any

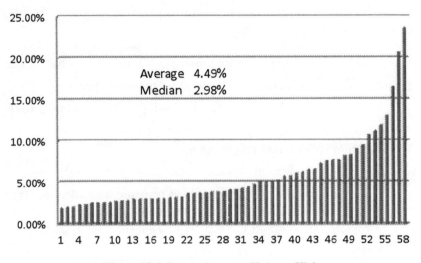

Figure 12.6 Conversions per Unique Click

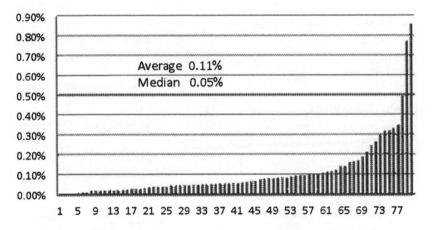

Figure 12.7 Conversions per Delivered E-mail

e-mail file becomes obsolete every year. In addition, of course, many customers who sign up for e-mail newsletters and promotions get tired of them and unsubscribe. As a direct mail or e-mail marketer, you will find that your subscriber list is constantly melting away. To keep it current, you have to continually add permission-based e-mail addresses. You can correct the direct mail addresses through NCOA, and you can rent as many new-people postal addresses as you want.

There are many sources of new e-mail names, which can be broken down into six categories:

1. Web site visitors who register their e-mail addresses on the site.

2. Viral marketing subscribers who are recommended by friends.

3. Online sales customers (an e-mail is usually a requirement for an online purchase).

4. Store visitors who register their e-mail addresses while in your store.

5. Catalog purchasers who give their e-mail addresses when they're buying.

6. Reactivated customers who are enticed to come back after having disappeared or unsubscribed (note: these folks are usually reached by a direct mail to avoid consumers considering the e-mail to be spam).

Each of these acquisition sources has a different rate of registration. Most people who come to your Web site do not register their address. Most online purchasers, however, give their e-mail address as part of the purchase process. Online catalog purchasers give you an address. Those who use mail or phone often don't. And store visitors seldom give you an e-mail address, unless you offer some sort of discount to the visitor or an incentive to your sales clerk to get the address. The monthly source of your new e-mails can be entered as shown in Figure 12.8.

The subject of customer and subscriber acquisition is so important that a whole chapter is devoted to it (Chapter 4).

New Subscriber Programs	
Catalog Registrations	4,518
Retail Store Registrations	5,986
Web Site Registrations	6,758
Reactivated Subscribers	294
Total New Subscibers Added	17,556
Amount Spent to Acquire New Subscribers	$426.00
Cost of Acquiring one Opt-in Subscriber	$0.02

Figure 12.8 Monthly New-Subscriber Sources for a Typical Company

Measuring List Growth

If you can add a lot of permission-based e-mail addresses in a month, you can't assume that your registration database will increase at the same rate. While you are adding people, many people on your existing database will be unsubscribing or changing their e-mail addresses without letting you know.

Suppose you begin with a database of 1 million. If you are like most e-mail marketers, you will find that only about half of these are actually active e-mail addresses you can market to. Why? When customers unsubscribe, you have to stop sending them e-mails. But instead of wiping them off your list, you mark them as unsubscribers and keep them on the list. You want to use their records as a suppression file for the next few weeks to be sure you honor their request.

When e-mails become undeliverable, you don't just wipe them off the database, either. In some cases you may have the name and address, and you may want to send these people a direct mail letter, postcard, or catalog to try to get them back at some point. Possibly, they've changed their e-mail address but still want to get your newsletter. In life's fast pace, they didn't notice that your newsletter wasn't getting through to their new e-mail address. They may even have been an active buyer. So you keep them in your database. You may pay an outside service like FreshAddress to append their new e-mail address so that you can reconnect with them.

In this way, over time, your database fills up with inactive e-mail addresses. The list growth of a typical company is illustrated in Figure 12.9.

List Growth Measures	
Address List Including Inactives	448,775
Mailable E-mail Addresses Start of Month	359,221
Percent Mailable	80.04%
New Subscribers Added	17,556
Unsubscribed in Month	6,262
Permanent Unsubscribed in Month	2,567
Apparent Change in Subscribers in Month	8,727
Average E-mails per Subscriber in Month	6.93

Figure 12.9 Growth of Inactive E-mail Addresses

Over the course of a month, you lose some subscribers through unsubscribes and many from changes of address. If you can accumulate enough new names to compensate for the losses, you are doing well. Active subscribers are the only ones that you can send newsletters and promotions to.

The Television-e-mail Paradox

E-mail marketing has one thing in common with TV advertising: it builds the brand. E-mail produces millions of orders for products and services, some of which can be tracked directly to the particular message that produced the sale. With television, ads can't be tracked as easily. This situation leads to a paradox:

We can't be sure of any specific result from TV ads, so we spend a lot of money on them. We can be absolutely sure of some of the results of e-mail promotions, so we spend much less on them.

Television advertising can be very powerful, but it can't be measured with the same exactitude as e-mail advertising. TV advertising is typically brand building. Because of TV ads, millions of people recognize Geico's gecko and its cavemen. They also remember the banker who said, "I lost another loan to Ditech!" We know that ads like these influence millions of people to call or go to a Web site or drive to a mall and buy. What we almost never find out is that Sarah Williams bought a specific product through a TV ad on a specific program as a result of a specific ad on a specific day. We marketers accept the idea that TV ads work, but we also accept the idea that how they work in any particular case can never be proved. As a result, billions of dollars are spent on preparing and broadcasting TV ads and programs with no proof of exactly what happens when they are viewed.

When e-mail marketing and search engine marketing came along, for the first time, we could prove that as a result of a particular e-mail or search engine placement, Sarah Williams bought a particular book from Amazon on a certain day. Because we can know these things, many companies have based their e-mail marketing budgets only on the resulting online sales. What a mistake.

The fact is that e-mail promotions are in many ways like TV ads. They build the brand. They lead recipients to visit a Web site, make a phone call, purchase from a catalog, or purchase at a mall—just like a TV advertisement. Seventy percent of online users today research products using e-mails, Web sites, and Google, before they buy offline. But normally that offline sale can't be tracked to the e-mail that produced it. Furthermore, a significant number of e-mail promotions never sell anything online. Are these marketers crazy? No. They are using e- mails to build their brand.

Major companies don't take an e-mail promotion's ability to generate offline sales into account when they determine their e-mail promotion budget. They know that e-mail promotions build the brand. They just don't use that knowledge in budgeting. As a result, e-mail budgets in most corporations are far lower than they would be if the true effect of e-mail promotions were taken into account.

Measuring On- and Off-line Sales from E-mail Promotions

In this analysis, we begin with a verifiable fact: a particular group of e-mail campaigns resulted in a certain number of sales. We then make an estimate of the Web site and offline sales through catalogs, retail store visits, phone calls, and indirect sales *resulting from the e-mail.* An indirect sale occurs when a customer buys a pair of Nike sneakers from, say, Macy's Web site or retail store rather than from a Nike-owned store or Web site. These retailers rarely, if ever, report to product manufacturers which products they sell, how much they've sold, to whom, when, and through what channel. Yet for many products, indirect sales are far greater than direct sales.

To know e-mail promotions' true effect, we have to estimate all sales that result from those promotions. This isn't as difficult as it might seem at first—and is much easier than learning a TV ad's effect.

If the e-mail marketer has a catalog sales department, she can learn which catalog sales were assisted by e-mail promotions with a simple coding system. The numbers can be backed up by verifiable statistics as shown in Figure 12.10.

Results of an E-mail Campaign	Sales
Sales in E-mails	1,264
Store Sales Using E-mail Coupons	3,780
Off-e-mail Sales Due to E-mails	2.99

Figure 12.10 Off-e-mail Sales Due to E-mails

Many e-mail marketers with retail stores already include promotion codes in their e-mails. These codes can be entered into the POS system at the stores so the retailer will learn which e-mail produced which retail sale. Other retailers use the 10-day rule: If Arthur Hughes received an e-mail about a specific product and that same Arthur Hughes bought that product at a company-owned retail store within 10 days of his receiving the e-mail, then that e-mail gets credit for the sale.

Indirect sales can also be estimated with some precision—much more precision than sales resulting from TV ads. For example, many retailers include electronic coupons in their e-mails. Such coupons may be effective in selling products in their stores, and retailers can learn a lot from e-mails with such coupons. The product manufacturers, however, will probably learn nothing. By doing a bit of research, any company sending promotional e-mails can make an informed guess about the offline sales that result from their e-mail promotions.

It's also useful to know how many people have been influenced by an e-mail promotion. When customers come into a department store as a result of an e-mail promotion, for instance, they may buy the promoted product. But some of them will buy other products as well. This almost always happens, and you can count on it if you drive traffic to your stores. With a little research, you can estimate the total orders per e-mail-driven customer. This number can be used to estimate indirect orders or unique customers resulting from an e-mail.

Once armed with the estimated number of buyers resulting from an e-mail promotion, you can estimate the percentage of those subscribers in your database who become buyers as a result of your e-mail promotions. The result is the Off-e-mail Multiplier (See Chapter 3).

These numbers can, and should, be used to estimate e-mail promotions' true effect. They should be used to determine the e-mail promotion budget. Far too few companies do this kind of analysis. With this book, you will realize the power of e-mail marketing and adjust your budget accordingly.

Measuring Order Value and Margins

If we are going to determine our success in database marketing, we have to know how much gross and net revenue is generated. We have to know things like those shown in Figure 12.11.

The AOV may be difficult to establish in many instances, but it is vital to measuring e-mail marketing's effectiveness. One customer may buy a $4,000 HDTV set, while another buys a $2 pair of socks. Adding these

Order Channel	Average Order	All Costs	Profit Margin	Total
Online Order	$51.76	30%	70%	100%
Catalog Order	$58.34	40%	60%	100%
Retail Order	$53.77	60%	40%	100%
Indirect Order	$32.78	30%	70%	100%

Figure 12.11 AOVs and Margins

together doesn't seem to make sense, but try it: Add up all the online sales in a month or a year; say it's $118.3 million. Then add up the online transactions; we'll say 1,003,368. Divide the sales total by the transactions, and you get $117.43. You may have no product whose sale price is $117.43, but that average number is a really good way to measure your e-mail marketing effectiveness. Use it.

The net margin on a sale is also a difficult number for many marketers to determine. The margin measures how much out of every dollar of sales a company actually keeps in earnings. In a retail store, there is often a 100 percent markup. That means you buy a dress for $50 and sell it for $100. A 100 percent markup means that your net margin is 50 percent. But you have other costs to consider: salaries, rent, utilities, advertising, and so on. Your cost to sell that dress may be quite high. A typical supermarket today earns a profit of only about 1 percent of the sale price of any item.

Dress stores make much more. In Figure 12.11, the net profit margin on a retail order (40 percent) represents the sale price less the cost of goods sold plus all other marginal costs for a retailer. Determining the average cost per sale in insurance, automobile rental, or airline travel may be complex. Don't make it a massive research project. Look at your annual report. Take the total profit before taxes made by your firm as a percentage of total sales, subtract from 100 percent, and you get the average cost per sale: $100 million in sales minus $8 million profits is $92 million. Your average cost per sale (rate) is 92 percent. That's good enough for a chart like the one in Figure 12.11.

E-mail Costs in Month	CPM	Delivered	Cost
Outsourced E-mail Expenses	$6.32	2,491,045	$15,738
Internal E-mail Expenses	$5.02	2,491,045	$12,500
Total E-mail Expenses in Month			$28,238
Cost of Acquiring New Subscribers	$0.02	17,556	$426

Figure 12.12 E-mail Mailing Expenses

Measuring E-mail Delivery Costs

What you pay for e-mail marketing is really based on two numbers: internal and outsourced e-mail service:

In most cases you pay a specific dollar amount for the development of the month's e-mail campaign creative. If the creative is done in house, the marketer can enter the total cost of salaries and overhead as part of internal e-mail expenses. Most ESPs encourage their clients to manage their own programs, using advanced self-service software that's used to select the names for each campaign, the content, the personalization, the links, and so forth. In other cases, the ESP does everything, based on general instructions from the client's e-mail marketing staff.

E-mail delivery is usually paid on a per-thousand basis, anywhere from $2 to $6, depending on how many e-mails are sent. Some ESPs charge based on e-mails sent, others based on e-mails delivered. These numbers are multiplied by the delivery rate to come up with the cost.

Underlying any e-mail or direct marketing program is the customer marketing database, such as the one in our earlier example the 1 million names, including actives and inactives. This database permits segmentation, personalization, and tracking of visits to your Web site, purchases, and preferences. This database is so important that we have devoted a significant part of the next chapter to discussing how it is set up and maintained.

Measuring This Month's Results

After we have entered all the data listed so far in this chapter, we can see some monthly results that jump out at us. Take a look at the numbers in Figure 12.13.

We delivered 2.49 million e-mails during the month—newsletters, promotions, transactions, triggered, and so forth. We made 1,264 online sales at an average price of $51.76 each, giving us a total e-mail revenue of $65,419. We learned something else: the e-mails delivered resulted in $196,257 of non-e-mail purchases. That's a reasonably good outcome. Some marketers can get that number considerably higher.

With these numbers, we are at last able to measure our e-mail promotions' effectiveness in a way the CFO can understand.

Monthly Results	
E-mails Delivered	2,491,045
E-mails Delivered per Campaign	146,532
HTML E-mails Opened	256,252
Unique Clicks	28,238
Total E-mail Conversions	1,264
Total Revenue from E-mail Conversions	$65,419
Total Offline Revenue Resulting from E-mails	$196,257
Total E-mail Induced Revenue	$261,676
Cost of Goods Sold Plus Overhead	$78,503
Total E-mail Costs in Month	$28,664
Net Profit from E-mail Operations	$154,509

Figure 12.13 Monthly E-mail Results

ROI Calculation

We now can put all the data in Figure 12.14 into a table that gives important information about our e-mail programs' success. Only e-mails can produce numbers like the ones shown in the figure.

These are wonderful numbers. Unfortunately, most e-mail marketers don't have numbers like these for their campaigns. They are a picture of what the most successful e-mail marketers get from an advanced ESP.

Return on Investment	
E-mail Spending This Month	$28,664
ROI per $1 Spent on E-mails	$5.39
Cost per Delivered E-mail	$0.012
Cost per Opened E-mail	$0.112
Cost per Unique Click	$1.069
Cost per E-mail Conversion	$22.68
E-mail Conversions per Campaign	74
Cost per Campaign	$1,686
Online Revenue per Delivered	$0.105
Monthly Revenue per Active Subscriber	$0.728
Offline Revenue per E-mail	$0.546
Annual Revenue per Active Sub.	$0.728
Monthly Profit per Active Sub	$0.430
Value of an Opt-in E-mail Address	$13.42

Figure 12.14 E-mail Marketing ROI

Where Does the Data Come From?

All the data described in this chapter are known to someone in any direct mail or e-mail marketing operation. The problem is that the data aren't all normally known to any one individual. They are spread between the marketers, the ESPs, the Web site managers, the retail store vice president, the CFO, IT professionals, and others. How can the information be assembled so that we can produce the kind of effectiveness measures shown here?

E-mail marketing managers should make the first move. They should fill in all the information they have at their command right away. That will indicate what they don't know. At that point, they should form a committee of all those involved in e-mail marketing to discuss how the missing data can be made available on a regular, automatic basis so the reports shown in the figures can be produced each month.

An alternate solution is to have your ESP collect the data and send it to everyone involved on a monthly basis. Most of the data can be collected from existing sources. Some of the numbers have to be estimates based on research. Data that have to be estimated at first include:

- Web site and viral subscription rate
- Store visitors and their subscription rate
- Catalog purchaser subscription rate
- Direct mail sent to lost subscribers and the reactivation rate
- Average cost per sale
- Percentage of offline sales from online promotions

For the first round of reports, make reasonable estimates of each number so that the reports can be prepared. It will soon become clear whether these initial estimates are realistic—and what can be done to get the data to make them representative of the actual situation.

Putting All the Data on One Chart

All the campaign data discussed in this chapter can be put together to provide a monthly view of e-mail marketing's ROI. It could look something like the table shown in Figure 12.15.

This is as complete a picture of e-mail marketing campaign performance as you are likely to get. Every e-mail marketer should have a chart

Typical E-mail Marketer	
A. Costs of Service	
E-mail Delivery Expenses	$15,738
Internal E-mail Expenses	$12,500
Total E-mail Expenses in Month	$28,238
New Subscriber Acquisition Spending	$426
B. E-mails Sent	
Campaigns in Month	17.00
Total E-mails Sent	2,507,549
Total E-mails Delivered	2,491,045
Delivery Rate	99.44%
C. Monthly List Growth Measures	
Deliverable Subscribers in Month	359,221
Gained in Month	17,556
Unsubscribed in Month	6,262
Perm. Undeliverable in Month	2,567
Apparent Change in Subscribers in Month	**8,727**
Average E-mails per Subscriber per Month	**6.93**
D. This Month's Results	
E-mails Delivered	2,491,045
E-mails Delivered per Campaign	146,532
HTML E-mails Opened	256,252
Unique Clicks	26,803
Total E-mail Conversions	1,264
Total Revenue from E-mail Conversions	$65,419
Total Off-line Revenue due to E-mails	$196,257
Total E-mail Induced Revenue	$261,676
Cost of Goods Sold Plus Overhead	$78,503
Total E-mail Costs in Month	$28,664
Net Profit from E-mail Operations	$154,509

Off-e-mail Multiplier	3.0
E. Opens and Conversions	
Open Rate (HTML) % of Delivered	10.29%
Unique Clicks as % of Opens	10.46%
This Month Unique Buyers	1,242
E-mail Conversions % of Unique Clicks	4.72%
Unique Buyers % of Mailable Addresses	0.35%
F. Clicks	
Total Clicks	34,576
Percent Unique Clicks per Open	10.46%
Total Unique Clicks	26,803
Percent Conversions per Unique Click	4.72%
G. Value and Costs	
Average Order Value	$51.76
Cost of Goods Sold Plus Overhead %	30.00%
H. Return on Investment and Costs	
E-mail Spending This Month	$28,664
ROI per $1 Spent on E-mails	$5.39
Cost per Delivered E-mail	$0.012
Cost per Opened E-mail	$0.112
Cost per Unique Click	$1.069
Cost per E-mail Conversion	$22.677
E-mail Conversions per Campaign	74
Cost per Campaign	$1,686
Online Revenue per Delivered	$0.11
Monthly Revenue per Active Sub.	$0.73
Offline Revenue per E-mail	$0.55
Annual Revenue per Active Sub.	$0.73
Monthly Profit per Active Sub	$0.43
Value of an Opt-in E-mail Address	$13.42

Figure 12.15 Monthly E-mail Summary

like this produced automatically every month. It should go to the CFO, the CEO, and the CMO. Arising from this form should be graphs that compare the performance of each value month by month. Graphs can be prepared that show progress—or lack of it.

Data like this can be used to produce Lifetime Value and Return On Investment reports similar to those in Chapter 3 of this book. These tables and graphs are useful for Marketing Management to see the effectiveness of their e-mail marketing program.

Take-Away Thoughts

- Database marketing is conducted by campaigns: groups of messages with a common theme such as "Pre-Christmas Mailing."
- Each campaign stands on its own and can be analyzed by its open, click, and conversion rates.
- There are many different types of customer and subscriber communications, including promotions, transactions, triggers, reminders, thank yous, surveys, welcomes, and reactivations.
- Successful direct mail response rates are around 2.6 percent. E-mail conversion rates average about 0.11 percent.
- Direct mail names can be rented legally and ethically. E-mail subscribers have to agree to receive your messages.
- The average e-mail marketer sends about 50 campaigns a month. The median is 28.
- Typical e-mail subscribers get about 10 e-mails per month from each company they have given their name to.
- The average open rate for e-mails is about 11 percent. That means that almost 90 percent of e-mails never get read by anybody.
- For those e-mails that get opened, subscribers click on about 24 percent of them. A click means that the subscriber is actually reading the message.
- Conversions (sales) average about 4.5 percent per click. They average about 0.11 percent per delivered e-mail.
- The TV–e-mail paradox: we can't accurately measure what a TV ad does, so we spend a lot of money on TV. We can accurately measure what e-mail does, so we spend very little.

- E-mails usually produce more off-e-mail sales than sales within the e-mail. From this we derive the off-e-mail multiplier.

- Online sales usually have a higher profit margin than retail store sales.

- Monthly campaign reports are essential to successful e-mail marketing.

A quiz on this chapter and all figures can be found at www.dbmarket ing.com/STM4. Those taking all the quizzes can receive a Successful Completion Certificate from the Database Marketing Institute which can be used in their résumé.

13

Analytics and Modeling

Predictive modeling makes it possible for businesses to react to what their customers are going to do rather than what they have already done. It begins by identifying a problem or opportunity—losing too many valuable customers or a need to grow the customer base, for example—and possible actions to address it.
It models each customer's likely response to various possible actions and helps the marketer choose the most appropriate action for each of those customers.

—MICHAEL J. McDERMOTT

There has been a strong push back on analytics with marketers. It's not to say that analytics isn't important, but if all decisions came back to what the analytics told us, then marketers wouldn't be needed. Creativity, gut instinct, anecdotal data, why customers do what they do, and emotional response cannot be addressed by looking in rear view mirrors of analytics reports.

—AARON KAHLOW

What if you could predict how a large group of prospects or customers would react to an offer from you? If you could separate people likely to respond and buy from those unlikely to respond and buy, you would be much more successful as a marketer. This is what predictive modeling can do for you. With a good predictive model, you can determine:

- Which customers and prospects are likely to buy, and which are unlikely to buy.

307

- Which customers are in danger of leaving you, and which are likely to stay.

- Which products they are more likely to buy.

The ideas behind database marketing predictive models rest on some simple principles:

- *Prospects and customers in many segments react in predictable ways.* This predictability is vital. If everyone had unpredictable reactions to your services and marketing efforts, a model could not provide reliable predictions.

- *Clues to expected customer behavior can sometimes be discerned in customers' previous behavior and their demographics.* The behavior used in predictions can usually be stored in your database in the form of transactions. The demographics can be appended from an outside source. This does not always work. It is not always possible to predict customer behavior based on the data you can collect in a database.

- *A predictive model is usually developed from the response to previous promotions.* It is difficult to run a successful predictive model unless you have already sent a promotion to your customers or prospects and gotten a reaction from them. What this means is that you usually cannot just take a file of names and addresses and do a model to determine which ones will be more interested in your product. For example, what kinds of customers are more likely to want to purchase a recreation vehicle? You can make some assumptions (over 65, lower middle income, perhaps), but without the results of an RV promotion to a number of prospects, you won't be able to build a model that gives you reliable predictions.

Once you have built a model that works, you can improve your response rates. The basic use of a predictive model is to concentrate your attention on those most likely to respond and purchase, and to avoid promotions to those least likely to respond. Say that you send a promotion to 100,000 people offering a product. You get a 2 percent response rate.

Using the results of this promotion, you build a statistical model which successfully identifies the characteristics of the responders and the non-responders. You use that model to compile a new batch of 100,000 names. If you mail only to the 50,000 who the model identifies as the most likely responders, you should get a response rate of more than 2 percent—perhaps 3 percent or more. This will be much more profitable for you, and it will avoid bothering people who are not interested in your product.

How Modeling Works

How does predictive modeling work? There are some simple steps:

1. *Do a promotion, or use a previous promotion as your base.* You will need enough customers in your model to get statistically valid results. A promotion to a few hundred people is seldom adequate as a base for a model. I use a rule of thumb for an adequate test file size: as a base for a typical model, you need about 500 responses, conversions, or sales. If, for example, you typically get a 2 percent response and sale rate, for a valid model then you need to send your promotion to 25,000 people (500/0.02).

2. *Append demographic and behavioral data to your responders and non-responders.* There are several companies that provide demographic data. AmeriLINK from KnowledgeBase Marketing is one example. It maintains a file of 236 million U.S. consumers with exact age, estimated income, shopping behavior, and about 20 other pieces of data. For a modest cost, you can get some or all of this information appended to your file of 25,000 consumers. Figure 13.1 is taken from AmeriLINK, but it is typical of the data available from other suppliers.

	Millions
Age	236
Income	236
Auto Loan	84
Census Data	236
Dwelling Type	236
Gender	236
Glasses Wearers	19
Height	61
Weight	55
Home Ownership	153
House Value	123
Length of Residence	185
Mail Order Buyer	108
NonProfit Donor	84
Persons in Household	236
Occupation	90
Religion	208
Student Loan	22
Wealth	236

Figure 13.1 Data Available for Appending

3. *Add geographic data.* Some of the data in Figure 13.1 is demographic (age, income). Some data is behavioral (mail order buyer, nonprofit donor). You can also add geographic data: code people by whether they live in rural areas, suburban areas, or urban areas. You may find differences in people who live in the north, south, east or west. Those who live near the ocean or a lake may differ in their response from those who live inland. Do they have a listed telephone or an unlisted telephone? This phone listing may seem irrelevant, and may be so, but for some products, marketers have found that those with unlisted phones respond differently from others. Besides this appended data, you should add previous purchase history with your company to your mix of data grouped with every customer record that you plan to use in your model.

4. *Divide your data into two parts.* Before you begin to create your model, you should divide your customer data in two parts: a test group of 12,250 non-responders and 250 responders and a validation group of 12,250 non-responders and 250 responders (see Figure 13.2). Both groups should have exactly the same type and variety of people.

   The validation group is set aside for now, and the model development process works with the test group.

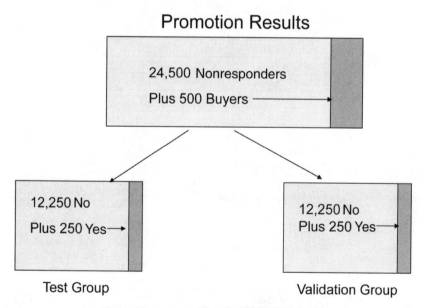

Promotion Results

24,500 Nonresponders

Plus 500 Buyers

12,250 No

Plus 250 Yes

12,250 No

Plus 250 Yes

Test Group   Validation Group

Figure 13.2 Splitting out a Validation Group

5. *Discard the outliers.* The modelers will first discard the "outliers." These are customers whose purchases were so unusual that they will distort the outcome. For example, if the average customer bought one or two items for an average sale of $200, you would consider as an outlier a lone customer who bought 482 items and spent $96,400. You should toss out this customer's records in building your model.

6. *Construct your model.* Now that you have a file rich with appended data, you are ready to construct a predictive model. As a first step, you will typically use a multiple regression model. (We discuss CHAID later in this chapter.) A regression is an equation that describes the relationship between a dependent variable and more than one independent variable. The dependent variable is the purchase that the customer made as a result of your promotion (500 bought, and 24,500 did not). The independent variables are the behavior and appended data listed above. Which of the independent variables will be most valuable in predicting who will buy and who will not buy? That is what the model is designed to find out.

The model is typically run on a PC using the software products SAS or SPSS. When the model is run, it applies weights to each of the independent variables. A weight is a number that indicates how important (weighty) each variable is in predicting the desired result (they bought the product). Typically a weight of "0" means that the variable has no discernable influence on the consumer's decision process. A negative weight means that the variable influenced the purchase process in a negative way. (The higher the negative value, the less likely the person is to buy the product.) Higher weights mean that the factor is more likely to influence the outcome. A weight of 0.89 (for income, for example) may be higher than 0.52 (for age) in determining whether the customer will buy the product.

Figure 13.3 is a sample table of weights created by a regression model. There were 24 independent variables with weights from minus 4.88 up to plus 0.69. Some are positive (+) and many are negative (−). If, for example, the customer said that he did not want to receive e-mails, he was unlikely to buy the product. Note that almost all the positive variables are related to recency. This table tells you that for this particular promotion, the mailer should probably have used RFM (see Chapter 5) and saved the money she spent on modeling.

7. *Determine the weights for each variable.* Using the weights determined by the model, you may want to concentrate on using in the model those

Variable Description	Effect	Contribution %	Coefficient
Last Product = Other	−	15.87%	−0.8988
Customer E-mail Flag = N	−	14.22%	−0.6856
Sales Item Amount LTD $0–$100	−	12.72%	−0.8494
Last Registration Recency 25–36	+	7.90%	0.5511
Sales Last Order Recency 0–6	+	5.13%	0.5330
Last Registration Recency 7–12	+	5.01%	0.5953
Sales Item Amount LTD $101–$250	−	4.87%	−0.5232
Last Registration Method = Broadband	−	4.06%	−0.4365
Customer Type = Unknown	−	3.66%	−4.8778
Last Registration Method = Dial Up	−	3.57%	−0.4432
Customer Type = Organization	+	3.35%	0.6922
Sales Last Order Recency 7–12	+	2.95%	0.3867
First Registration Method = Paper	+	2.63%	0.2668
Sales Last Order Recency 61+	+	2.35%	0.6308
Sales Last Pay Method = Credit Card	−	2.32%	−0.2889
First Product = Other	−	1.98%	−0.4011
Sales First Order Recency 0–6	+	1.46%	0.6904
Sales Item Amount LTD $251–$500	−	1.22%	−0.2690
Last Registration Recency 0–6	+	1.15%	0.2837
Sales Item Amount LTD $1001+	+	0.96%	0.2885
Sales Last Item Amount $20.00–$39.99	+	0.77%	0.1655
First Registration Recency 25–36	+	0.67%	0.2151
First Registration Use = Business	+	0.61%	0.3022
Sales First Pay Method = Credit Card	−	0.57%	−0.1337
		100.00%	

Figure 13.3 Weights Assigned by a Regression Model

independent variables that have a high weight in determining the outcome. You can ignore those variables whose weight is very low. So instead of using 30 different variables (age, income, religion, student loan, etc.) you may build your model based on the five or six variables that provide the greatest predictive power. This may save you money later on when you have to append data to a large file so it can be scored using the model.

8. *Develop an algorithm.* The final outcome of the model is an algorithm. An algorithm is a mathematical routine used to perform computations.

In the case of a statistical model in marketing, the algorithm usually includes the computer code that creates a score for each customer or prospect record. The scores may vary from 95 percent certain to buy the product down to 5 percent (unlikely to buy). Figure 13.4 shows a sample ranking of deciles from an actual mailing showing the response rates.

Decile #	Mailings #	Responses	Response %	Index
1	15,853	1,085	6.84%	297
2	15,853	640	4.04%	175
3	15,853	564	3.56%	154
4	15,853	390	2.46%	107
5	15,853	286	1.80%	78
6	15,853	279	1.76%	76
7	15,853	193	1.22%	53
8	15,853	142	0.90%	39
9	15,853	69	0.44%	19
10	15,853	9	0.06%	2
Total	158,530	3,657	2.31%	

Figure 13.4 Scoring the Test File into Deciles

9. *Score the validation group.* Using the algorithm that emerges from your modeling of the test group, you can "score" the validation group. Now, bear in mind that the validation group has already received promotions. You know the outcome (2 percent bought, and 98 percent did not buy). So if the algorithm developed for the test group is going to be useful in predicting, it should correctly identify most of the people in the validation group who bought (with a high score) and those who did not buy (with a low score). If the algorithm does correctly score the validation group, then you have a successful model that can be used to predict customer response in your next promotion.

In Figure 13.5, look how closely the validation group response rates came to those of the test group. This was an excellent model that was used to accurately predict the response to a large mailing. The breakeven response rate was about 2.3 percent. From the figure you can see that deciles 6–10 should probably not be mailed to (depending on the profit from the purchased items).

Decile #	Mailings	Responses	Response %	Index
1	15,984	1,092	6.83%	292
2	16,265	618	3.80%	163
3	15,528	524	3.37%	144
4	15,900	397	2.50%	107
5	16,391	339	2.07%	89
6	15,378	295	1.92%	82
7	15,812	217	1.37%	59
8	15,471	128	0.83%	35
9	18,258	89	0.49%	21
10	13,542	4	0.03%	1
Total	158,529	3,703	2.34%	

Figure 13.5 Validation File Scored by the Algorithm into Deciles

What If It Doesn't Work?

If the validation process is unsuccessful, of course, you either have to redo your model or give up the whole process as a bad job. It may be that with the data you have available, a model cannot predict the responders. This is very often the case. Modeling does not always work.

Most direct marketing dilemmas cannot be solved by predictive modeling. Why? Because the answer may not lie in the available data. For example, it could be that purchasers of your product cannot be determined by age, income, presence of children, or any standard demographic factors. Why not? Well, suppose you are selling cold remedies, or snow tires, or vacuum cleaners. It is highly possible that these demographic variables will not show a difference between purchasers and non-purchasers. If this is the case, all the modeling in the world won't help. A general rule: if the solution does not seem to make sense to you, then it probably doesn't make sense. Modeling is not magic. It is only a quantification of intuitive logic.

Many models take weeks to develop. This is because the modelers are constantly tweaking them to get more and more predictive results using different variables.

What You Can Do with Your Model

If you have a model that works, you can use it to generate profits. There are two main uses for predictive models:

- Determine who will buy a product or service and which product to offer them.

- Determine which customers are most likely to drop your service and when they are most likely to depart.

Who Will Buy?

To use your model, you could start with your next planned promotion (of the same product). Score the mail file. After scoring a file of prospects or customers, you typically divide the scored file into deciles based on the score. The top decile (10 percent of the file) contains those people most likely to buy. You will be able to arrange your customer or prospect data as shown in Figure 13.6.

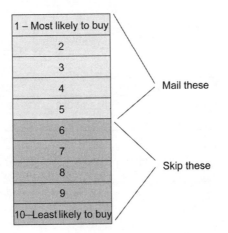

Figure 13.6 Predictive Deciles

In this figure, deciles 6–10 are your worst performing deciles. You probably should not mail to this group. You should, however, mail to a few (5 percent) of each of these low performing deciles just to prove to yourself, and to your management, that the model is still working properly and actually does predict the buyers correctly.

The result of mailing only to the higher deciles is that you will get a higher response rate overall. The picture should look something like the one shown in Figure 13.7.

How does this work in practice? An automobile insurance company engaged The Summit Marketing Group to build a model to predict the

	Previous Mailing	Modeled Mailing
Number Mailed	500,000	500,000
Cost @$0.50	$250,000	$250,000
Response Rate	2.0%	3.5%
Number Sales	10,000	17,500
Sales @$100	$1,000,000	$1,750,000
Gross Profit	$750,000	$1,500,000

Figure 13.7 Profit from Use of a Predictive Model

response to its monthly mailings to acquire new customers. Summit prepared a model and used the algorithm to select prospects for each mailing. See Figure 13.8. As a result, the insurance company almost doubled its monthly profits.

	Control Group	Optimized Group	% Change	# Change
Total Mailed	1,264,571	1,264,571	0%	0
Cost of Mailing	$547,559	$547,559	0%	0
Number of Responses	13,366	16,090	20%	2,724
Response Rate	1.06%	1.27%	20%	0.22%
Number of Sales	1,599	2,323	45%	724
Sales Rate	12.00%	14.40%	21%	2.47%
Total Revenue	$2,605,603	$3,158,151	21%	$553,208
Profit	$95,896	$187,851	96%	$91,955
Return on Promotion	18%	34%	96%	16.80%

Figure 13.8 Insurance Mailing Using a Model

Do Analytics Work with E-mail Marketing?

There are two broad methods of using analytics to support e-mail marketing: subscriber analytics and clickstream analytics. Both are useful and can be profitable.

Subscriber analytics is more than 30 years old and support most of the marketing methods discussed in this book. They are familiar to anyone who has participated in database or direct mail marketing. Clickstream analysis is very new and applies only to Web sites and e-mails. Because it is so new, many people starting out in e-mail marketing assume that clickstream analysis is all there is. Wrong. If you are going to do database marketing, you start with subscriber analysis.

To analyze e-mail subscribers, build a database and track what your subscribers are like, what they want, and what they do. In addition to studying what the subscribers do when they receive your e-mails, study their demographics and offline behavior. Typically, if you have the subscriber's postal address, you can append more than 100 fields of data, such as age, income, presence of children, and time at residence. This data, combined with opens, clicks, and purchase history enables you to create segments, to customize and personalize your e-mails, and to increase profits.

Is E-mail Subscriber Analysis Necessary?

Some people maintain that subscriber analytics is useless for e-mail marketing. Their reasoning goes like this: Subscriber analytics was developed for direct mail, where each letter has an in-the-mail cost of $0.50 or more. By sending your promotions to those most likely to buy, you are saving the cost of mailing to those less likely to buy. These savings don't apply to e-mail, where the cost per e-mail is a fraction of a penny.

Let's take a practical example. The average conversion (sales) rate for a typical e-mail marketing program is about 0.152 percent as shown in Figure 13.9, which was derived from our 80 test e-mail marketers:

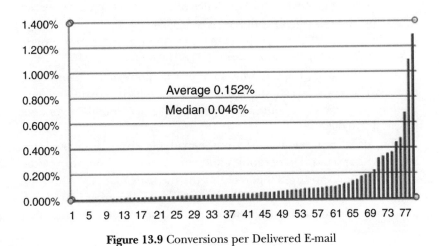

Figure 13.9 Conversions per Delivered E-mail

Now consider the table in Figure 13.10. The table compares direct mail with e-mail marketing. With direct mail, we have a house file of 1 million names. We send a promotion that has an in-the-mail cost of $600 per thousand ($0.60 per piece), including printing and postage. With a 2.04 percent response rate and a $50 profit per successful sale, the net profit is $420,000.

Comparison of Analytics Results	Mailed	Promotion Cost	Analytics Cost	Percent Sales	Total Sales	Revenue @ $50	Net Profit
DM Without Analytics	1,000,000	$600,000	$0	2.04%	20,400	$1,020,000	$420,000
DM With Analytics	600,000	$360,000	$80,000	2.96%	17,760	$888,000	$448,000
E-mail without Analytics	1,000,000	$6,000	$0	0.152%	1,520	$76,000	$70,000
E-mail with Analytics	600,000	$3,600	$80,000	0.228%	1,368	$68,400	-$15,200

Figure 13.10 Subscriber Analytics Results for Direct Mail and E-mail Programs

We then add in analytics to the mailing program, developing a predictive model that we apply to our file. This model predicts those customers most likely to buy. We drop from the mailing those less likely to buy, 40 percent of the file, and our sales rate goes up from 2.04 percent to 2.95 percent. Our net profit has risen by $28,000. To do the analytics, we had to spend $0.07 for each name for the demographic data appending and $10,000 for the model—a total of $80,000.

With our e-mail program, we also have 1 million names. Using batch and blast, it costs $6 per thousand ($0.006 each) to create and send them e-mails. We get a conversion rate of 0.152 percent, giving us a net profit of $70,000.

Now let's apply analytics to our e-mail file. We spend the same $80,000 to append demographics and run a model. Using this model, we select the responsive 60 percent of the file for e-mailing. With these better responders, we get a response rate of 0.228 percent. What has happened, however, is that the cost of appending and modeling,

$80,000, has cut deeply into our net profit. We have lost money by doing analytics.

These numbers are typical of what any e-mail marketing operation will find. Analytics is great for direct mail projects because you save postage. It fails with e-mail promotions because of the steep cost of appending demographics.

Saving Subscribers

There are some uses for analytics with e-mail other than saving postage. Because we have eliminated mailing to 400,000 subscribers who the model showed were less likely to buy, we have also reduced the unsubscribes, undelivers, and spam reports that would have come from those subscribers if we had e-mailed them something they didn't want. These unmailed subscribers are available for a promotion for something that would be more to their liking. The normal unsubscribers resulting from e-mail delivery are shown in Figure 13.11.

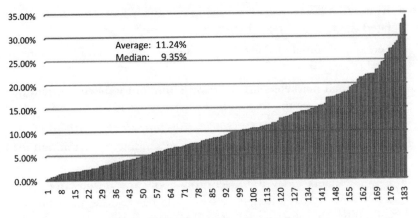

Figure 13.11 Annual Unsubscribe Rate

If we have determined that the LTV of our e-mail subscribers is $22.50 each, then, if we have decided to do analytics for some other reason, we might be able to reduce our unsubscribers by not sending them irrelevant mail. The result might look like the information in Figure 13.12. The figure shows that by sending e-mails only to those most likely to be interested, we have reduced our annual unsubscribe rate from the average of 15.1 percent to the median rate of 12.9 percent thus cutting our losses from unsubscribes by $495,000. Analytics has proved to be highly profitable.

Comparison of Analytics Results	Subscribers	Annual Unsub Rate	Unsubs	Loss due to Unsubs @ $22.50	Loss Reduction
E-mail without Analytics	1,000,000	15.10%	151,000	$3,397,500	
E-mail with Analytics	1,000,000	12.90%	129,000	$2,902,500	$495,000

Figure 13.12 Saving in Subscriber Loss through Mailing
Only Those Interested in Our Offer

How many e-mail marketers are doing this kind of sophisticated analysis by including the cost of lost subscribers in their overall campaign planning? From my experience, I would say, today, less than 5 percent. Why?

- In the first place, few e-mail marketers today have accurately calculated the LTV of their subscribers.

- Few have estimated the effect on subscribers of sending irrelevant mail.

- Most e-mail marketers are so busy getting out tomorrow's mail that they do not have the time to make these calculations.

- Management in most companies is interested only in boosting next quarter's revenue. Building models and sending more relevant mail does not fit into a quarterly revenue growth plan.

- Few marketers today think seriously about the unsubscriber problem—viewing it as a long-term cost of doing business, rather than as something that they can affect by their actions today.

E-mail marketing is here today. It is established. It is high time for e-mail marketers to take it seriously as the quantifiable long-term strategy that it is.

E-mail subscriber analytics, thus, has two benefits: It boosts the conversion rate by letting us send customized e-mails to segmented subscribers. And it helps us avoid sending e-mails to people for whom the promotion isn't relevant, saving them for a promotion they will consider relevant. But, if you lose money by doing subscriber analytics, there is little point in doing it.

Why Does Direct Mail Get Higher Conversion Rates?

There are several significant reasons why direct mail gets higher conversion rates than e-mail. First, a direct mail letter's shelf life is several days. For catalogs, it is several weeks. An e-mail's shelf life is seldom more than one day. The longer the direct mail letter, catalog, or postcard kicks around the house, the greater the chance someone will read it and will buy something as a result of reading it. It can be carried from room to room. E-mails are almost never printed out. They can't be carried around. They sit with a hundred other e-mails in an in-box where only one or two people in the house ever see them.

This does not apply, however, to e-mails sent to mobile subscribers. Their results may be higher because the subscribers are carrying the e-mails around with them and can read them in their spare time. Whether this will affect the overall open, click, and conversion rates needs to be determined by detailed study of the results. Unfortunately, I do not know of anyone who has done this study to date.

Another e-mail–direct mail difference is that everyone in the country gets direct mail. Roughly one-fifth of all U.S. households is not connected to the Internet and has never used e-mail, according to a 2008 Parks Associates study. Although the number of non-connected households is slowly going down, age and education remain factors in this divide. One-half of those who have never used e-mail are over age 65, and 56 percent have no schooling beyond high school. On the other hand, many Americans over age 65 are active responders to direct mail.

Another reason e-mail's conversion rates are low is batch-and-blast e-mail campaigns. People are sick of getting too many e-mails. The same isn't true of direct mail. People get only five or six direct mail pieces a day. The average person gets many more promotional e-mails a day. Batch and blast reduces the attention span and response rates.

Finally, because of the cost of a direct mail letter, all direct mail today is targeted at people likely to respond. Because of the low price of marketing e-mails, less than 10 percent are targeted. Most e-mail marketing is like hunting: set a trap (e-mail blast to everyone) and see what you can catch.

Doing the Math on Modeling

If you are paying a service bureau to build your model, you may pay between $5,000 and $50,000, depending on complexity. An additional expense is the appended data necessary for your model to work. You can get appended data from several different sources. You can expect to pay between $7 and $35 per thousand records for the appended data. This is an additional cost. For example, if you are going to append data to 1 million records, as in the previous example, at $7 per thousand, the data will cost you an additional $70,000.

But this does not tell the whole story. If you are going to use your model to discard prospects with low scores, you may have to pay for the discarded records. See Figure 13.13 for an example.

	Quantity	Price/M	Cost
Rented Names	1,000,000	$70	$70,000
Model	1	$10,000	$10,000
Appended Data	1,000,000	$20	$20,000
Scoring	1,000,000	$5	$5,000
Total Cost			$105,000
Names Used	500,000		
Cost per Name			$0.21

Figure 13.13 Cost of Names Using a Model

Putting all the costs together, you will pay $0.21 per name ($210 per thousand) for names produced from a model. For companies that are used to paying less than $70 per thousand for rented names, the model will be a tough sell. However, there are ways around these additional costs.

You Can Negotiate a "Net Name" Arrangement with Your List Brokers

This means that you have to pay them only for the names you actually mail, not for the names that you used in the model and discarded. Net name arrangements are usually granted when the rented name is a duplicate of another name that you already have on your house file or on another rented list. You will have to do some fast talking to convince the broker that you do not have to pay for names that you used in your modeling process but did not mail.

You Can Purchase Compiled Names Based on the Model

Purchasing compiled names brings up a whole new marketing technique using your model. Typically, mailers rent prospect names from companies that have proved the worth of the names by actually selling products to them. These lists are called "response lists." The people on the lists may be subscribers to publications, purchasers from catalogs, direct mail buyers, or retail store buyers. A response list usually produces better results than a "compiled list." A compiled list is typically a list of all the consumers in a city or in the whole country. (See Chapter 4, Customer and Subscriber Acquisition.) Since only about half of all U.S. households ever buy anything by mail, a response list will usually produce twice the responses per piece mailed as a complied list.

Your model changes the picture. Your model has identified six or a dozen characteristics of buyers of your product that differentiate them from non-buyers. If you run your algorithm on a compiled list that has the necessary data appended, the scoring process will yield a table that divides people by deciles indicating likelihood of purchase. People in the top deciles will buy your product. People who do not buy goods through the mail will be ranked low.

Some suppliers of complied names have already appended census and other demographic data to the names. They will let you select names from their database using your model. In some cases, they will build your model free if you use it to select their names. The resulting prices can be very rewarding (see Figure 13.14).

If you rent a compiled list from a savvy supplier, you may pay nothing for the model and nothing for the appended data (since their compiled file already has data appended). You may pay only for scoring and selecting the records based on the model. Seven and a half cents per record is much cheaper than twenty-one cents per record.

Are these compiled names selected by a model less responsive than rented names selected by the same model? Not necessarily. If your compiler has a large file that includes almost all U.S. consumers, the model should select, in many cases, almost exactly the same names that you would produce using the model on a response list.

	Quantity	Price/M	Cost
Rented Names	600,000	$70	$42,000
Model	0	$0	$0
Appended Data	600,000	$0	$0
Scoring	600,000	$5	$3,000
Total Cost			$45,000
Names Used	600,000		
Cost per Name			$0.075

Figure 13.14 Reduced Costs with a Compiled List

Using the Model for Cross-Sales

Models can be particularly useful in determining which of your current customers will buy again—and what products they are most likely to buy. The advantage of using a model on your current customers is that you usually have much more relevant data to work with than you do with prospects. In a model, behavioral data typically is more powerful than demographic data. In other words, you can better predict what people are going to do in the future based on what they have already done in the past than by basing your model on who they are (age, income, home value, etc.).

MSDBM in Los Angeles (now SourceLink) created a customer purchase behavior model for Isuzu midsized commercial trucks. Scores were grouped into three ranges to indicate high, medium, and low purchase likelihood. The model predicted the propensity to purchase based on four variables:

- Number of employees in a business
- Vocation: for example, landscaping, electrical contractor, towing, and so on
- Time since last purchase
- Total number of trucks owned

Using the model scores, the customers (companies) were divided into three groups showing the likelihood of their purchasing a new truck:

- High probability
- Medium probability
- Low probability

Isuzu decided to use the models to create a mailing designed to drive selected small business owners to Isuzu dealers. The total number mailed was 6,000. In addition, 520 companies were set aside as a control group to monitor the success of the promotion.

This test mailing proved that the scoring methodology developed was highly accurate (see Figure 13.15). As a result Isuzu used the same methodology to score its entire customer file for a follow-up mailing. This gave Isuzu the ability to target key customers and ensure a sale of a vehicle with very little cost, compared to normal prospect acquisition costs.

Isuzu Trucks	Group Totals	Companies Buying	Buying Rate	Trucks Sold
High Score	1,899	97	5.10%	107
Medium Score	1,855	32	1.70%	34
Low Score	1,890	15	0.80%	16
Control Group	520	3	0.60%	3
Total	6,164	147	2.38%	160

Figure 13.15 Trucks Sold

Based on its previous experience, Isuzu had expected to sell only 85 trucks to 6,000 prospects. The industry estimates that it costs a manufacturer about $1,000 in marketing and sales effort to sell one midsized truck. Using the database, Isuzu was able to sell the trucks for half that amount.

Using a Model for Upgrades

A software manufacturer was interested in identifying the most likely customers for an upgrade to a new product version. Using the client's customer database going back three years, KnowledgeBase Marketing built some models that predicted which customers were most likely to purchase the upgrades. Using the model, the customer base of 2,452,549 was divided into three groups: high probability, medium probability, and low probability of responding positively to the offer (see Figure 13.16).

The response rate of the low probability segment showed that marketing to this segment would not be profitable for the company. A second mailing to the same group produced equally definitive results. At a cost of about $0.40 per piece mailed, the company could save about

$155,379 by not mailing to this group. The model split the combined second and third mailing into 20 segments, from most probable to least probable. The actual results proved the validity of the model.

	Mail Qty	Orders	Response Rate	% of Total Orders
High Probability	1,027,914	13,465	1.31%	64.35%
Medium Probability	1,036,188	6,210	0.60%	29.68%
Low Probability	388,447	1,249	0.32%	5.97%
Total	2,452,549	20,924	0.85%	100.00%

Figure 13.16 Direct Mail Results

What Data Should You Include in Your Database?

The power of prior behavior is one reason why it is important that you keep in your database as much of the customer transaction and promotion history as possible. Keep track of every communication with customers: letters, brochures, e-mails, products purchased, services, phone calls. Keep track of all the transactions: what they bought, when, as a result of what offer, product type, price, quantity, how they bought (Web, mail, phone, retail visit). Be sure you record how they paid for the product or service: check, purchase order, credit card, and so forth. Almost all this data can be used in constructing a predictive model.

The Next-Best Product

By using a model, you can determine what the next-best product for every customer should be. Banks, for example, have a lot of data about their customers. They can use their database to examine customers who have only checking accounts. From the data they can determine whether the next product should be a home equity loan, an auto loan, a savings account, or mutual funds. How do they do this? By using a model to see what thousands of their depositors who have purchased mutual funds look like in terms of behavior and demographics, and how they differ from those depositors who have been offered mutual funds but have not bought them. The model is used to score all the depositors. Those depositors whose scores resemble the mutual fund buyers are likely targets for a mutual fund promotion. Mutual funds are their next-best product. The next-best product is put into the customer record and called up on the teller's screen when the customer comes in to cash a check or make a deposit. It is also used in mailings to depositors. The bank does the same thing for savings accounts, auto loans, home equity loans, and so on. The product that has the highest score for each customer is that customer's next-best product.

Not only banks, but insurance companies, airlines, hotels, and Web sites use next-best product models. It is powerful stuff. You can prove the effectiveness of the next-best product by comparing the response to a personalized offer based on a next-best product model with an offer based on the "product of the month."

A nationwide insurance company developed a next-best product model that was designed to bundle the customer's current premiums with the premium on the next-best product. An auto insurance customer, for example was offered a monthly saving of $X on his auto policy if he purchased life insurance. Another customer was offered $X saving on the auto policy if she purchased long-term care insurance. As a result of the model:

- The top decile of scored households had a sales rate of 68 percent higher than the overall average and 195 percent higher than the bottom decile. Two-thirds of all sales came from the top 50 percent. This meant that focusing attention on this group saved marketing dollars.

- Households that were sent the next-best product mailings had a sales rate 11 percent higher than those who got the regular "product of the month" mailing.

Using a Model to Predict Churn

Long distance and cell phone companies, credit card companies, banks, insurance companies, retailers, and scores of other businesses that provide regular services suffer from churn. Customers may switch to a different service provider because of a better price, quality of service, quality of customer care, equipment and technology, billing issues, or simply more effective marketing campaigns. The percentage of customers who churn in a particular time period is defined as the churn rate. In the United States recently, the churn rate in telecom was 2.9 percent per month, or 35 percent per year.

Modeling Using CHAID Analysis

In addition to regressions (discussed earlier in this chapter), modelers use CHAID, or chi-square automatic interaction detection. CHAID is a classification tree technique that displays the modeling results in an easy-to-interpret tree diagram going from top down instead of from the bottom up. SmartDrill in Ashland, Massachusetts (www.smartdrill.com), is an expert in this technique.

The segments in the tree diagram can be shown in a "gains chart." The gains chart shows how "deep" into a file one must go to select prospects that have the results you are looking for in terms of dollar value or response rate. Financial data or assumptions can also be incorporated into the predictive CHAID model results, to generate return on investment, mail cost savings, and so on.

When the outcome we are trying to predict has only two values such as mail responder versus non-responder, modelers can generate what is called a "nominal" CHAID model. CHAID is useful in picking the best prospects for a direct mail effort. And it may be useful to score the remainder of the file using a regression model, if we wish to identify good prospects beyond about the top 8 percent. Modelers can first generate a CHAID model and then follow this up with a regression model.

Figure 13.17 is a small, simplified example of an ordinal CHAID tree diagram provided by SmartDrill. The diagram begins at the top with a box representing the entire modeling sample of 81,040 households to which a consumer product was marketed via direct mail. Also included in this first box is the average profit per household generated by the initial mailing (75 cents). Household size is identified by CHAID as the best predictor around which to begin segmenting the prospect market.

We can see that a household size of two to four persons returns an average profit of $1.64, which is twice the profit generated by a one-person household, and nearly seven times the profit generated by a five-to-six-person household. CHAID then shows us that if a two-to-four-person household has a bank card, the average profit jumps to $3.58. If it does not have a bank card, the average profit return is only $1.29. However, among this non-bank-card group, if the head of household's occupation is white collar, profitability rises to $2.25.

This figure is supplemented by a gains chart (Figure 13.18) that shows the gains from each of the segments identified on the CHAID diagram.

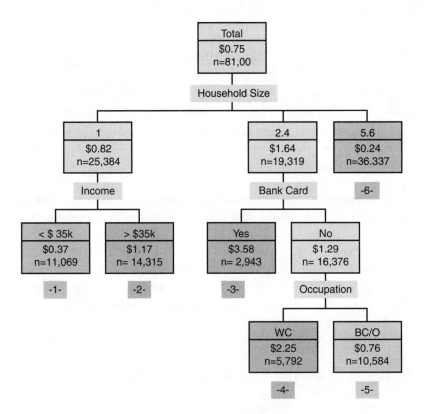

Figure 13.17 CHAID Diagram

1 Segment ID	2 Segment Count	3 Percent of Total	4 Average $ Value	5 Segment Index	6 Cum. Count	7 Cum. Percent	8 Cum. $ Value	9 Cum. Index
3	2,943	3.6	$3.58	476	2,943	3.6	$3.58	476
4	5,792	7.1	$2.25	298	8,735	10.8	$2.70	358
2	14,315	17.7	$1.17	155	23,050	28.4	$1.75	232
5	10,584	13.1	$0.76	101	33,634	41.5	$1.44	191
1	11,069	13.7	$0.37	49	44,703	55.2	$1.17	156
6	36,337	44.8	$0.24	31	81,040	100	$0.75	100

Figure 13.18 Gains Chart from CHAID

The fourth column in the figure shows the average profit per household for each segment. The fifth column represents this profit number as a relative index, with the average for the entire modeling sample set at 100. Thus the best segment has an index of 476, which means that it performs at a profit level of 4.76 times the average for the entire modeling sample and more than 15 times the profitability of the worst segment.

Columns six through nine are cumulative representations of the data from columns two through five: cumulative household count, percent of modeling sample, average profit per household, and profit index. Among other things, the gains chart shows us that the best three segments (segments 3, 4, and 2) represent 28.4 percent of the total sample, have an average profit of $1.75 per household, and are therefore 2.32 times as profitable as the average sample household.

The gains chart is a handy tool for seeing what levels of expected profitability would result from going increasingly deeper into a prospect file. This is useful for planning direct marketing campaigns, since it helps determine mailing quantities, and provides information for calculating return on investment.

CHAID helps to create market segments. The tree diagram predicts the performance of each segment. This helps advertising agency personnel and media planners visualize and define market segments. CHAID model algorithms are used to score a master database. As with regressions, new records added to a file can be scored quickly once the basic scoring algorithm is established.

Descriptive Modeling or Profiling

Even if predictive modeling does not work for you, you should have a profile done of your customer base. This is accomplished by descriptive modeling. It is amazing to note how many companies really know very little about their consumer customers. Any modeler can create useful profiles such as the one shown in Figure 13.19.

The figure shows the household income of the purchasers of the company's products. The company has a much higher percentage of the upper income consumers than the national average.

Clickstream Analytics

Clickstream, or Web, analytics is the science of analyzing what customers do when they read your e-mails or come to your Web site. The goal is to

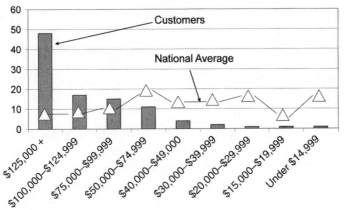

Figure 13.19 Household Income of Customers Compared to the National Average

make e-mails and Web sites more user-friendly and encourage more opens, clicks, and conversions. It requires specialized software. It also requires analysts who review the data and come up with methods for using the results to improve the e-mails and Web sites. Web analytics is so specialized that the process should probably be outsourced. It is not simple, easy, or cheap to do. Done right, however, it can have a tremendous return on investment.

How Are E-mails Tracked?

Little invisible Web beacons are embedded in outgoing HTML e-mails. These beacons are used to track what happens to the e-mail after it arrives. Whenever the user opens the e-mail, the beacon sends a packet back to the server that originally sent the e-mail. This lets the server know that the e-mail has been opened. Similar beacons are embedded in all links within the e-mail. As a result, the organization running the server is informed of all the links the subscriber clicks on.

Using Clickstream Data

Clickstream data is the history of the links a consumer clicked on when she read your e-mail or looked at your Web site. Storing clickstream data concerns privacy watchdogs, especially since some companies have begun selling users' clickstream data as a way to earn extra revenue.

Several companies purchase this data, typically for about $0.40 per month per user. While this practice may not directly identify individual users, it is often possible to indirectly identify them. Most consumers are unaware of this practice and its potential for compromising their privacy. Reputable companies that use major outsourced e-mail agencies highly rated by Forrester Research never sell user clickstream data to others. They advertise that fact on their Web site and in their e-mails. I do not recommend selling clickstream data.

Internal analysis of clickstream data, however, has become important to profitable e-commerce. It tells you how your e-mails and Web sites are being received by users. It also tells you something about subscriber behavior. You can use clickstream data to create or enhance subscriber profiles. For instance, you could use clickstream analysis to predict whether a particular subscriber is likely to make a purchase from your site. You can also use clickstream analysis to improve subscriber satisfaction with your e-mails and your company.

Using Clickstream Analysis

Once it is possible to capture what your subscribers are doing when they receive your e-mails, you can use the information to understand how your e-mails are being received. One of the best ways to understand the data is to create dashboards that summarize the subscriber's activity in ways that enable you to make changes to improve your e-mails.

Figure 13.20 is a clickstream analysis showing the results of an e-mail campaign that featured five product categories: children's, women's, kitchen, stationery, and bargains. The marketer sent 1.8 million e-mails that produced $373,949 in sales. The figure compares this e-mail to the 12-month average of e-mails sent by the company. The graphs show which site sections were most visited by subscribers, time on site, new visits, abandoned cart percentages, revenue, and average sales.

Your ESP can help you set up your own dashboard. The important part of the analysis is using the data to improve e-mails in the future. This is where many e-mail marketers fail today. They are so busy creating and sending new e-mails that they don't take the time to see what was good or bad about the current e-mails so that they can make their new ones better. In this example, the cart abandonment rate in women's clothing is particularly striking. If the abandonment rate could be brought down from 31 percent to 21 percent, for example, total sales

Clickstream Analysis of July 13 Campaign

	Delivered 1,874,223	Opens 356,102			8,582 Clicks		24,682 Conversions		12,217
Click Category	Subscriber Visits	Avg Pages Visited	Time on Site	Unique Clicks % New Visits	Avg Cart Items	Avg Abandon	Items Checkout	Average Item Price	Total Revenue
Childern's	969	1.97	1.48	76.47%	1.2	48.0%	605	$37.44	$22,638
Women's	1,218	2.68	1.52	65.91%	2.2	31.0%	1,849	$108.33	$200,294
Kitchen	787	2.50	2.48	63.63%	2.4	11.0%	1,681	$18.01	$30,275
Stationery	484	2.24	2.22	71.43%	1.3	18.0%	516	$38.33	$19,776
Bargains	1,997	3.11	3.22	44.87%	2.8	12.0%	4,921	$18.32	$90,146
Elsewhere	3,127	1.88	2.01	44.67%	0.9	6.0%	2,645	$4.09	$10,820
Total/Avg	8,582	2.88	2.59	73.40%	2.16	25.2%	12,217	$30.61	$373,949
Annual		1.97	2.01	44.60%	1.77	21.74%		$36.40	
% Change	45.99%	28.66%		64.57%	22.03%	15.92%		-15.91%	

This Campaign vs 12 Month Average

(Categories: Item Price, Abandonment, Average Cart, Time on Site, Page Visited, %New Visits; axis: -20.00%, 0.00%, 20.00%, 40.00%, 60.00%, 80.00%)

Visits This Campaign

(Categories: Elsewhere, Bargains, Stationery, Kitchen, womens, Childrens; axis: 500, 1,000, 1,500, 2,000, 2,500, 3,000, 3,500)

Figure 13.20 Illustrative Clickstream Analysis Dashboard

might go up significantly. Why were so many carts abandoned, and what could the marketer have done about it? Developing and studying such a dashboard is very important to success in e-mail marketing.

Key Performance Indicators

To create a useful dashboard, begin by identifying the key performance indicators (KPIs) that are important to your business. Then add the reports that contain those KPIs to your dashboard. Which are the most useful e-mail KPIs? Here are several from different industries:

- E-mails sent and delivered
- Percentage of delivered e-mails that are opened
- Clicks compared to other campaigns
- Percentage of opens that are clicked
- Churn rate (percentage of unsubscribes or undeliverables)
- Viral rate (e-mails sent to a friend)
- Opens and clicks by ISP domain name

  You may also include:

- Total sales by campaign, month, quarter, or segment
- Profit per delivered e-mail
- Sales per delivered e-mail
- Cost per delivered e-mail
- Average order value (AOV)
- Number of orders
- Conversion rate of opens or click-throughs
- Number of site visits
- Cost per visitor
- Number of leads by entry page
- Average page views
- Length of site visit by source

  If you are interested in generating leads for your sales force, you may have these KPIs:

- Number of leads (by product/client type)
- Number of downloads
- Site visits
- Google PageRank
- Cost per lead
- Conversion rate
- Membership, subscriber, or database growth

Using Clickstream Data to Improve E-mail Campaigns

Suppose we send a promotional e-mail to 1.5 million customers on Tuesdays and Fridays, which research has shown us to be our best days. Our e-mail program is outsourced to a large ESP highly rated by Forrester Research. The ESP has an excellent clickstream analytics staff. For example, the ESP receives reports from the Tuesday mailing on Wednesday. Staff members spend Wednesday afternoon analyzing the results, and their creative team and our creative team spend Thursday redoing the material on the home page based on what the clickstream analysis tells us.

The e-mail, diagrammed in Figure 13.21, has eight sections with links. A is a search box. B is a place to change your profile or preferences.

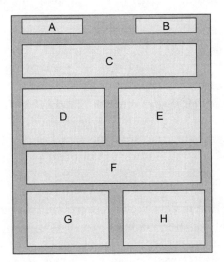

Figure 13.21 Diagrammed E-mail Sections

C is the main message, a welcome offer. D is a download offer, E is a discount offer, and F is a second main subject area. G is a product directory with links to many other areas, and H is viral information. Clicking on any of these sections leads readers to more information on the site, where there are additional links to click on. (A well-crafted e-mail has at least a dozen or more links. These complexities are why e-mail tracking is so specialized that it should be outsourced.)

Twenty-four hours after we send those 1.5 million e-mails out, we get a report on the results. We design our dashboard to provide us with information on what the subscribers did with the e-mails we sent. Figure 13.22 shows us how we might arrange the statistics.

At first, this figure might seem like a bunch of numbers that don't tell much of a story. Only 3,655 subscribers (0.7 percent of the openers) clicked as many as eight times on the links. But graphs can help show some productive actions we might take. Figure 13.23 shows the first clicks, and Figure 13.24 shows the second clicks.

What do we learn from these two graphs? Subscribers go first to the discount offer (section E), which is in the middle of the page on the right. After that, most people appear to go to the search box to find something else, rather than going to the product directory (G) or to another area in the e-mail. We can reasonably conclude they are looking for something that is not on the home page.

What are they are looking for? Our Web analytics can tell us what subscribers put into the search box. If we find that most people are searching for a similar product, that product should be featured in the next e-mail—and we should revise the product directory to include that product, since it clearly isn't there. Besides revising the directory, where in the e-mail should we feature this missing product? What should we displace?

The graphs also tell us that the download offer (D) isn't a winner. It occupies valuable space to the left of the discount offer, our most popular click. We are wasting that space on something of lesser interest to our subscribers. Let's find out what most people are searching for and feature that in space D.

If you can get your ESP to give you dashboard charts like these, you are home free. Get the data, figure out what it tells you, and take the actions suggested. Create profitable e-mail marketing. If you do this correctly, you can correct 90 percent of what can be fixed using this type of analysis. Don't waste money by trying to fix the remaining 10 percent.

April 15 Promotion Sent Delivered Title	1,502,116 1,437,223 No. Clicks	Opens Percent Total Clicks	501,223 34.9% First Click	Unique Clicks Percent Second Click	335,819 67.0% Third Click	Fourth Click	Unsubs undels Fifth Click	9,823 55,070 Sixth Click	Seventh Click	Eighth Click
A Search Box	291,219	210,004	35,700	27,801	6,300	4,200	3,360	1,680	1,260	420
B Registration	428,662	72,561	12,335	1,887	2,177	1,451	1,161	580	435	145
C Welcome Offer	191,113	310,110	52,719	11,730	9,303	6,202	4,962	2,481	1,861	620
D Download Offer	415,552	85,671	14,564	3,038	2,570	1,713	1,371	685	514	171
E Discount Offer	82,222	419,001	71,230	14,858	12,570	8,380	6,704	3,352	2,514	838
F Second Product	290,884	210,339	35,758	15,414	6,310	4,207	3,365	1,683	1,262	421
G Product Directory	191,337	309,886	52,681	21,977	9,297	6,198	4,958	2,479	1,859	620
H Viral Invitation	291,338	209,885	35,680	12,900	6,297	4,198	3,358	1,679	1,259	420
Total			310,667	109,605	54,824	36,549	29,239	14,620	10,965	3,655

Figure 13.22 Clicks on E-mail Locations

337

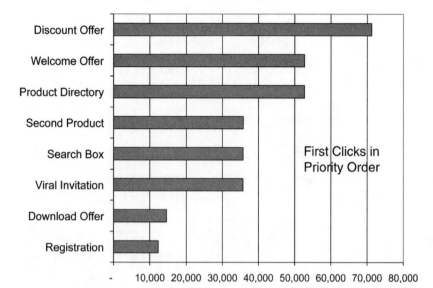

Figure 13.23 First Clicks by Priority

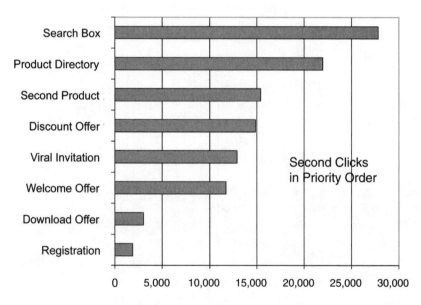

Figure 13.24 Second Clicks by Priority Order

Should You Outsource Your Modeling?

If you already have an experienced modeler on your staff who does good work and likes it, hang onto her. Good modelers are hard to find. If, however, you do not have such a person, you should not necessarily rush out to recruit one. There are many companies that will do modeling for you for a reasonable price (from $5,000 to $25,000). In addition some list providers such as Abacus or KnowledgeBase Marketing may include a custom model in the cost of the names that you purchase, so the models are essentially free. In general, I favor outsourcing for two reasons:

- Outsourcing is usually less expensive in the long run.
- You will learn what is state-of-the-art in a rapidly changing field.

Few mailers can keep an in-house modeler busy all the time, whereas outsourced modelers can be developing models for dozens of clients at once. In-house modelers come to you with the skills they have learned. They will not learn as many new things working only for you as they would if they worked at a service bureau with 20 different clients.

Take-Away Thoughts

- Analytics helps you to predict which recipients of your direct mail will buy your products, and which are not likely to buy. At $500 per thousand pieces, analytics can save you a lot of money.
- Analytics is not as useful for e-mail marketing. The cost of appending data and the modeling often results in a loss, since the cost of mailing is only $6 per thousand.
- Predictive models are based on previous promotions. You add demographic data (age, income, value of home, etc.) to a sample of your file and determine the differences between responders and non-responders.
- Predictive modeling uses multiple regressions. It results in an algorithm—a mathematical formula that can be used to "score" any direct mailing file that has demographics appended, and predict, before you mail, which ones are going to respond.

- Modeling does not always work. Sometimes what makes people buy is not based on demographics.

- Analytics can be used to reduce unsubscribes. If you have done LTV and know the value of your subscribers, you can calculate how much analytics would save you by not mailing unwanted material to some subscribers.

- Very few e-mail marketers are doing any predictive modeling today, with good reason.

- Direct mail gets higher response rates than e-mail partly because the shelf life of a direct mail piece or catalog can be weeks or months. An e-mail's shelf life is one day or less.

- Modeling can be useful for cross-sales—determining what other products your customers might buy.

- Next-best product analytics and churn predictive analytics can be very profitable.

- CHAID is very useful for dividing your database into segments containing people with different interests and response rates.

- Descriptive analytics is useful for advertising campaigns, but seldom useful for direct mail.

- Clickstream data analysis can be very useful in planning the layout of a Web site or an e-mail.

- Key performance indicators (KPIs) can help you determine the relative success of e-mail programs.

A quiz on this chapter and all figures can be found at www.dbmarket ing.com/STM4. Those taking all the quizzes can receive a Successful Completion Certificate from the Database Marketing Institute which can be used in their résumé.

14

Testing and Control Groups

Almost any question can be answered, cheaply, quickly, and, finally, by a test campaign. And that's the way to answer them—not by arguments around a table. Go to the court of last resort—the buyers of your product.

— CLAUDE HOPKINS
Scientific Advertising, 1923

The Holy Grail of direct marketing is the single-variable test. You want only one thing to change in each test. If you're going to test price, then you test two packages that are the same in all respects except for price. ... The goal is to make sure that when something wins or loses on a package or panel, you know the cause of the difference so you can repeat it if it wins.

— DON NICHOLAS in *2,239 Tested Secrets for Direct Marketing Success*
(Hatch and Jackson, 1998)

Testing is the unwanted stepchild in both direct mail and e-mail marketing. Everyone says that testing is essential, but most marketers postpone the tests until they are not so busy and when they are not under pressure to make this quarter's revenue goals. Let's face it. Testing takes time away from getting out tomorrow's e-mail or next week's direct mail campaign. It requires setting up control groups that get something different from what everyone else gets. If your control group does worse than your main mailing, you will have lost money that you needed for this quarter's revenue. If it does better, someone will say, "You blockhead! Why didn't you send this great piece to everyone?"

E-mail marketing makes testing very simple and accurate; and the results come back in 24 hours. Direct mail tests often take weeks before the results come in. Direct mail tests are usually more expensive, because you have to arrange to print different copy for your test group. With e-mail, different copy (such as subject lines) is very easy and inexpensive to create. Yet not much testing is done by either group.

E-mail testing is usually short run—which subject line gets the most opens. Direct mail testing is usually longer run—which piece sells the most products.

Why Testing Is Important

The market is constantly changing. What worked last year does not work as well this year and may not work at all next year. Capital One pioneered the "teaser rate" for credit cards. It was the first to make an introductory offer of a 3.9 percent annual percentage rate to get people to switch to its credit cards. It was wildly successful. Capital One card memberships and profits grew at a phenomenal rate. Of course, after a few months, the teaser rate expired. The card interest rates for each new member went up to 18.9 percent. The company lost some customers, but kept most of them. Soon, everyone was offering teaser rates. In a couple of years, the idea lost its luster. People were no longer fooled. Capital One, again ahead of the market, shifted to offering a firm 9.9 percent permanent rate, while the rest of the world was still offering teasers.

The object of testing is to learn how well you are doing so you can modify your marketing strategy. The goal is to constantly get better and better at what you are doing.

Why Management Resists Testing

You have 400,000 customers to whom you can make an offer. You are pretty sure of what that offer should be and which customers should get the offer. But you want to test your theory before you blow your whole budget on a hunch. You want to send two different offers of 25,000 each, and then roll out the best offer to the remaining 350,000. Management will resist the idea. "Our goal is to increase sales this quarter. Your tests will delay the results until next quarter. Forget the test. Take your best offer, and roll it out. You can test later."

It might seem best not to argue with your managers. But postponing testing could cost you your job. Without tests, you cannot learn anything. If you cannot learn, you cannot improve, while your competition may be learning a great deal. There is a danger in not testing. If you are not really on top of things, you may not be around next year after company profits take a nose dive and management looks around for something to cut.

Fortunately, database marketing is in a much better position to test and prove its contribution to profits than advertising, customer relations, corporate planning, R&D, and most other staff functions. We just have to go about it in an organized way.

Questions before You Start to Test

Before running any test, make certain that you know how you will use the results to develop a more effective program. Too many tests are "nice to have" information, but the information is not directly applicable to the next direct mail or e-mail. There are some basic things to do before you begin testing. Ask yourself these questions:

- If the test is successful, can we roll it out in future mailings? Can we generalize the results? Too often tests are conducted for small things that will not matter for future mailings such as color, size of lettering, or day of the week. Testing by RFM makes sense in direct mail. It makes little sense in e-mail marketing since you will probably send mail to everyone anyway.
- Who will listen to your results and run with them? Are you alone?
- How much will the test cost?

Marketing Objectives

The first step in any testing program is to determine what you are trying to accomplish. The goal of database marketing programs is usually to:

- Increase sales to existing customers
- Reduce attrition
- Gain new customers

Let's begin by devising a direct mail test for a department store. Let's assume that your department store has a house credit card which is tied in to a customer database. This house card permits you to capture data about purchases. You are planning a new offer to increase sales. The question is how much does the offer actually increase sales, and what is its effect on lifetime value?

To set up a test, you need two groups of customers: a test group (which gets the offer) and a control group (which does not get the offer). Without the control group, you will learn very little.

Assume that your department store has 400,000 customers who use the store credit card. The store has brought in a new line of high-fashion clothes for women. They are being promoted through print ads. You want to test the effectiveness of a direct mail offer to female customers. For the purpose of the test, you have decided to mail your offer to 20,000 women.

As a first step, you query your database to see how many women have credit cards in their name. There are 200,000. You must select two groups: a test group of 20,000 that will get the mailing and a control group of 20,000 that will not get the mailing. Control groups do not have to be the same size as test groups. They could be larger or smaller. They have to be big enough to provide valid results, and they have to be exactly the same type of people as those in the test group in demographics and purchase behavior. To create these two groups, you use a procedure called an Nth, described in Chapter 5.

Use an Nth to separate the 40,000 into two groups of 20,000: a test group and a control group. You will have to come up with an organized coding system so that you can remember who was in which group. You must keep other marketers in the organization from ruining the validity of your test by sending some other promotion to your test or control group during the test period.

Control Group Problems

A major retailer set up a special program designed for the top 10 percent of its customer base—about a half a million customers in all. To measure its success, it needed a small control group. Here is how the retailer went about constructing a control group, as described by the master marketer who created it:

> To prove that the money spent on the program was paying off, we had a control group. The company had never had one

before. It is difficult to measure a program unless you have a control group. When we set up the control group, we made sure that no store executives were in it, no board members, no employees, but we did not have a smart enough database to tell us who was the next door neighbor and best friend of the President's wife. She was in the control group. We got some angry calls from people who were in the control group. We didn't tell them that they were in a control group, of course. We just told them that there had been "a terrible mistake," and shifted them to the test group. These people were tagged as the "out of control group." Others called to complain about being left out who were not qualified for the program. We explained that you have to spend so much to qualify. Most said OK, but for those who were adamant we made exceptions."

Control Group Size

How big should a test or a control group be? Cost considerations say to make them small. Statistical accuracy says, make them big. As a good rule of thumb, each group must be big enough so that you can antici-pate a minimum of 500 responses from the promoted group.

$$\text{Control group size} = 500 \div \text{anticipated response rate}$$
$$= 500 \div .02 = 25{,}000$$

If you anticipate a 2 percent response rate, then your test group must have at least 25,000 people in it. If you have too few respondents, the test may give you invalid results for making predictions. The control group can be smaller than the test group, but still must be large enough for sta-tistical accuracy.

Control Group Substitutes

Sometimes it is not possible to set up a control group. One example is the Travelers Property and Casualty case study. In this exercise, a series of com-munications were sent to customers of participating independent agents. The control group was designed to answer this question: "Will these com-munications improve the retention rate of these customers?" The perfect control group would be 20 percent of each participating agent's customers who would not be sent messages. Independent agents, paying for the pro-grams with their own money, would not willingly participate in such a test.

Alison Bond, who ran the original Travelers program, used the retention rate of non-participating agent customers as the control group. Using the customer data from these agents, she was able to show that her program increased the retention rates by about 5 percent. A statistician might object to this control group. Perhaps the participating agents were more customer-friendly than the nonparticipating agents. If this were so, the higher retention rates were a result of the agent's effectiveness, not the communications. Control groups are almost always a compromise, but this does not mean that you can do without them.

When the groups are set up, a promotional offer is made to the test group. The control group is treated like everyone else but does not receive the promotion or other related communications. Members of the control group do, of course, get all other normal communications that customers get. In the example we are using here, members of both groups are on the database and use the store's credit card. Their purchase behavior is registered in the marketing database. A month later, the purchases of the two groups are compared. The effectiveness of the promotion is measured by the difference in purchases by the test group from purchases by the control group.

Let us assume that we are promoting a woman's suit that costs $150. Let us assume that 1,000 of the 20,000 test households (5 percent) took advantage of the offer, buying a net average of $150 worth of promoted items (the suit) plus $80 worth of non-promoted items during the month. The remainder of the test group (19,000 households) bought an average of $30 of non-promoted items during the same month. Let us assume that during the same month, the controls bought an average of $2 of the promoted items (the suit—even though it was not promoted to them) and $22 of non-promoted items during the same month. How successful was the test? (See Figure 14.1.)

Overall, sales resulting from the test increased by $320,000, and profits increased by $118,000. Consider these questions:

- Why did sales of non-promoted items increase in responding households? The answer is that when the customers went into the store to look at the suit, they saw other items and bought them too.

- Why did sales of non-promoted items to non-responding test households increase over sales to control households? Because some of the non-responding customers went to the store because of the promotion, did not buy the suit, but bought something else.

| Group | Number of Customers | Average Sale of: | | | Total Amount |
		Promoted Items	Non-Promoted Items	Combined Sales	
Responders	1,000	$150.00	$80.00	$230.00	$230,000
Non-responders	19,000	$0.00	$30.00	$30.00	$570,000
Controls	20,000	$2.00	$22.00	$24.00	$480,000
Total	40,000				$1,280,000
Total Sales to Test Group					$800,000
Total Sales to Control Group					$480,000
increased Sales Resulting from the Promotion					$320,000
Gross Profit from Sales @40%					$128,000
Cost of Promotion to Test Group @ $500/M					$10,000
Net Profit					$118,000
Return on Investment $118,000 / $10,000					11.8

Figure 14.1 Sales to Control and Test Groups in First Month After a Promotion

The return on investment from this promotion was $11.80 ($118,000 ÷ $10,000). Since the test generated a clear $118,000 profit over the cost of the promotion itself, the promotion can now be repeated with other customers with, presumably, equal success. So far, however, what we have done is straight direct marketing using a database. What follows is real database marketing.

In database marketing we consider the long-term effect on the customers of every customer contact. This promotion was a success in that it increased profits by more than the cost of the test. This is not the end of the impact on the customers, however. We must look at the results on the test group in the following months. After all, the test resulted in bringing many more than 1,000 women into the store: the 1,000 test respondents plus an unknown number of non-respondents. Many of these women might not otherwise have come into the store that month. How do we know that? Because most of the women in the control group stayed at home. As a result of this promotion, the women who did respond moved to higher RFM cells. They all became recent buyers, they probably became more frequent buyers, and their monetary scores probably advanced. A woman responder whose RFM cell was 423 before the promotion, could have become a 534 because of her purchase of the suit. The same type of thing probably happened to almost all of the 1000+ respondents. In addition, the lifetime value of the respondents probably went up as well. We can see this from their subsequent behavior.

In the following months, some of those in the test group who moved to higher RFM cells will probably visit the store again. Why? Because of increased recency, frequency, and monetary scores. See figure 14.2. These responders (and some of the others) have become recent buyers because of the promotion. Recent buyers (we remember from RFM principles) are the most likely customers to buy again soon. This is normal behavior. This subsequent behavior can also be measured:

Group Name	Number	Sales per Customer	Total Sales
Test-Resp	1,000	$30	$30,000
Test Non-resp	19,000	$21	$399,000
Controls	20,000	$20	$400,000
Total	40,000	$20.73	$829,000
Increased Sales from Last Month's Promotion			$29,000
Cost of Promotion (This Month)			$0

Figure 14.2 Sales to All Groups in Second Month after Promotion

Total sales this month are down. Why were sales to control groups only $400,000 during the second month? Who knows? This was a slower month, for reasons unrelated to the test. If the controls had not been followed, however, and only the test group had been measured, one could have concluded that the test promotion depressed sales in the following month, which, of course, was not true. The testing shows that even in a slow month, the test in the previous month helped overall sales in that month. Consider these questions:

- Why did the respondents buy more than the controls in the second month? They received no promotion. The reason: recency (and possibly frequency and monetary). They had moved to higher RFM cells. This is the long-term effect of any promotion and shows the difference between direct marketing and database marketing.

- Why did the non-respondents buy more than the controls in the second month? For the same reasons. Some of them had become recent buyers because of the promotion, even though they did not buy the suit. Database marketing works.

Control Group Failure

I worked with a large financial services company that was persuaded by its advertising agency to issue plastic "preferred member" cards to its customers who had used its services three times or more. The cards gave their holders check-cashing privileges and other benefits. There seemed to be a definite spike in sales from holders of the cards, so the company was happy with the results. A couple of years later, the marketing staff of the company was changed, and the new managers asked the direct agency to show them evidence that the results from the preferred member cards was worth the money spent on them. The agency came to our company for help, since we were maintaining the database. "We know that the cards are valuable, but how can we prove it?" they asked.

"By comparing the performance of the cardholders with the performance of your control group that did not get the cards," I explained.

"What is a control group?"

"It is those people who used the service three times or more, but were not issued cards to measure the performance of those who got the cards."

"There is no such group. We gave the cards to everyone who deserved them."

"Then you are out of luck. You can't prove that the cards have done any good."

The agency lost the account.

Let that be a lesson to you. Using test and control groups can mean the difference between keeping your job and losing it. You must have a control group every time you do testing, especially if it involves the expenditure of money.

Using Half-Life in Tests

One difficulty in testing is the length of time that it takes to learn the results of a direct market test. If you sent out a promotion, it may take many weeks before all the responses have come in. This is why half-life analysis is so useful in testing.

As soon as you launch any direct mail test, you should record how many responses have come in every day—both the number of responses, the quantity sold, and the amount of money received. Let's say that you send out a catalog. If you don't have a definite cutoff date, the catalog may result in sales coming in over a period of many months. Let's say that you get 2,000 orders from the catalog over a period of five months. If you have recorded your daily sales, you will find that there is one day on which the 1,000th response was received—exactly half of your total. That is your "half-life day." Typically, the half-life day comes within the first 30 days after any promotion. On your next promotion, you will find that the half-life occurs on approximately the same day. Sears Canada, for example, mails out 13 different catalogs every year. It has discovered that its half-life day is day 20. That is the day on which the company has received half of the dollars that it will eventually receive from each catalog. All it has to do is multiply the amount taken in by day 20 by two, and the company knows the results of the catalog—several months early.

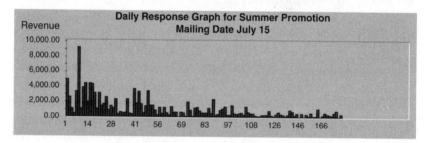

Figure 14.3 Daily Response of Typical Promotion

In this illustration of the response to a typical promotion, the days since the first response are plotted across the bottom. The revenue received is on the left. It took 197 days before the full revenue of $133,986.00 from the promotion was received from all purchasers.

The details are shown in Figure 14.4.

On the thirty-fifth day, in this example, you have taken in $67,000 that is exactly half of what you will receive from the entire catalog, after waiting some 197 days.

	Days	Revenue
Total	197	$133,986.00
Half-Life	35	$67,007.17
Third	15	$45,493.47
Quarter	12	$33,557.45

Figure 14.4 Details of the Results of the Summer Promotion

The beauty of half-life analysis is that you can conduct many more tests and learn the results of your tests much faster. If you are doing tests—and you must, if you are going to be successful at database marketing—you must learn to do half-life analysis. Free software available from The Database Marketing Institute (RFM for Windows) enables you to do half-life analysis (www.dbmarketing.com).

Outboard Motor Sales Test

A couple of advanced database marketers conducted a nationwide launch of a new outboard motor. In this launch, of the 250,000 selected for the first mailing, 20,000 were set aside as a control group. Members of this group received no mailing, but were tracked in their purchases. It was this group that permitted the marketers to learn the effectiveness of their entire program.

Once they began their rollout, the marketers, David Christensen and Stanton Lewin, did 32 mailings a year, setting aside 32 control groups to validate their results. They used their system not only to sell the new motors, but also parts and accessories. The result was that they learned that parts sold 24 percent more to the test groups than to the controls.

They mailed 2 million pieces a year for the next three years, using the controls to validate their results. Some boat dealers experienced an 8 percent response to the mailings. The average response rate was 2.83 percent.

Failure in Testing of Existing Bank Customers

Several years ago, I took out a home equity loan with the Chevy Chase Bank in Maryland. The program was widely advertised; and the rates were low. I used the loan to finance the building of a barn, a swimming pool, and an addition to my house.

Some time after I took out the loan, Chevy Chase sent me a preapproved invitation for a Master Card at low interest rates. I have received dozens of others over the years, which I routinely toss in the trash. I responded to Chevy Chase because I had formed a favorable opinion of the bank from the home equity experience. I canceled my American Express Card. American Express, by the way, did an excellent job of trying to keep me. It just couldn't accept the idea that anyone would voluntarily drop the card. I got three different telephone calls and more than four letters on the subject before they finally gave up.

A couple of years later, I noticed that my broker was handling Chevy Chase bonds. They were selling at about 40 percent of par because of the national savings and loan problem. I asked the broker to buy some for me, because I had such good feelings about the bank. In a couple of years the bonds came up to 104 percent of par value, besides paying a 13 percent rate of interest. I became a loyal Chevy Chase customer.

The point of this personal story is to illustrate the way in which customer lifetime value builds up based on the way that the customer is treated by the institution in more than the specific situation under review. Chevy Chase, if it calculated lifetime value at all, could see me as a cardholder, home equity customer, and bondholder, each one of which contributes to overall bank profits.

In fact, Chevy Chase was not doing much of a job in profiling its customer base. A very persistent Chevy Chase telemarketer called me at dinnertime one night telling me that "as a long-time cardholder with an excellent record" I was being awarded two months of free life insurance with no preconditions. After the two months, the policy would be charged to my credit card at the rate of $14.40 per month unless it was cancelled by me. I asked how much the policy paid, and was told $2,000—a ridiculously small amount of life insurance. The worst part of the call was that Chevy Chase knew that I had $300,000 worth of insurance for which I was paying about $180 per month. How did it know? Because I had to provide this information in my credit application for the home equity loan. I got off the phone angry with Chevy Chase for bothering me with a totally irrelevant offer. It saw me as a name on a list, not as the valuable customer that I thought I was. After a few months, I left Chevy Chase and have never gone back.

Most companies, like Chevy Chase, have data about their customers buried in their files somewhere. Digging that data out and putting it into their database to use in customer profiling and testing would be an inexpensive and profitable strategy to adopt before they ruin their customer base with worthless outbound telemarketing calls.

Summary of Direct Marketing Testing

To know if a marketing program is successful, you must test it properly. The steps are to:

- Determine the objectives of the marketing program and be sure that it will result in a positive return on investment.

- Test one thing at a time. Create a test group big enough so that there will be a minimum of 500 responders. You will need a control group of roughly the same minimum size.

- Develop a method to measure sales. This may be easy, or it may be the most difficult part of the whole effort.

- Carry out your marketing program with the test groups. Treat the control groups normally, except don't promote to them.

- Measure the incremental sales by comparing sales in the test groups with those in the control groups.

- Calculate the direct costs of your program.

- Figure the short-term net profitability of your program and the return on your investment.

- Figure the long-term net profitability of your program based on change in the lifetime value of your customers.

E-mail Marketing Testing

With e-mail testing things move much faster. We can test something on Monday and get most of our results by Wednesday. What can we test?

- The subject line
- Calls to action
- The offer
- The price
- The day of the week of the offer
- Personalization
- The arrangement of the home page

But what do we use as the proof of success? In direct mail the proof is, "Did they buy the product?" In e-mail we know much more, and we can look at many proofs:

- Opens
- Clicks
- Conversions
- Unsubscribes
- Cart abandonment

In a Marketing Sherpa survey of 623 e-mail marketers, 37 percent said that they never test. Most of the remaining 63 percent did some, but not extensive testing.

Use Your Best Previous Promotion as Your Control

Use your best newsletter as your newsletter control. Select your best welcome e-mail as a second control. Find your winning transaction message as a third control. In other words, for each type of campaign you send out, look for your best and try to beat it.

Define What Was Best about the Control E-mail

Was it opened? How many clicks did it get? Did it have a lower rate of unsubscribes or high conversions? Be sure you have a concrete definition of *best*.

Create Test Groups

Creating a test group isn't as easy as it sounds. The people in your test groups should be representative of your entire customer base—if you will use their responses as representing how everyone would respond to a similar newsletter or promotion. To define a test group, you need criteria, such as:

- Buyers versus non-buyers
- Length of time as subscribers
- Source of the subscriber
- Demographics (more about this later)

If you don't have any test groups, you can simply use an A/B split and send version A to half your e-mail file and version B to the other half. You'll need to keep track of which group got which version. This is a good way to begin and should give you valid results. It costs nothing to do this, since everyone gets an e-mail.

When you want to get more sophisticated, however, you will need test groups. Why? Suppose version B delivered a 4 percent conversion rate and version A delivered a 2 percent conversion rate. Version B is so much better that you will want to use that version from now on. But to test something else, you don't want to risk losing a lot of sales by restricting the number of people who get your best e-mail. You will want to test your new ideas on only a small portion of your database. Hence, use a small test group, and everyone else is your control.

How Many Things Can You Test in One E-mail Promotion?

The best test is the single-variable test. Test only one thing with each e-mail promotion. Some people make the mistake of testing many things. In the e-mail marketing business, we are all very busy. We may be sending out e-mails every day. We can build in lots of tests, but when do we have the leisure to study the test results to determine which was the best and what we should do now?

What Should You Test First?

The first thing to test is always the subject line. This line is all that most people see before they delete your e-mail. If it isn't good, most subscribers won't see anything else. No matter how well your subject line performed in the past, always test another version on a small test group. Your competition is looking at your e-mails, and it may be copying what you are doing. It may have worn out the words that once brought you such success. You want to keep one step ahead.

Do a Quick Subject Line Test

You have six possible subject lines. Which is the best? Let your readers tell you. Here's how. Pull together a random 10 percent of your file, dividing it into six equal segments. Try one subject line on each segment. Mail 'em. Wait six hours. Look at the open rates for each. Then send to the remaining 90 percent of your file using the winning subject line. This is a very quick way to win the subject line battle early.

What Are You Trying to Prove?

Before any test, write down a statement of what you're trying to prove or disprove with the test. For example: "Our hypothesis is that showing the product price above the fold will produce more conversions than the present system of showing the price only in the checkout process."

Also before the test, determine your decision metrics and the rollout plans. "If the new e-mail page arrangement increases conversions by at least 10 percent more than the control, we'll use it in the rollout." After the test, write down your numeric results, your interpretation of their meaning, and your decisions as to what the next steps will be.

Keep a test notebook. It becomes your marketing department's shared institutional memory. It is worth keeping it electronically.

Separate Significant Results from the Noise

All tests have some element of random statistical noise. To find out what it is, randomly split a mailing list of 10,000 people into two cells of 5,000 people each, and on the same day mail each cell exactly the same e-mail. It is almost certain that one cell by chance alone will have a higher open, click, or conversion rate. Let's say that the variation in opens is 15, that is one file gets 15 more opens than the other file. Statistically, this difference amounts to 0.3 percent. Once you know this, you have established the level of statistical noise. To use this knowledge in future tests, you might use a rough rule of thumb: "A test needs to increase conversion or CTR by more than 1.5 times the level of statistical noise to be considered significant." Any difference of less than 4.5 percent shouldn't be taken as a significant difference (15 times 0.3 percent is 4.5 percent).

Assign Unique Mail Codes

To understand your tests, give each e-mail cell a unique mail code. Come up with a system, and record your system in your testing notebook. Enter the meaning of each code on a spreadsheet. Your spreadsheet should be available to your marketing team and preserved so you can go back and check your work. This is important when you try a similar test a year from now and want to see what you learned in the past.

Don't Expect Amazing Results

If you are doing a lot of tests (and you should), many tests will fail to prove anything significant. That's OK. Be patient and try again. Make sure your management understands that most tests don't produce surprising results. If you have been doing testing for some time, your current e-mail program has been improved by years of step-by-step adjustment, so each additional test may not be earth-shaking. The more successful your testing has been, the harder it becomes to move the needle.

For example, a hunting-products retailer tested the value of designing content for images. It tested an all-images design against one that contained images but whose main message was in the text. The retailer found that the second e-mail produced almost four times more revenue. Why? Because it worked well for subscribers who blocked images.

The Quality Paperback Book Club tested two different headlines in its e-mails. One was, "Click here to see ..." and the other was, "Get ..." "Get" had a 47 percent higher conversion rate. How could you possibly know that this would happen unless you tested it?

Testing Many Ideas at Once

The rule of testing only one thing at a time doesn't prevent you from trying many different concepts at once. Say that your creative staff has developed five different approaches to selling a product using e-mail. Don't have a committee meeting to choose the best one. Divide your subscriber list into five parts and test them all at once. The results may be surprising. One of them may prove to be much better than the other four—a result that your committee members would never have been able to guess. In fact they might have rejected the idea because it seemed unusual.

Set Aside Time to Study Every Test's Results

E-mail marketers who fail to study the results of previous tests are making a huge mistake. It takes time. It takes imagination. It takes persistence. We worked with the CMO of a large corporation that mailed 25 million e-mails a week. When we began, we asked what the first tests were to be. She answered, "Oh, we don't need to waste our time with tests. We already know what works." Since she was the client, we didn't argue with her. Later, however, we were able to introduce some tests that did about 15 percent better than the e-mail copy that she was using. She began to see the value of experimentation and testing.

The great thing about e-mail marketing is that test results can often be learned within 24 hours. With direct mail, the results may take weeks. Since good analytic software can give you results quickly, you have to build in time to study those results and apply them to the next few e-mails. Tomorrow you may be busy getting out the next e-mail. You don't have time to figure out what to do with the results of yesterday's test. That is a shame. You might have learned something valuable.

Testing Personalization

Suppose you want to test the effect of personalization by using the subscriber's name in the message's salutation. In one case study, the client had been using a straight message with no salutation or per-sonalization. As a test, it began with "Dear Customer." Just that little change provided a 4.1 percent lift in the click rate over the previous version.

Since that little change worked so well, the client decided to dig up the first names of many subscribers and test, "Dear [Name]" with a sim-ilar offer. However, the entire subscriber list had gotten used to the "Dear Customer" salutation. The offer had to be changed slightly. No matter. With a similar offer, the personalized salutation increased the click rate by 13.0 percent over the original version. This case study shows the importance of constant testing.

Fixing Bad Names

Many marketers are unwilling to use subscriber's names in their e-mails because they have learned from experience that some of the name data is bad. "Dear G7", or "Dear M—G". They do not want to look foolish, so they do not use names at all. What a mistake! There are service bureaus that can correct your names in a couple of days. I did this work for a client a few years ago. I took his file of 1,200,000 names and matched it against a perfect first name file that I had available from a previous job. On the first run, I matched about 80 percent of the client's names with valid names. I marked the good and bad names with a code. From then on, the client was able to use the good names in their mailing, and use Dear Customer for the rest. For $300 they had a file that yielded them about $4,000 more on each mailing.

Testing the Offer

EVO Gear tested an identical offer of Wake Packages: one version with $50 off and the other with 15 percent off. Pricewise, the offers were almost identical. However, the $50 off e-mail generated 170 percent more revenue and a 72 percent higher conversion rate. Conclusion: many people still don't understand percentages. Everyone understands dollars.

The Click-to-Open Rate

In testing, we have to know what we are using as a measurement. There are three standard measurements: opens, clicks, and conversions. There is another way of using these numbers that can give you positive results, suggested by e-mail expert Jeanne Jennings[1] of JeanneJennings.com: the click-to-open rate (CTO). The CTO can be compiled by dividing the unique number of clicks by the unique number of opens. Figure 14.5 offers an example.

	Control Group	Test Group
Number Delivered	1,000,000	1,000,000
Unique Opens	300,000	250,000
Unique Clicks	80,000	80,000
CTR %	8%	8%
CTO %	26.70%	32%

Figure 14.5 CTR versus CTO[1]

In the figure the click-through rate (CTR) is identical for the control group and the test group, but the CTO rate of the test group is better because an equal number of clicks was produced from a smaller number of opens. Opens are nice, but clicks are better.

Mistakes You May Make in Testing

To run a successful test, avoid the following mistakes.

---

[1] Jeanne Jennings, "Dear John: Tips for Testing Personalized E-Mail Salutations," *The ClickZ Network* (February 13, 2006), http://www.clickz.com/showPage.html?page=3584001.

Mistake 1: Making Too Many Changes at Once

When you change several items in one version of an e-mail and test it against your control, you won't learn much. Suppose that in the two versions the layout, promotions, copy, and even products are completely different. Any one change might have helped or hurt responses, but by putting them all together, you can't tell what was doing what. One change might have helped opens by 10 percent, but another change in the same e-mail might have reduced clicks by 10 percent. Rule: test only one element at a time.

Mistake 2: Looking Only at Conversions

There is a logical sequence for e-mail readers: They are attracted by the subject, so they open the message. They like the way the salutation greets them when they open. The copy is interesting, and the offer stimulates them. They click on a couple of links and finally order a product. At any point, your e-mail can fail: bad subject, bad salutation, bad offer, weak link, poor products or pricing, or confusing order form. Which of these things was responsible for the low conversion rate? You will never know if you look at the conversion rate by itself.

Test each part separately. First, select a subject line that works better than others. Then get your best salutation. Now you are ready to try different versions of the copy. You also need to test pricing and then your order form. We never said testing was easy, particularly if you don't test elements separately.

Mistake 3: Offering Too Many Choices

There is an old saying in the direct mail business: "Choice kills response." Time after time, direct mail marketers have tested a direct mail piece that offers readers two or more choices against a mail piece that offers only one possible answer: take it or leave it. The one choice always beats more choices. For example, a company selling low-cost tours leading to the sale of a timeshare tried two approaches: "Only $69 for a family vacation weekend in Fort Lauderdale, Florida. Chose any of the following six weekends, and the vacation is yours." And, "We have only one available family weekend for $69 left in Fort Lauderdale, Florida: March 12–14. Call right away." The second message always beat the first by a large margin.

Just because you are doing e-mail marketing, don't assume that you can't learn from the direct mail folks. There are a lot of fundamental truths about marketing that have already been learned. Choice kills response is a fundamental truth. Don't make the mistake of giving readers a choice.

Mistake 4: Not Knowing the Territory

There is a wonderful song in *The Music Man*: "Whaddaya talk, whaddaya talk? ... You gotta know the territory." In e-mail marketing, you will get better results if you know whom you are sending your e-mails to. Are they affluent seniors or college students? Are they married women or single men? Do they live in big cities or way out in the country? Are they previous buyers or registrants who have never bought anything?

The new elements you test may attract some people but alienate others. If you know nothing about your audience (i.e., you have only the e-mail address and not the name or demographics), you should stick with big, significant changes in your testing, such as a dramatic ease of navigation or a promotion that is of general interest to all.

If you *do* know the territory, then you can show different content to different segments of the market that are reading your e-mails. Run different tests for each segment. You'll get a cleaner answer on your tests if the population who sees the test is consistent.

Mistake 5: Testing by Committee

The worst group to create an e-mail program is a committee representing different departments in your company. Some people like one idea, and others like something else. You compromise on an e-mail that no one likes very much but has the fewest negatives. Good ideas are edited out of the process during meetings as being bad ideas before they can be tested. The result is a test that is really an A/A test—there may be a little tweak here or there, but the two versions are really the same.

A better approach is to let your subscribers kill bad ideas and reward good ones. Let your creative people loose to try new ideas. Are you in business to create peace in a committee or to build customer loyalty and sales? After all, it's only an e-mail. Your whole company's reputation doesn't hang on every word. Cut loose. Try something new. Use what you learn.

Mistake 6: Using Personalization in the Subject Line

Since personalization in the body of the e-mail improves clicks and conversions, why not use it in the subject line? At one time that was a good idea, but spammers have ruined it. By now millions of people have received e-mails from unknown people who seem to know the receiver's first and last name. The spammers picked them up from a phishing expedition. If you use the subscriber's name in the subject line, you may be deleted as spam.

Keep a Log of Your Mailing Statistics

Tests have to be compared with the results of other tests in order for you to know whether you are doing better or worse. Is an open rate of 16 percent good or bad? It is better than an overall industry average of 13 percent, but what if your e-mails last year had an open rate of 28 percent? You need to know this.

Set up a systematic log of all e-mail statistics that are posted after every e-mail that is sent out, organized by type of e-mail. It might look something like Figure 14.6.

Figure 14.6 is the result of a single mailing. It could be created a few days after the actual mailing. Remember, an e-mail's shelf life is usually less than a week. In this example, we compare two different subject lines. Everything else in the two e-mails should be exactly the same if the test is to be valid. Based on this test, you can determine that subject line B is better than subject line A.

Next we could try two different salutations using subject line B. One might be, "Dear Valued Customer," and the other might be, "Dear [Name]." We can bet that "Dear]Name]" will win, but we can't predict by how much. If "Dear [Name]" wins, then you can test two different offers in the body of the e-mail using the winning subject line and salutation.

The examples make the process seem simple, but it isn't simple. If you have only 2.3 million subscribers, you can't keep sending them the same e-mail advertising the same cocktail dress if you want to remain relevant. Each e-mail will have to be different. The difference will affect your open, click, and conversion rates. This doesn't mean that you will never learn anything lasting. You will learn how to create a productive subject line. In time, you will perfect your salutation. Finally you will learn the best way to sell your products.

Type of E-mail	Promotion	Promotion	
Name	Cocktail Dress/A	Cocktail Dress/B	
Date	Jun 3 2009	Jun 3 2009	
Item Tested	Subject Line	Subject Line	
Mailed	1,172,839	1,172,839	
Delivered	1,129,444	1,138,827	
Del %	96.3%	97.10%	Percent of Mailed
Opened	242,830	268,763	
Open %	21.50%	23.60%	Percent of Delivered
Unique Clicks	44,681	54,559	
CTR	18.40%	20.30%	Percent of Opens
COTR	18.4%	20.3%	Clicks/Opens
Conversions	1,385	1,582	
Conversion Rate	3.1%	2.9%	Percent of Clicks
Total Sales	$169,551	$190,498	
$ per Delivered	$0.15	$0.17	
Average Order	$122.41	$120.40	
Mailing Cost	$10,555.55	$10,555.55	
Cost per Open	$0.043	$0.039	
Cost per Click	$0.236	$0.193	
Cost per Sale	$7.621	$6.671	
Conv. %	3.30%	4.10%	Conv as % of Delivered
Unsub %	1.20%	1.10%	As % of Mailed
Undel %	2.50%	1.80%	As % of Mailed
New Viral Names	4,877	6,120	
Viral %	0.43%	0.54%	As % of Delivered

Figure 14.6 E-mail Statistic Log

Figure 14.6 shows why we say that every single e-mail you send should be a test. Because you can test only one thing with each e-mail, you really need a lot of tests to become an e-mail marketing expert.

Does it seem as if recording each test's results is a lot of work? It is, but not necessarily for you. If you have your e-mail delivery outsourced (and we highly recommend that you do), you can ask your e-mail service provider (ESP) to prepare this chart for you automatically for every e-mail you send. This way you can concentrate on the marketing aspect of your e-mail program and leave the drudgery to your ESP.

Testing by Analyzing the Audience

The testing we have been discussing has been about the effect of our e-mails on an audience. We haven't defined the audience, other than to say that it comprises opt-in registrants. E-mail analysis can be quite sophisticated. It is much more sophisticated than what direct mail marketers can do because we know so much more. We know that our e-mails have been received, opened, clicked on, and purchased from. In direct mail we only know if the recipients bought something.

However, direct mail marketers have become very sophisticated in their audience analysis. E-mailers can do the same thing. In general, though, e-mail marketers haven't done much audience analysis. They are so excited by the instant results they get from the e-mail analysis that they haven't bothered to take the next step. Many of them know nothing all about their audience other than e-mail addresses.

However, a rich harvest can come from taking that next step and appending demographics. We can break our audience into segments based on a number of factors:

- Type and value of products purchased
- Recency, frequency, and monetary of purchase (RFM)
- Demographics, including:
  - Age, gender, income, wealth, marital status, children
  - Housing type, value, own versus rent, length of residence
  - Occupation, ethnicity, lifestyle

For e-mail tests, therefore, you must assign segment codes to your subscriber lists and study the test results by segment. (For more on segmentation, see Chapter 10.)

If you want to test using demographic data, start with people who have provided you with their home address, either because they have bought something or because you included the address field in your e-mail registration form. Let's say that you test 120,000 consumers with appended data, and the data cost you $6,000. You are trying to sell life insurance to a group of auto insurance customers. Your goal is to get the e-mail readers to fill out a life insurance application. Figure 14.7 illustrates the type of results you might get from an identical e-mail sent to everyone on your list broken down by age range:

Age	Result of an Insurance Mailing to 118,065 Subscribers							
Range	Delivered	Opened	Clicked	Applied	Open %	Click%	Appl %	Success
Under 20	3,305	264	58	5	8%	22%	9%	0.16%
21–40	24,331	4,136	745	171	17%	18%	23%	0.70%
41–55	31,882	11,478	3,214	996	36%	28%	31%	3.12%
56–65	28,774	6,330	2,785	1,114	22%	44%	40%	3.87%
66+	29,773	8,634	3,195	1,757	29%	37%	55%	5.90%
Total	118,065	30,843	9,996	4,044	26%	32%	40%	3.43%

Figure 14.7 E-mail Results by Age Range

The figure shows us that your message resonated with subscribers ages 66 years or older. You aren't doing well with those under 41. With direct mail, we might conclude that mailing to those under 41 was a waste of money. But with e-mail marketing, we can come to a different conclusion. We keep the message for those 66 and older, but we change our message for the under–41 crowd and perhaps for those 41 to 65. We have a control. We want to beat a success rate of 5.9 percent.

We aren't done yet. Let's look at exactly the same mailing to the same people by income (see Figure 14.8). We don't have to mail to them again. All we have to do is compile the statistics in a different way.

Income	Result of an Insurance Mailing to 118,065 Subscribers							
Range	Delivered	Opened	Clicked	Applied	Open %	Click%	Appl %	Success
Under $20 K	35,664	9,629	2,359	873	27.0%	25%	37%	2.45%
$21K-$40K	35,663	8,238	2,065	558	23.1%	25%	27%	1.56%
$41K-$75K	20,859	5,006	1,652	661	24.0%	33%	40%	3.17%
$76K-$125K	16,774	6,877	3,439	1,685	41.0%	50%	49%	10.05%
$126K+	9,105	1,093	481	269	12.0%	44%	56%	2.96%
Total	118,065	30,843	9,996	4,044	26.1%	32%	40%	3.43%

Figure 14.8 E-mail Results by Household Income

From this we can see that the e-mail appealed mainly to people whose income was $76,000 to $125,000. We have a winner here. For other income ranges, perhaps we should change the offer or the e-mail content in some way to improve the success rate. We have an e-mail that appeals to people over 66 whose income is from $76,000 to $125,000.

And we're still not through. We could look at the data by gender; women and men have very different reactions to life insurance offers. We could look at people by section of the country or length of residence, and we would get still another picture. People who have lived at a residence for a short time are much more likely to respond to such an offer than people who have lived a long time in their homes. There may be six or more ways to break the audience down based on this one mailing. You will learn something from each analysis, but you had to do only one mailing.

Testing by demographics for certain kinds of products and services can be very powerful. Once we know how to write winning subject lines, salutations, and e-mail copy, we can get more deeply into audience analysis testing—a process that can be highly profitable.

Take-Away Thoughts

- Everyone agrees that testing is essential, but few people do it.

- Use half-life in direct mail testing.

- Consider both the short-term and long-term effect of everything that you do.

- The formula for a control group size is Control group size= 500÷anticipated response rate.

- In e-mail testing, the results come back in 24 hours. You can test the subject line, calls to action, the offer, the price, and the day of the week. You can also personalize or the arrangement of the home page.

- Use your best previous promotion as your control.

- Define what was best about the control e-mail: Was it opens? Clicks? The lower rate of unsubscribes or the high conversions? Be sure you have a concrete definition of best.

- The best test is the single-variable test. Test only one thing with each e-mail promotion.

- Start with a quick subject line test. Create a random 10 percent of your file, dividing it into six equal segments. Try one subject line on each segment. Mail the test. Tomorrow you will know which was best. Use that.

- Before any test, write down a statement of what you're trying to prove or disprove by the test.

- Separate significant results from the noise.

- If you are doing a lot of tests (and you should), many tests will fail to prove anything significant.

- Set aside time to study every test's results. One of e-mail marketers' great sins is the failure to study the results of previous tests.

- Mistakes you can make in testing:

  - Too many changes at once.

  - Looking only at conversions. Look at opens and what customers click on.

  - Testing by committee rather than by the customers.

- Keep a log of your mailing statistics. Tests have to be compared with the results of other tests to know whether you are doing better or worse.

- Test by the demographics or behavior of your audience.

A quiz on this chapter and all figures can be found at www.dbmarket ing.com/STM4. Those taking all the quizzes can receive a Successful Completion Certificate from the Database Marketing Institute which can be used in their résumé.

15

Social and Mobile Marketing

Tri Tang, a 25 year old marketer, walked into the Best Buy Co. store in Sunnyvale, Calif., and spotted the perfect gift for his girlfriend. Last year he might have just dropped the $184.85 Garmin global positioning system into his cart. This time he took out his Android phone and typed the model number into an app that instantly compared the Best Buy price to those of other retailers. He found that he could get the same item on Amazon.com Inc.'s web site for only $106.75, no shipping, no tax. Mr. Tang bought the Garmin from Amazon right on the spot. ... Mr. Tang's smartphone reckoning represents a revolution in retailing—what Wal-Mart Stores Inc. Chief Executive Mike Duke has dubbed a "new era of price transparency" and its arrival is threatening to upend the business models of the biggest store chains in America"

—MIGUEL BUSTILLO AND ANN ZIMMERMAN, WSJ

How many friend and friend details can we possibly track? With how many friends—or brands—can we sustain meaningful engagement? Using a loose definition of "friend" including those whose updates or status we follow on Facebook, Twitter, LinkedIn, Foursquare, and other social networks or communities, the attention required to manage all those updates has grown in multiple, exponential ways. Not only do we have many, many more friends but each friend has many, many more updates across many, many more devices, apps, and platforms. Just about every online activity has a social component or implication. How

*long until we get lost in a cacophony of noise and
what filters do we have besides our time and effort
(precious commodities) to help us find relevant nuggets
that actually bring value to our lives? Exponential
growth is already astounding and while the trend for
social media participation is undeniably sharply
positive, some people are dropping out of this race that
has no finish line.*

—ROBIN NEIFIELD, CLICKZ

*According to Mark Cuban, who sold Broadcast.com to
Yahoo in 1999 for close to $6bn, what we're seeing
today isn't a bubble, it's a Ponzi scheme. The question
is how much companies like Facebook and Twitter are
really worth, and whether or not the newest investors in
them are motivated more by their long-term potential or
by making a quick buck selling to even greater fools
(perhaps retail investors) in a year or two. Unlike in
the first .com boom, when the value of the web was
largely perceived to be correlated with the immediate
prospects for overhyped, overvalued companies, the
internet's worth today isn't determined by the value of
Facebook, Twitter or the "next big thing." Plenty of
entrepreneurs, developers and companies are profiting
daily from the internet using proven online business
models, and the vast majority of them wouldn't lose a
wink of sleep, or a penny, if Facebook and Twitter
folded tomorrow.*

—PATRICIO ROBLES

Social media involve reaching consumers using Web sites like Facebook
and Twitter, plus many other Internet forums. In general, social media
are used by a younger audience. This is illustrated by surveys like the one
shown in Figure 15.1.

When social media began, many companies assumed that the process
would be similar to other marketing platforms: you set up a page on
Facebook, describe your products, and sell them. Experience over time
showed that with the social media audience, this method did not work
particularly well. What members of the social media audience want to do
is to interact with you. They want to tell you (and the world) what they

	% of Respondents					
	18–24	25–34	35–44	45–54	55–64	65+
Facebook	76%	70%	52%	43%	27%	24%
E-mail	70%	78%	86%	92%	96%	97%
Telephone	17%	23%	20%	24%	29%	37%
Twitter	11%	7%	6%	2%	1%	0%
Mail	6%	7%	7%	7%	9%	17%
Blog It	5%	9%	4%	1%	1%	0%
Print Out	5%	5%	4%	8%	7%	9%
Linkedin	2%	2%	2%	2%	0%	1%
None of These	3%	2%	1%	0%	0%	0%

Note: n = 1,391
Source: Chadwick Martin Bailey, "Social Sharing Research Report," Sep 28, 2010

Figure 15.1 Ways US Internet Users Share Content, by Age, Aug 2010

think about your products, company, customer service, and so on. Sometimes what they say is not what you want to hear or what you want the world to hear. Companies learned to use social media to listen more than to speak. They began to tabulate how many mentions there are on media of their company and its products. Gradually, these companies began to interact with commenters, building up a social blog of interest to many who visited the sites. These companies found that the idea of social media was to participate in a public dialogue—to get noticed and talked about.

Future historians will be better able to explain why, in 2010, Facebook has emerged as the unchallenged de facto home address for almost 500 million users worldwide. But it undeniably has. Born in a Harvard dormitory, Facebook has moved off-campus and now everyone from the original teenagers to their great grandparents check their pages regularly. Not all of the pages belong to people. Businesses can also create and maintain pages. Today, given the monstrous size of the Facebook market, a page is becoming an essential online channel. Just as a media conglomerate must have a presence in New York, a fashion designer Milan and a global bank Hong Kong, businesses that operate online now need to have at least a window onto Facebook.

—JEFF ENTE, DIRECTOR, WHO'S BLOGGING WHAT

One company that succeeded in social media was bakeware and cake-decorating accessory company Wilton which used social media to interact with its audience rather than to sell to it. It supplemented its regular e-mail marketing tactics with a blog, a Facebook page, and a Twitter feed. To reach this audience, Wilton used several strategies.

At first, Wilton assumed that the same people who read its e-mails would also follow the company on Facebook. To prove this, it surveyed its e-mail newsletter subscribers to ask which social media sites they used. Wilton discovered that only about half of the company's Facebook fans and Twitter followers subscribed to its e-mail newsletter. It also discovered that the e-mail and social media participants had different interests. By monitoring Facebook discussions, it found that Facebook fans were less engaged with Wilton products than e-mail subscribers. Most had never taken a Wilton class. They had come to the Facebook page because of their interest in baking and cake decorating. The company's e-mail fans were most interested in how-to content, such as party planning ideas, baking projects, and decorating tips. For them, product promotions in the e-mail newsletters got a much lower response rate because e-mail subscribers already owned Wilton products. Not so with social media followers. They had a greater interest in new product announcements.

Since many social media fans were not e-mail subscribers, Wilton promoted its e-mail newsletters to Facebook fans. At the same time, it used its e-mail newsletter to boost awareness of the Facebook page. It added buttons to its e-mail newsletter to encourage subscribers to follow the brand on Facebook and saw a 325 percent increase in new Facebook fans on the day it sent the newsletter. (See Figure 15.2.)

For Facebook fans Wilton created a Facebook wall post that encouraged fans to opt in. As a result, it got a 225 percent increase in newsletter subscriptions compared to the average daily sign-up rate.

Starbucks had 18.5 million Facebook fans as of November 2010. Alexandra Wheeler, director of digital strategy, explained, "It's about making sure that we do our job every day to give those fans some sort of meaningful value. Having 10 million people on Facebook who like us would be useless if we did nothing with it."

Social media marketing agency Cone found that 77 percent of new media users want brands to offer them incentives or to be entertained online. For example, Coca-Cola, with 19.8 million Facebook fans, used a year-long social media campaign, Expedition 206, to keep its Facebook page constantly updated with new content. Oreo launched an interactive game on its Facebook page in September 2010. As a

Figure 15.2 Wilton Facebook Page

result it jumped from 8.5 million fans in August to 15.2 million in November.

How Do You Measure Social Media's Impact?

Social media can be measured—and we show how to measure them later in this chapter. There are those, like Dr. Augustine Fou of Omnicom's Healthcare Consultancy Group (HCG) who maintain that "The ROI of Social Media is Zero." He pointed out that in surveys nearly half the respondents said that they were not able to measure the return on investment of social media activities or even compare it to the return of other marketing activities. This is because they have not yet read this book. As we show, social media, if successful, get people more interested in your company and its products. As a result you will acquire more e-mail subscribers. You will experience higher open, click, and conversion rates. The rate of product returns will go down, as well as the number of your unsubscribes. All these things can be measured.

Generally speaking, social media are not used for selling products—which can be measured. Fou points out several valuable features of social media: Dell has built up a following on Twitter over time so it can now tweet last minute deals and clear out unsold outlet inventory very efficiently. It made more than $6.5 million in one year doing this. Netflix has built up a large fan base on Facebook and uses it to interact with fans, get feedback, and announce new features or content. JetBlue and Best Buy use Twitter for customer service and have thus built up a large enough following to use Twitter as a free launch or awareness channel.

Fou explains that social media cannot be controlled; people won't necessarily talk about the product the way the advertiser wants the product or brand to be talked about; and they certainly won't use "on brand" terminology.

Develop a Plan

Before you create a Facebook page for your business, have a strategy in place. What are you trying to accomplish with this page? How are you going to achieve it? There are several ways to customize your page on Facebook. Your pages have multiple tabs. Default tabs include the Wall tab, which is for exchanging information with your fans and the Info tab, which is for sharing content. If you learn more about your social media fans, you can create better dynamic content in your e-mails.

One of the most important effects of social media activity is to increase brand name recognition. Much of consumers' business is given to certain companies because they recognize and trust the brand names and what that branding implies. People go to Wal-Mart because the company promises low prices. People trust UPS to deliver their packages on time. Branding is vital for building name recognition and the expanding customer base. And it entails much more than just a logo.

For example, NASCAR launched the "Fan Council," a prequalified online community of 12,000 members, to listen to and to engage fans. As a result of what it learned, NASCAR changed some of the rules in the sport. As a result of the council, NASCAR reported that it increased key brand attributes like "thrilling and exciting," "down to earth," and "good public image" by 10 percent or more.

The fact is that millions of people go to Facebook and Twitter daily. Some of them will interact with your page. You can measure this. Some of the interaction will build your brand name in their minds. It takes a long time and is hard to measure, but it has value. There is one way, however, to get a direct measurement of the value of social media: by using media to build your e-mail subscription base. As you know by now, e-mail subscribers have a measurable LTV.

Faster Internet connections at home and at work have made it easier for millions of people to interact with each other. They are creating their own online content. They are watching online videos. They are texting each other. A Pew survey found that 48 percent of Internet users watch Web videos, 39 percent read blogs, 30 percent post online reviews, and 16 percent participate in social networking sites like MySpace, Facebook, and Friendster. Social networking and social computing are growing. Consumers today are more connected to other consumers, and they trust other consumers.

If you want to reach young people, go with the flow. Create ways to leverage social networks to promote your e-mail program. For example:

- Create a Facebook page for your company, and capture e-mail addresses on it.
- Use social media sites to communicate news.
- Test messages, calls to action, and creative on social networking sites.
- Use e-mail to drive initial traffic to these sites or your features on them.
- Send messages that can be read on their iPhones and Androids.
- Inform subscribers through e-mail when you launch new social network initiatives.

Steps in Getting into Facebook

I am afraid that you can't avoid it today. You have to have a "social presence" which entails a page of Facebook and Twitter. Social media won't make you rich, but if you do it right it will get you notices. Here are some steps to take:

- Choose a name for your page that your customers can identify with.
- Use a vanity URL that your fans may guess to find you. You can allocate a vanity URL by going to facebook.com/username.
- Give your followers information about you and make sure to offer keyword-rich text so that your Facebook presence shows up in search engine queries for your business.
- Personalize your page: One of the ways to do this is to create a Facebook page with FBML, Facebook markup language.
- Let your customers know where to find you. Make sure to encourage your followers to find you on Facebook. Add links to your Facebook profile (and any other major social presences) in your e-mail signature. When people become a new fan, it shows up in their news feed, so others can also find out where they've been. This could potentially have a viral effect. Being actively engaged is a critical part of success on Facebook.

Before you spend a lot of money on such applications, be wary. Many consumers go to these sites primarily to socialize, not to shop. Ads on social networking sites so far have generated relatively few sales. In 2008, Forrester Research reported that the average cost of an order from an ad on a social network site was $50.11, compared with $19.33 for paid search ads and $6.85 for e-mails to subscribers.

Source	15–17	18–24	25–34	35–44	45–54	55–64	65+
Regular Mail	58%	59%	72%	77%	82%	88%	92%
E-mail	42%	56%	65%	66%	69%	79%	73%
Phone	23%	14%	26%	26%	35%	32%	32%
Text Message	13%	9%	10%	4%	2%	3%	0%
Social Networking	12%	10%	11%	5%	3%	1%	1%
Instant Message	11%	5%	7%	2%	4%	1%	0%
RSS	4%	4%	3%	2%	1%	1%	0%

U.S. Internet users who have made purchases because of marketing messages. Feb 2008
n = 1,555 people who own a mobile phone
Source: Exact Target 2008 Channel Preference Survey

Figure 15.3 Messages That Lead Consumers to Buy by Age Group

Figure 15.3 is an interesting chart. Notice that regular mail always beats e-mail in getting customers to make purchases—but not by much—and e-mail beats everything else. The cost of direct mail is about $600 per thousand. The cost of e-mail is less than $6 per thousand. So, for any age group, including seniors, e-mail marketing is more cost-effective than any other direct marketing method.

Companies that have invested in social media find that there are secondary effects on subscriber acquisition. The fact that there is an active company Facebook page induces many visitors to sign up for e-mails. These subscribers, in turn, purchase products. This secondary effect can be measured.

A survey by Lyris showed that many companies are using social media marketing to help build their opt-in e-mail lists. Twenty-one percent said social media drove the greatest opt-in rates, after Web site registration forms and e-mail marketing itself.

The measurement process is straightforward. Using LTV analysis, you might determine that each of your e-mail subscribers is worth $26.57. You have various campaigns going on to generate more subscribers. Suppose that you are currently adding 44,000 subscribers per month using your current methods. Your social media team gets the Facebook page working and uses it to acquire more subscribers. As a result, you can measure the increase: an additional 12,000 per month—or 144,000 per year. (See Figure 15.4.) The value of these subscribers added $3,826,080. If you are spending $500,000 per year on your social media activities, you have a powerful ROI to present to your CFO to justify your social media budget.

	Annual Subscriber Acquisition	Value of Each Subscriber	Annual Gain
Before Facebook	528,000	$26.57	$14,028,960
After Facebook	672,000	$26.57	$17,855,040
Gain from Facebook	144,000	$26.57	$3,826,080

Figure 15.4 Gain from New Subscribers Due to Facebook

Social media are moving out of the experimental stage and are becoming a mainstream marketing strategy. They are moving so fast that most marketers cannot keep up. ExactTarget commissioned a study on smartphone Internet usage. The study found that the rise in social media adoption has led to an *increase* in how much we e-mail from our mobile devices—not the decrease many analysts were predicting.

A Nielsen study showed that social media make users consume more e-mail, not less. More and more users treat services like Facebook as replacements for an e-mail in-box. E-mail is still more versatile, but for some users social networking services offer a more convenient messaging experience.

The North Face created a mobile alerts program called Summit Signals which gave customers store level text on their mobile phone. Participants can specify how frequently they want to get alerts. The North Face sends out two surveys. Those who fill out both surveys (sent within 30 days of each other) receive a $25 gift card good for The North Face products. The social media focus is shifting from short term to long term. Marketing investments like social media are not intended to furnish immediate financial results but instead create long-term brand value. The greatest and most valuable brands weren't created from quarter to quarter but with an eye toward building lasting relationships with customers. Smart marketers are coming to recognize the way social media marketing can deliver on those same long-term values and are building programs with strategies and metrics to suit.

Not every social media program needs ROI to deliver business benefit. What is the ROI of a company's Web sites? Even though we are well into the Internet age, most organizations still have not measured the financial return they receive from their Web properties. But even though there is no measurement system, companies continue to invest in redesigns, new sites, and Web technology. Why? To keep up with customer expectations and the competition. Many social media activities— such as a presence on Facebook or listening programs—are becoming standard marketing techniques even though there are not currently available ways to measure their value.

Finally, few companies have figured out a way to meld their social interactions with consumers into their marketing databases. Until this is done, it will not be possible to have real interactive conversations with customers and subscribers, which is the real benefit of database marketing.

> *In the bigger-is-better mentality, we lose sight of the fact that the marginal value of more friends might actually be negative. Having more friends creates more noise and more management load and might in some cases actually reduce the value of your network and create a disincentive to participate. It's becoming increasingly difficult for consumers to manage these varying social media needs.*
>
> —ROBIN NEIFIELD, CLICKZ

> *No need to do any social media efforts unless you have some good content to share. Just don't do it. You'll denigrate your brand and water down what's really important.*
>
> —AARON KAHLOW

The Return on Investment from Social Media

Figure 15.5 is a picture of a company before getting involved in social media. Figure 15.6 shows what could happen with social media. The company has 500,000 subscribers and $9.7 million in sales has an e-mail marketing program but has not invested in social media.

Now let's look at the LTV after we create a Facebook page and get a lot of Web visitors interested in what we have to say. Figure 15.6 shows a revised picture.

LTV before Social Programs		This Year	Next Year	Third Year
Subscribers		500,000	425,000	361,250
Unsubs & Undels	15%	75,000	63,750	54,188
Delivered E-mails	104	52,000,000	44,200,000	37,570,000
Opens	11%	5,720,000	4,862,000	4,132,700
Unique Clicks	15%	858,000	729,300	619,905
Conversions	3%	25,740	21,879	18,597
Non-e-mail Conversions	2.00	51,480	43,758	37,194
Total Conversions		77,220	65,637	55,791
Revenue	$126.43	$9,762,925	$8,298,486	$7,053,713
Costs	40%	$3,905,170	$3,319,394	$2,821,485
Returns	8.7%	$849,374	$721,968	$613,673
Acquisition Cost	$0.10	$50,000		
E-mail Creation & Delivery	$8.00	$416,000	$353,600	$300,560
Database Cost	$2.00	$1,000,000	$850,000	$722,500
Total Costs		$6,220,544	$5,244,963	$4,458,218
Profit		$3,542,380	$3,053,523	$2,595,495
Discount Rate		1.00	1.10	1.21
NPV Profit		$3,542,380	$2,775,930	$2,145,037
Cumulative NPV Profit		$3,542,380	$6,318,311	$8,463,348
Lifetime Value		$7.08	$12.64	$16.93

Figure 15.5 LTV before Social Media Programs

The changes follow:

1. We gave gained 100,000 subscribers because of our popularity on Facebook. This is one of the main ways that social media help marketers.

2. Our unsubs and undelivers have gone down from 15 to 13 percent. This too is a common result of the success of social media.

3. The open rate has jumped from 11 to 13 percent.

4. The unique clicks have gone from 15 to 16 percent. We are reaching our audience members and understanding them. Result: they click more on our product offerings.

5. Our conversion rate has jumped from 3 to 4 percent—a jump of 33 percent.

6. Our product returns have gone down. People understand us, like us, and do not return products as often. The National Retail Federation estimates that approximately 8.7 percent of all goods purchased in 2008 were returned.

7. The social media program has cost us $1 million per year.

LTV with Social Programs		This Year	Next Year	Third Year
Subscribers		600,000	522,000	454,140
Unsubs & Undels	13%	78,000	67,860	59,038
Delivered E-mails	104	62,400,000	54,288,000	47,230,560
Opens	13%	8,112,000	7,057,440	6,139,973
Unique Clicks	16%	1,297,920	1,129,190	982,396
Conversions	4%	51,917	45,168	39,296
Non-e-mail Conversions	2.00	103,834	90,335	78,592
Total Conversions		155,750	135,503	117,887
Revenue	$126.43	$19,691,523	$17,131,625	$14,904,514
Costs	40%	$7,876,609	$6,852,650	$5,961,806
Returns	7.0%	$1,378,407	$1,199,214	$1,043,316
Acquisition Cost	$0.10	$60,000		
E-mail Creation & Delivery	$8.00	$499,200	$434,304	$377,844
Database Cost	$2.00	$1,200,000	$1,044,000	$908,280
Social Media Costs	$1.67	$1,000,000	$870,000.00	$756,900.00
Total Costs		$12,014,216	$10,400,168	$9,048,146
Profit		$7,677,307	$6,731,457	$5,856,368
Discount Rate		1.00	1.10	1.21
NPV Profit		$7,677,307	$6,119,507	$4,839,973
Cumulative NPV Profit		$7,677,307	$13,796,814	$18,636,787
Lifetime Value		$12.80	$22.99	$31.06

Figure 15.6 LTV Using Social Media

Summary of the Return on Investment from Using Social Media

The ROI is $2.44 for every $1 invested. Not overwhelming, but significant. This is an answer to those like Professor Fou who maintain that the

ROI is zero. Using reasonable assumptions, a successful social media program can produce measurable results. Figure 15.7 shows what this company might gain through its investment in Social Media. The gain is shown in LTV before and after. The last line shows that you gain more than $2 in profit for every $1 invested.

	This Year	Next Year	Third Year
Before Social Media	$7.08	$12.64	$16.93
With Social Media	$12.80	$22.99	$31.06
Gain	$5.71	$10.36	$14.13
With 600,000 Subscribers	$3,426,451	$5,406,912	$6,419,095
ROI	$3.43	$2.89	$2.44

Figure 15.7 ROI from Social Media

The Effect of Mobile Technology on Database Marketing

The Apple iPhone has changed the world forever. All other phones have to be redesigned to catch up. Not just touchscreen, but an entire phone that you can touch with your fingers. Phones in the past used a stylus or other devices. With the iPhone, you can use multiple fingers to have two different points of reference at once. It is the iPhone's claim to fame, and we don't know how we ever lived without it. Turn it on its side and see the extra room in landscape mode. And who else but Apple would have thought to shake your device to undo, shuffle, and more. The iPhone could be the first smartphone where people actually use their phone to watch TV, and movies. What other phone allows you to record, edit, and upload to YouTube all on your cell? Finally, an online store with applications to download for your phone. It was simple, consumer-friendly to browse and purchase, offering free and paid apps for every one of your everyday needs. More than 1 billion apps were downloaded in the first 9 months of its inception.

—*Nick Mahar at T3CH H3LP*

The success of the iPhone has made the mobile use of the Internet grow faster than any previous Internet platform. It produced 120 million subscribers worldwide within three years after its initial launch. At the same time the Android popularity has surged, and the loyalty of its users has increased to match that of iPhone users. eMarketer estimates that after exploding from just 6 percent of the U.S. smartphone market in 2009 to 24 percent in 2010, Android will continue to gain market share through 2012, when 31 percent of all smartphone users will own a device running on the Google operating system. That same year Apple's share of the market will hold steady at 30 percent.

Database marketing is about communicating with customers. How do you communicate? With direct mail, phone calls, e-mails, social media, and mobile devices? Companies that have just learned to use e-mails effectively now have to learn how to communicate with mobile phones as well.

Texting Is Growing

SMS stands for short message service, or texting. It is a method for sending messages to a cell phone from another cell phone, a computer connected to the Internet, or a regular landline. It was invented by Friedhelm Hillebrand and Bernard Ghillebaert in 1984. Each text message is limited to fewer than 160 characters.

SMS messages may be sent either from one point to another point or to all devices within a specific geographical region. They can be used between individuals communicating with each other or may be used to broadcast public or commercial messages to a large number of people.

By 2010 there were more than 4 billion mobile phone subscribers worldwide. The majority of these users had SMS capable devices and an increasing number were adopting Web-enabled smart phones. Worldwide more than 700,000 customers abandoned their landline telephones each month. For many, the phone is no longer just about voice calls.

Young people are texting. A 2009 Nielsen survey found that the average American teenager is sending and receiving more than 2,800 text messages per month. This average is even higher for teens in other areas of the world. Texting is second nature to the next generation of consumers.

In-Stat reports that more than 2 trillion mobile messages are sent per day globally. While teens account for a large portion of SMS usage, they are not alone. Limbo reports that 50 percent of SMS users are age 35 or over. How does this texting produce an opportunity for marketers?

SMS is a killer call center application. It is user-friendly, personal, and inexpensive. Using SMS for customer interactions costs a fraction of the cost of phone reps. ContactBabel estimated that live phone rep service calls average about $12 per call, while SMS costs pennies per message.

SMS is particularly good for routine inquiries and outbound notifications. Some companies already use SMS to let customers get their bank account balance, order status, mobile minutes usage, the amount of a utility bill, or the nearest store location.

For the customer, SMS saves time and provides her with a record of the response so she can refer back to the requested information later:

> *Now that the boundary between the Internet and cell phones has become so blurred as not to exist, it makes perfect sense for teenagers to text each other even when they're at the same party, or sitting at the same couch. For one thing, nobody can overhear them. And texting gives them time to frame their words more carefully, even if they're using shorthand their parents don't understand, like "imo" (in my opinion) or "aaf" (always and forever).*
>
> —ORSON SCOTT CARD
> *in The Wall Street Journal*

How Short Codes Work

A common short code (CSC) is a five- or six-digit number approved by the cell phone carrier that mobile phone subscribers use to send SMS messages to receive information, promotions, alerts, and branded content on their mobile devices. The implementation of short codes helps both consumers and brands because it establishes a two-way communication channel. By using these codes, wireless subscribers can participate in voting and polling, customer feedback, database enrollment, news and offer alerts, contests, surveys, chat, games, direct marketing, and mobile commerce. Short code campaigns are becoming more and more popular because the code is simple and can be used by anyone with a mobile device. Over 96 percent of cell phones are capable of receiving SMS messages.

As of 2011, many SMS-based campaigns were achieving over a 90 percent opt-in rate, compared to 22.1 percent for e-mail. The average SMS response rate typically ranged between 15 to 30 percent, compared to

5 percent for e-mail and 2.61 percent for direct mail. Look at some of the success stories:

- Chicago's Shedd Aquarium ran several TV commercials that directed viewers to a Web site to register for a contest. One commercial gave viewers the option of entering by sending a text message to a short code. The short code campaign generated 325 percent more entries than the Web-based campaign. While it ran in only 25 percent of the ads, the short code campaign generated 52 percent of the total entries.

- Ashley Furniture HomeStore held a four-day secret sale that was promoted only by e-mail and SMS. After subtracting the discounts from coupons, the store sold $122 dollars of merchandise for every dollar spent on SMS and $76 for every dollar spent on e-mail.

- In Coca-Cola's "My Coke Rewards" program, consumers text unique codes found under the caps of various Coke products to gain points. They use these points to redeem rewards.

- Jiffy Lube ran an SMS contest to win a year's worth of oil changes. Half of those who redeemed the coupon were new customers.

- Planet Funk ran a mobile coupon campaign to drive traffic to its clothing store. The campaign generated a 91 percent redemption rate on 2,000 issued coupons—20 percent of December's total revenue. Overall, the store calculated a 377 percent return on investment as a result of increased sales.

- Pizza Hut ran an SMS contest for a chance to win a Pizza Hut pizza once a month for a year. Within two weeks the campaign had received more than 2,000 consumer e-mail addresses, and 54 percent moved on to double-opt-in.

To create a short code campaign, a business must file an application form for leasing a short code from the Common Short Code Administration (CSCA) at www.usshortcodes.com.

Face-to-Face Campaign

British Airways ran a contest called "Face of Opportunity" to build up its e-mail database. It gave away free trips to small business owners anywhere they needed to go. (See Figure 15.8.) Announced by ads in the press, the contest invited small business owners to text their e-mail address to 21713.

"Small business is the lifeblood of the American economy. We believe face-to-face meetings are the most effective way of growing those businesses," said Anne Tedesco, vice president of marketing for North America at British Airways, New York. "We are reaching out to companies under 250 people and asking them to make an elevator pitch justifying an overseas trip which might help them grow." Using a mobile short code generates an instant response e-mail. It is much easier than asking people to fill out a form or make a mental note to come to the Web site later.

As part of our face to face program, we're giving hundreds of small business owners free flights and seats at exclusive conferences led by business pioneers and celebrity speakers. Give us your best pitch on why you should be one of them. Visit Ba.com/contest or text your email address to 21713 for more details.

BRITISH AIRWAYS

Figure 15.8 British Airways Mobile Contest

The Gap and Your Visa Card

The Gap created a text messaging promotion together with Visa. They sent out an e-mail marketing piece urging shoppers to sign up online on a secure Visa.com page for Gap Mobile 4 U. Shoppers entered their mobile phone number and their Visa card number. They agreed to receive up to two text messages with customized offers per week.

The Visa card was not used for payment. To create the offers, Visa scours the shoppers' transaction history at Gap and elsewhere, looking for buying trends. Using that data, Gap sends out text message promotions based on what the shoppers actually buy.

Triggers for the messages can include where you use your enrolled Visa card to make a purchase (at a store or online); the type of merchant you buy from, the time of day of your transactions, the number of purchases, and the transaction amounts.

Instant Messaging (IM)

Instant messaging is similar to, but a different application from, texting. With IM, you keep a list of people you interact with. You can IM with anyone on your contact list as long as that person is online. You type messages to each other into a small window that shows up on both of your screens. Most IM programs provide these features:

- *Instant messages:* Send notes back and forth with a friend who is online.

- *Chat:* Create a chat room with friends or coworkers.

- *Web links:* Share links to your favorite Web sites.

- *Video:* Send and view videos, and chat face to face with friends.

- *Images:* Look at an image stored on your friend's computer.

- *Sounds:* Play sounds for your friends.

- *Files:* Share files by sending them directly to your friends.

- *Talk:* Use the Internet instead of a phone to actually talk with friends.

- *Streaming content:* Real-time or near-real-time stock quotes and news.

- *Mobile capabilities:* Send instant messages from your cell phone.

Gartner, Inc. is the world's leading information technology research and advisory company. They predict that by the end of 2013, IM will be the de facto tool for voice, video, and text chat in 95 percent of global organizations. Mobile IM is growing because of the availability of handsets with QWERTY keyboards.

Customer self-service using interactive instant messaging is carried out with intelligent IM automated agents that provide real-time responses to customer inquiries, including package tracking, emergency notifications, interactive games, customer surveys, and identity verification. IM saves money. On average, an IM call is one-tenth the cost of IVR and one-hundredth the cost of a live agent.

Banks have made major use of mobile transactions. Balance requests are cited as the number one type of mobile banking transaction today, followed by fund transfers. Informa predicts that by 2013 over 977 million people will access banking services via their mobile phones, performing an estimated 300 billion transactions. Unlike PCs and laptops, the 4 billion mobile phones deployed globally are with consumers at all times.

Modern 3G mobile phones not only support voice calls and Web surfing, but also are capable of displaying streaming self-service videos.

Managing Mobile Subscriber Preferences

Of mobile e-mail consumers surveyed in 2010, 17 percent stated that they do not open and read messages that they have opted into because the marketer did not understand their preferences. This percentage is higher than for non-mobile users. Since more and more subscribers are using mobile devices, marketers must begin to change their e-mails so that they show up properly on cell phone screens. This is particularly important for travel companies where subscribers are interacting with the travel provider during their trip. One way to reach these mobile subscribers may be with contests like the American Airlines million mile contest in Figure 15.9.

Figure 15.9 American Airlines Mobile Sweepstakes, www.thefind.com

Mobile Search Is Exploding

According to Google, mobile search query volumes grew by a factor of 300 from 2007 to 2010. It is clear that the consumers are using their phones both online and offline at the same time. Booz reported that in 2010, 16 percent of consumers were using their handsets to influence their shopping experiences. This is an opportunity for database marketers.

The new mobile ad formats make it easy for retailers and brands to learn where subscribers are geographically so that they can deliver information to consumers on local store addresses and phone numbers—and even fill them in on specific product stock levels in stores close by. In 2009 consumers using mobile devices accounted for just 0.1 percent of visits to retail Web sites, according to Coremetrics. In 2010, they accounted for 5.6 percent, for a 50-fold increase. Dozens of mobile shopping apps are already available, and many more are being developed.

The new smartphones enable consumers to take a picture of a print ad, bar code, or physical object, and receive all sorts of additional information on the product or place. For instance, a snapshot of a Buick ad taken with a smartphone can result in a promotional video, a dealer locator, or a request for additional information by clicking the phone.

If shoppers use the find's free app to compare prices, the phone captures the data from their search and shows them ads of similar electronics for sale elsewhere.

Mobile Commerce Is also Expanding

By 2014, mobile commerce will generate $5.5 billion worth of sales in the United States according to Booz. By this date more than half of U.S. shoppers will use their mobile phones to make their shopping decisions. Brands are signing up for the new Google mobile ad format. They see the value in being present with highly relevant content when consumers are looking for a shop or are even in the aisle, moments from the actual purchase.

So what should database marketers do today with the new mobile platform?

- Make sure that the messages and the call to action of all print and outdoor campaigns use the consumers' online presence.
- Get consumers' cell phone addresses as well as their e-mail addresses.

- Coordinate print campaigns with online campaigns.

- Use new metrics from companies like Marketing Evolution and comScore to measure the effectiveness of online campaigns.

- Make sure you can deliver on your mobile promises.

- Partner with retailers to capture product inventory data at the store level so that you can provide in-stock data to consumers' smartphones while they are shopping.

High-Speed Connections Are the Norm

By the end of 2010 it was estimated that 91 percent of online households were connected through broadband. While there is still a technology gap for the households that don't have home access, the gap is disappearing among the connected. Worries about the user experience of dial-up versus high-speed are gone.

Time Spent with TV and the Internet Is Now Equal

By 2011, the amount of time U.S. households report watching TV offline in an average week (13 hours) equaled the amount of time they spend online. The leveling is driven by the huge growth in time spent with the Internet. General activities like e-mail are attractive because of their integration with consumers' existing lives. Once consumers understood the concept of sending electronic messages, for example, it became easy to substitute traditional letter writing (or even phone calls or in-person meetings) with a quick e-mail, or instant messaging (IM) for the younger generations. In 2010 60 percent of online respondents were shopping online according to Forrester. People take to e-commerce because, like e-mail, it is based on a behavior that consumers are already doing: shopping.

Social Networking Now Connects 62 Million U.S. Adults

Forrester also notes that next to e-commerce, social networking site usage has seen the biggest jump in usage since 2007. Although only one-third of all U.S. online adults visit social networking sites—and most of them are under 30—the future is wide open for this type of social medium.

- The increasing availability of mobile-Internet-capable phones and unlimited data plans translates directly into the possibility for consumers to connect to the Internet through their mobile devices. The percent of mobile users who report texting on a monthly basis was 61 percent by 2011, with more and more older users doing more than voice calls.

- By 2011, one-quarter of online mobile owners now log onto the mobile Internet. Social networking sites have proven to be one of the most popular types of sites that users are accessing. Facebook claims that as of 2010, 200 million global consumers now access the site through a mobile device.

- In 2008, only 5 percent of online mobile owners were listening to music on their mobile devices. That number grew to 17 percent by 2010. Video watching by mobile consumers has been growing fast—16 percent of online mobile users now use their mobile phones to check news, sports, or weather, and 13 percent look up directions or maps. Sixty percent access the mobile Internet at least weekly.

- Nielsen reports that Google Search is the top Web site accessed on mobile phones. Such mobile users, according to Forrester, tend to be male and college-educated, with a household income of more than $92,000. In view of these trends, marketers need to cater to the behaviors of these valuable mobile users who like to create media content, write ratings and reviews, and blog. What would make the process of doing these things easier for them?

Conclusions

While personal computers are not going to disappear altogether, the trend lines are clear. Gartner, the market research company, predicts that by 2013 the number of smart phones will surpass PCs, 182 billion to 1.78 billion. And that's not counting the tablets. ... We want to be mobile, but we still want to remain connected to the people and things we care about. Nothing currently fulfills that psychic hunger better than a fully loaded tablet or smart phone in your pocket. There's also an inherent appeal to the culture of these devices: Compare the dry utility of a personality-free PC to the candy-colored array of app icons on the iPad user interface. Which one would you like to wake up to every day?

—MIKE MALONE AND TOM HAYES, WSJ

Database marketing today involves more than ever the way that we communicate with our customers. Social media and mobile devices have, for many customers, replaced direct mail, e-mails, and Web sites on PCs. Social media do not, in general, sell products the way that direct mail and e-mails do. They modify the way people think about their suppliers: they increase e-mail subscriptions and open, click, and conversion rates. They reduce unsubscribes and product returns.

Mobile devices, particularly the iPhone, involve a new way to reach customers. Instead of reaching them while they're seated at their PCs, they are available 24/7 attached to their bodies. Through their mobile devices they can get e-mails, text messages, instant messages, coupons, videos, and brand advertising. Any database marketing practitioner has to use all means of communicating with his customers if he is going to succeed in today's world.

Take-Away Thoughts

- Social media are largely used by younger people. E-mail is used by everybody.
- Starbucks had 18.5 million Facebook fans as of November 2010.
- Oreo created an interactive game on its Facebook page that jumped its fans from 8.5 million to 15.2 million in three months.
- Dell sells unsold inventory using Twitter, making $6.5 million in one year doing this.
- Most people go to social media to socialize, not to shop.
- In 2008, Forrester Research reported that the average cost of an order from an ad on a social network site was $50.11, compared with $19.33 for paid search ads and $6.85 for e-mails to subscribers.
- A Nielsen study showed that social media leads users use more e-mail, not less.

- The iPhone and the Android have revolutionized mobile communications.

- American teenagers are sending and receiving more than 2,800 text message per month according to In-Stat.

- Short codes have become very popular for cell phones—used by Coca-Cola, Jiffy Lube, and Pizza Hut.

- British Airways gave away free flights to small business owners if they text their e-mail.

- Gartner predicts that by the end of 2013, IM will be the de facto tool for voice, video, and text chat in 95 percent of global organizations.

- By 2014 mobile commerce will generate $5.5 billion worth of sales in the United States according to Booz. By this date more than half of U.S. shoppers will use their mobile phones to make their shopping decisions.

- Any database marketing practitioner has to use all means of communicating with his customers if he is going to succeed in today's world.

A quiz on this chapter and all figures can be found at www.dbmarket ing.com/STM4. Those taking all the quizzes can receive a Successful Completion Certificate from the Database Marketing Institute which can be used in their résumé.

16

How Often Should You Communicate?

When asked why recipients stopped subscribing to opt-in e-mails, more than one half said the content was no longer relevant, and 40% said they were getting too many offers.

—*JUPITERRESEARCH (2007)*

Sixty percent of online retailers conduct between one and three campaigns each month. 32.8% coordinate 4 to 15 campaigns each month; 7.2% conduct more than 15.

—*INTERNET RETAILER (2007)*

37.4 percent of Internet users say they receive more e-mail than they expected when they signed up.

—*RETURN PATH (2007)*

For years, consumers complained about "junk mail" referring to the number of postal pieces they received each day. They didn't know what junk mail really was until they got a PC and began receiving e-mail spam. Junk e-mails exceed junk postal mail by more than 100 to 1.

Fortunately, most Internet service providers (ISPs) like AOL or Yahoo! recognize much of the spam and prevent it from reaching the helpless consumers. PC e-mail software, like Microsoft Outlook, has filtering provisions so most of the spam that gets through the ISPs is routed to a junk mail folder. But despite these filters, most consumers receive more legitimate commercial e-mail than they want or can possibly read. When they unwittingly signed up for this e-mail, they did not realize the volume that they would receive. In general, they like the companies and their products that are sending this material, but they get more e-mails than they bargained for.

Figure 16.1 shows a chart of the number of e-mails sent per month to each subscriber for the 80 sample e-mail marketing companies we have been following in this book.

E-mails Delivered to typical subscriber per month

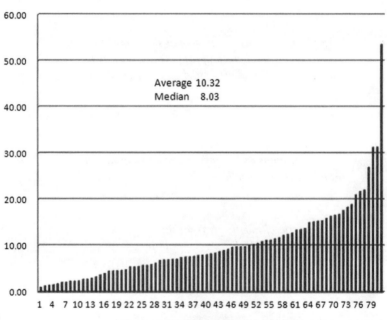

Figure 16.1 E-mails per Month

An average of 10.3 means that the average subscriber is receiving an e-mail from the average company more than twice a week. No wonder people are upset. No wonder they fail to open their e-mails.

The chart shown in Figure 16.2 is typical of the frequent surveys of e-mail subscribers. Frequency is an important issue in the database marketing business. In this chapter, we take a look, first, at the direct mail situation. Then we discuss the real problem: frequency of e-mails.

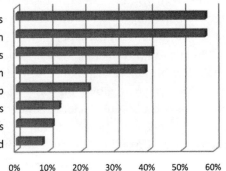

Figure 16.2 Why Don't You Open and Read E-mail Messages?

Direct Mail Calculation

Consumers are lucky with postal mail. It typically costs commercial mailers $0.50 a piece or more to deliver postal mail to the public. This cost places a limit on the number of pieces that can profitably be mailed. Some people may complain about their mailbox load, which is more than they may want, but the cost of mailing creates natural limits to the volume. For this reason, the volume of direct mail tends to stay at a manageable size.

How often should you send direct mail to your customers and prospects? Answer: as often as it is profitable to do so. From previous mailings, you should have an idea of how your customers respond to your direct mail offers. There are several types of response to direct mail today. People can:

- Pick up the phone and place an order.
- Go to one of your stores and use the coupon in the mail piece.
- Use the URL on the mail piece to log on to your Web site and order something.
- Mail in your return card or envelope with a check, credit card number, or a "bill me."

To communicate profitably, you keep everyone whom you send messages to on a database so you can know whom you mailed to and what they did. From this you can determine the response rate—which should be, if you are doing things right, about 2 percent. This means that 98 percent of your audience will chuck your mail piece out. You make your profits on the 2 percent.

The next step is essential: you need to use your database to figure out what kind of people responded and what kind did not. Let us say that you have 1,730,050 people on your database—including customers and prospects. Ideally your database contains pertinent information such as postal address, age, income, family size, housing type, RFM cell code, and so forth. If you are big enough, you will have a statistician on your staff or available to you who can take all this data and do some analytics based on previous responses to your promotions. This can divide your list of customers and prospects into deciles based on the likelihood of response.

How Many Should You Send?

You can derive the number of pieces to send mathematically from the break-even rate. This rate is calculated by this formula:

$$BE = (\text{cost per piece}) \div (\text{net profit from a single sale})$$

Suppose your average order size is $146 and of this total, $41 is profit. If your mail cost per piece is $0.64, then your break-even rate is

$$BE = (\$0.64) \div \$41 = 1.56 \text{ percent}$$

You can use RFM (Chapter 5) to score your database based on previous promotions. Figure 16.3 shows the breakdown of your database by RFM cell code which is compiled from previous promotions to your database; you can see that you can afford to mail the first four deciles. Your response rate for each decile is above 1.56 percent, which is above your break-even rate. If you go into the fifth decile, you will lose money.

You could divide your database on some other basis, such as geography, age, income, or any other factor that you have available. From this you can make up a similar chart, mailing only to those deciles that will be profitable for you.

Decile	RFM Range	Quantity	Response Rate
1	555–542	173,005	4.12%
2	541–511	173,005	3.03%
3	455–433	173,005	2.02%
4	432–413	173,005	1.89%
5	412–333	173,005	0.97%
6	332–311	173,005	0.86%
7	310–233	173,005	0.71%
8	232–211	173,005	0.64%
9	210–133	173,005	0.53%
10	132–111	173,005	0.27%
Total		1,730,050	1.50%

Figure 16.3 Direct Mail Mailing Chart

E-mail Marketing Calculation

With the same situation, let us assume that you have opt-in e-mail addresses from all 1,730,050 on your database (a very unlikely situation). How many should you mail to based on your direct mail decile chart? What is your break-even rate? Using the same formula with a cost per piece of $0.0064, your break-even rate is 0.016 percent.

$$BE = (\$0.0064) \div \$41 = 0.016 \text{ percent}$$

Figure 16.4 is the comparable chart for e-mailing.

Decile	RFM Range	Quantity	Response Rate
1	555–542	173,005	0.906%
2	541–511	173,005	0.667%
3	455–433	173,005	0.447%
4	432–413	173,005	0.416%
5	412–333	173,005	0.213%
6	332–311	173,005	0.189%
7	310–233	173,005	0.156%
8	232–211	173,005	0.141%
9	210–133	173,005	0.117%
10	132–111	173,005	0.059%
Total		1,730,050	0.33%

Figure 16.4 E-mail Mailing Chart

If your break-even rate is 0.016 percent, then you can afford to mail every single decile since they are all better than break even.

As you can see, e-mail response rates are much, much lower than direct mail response rates.

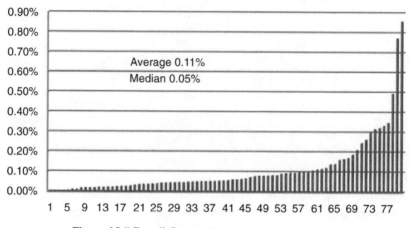

Figure 16.5 E-mail Conversions per Delivered e-mail

Your decision on whom to mail to, therefore, will not be based on the cost of delivery. "Mail 'em all," will be the CEO's instructions. This is probably the wrong command.

Relevance and frequency are related. A relevant e-mail sent too often can lose its relevant effectiveness over time. In a study by Merkle,[1] it was found that 66 percent of e-mail users list excessive frequency as a reason for unsubscribing. But the reverse doesn't necessarily hold true. If you send e-mails very infrequently, your customers may forget about you and consider your e-mails spam when they do arrive.

If you take one thing away from this chapter, it's this: make it easy for subscribers to tell you what they think, and listen to what they say and pay attention to what they do. They will usually tell you what frequency is best. Moreover, some of the best communicators of this are your inactive customers.

When your e-mail efforts are perceived as too frequent, you have a problem. Your customers, typically the best ones, may unsubscribe or mark your e-mails as spam. The basic problem relates to this. Should

---

[1] View from the Inbox™ 2008 Merkle www.merkleinc.com/user-assets/Documents/WhitePapers/ViewFromThe%20Inbox2008.pdf.

marketers analyze e-mail campaigns or e-mail subscribers? E-mail campaigns themselves are only one side of the equation. The communication's true value is often difficult to measure.

Imagine daily e-mails like a swarm of mosquitoes attacking a group of consumers resting outside a shopping mall. Some of the consumers will get in their cars and go home because of the mosquitoes. Others will go into the mall to shop to escape from the mosquitoes. But instead of studying what the consumers are doing, the e-mail marketers are studying the mosquito clouds on the group of consumers. This makes as much sense as an army analyzing the bullets being fired at an enemy rather than what the enemy is planning and doing.

Buyers can be a valuable long-term source of revenue. Your goal should be to woo them, to build long-term relationships with them, to make them happy with your company, your service, and your products. To become successful in the long run, you must analyze and understand all of your subscribers—what their preferences are and how you can create marketing messages that respond to these preferences. If you have a subscriber who might give you $2,000 a year for 10 years and you lose her within a few weeks through excessive e-mails, you have lost a lot of revenue—usually without even realizing it.

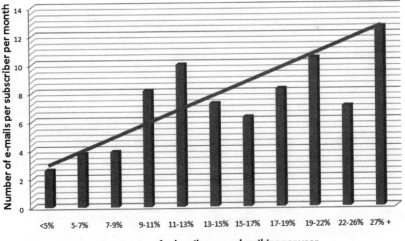

Figure 16.6 Percent Unsubscribed of Number of Delivered e-mails for 187 Companies.

This is a chart of 187 companies that sent 4.19 billion e-mails every month to 414 million subscribers. Some subscribers got less than one e-mail per month. Some got as many as 40 per month. As you can see from this chart, there is a direct correlation between the number of e-mails received and the unsubscribe rate.

Frequent E-mails Can Reduce Deliverability

It costs 5 to 10 times more to acquire a new customer than it does to retain an existing one (*Emarketer,* 2005). Frequent e-mails can generate so many additional unsubscribes and spam complaints that you could end up trading increased short-term gain for lost long-term revenue, as well as increased list attrition. You could potentially damage your brand and e-mail reputation. Any additional revenue, leads, downloads, trials, or other desired actions you generate could easily be wasted by the higher costs of replacing lost customers or prospects.

Following is a case study derived from data reported by Kirill Popov and Loren McDonald on The ClickZ Network.[2] Popov and McDonald list the four main reasons for losses resulting from increased frequency of mailing:

- Additional loss of subscribers
- Cost to reacquire these customers
- Potential lost revenue from lost subscribers
- Higher spam complaint rate that triggers ISP blocks

These were illustrated in their case study, which formed the basis for the numbers shown in Figure 16.7.[3]

This retailer had annual online revenue of $5.7 million and decided to increase the frequency of his e-mail marketing campaigns from 5 per month to 12 per month. Annual revenue increased by 38 percent to $7.9 million. Popov and McDonald looked more closely at the cost of this $2.2 million increased revenue and found that a number of things happened.

---

[2] "Calculating the Cost of Increased E-mail Frequency," Kirill Popov and Loren McDonald, *The ClickZ Network,* Jun 7, 2006, http://www.clickz.com/showPage. html?page=3611201.

[3] This chart is based on the published case study results but is not the same as the work of Popov and McDonald. We have extrapolated their numbers to illustrate the points in this chapter.

Online Retailer Increasing E-mail Frequency	5 per Month	12 per Month
Subscribers Start of Year	515,677	515,677
E-mails Delivered	32,161,000	79,890,000
Revenue per Delivered	$0.18	$0.10
Revenue	$5,788,980	$7,989,000
Revenue per Subscriber	$11.23	$15.49
Unsubscribe Rate	0.740%	1.770%
Monthly Spam Complaints	0.046%	0.646%
Monthly Address Losses	1.53%	3.55%
Annual Loss Rate	18.36%	42.60%
Subscribers Lost in Year	94,678	219,678
Subscribers End of Year	420,999	295,999
Cost of Replacing Lost Subscribers @ $15 Each	$1,420,174	$3,295,176
Lost One-Year Revenue from Lost Subscribers @ $11.23 Each	$1,062,857	$2,466,105
Cost of E-mails Creative and Dispatch @ $6	$192,966	$479,340
Total Present and Future Costs	$2,675,997	$6,240,622
Net Revenue and Present and Future Costs	$3,112,983	$1,748,378
Lost Profits from Increasing Frequency		$1,364,604

Figure 16.7 Effect of Increasing Frequency

The e-mails delivered went from 32 million to almost 80 million. This boost caused the monthly unsubscribe rate to increase, from 0.74 to 1.77 percent. Reported spam complaints increased from 0.046 to 0.646 percent. As a result, the retailer lost 219,678 subscribers instead of 94,678 subscribers during the year. This was a serious loss: revenue per e-mail went down from $0.18 to $0.10.

These permission-based e-mail addresses cost the retailer an average of $15 each to acquire. To keep his business going, he will have to replace these lost subscribers at a cost of $15 each. In addition, each lost subscriber costs the retailer an average annual revenue of $11.23, which he would have received if they hadn't disappeared. This amount was determined by what the company was originally getting per subscriber. Is this $11.23 correct? It could be that the subscribers who unsubscribed were less valuable than the average. On the other hand, sometimes the unsubscribers are more valuable than the customers who remain.

At the end of the year, the retailer had fewer than 300,000 subscribers left with the high-frequency mailing, whereas with the lower-frequency mailing, he had more than 400,000 left.

What Figure 16.7 doesn't tell is how much the perceived excessive frequency reduces the brand's value in subscribers' minds. When more than 100,000 consumers unsubscribe or otherwise become undeliverable as a result of what they considered to be too many e-mails, what do they think of the retailer who sent these e-mails? Are excessive e-mails not only reducing net revenue but also destroying the brand's image?

This experience is the same as my wife Helena's experience with Macy's. Its large store in the Galleria Mall is just 15 minutes away from our condo in Fort Lauderdale. She shops there often. On one visit, a store clerk asked for her e-mail. Shortly thereafter she began getting five e-mails per week from Macy's. She was surprised and annoyed. After a couple of weeks, she unsubscribed. She thinks much less of Macy's now, although she still, reluctantly, shops there. For Helena, that was strike two for Macy's. Strike one was when it refused to say "Merry Christmas" when it came around, instead saying "Happy Holidays." She refused to shop there at all that Christmas. Macy's has since mended its ways with Christmas concerts in its stores. Branding is important.

Test Frequency Changes First

By looking at Figure 16.7, we can see this retailer lost almost $1.4 million per year in profits by increasing his mailing frequency. The only way to know that increased frequency will affect profits is to do the analysis shown here before and after the increased mailing frequency.

Whenever you want to change your e-mail program, begin by making the changes to a test group. Compare the test group's open rates, CTRs (Click Through Rates), conversions, deliverability rates, and unsubscribe rates to those of the control group. Wait until you convince yourself that your change is a good idea. Then roll it out.

Easier said than done. Increasing frequency from 5 per month to 12 per month requires an increase in your creative and programming staff. Management won't give you the funds to hire additional staff just for a test. So how can you test additional frequency? If you have your e-mail delivery and part of your creative outsourced to an ESP, you can ask the ESP to help you increase your frequency for the test without you or your ESP hiring additional permanent staff for it.

Of course, increasing frequency isn't always a bad thing. Many companies don't send enough e-mail. To determine the right frequency, you need to study your customer situation one segment at a time.

The E-mail Experience Council's "2006 Retail E-mail Subscription Benchmark Study" showed that only 7 percent of retailers gave subscribers any kind of idea of how many e-mails to expect. In the study, only one retailer, Coldwater Creek, allowed subscribers to choose to receive a monthly e-mail.

Frequency and Bounces

Why do e-mails bounce? It may be because subscribers change jobs or e-mail addresses or because they get tired of receiving communications from you. Each factor is illustrated in MailerMailer data in Figure 16.8.[4]

E-mail Frequency	Bounce Rate
Daily or More	2.35%
Few Times a Week	2.02%
Once a Week	2.59%
Few Times a Month	4.91%
Once a Month	5.43%
Less than Once a Month	13.57%

Figure 16.8 E-mail Frequency by Bounce Rate

The numbers in the figure suggest that if you send e-mail to people less than once a month, they will forget about you and possibly consider your e-mails to be spam. Regular communications reduce the bounce rate. Using these numbers, you might conclude that daily e-mails are a good thing. But bounce is only one factor to consider.

Two Unsubscribe Case Studies

Take a look at this case study from Dan Wilson on the E-mail Experience Council's blog:

A few weeks ago, I enrolled in Saks Fifth Avenue Online Customer Care (I wanted to pay down my Saks Credit Card). At the end of the process, I opted in to receive Saks e-mails. Below is a day-by-day timeline of what ensued from the moment I hit "confirm."

[4] http://blog.e-mailexperience.org/2008/02/saks_fifth_avenue_how_to_almos.html.

Day 1: Opted-in—Redirect to a thank-you page, but no welcome e-mail.
Day 2: One day after sign-up, the welcome e-mail arrived. I would've liked to have seen it immediately, but a one-day lag time is not the end of the world. I thought the subject line, "Welcome to Saks.com. We have a special offer for you ..." wasn't great, but at least was very clear and direct. The body of the message contained a call-to-action that included a 10% discount. Pretty good overall.
Day 3: Not 1, but 2 messages from Saks in one day. Oops?
—Message #1: Subject Line—"SAKSFIRST Double Points + From the Heart," received at 10:31AM EST, Valentine's Day call-to-action.
—Message #2: Subject Line—"Get SAKSFIRST Double Points!" received at 3:53PM EST, Double Points call-to-action.
Day 4: Subject Line—"SAKSFIRST Double Points + Have-To-Have Handbags."
Days 5 and 6: Nothing (Super Bowl weekend).
Day 7: Not 1, but 2 messages from Saks. Hard to believe that they would make this same "mistake" only 4 days later.
—Message #1: Subject Line—"Dior ... Take it Away!" received at 10:08AM EST, Women's Shoes call-to-action
—Message #2: Subject Line—"Video Exclusive! Days 1 to 3 of Fashion Week," received at 4:51PM EST, Fashion Week call-to-action.
Day 8: Subject Line—"Fabulous Valentine's Gifts."
Day 9: Not 1, but 2 messages from Saks. Another "mistake" 2 days after the 2nd one (3rd double e-mail day in past 6 days).
—Message #1: Subject Line—"David Yurman Gifts," received at 9:47AM EST, Women's Shoes call-to-action.
—Message #2: Subject Line—"Day 4 Video of Fashion Week," received at 5:05PM EST, Fashion Week call-to-action.
Day 10: Subject Line—"NEW: Reyes, Wayne ... + SALE."
Day 11: I clicked on their unsubscribe/change preferences link, fully intending to unsubscribe. But, alas, they did it right! I was able to edit my preferences and elect to receive updates only "Once a Week."

Saved by an unsubscribe option! This is a safety net—a virtual last ditch for you to try to recapture your subscribers' hearts and minds. How many e-mail marketers provide this option? Not enough.

My second case study compares two actual companies that did some pretty extensive mailing one year. Figure 16.9 outlines the numbers.

	Company A	Company B
Subscribers	586,324	558,128
Delivered	42,407,835	50,173,347
Average E-mails per Year	72.3	89.9
Unsubscribed	43,652	59,031
Percent Unsub	7.45%	10.58%
Online Buyers	58,566	95,036
Percent Buyers	10.0%	17.0%
Total Online Orders	64,910	107,638
Average Order Value	$159.81	$101.77
Total Online Sales	$10,373,267	$10,954,319
Dollar Sales per E-mail	$0.24	$0.22
Sales per Subscriber	$17.69	$19.63
Conversions per E-mail	0.15%	0.21%
Spending per Buyer	$177.12	$115.26

Figure 16–9 Two Companies with Differing e-mail Frequencies

Both retail firms had several hundred stores in shopping malls; the numbers here cover only online sales. Both began the year with approximately the same number of registered subscribers in their databases. Company A sent more than 42 million e-mails, about 72 e-mails per address. Company B sent more than 50 million e-mails, about 90 e-mails per address. Company B's higher mailing frequency took a toll on its subscription rate: 10.6 percent of recipients unsubscribed, compared to 7.5 percent of Company A's recipients. However, 17 percent of Company B's subscribers became buyers, compared to only 10 percent of Company A's. The difference in the average order size may have been to the result of different merchandise rather than a result of less frequent mailing.

Interestingly, some of the subscribers who unsubscribed had made purchases before they disappeared. The total online purchases of all unsubscribers in each store was close to $1 million (see Figure 16.10). The most significant number is the average spend per unsubscriber. Company A's unsubscribers spent an average of $220, whereas all its buyers spent only an average of $177. Company B's lost buyers spent an average of $156, and all its buyers spent an average of $115.

Figure 16.10 reveals that the lost subscribers were more valuable than the ones who remained. The companies were losing their best

Company A	Unsubs and Undels		
Number of Purchases	Buyers	Revenue	$/Buyer
1	3,654	$528,140	$144.54
2	551	$181,528	$329.45
3	146	$79,704	$545.92
4+	156	$168,071	$1,077.38
Total	4,351	$957,443	$220.05
Not Leaving	58,556	$10,373,267	$177.15

Company B	Unsubs and Undels		
Number of Purchases	Buyers	Revenue	$/Buyer
1	4,054	$386,847	$95.42
2	753	$159,822	$212.25
3	262	$81,355	$310.52
4+	292	$207,911	$712.02
Total	5,361	$835,936	$155.93
Not Leaving	95,036	$10,954,319	$115.26

Figure 16.10 Two Companies' Unsubscribes and Undeliverables

customers. Company B was losing 292 customers who bought products four or more times before they disappeared. This kind of analysis shows the hidden costs of increasing mailing frequency.

What can we conclude from these numbers?

- The conversion rate from frequent e-mails was quite low—between 0.15 percent and 0.21 percent per e-mail delivered.
- Frequent mailing increased the number of sales.
- Frequent mailing probably increased the number of unsubscribes.
- Marketers need to analyze those who leave (through unsubscribing or through becoming undeliverable). If you are losing your best customers, you need to find out why and figure out what you can do about it.

How to Keep Your Best Buyers

You know two facts at this point. Frequent e-mails increase sales, but they can turn some people off. You can live with losing non-buyers; you can't live as comfortably if you lose frequent buyers, especially if it's because you send them too many e-mails. One way to improve the situation would be to treat your buyers better than your non-buyers.

This obvious solution wasn't easy for either company to adopt. Both had large stores and considered their e-mail program as a sideline. They fell into a trap because all they collected from subscribers in the opt-in process was the subscriber's e-mail address and first name. Using that name, they could personalize the greeting in the content, but that was all. Going forward, their buyers got exactly the same e-mails as the non-buyers. The retailers had their buyers' street addresses, of course. They could have appended data and created e-mails with very personal content just for the buyers. Why didn't they take advantage of the situation?

For both companies, the reason is a common one among e-mail marketers. They were so busy creating new e-mails that they had little or no staff resources available to create differentiated communications for buyers. Such mass e-mailers typically live hand to mouth. Each e-mail offered deep discounts as inducements to their subscribers. Their management was seeking the least costly way of delivering their e-mails. Any marketer who comes up with the idea of creating different e-mails for buyers will have a tough time convincing management that the extra expense is justified. But numbers don't lie. According to JupiterResearch, "Engaging in relevant communications increases net profits by an average of 18 times more than broadcast mailings" (2006). What can you do to get management's attention to this situation?

Frequent E-mails' Effect on Offline Sales

Not shown in figure are the offline sales attributed to these subscribers. (The Off-e-mail Sales Multiplier). E-mail campaigns sent by companies with several marketing channels, as these two companies have, will affect behaviors in all other channels. Typically, 75 percent of offline purchases made by customers who are active on the Web (as registered subscribers are) are made after some online research. Unquestionably, subscribers who got these e-mails were prompted (and encouraged) to go to the retail stores to see and try on the clothing before they bought. The offline sales resulting from these e-mails were significant. No one knows how significant, however. The reason these sales don't show up on the chart is that these companies didn't maintain customer marketing databases that showed sales from all channels. Creating such marketing databases would have cost more than $1 million per year. That kind of extra expenditure just doesn't fit into the business model of the heavily discounting mass e-mailer. If they had calculated their off-e-mail multiplier which was probably 2 or 3, they would have realized that their e-mails were generating $30 or $40 million in total sales, rather than the $10 shown in the e-mails themselves. With numbers like these, which they did not have, spending $1 million for a database would have made sense.

How can you find out how extensive are the sales due to the e-mails which are not shown in the e-mail shopping carts? Here are some ideas:

- Put coupons in your e-mails that are good in stores or on the Web site.

- Feature products in the e-mails that are not advertised elsewhere.

- Set up a loyalty program so that buyers will let you know when they are buying in any channel.

- Conduct surveys to find out what your e-mail subscribers are doing.

How Often Should You Mail?

For direct mail, the answer is: "As often as profitable." For e-mail you have to answer a more fundamental question first. What do you have to say that your subscribers might want to hear? Once you have that clearly in mind, you can explain it to your subscribers during opt-in. However, some subscribers will only be window shoppers at best and will more than likely disappear on you no matter what you do. You might experiment with the opt-in e-mail to ask them how often they want to hear about your subject, perhaps giving them a choice and letting them dictate the frequency that is right for them.

If you publish news, for example, subscribers might actually want to receive a daily newsletter, plus breaking news occasionally during the day. But most businesses don't publish news, so daily might be an overload. To get the answers you need, set up a preference center that makes clear what your e-mail newsletters or promotions will contain and how often they will appear. Break your content down into several newsletter options: daily, twice a week, weekly, or less often.

Don't bite off more than you can chew. If you advertise daily content, be sure that what you send matches the expectations you create in the preference form. To make sure readers actually get what they want, break your subject matter into categories that readers can get their minds around.

For example, you might have four different newsletters and a fifth that is a weekly summary of the other four. Some subscribers might opt for the weekly summary. It could have links that take readers back to material in any of the other four newsletters.

Retailers, on the other hand, are providing opportunities to purchase products and services in their messages. The e-mails will contain pictures of the products and links to detailed descriptions. They might have technical information on the products or nostalgia about how they are made. Have a brainstorming session to figure out what you will really give your subscribers so you can make it completely clear in the preference request form. Make sure you explain how often these e-mails will arrive. If you are frank in the opt-in process, there will be fewer disappointments and spam accusations later on. If you send more than your subscribers were expecting based on your preference form, many subscribers will get annoyed, or even angry.

> *No matter what you promise during the opt-in process, you must honor it throughout the lifecycle of your e-mail relationship with subscribers. Resist the temptation to sneak one or two "can't miss" e-mail messages through. You may get away with it once or twice, but keep it up, and you'll pay for your aggression with more spam complaints and less customer engagement.*
>
> —STEFAN POLLARD, CLICKZ

Conclusion on E-mail Frequency

Mailing too frequently can be dangerous for your e-mail marketing program. To be sure you are doing things the right way and not losing your most valuable customers, consider some of the following tests.

In addition to an unsubscribe link, test inserting an, "Are we sending you too many messages?" link. When subscribers click on this link, tell them how often you have been mailing them. Then offer them the opportunity to reduce or increase mailing frequency or limit mailings to specific topics.

Don't go crazy with this idea. Test it with a few of your subscribers first. Use RFM cell codes to suggest the ones to test this with. You might begin with subscribers with very low RFM codes to see if you could reactivate them.

Another test to try is with unsubscribers; they hold valuable information for you. They have an idea of what is wrong (if anything) with your e-mail program, as far as they are concerned. You have one last shot at these unsubscribers: the "you have unsubscribed" message. Try placing a survey in this e-mail to find out what why they are leaving and what you could do to make your e-mails better. Don't miss this opportunity. Take what you learn very seriously. Think about it, and act on it.

Take-Away Thoughts

- Junk e-mails exceed junk direct mail by 100 to one.

- Despite all the spam and junk filters, most e-mail subscribers receive more e-mail from legitimate companies than they want or can possibly read.

- A survey of 80 major mailers shows that their subscribers receive an average of 10.3 e-mails a month.

- Direct mail frequency is controlled by the cost. You should send as many messages as it is profitable to send.

- The break-even rate formula for direct mail is (Cost per piece) ÷ (Net profit from a single sale).

- Use the same formula for e-mail, and because of the low cost, virtually all mailings break even.

- The average conversions per delivered e-mail is 0.11 percent.

- Over-mailing increases the unsubscribe and undeliver rate. You may lose your best customers.

■ You may actually lose profits by mailing too often.

■ One solution: on your unsubscribe page, offer the possibility of lower e-mail frequency.

A quiz on this chapter and all figures can be found at www.dbmarket ing.com/STM4. Those taking all the quizzes can receive a Successful Completion Certificate from the Database Marketing Institute which can be used in their résumé.

17

Building Retail Store Traffic

*I can't believe the number of people who are actually
walking in our restaurants and redeeming the coupons.
Before I tried e-mail, I put a coupon in the local
newspaper and had fewer than 10 people redeem it.
Then, I put the same coupon in an e-mail and sent it
to 400 people and saw 100 of the e-mail coupons
redeemed that month! That's an outstanding rate,
given that only 400 were sent. I've also tried direct
mail and got such a low redemption rate that I won't
do it again. The e-mail coupons are being printed and
brought in daily and people are fighting to get on my
e-mail subscription list.*

—ABBY WEAVER,

Marketing Director, Fajita Grill

*Even if you don't have an online business you still
need to have an online presence for your business.
Why? Because consumers are increasingly searching for
information about a business or product online before
they decide to visit or buy. I have found myself
engaging in ROBO (Research Online, Buy Offline)
behavior for a number of years, but didn't realize how
widespread the trend was becoming until I saw the
results of a consumer study presented by Gillian Heltai
and Greg Stewart at the Search Marketing Expo East
Conference this year.*

*Stewart's company, 15 Miles, partnered with comScore
and observed nearly 25 million searches from a sample
of one million consumers who agreed to anonymous*

413

monitoring of their online habits. They found that consumers in all age groups tend to go online first for information about local businesses. 81 percent of the 18–34 year-old age bracket search online first, while a lower (but still very significant!) 69 percent of the 35–59 year-old age bracket search for local business info online before venturing out.

—WENDY CONEYBEER,
GannettLocal

Direct mail has been a way of creating retail store traffic for more than 50 years. Recently, e-mail has begun to take on that job. Most people think of e-mail marketing as a way of creating online transactions. Actually, e-mails do far more for offline sales than they do for online sales, as you will learn in this chapter. An Epsilon study reported that 86 percent of e-mail recipients said that they buy products and services at retail locations as a result of e-mails. In addition to online sales, marketing e-mails build the brand and drive catalog sales, phone sales, and brick-and-mortar sales. The percentages will surprise you.

In 2003, cataloger Miles Kimball did a pioneering test of e-mail to stimulate catalog sales. It sent 20,000 catalogs in three waves to previous online shoppers with an accompanying e-mail saying, "Look in your mailbox for ..." It also sent 20,000 catalogs in three waves without the accompanying e-mail to identical shoppers. Those who received the e-mail spent 18 percent more per household than those who did not.

Many catalogers now use e-mails to boost catalog sales. By 2007, 82 percent of 434 catalogers surveyed by the Direct Marketing Association (DMA) were using e-mail promotions. Today, more than 44 percent of all paper catalog sales are made on the Web, as opposed to phone or mail.[1]

A major video rental chain asked members to provide their e-mail addresses and asked them whether they wanted to receive e-mails about movies. When its database was big enough, it sent e-mail newsletters about movies to 204,000 members every two weeks, holding 16,000 as a control group who didn't receive the e-mails. After six months, the retailer discovered that those who got the e-mails spent 28 percent more per household than those who didn't. E-mails drive traffic to retail locations.

---

[1] *Multichannel Marketing in the Catalog Industry* (Direct Marketing Association, 2007), http://imis.the-dma.org/Bookstore/ProductSingle.cfm?p=0D440279 DD4D1CDA 3951319EF42A00D3DEA36CD0.

In 2008, Constant Contact reported that 88 percent of small-business owners surveyed used e-mails to build sales for Mother's Day. Thirty-seven percent of retailers found flowers to be the most popular gift, and 25 percent of gifts were a restaurant meal. Salon/spa appointments, jewelry, and clothing were also popular gifts. Most consumers spent from $25 to $75 on their gifts.

Why E-mails Boost Offline Sales So Well

E-mails are like TV advertisements. You may not buy from them, but if you open them you usually see product pictures and sales which stick in your mind, just like what happens when you see something on TV. Now that the thought is in your mind, it will affect what you do later that day or week. What's more, the e-mail may be much more cost effective than a TV ad.

- Direct mail and print are about 100 times more expensive than e-mail ($600 per thousand versus $6 per thousand).

- E-mail can be personalized and customized to individual subscribers.

- E-mails are completely measurable.

- E-mails are useful in building a relationship with individual subscribers.

A Harris Interactive poll conducted for Yahoo! reported that 66 percent of consumers shopped online before making an on- or offline purchase. Of that group, 75 percent said that going online to research products and services was their first stop in their holiday shopping experience, and 90 percent said that they had a better overall shopping experience when they researched products online before shopping in stores.

Multichannel customers have high expectations for what they think retailers should do for them. Many of them want to:

- Use loyalty cards, store cards, and gift vouchers through all channels.

- Get e-mail updates about special orders when they talk to a call center.

- Return to stores products that were bought online.

- Find out via the Web whether the item they want is available in any given store.

After doing their research on the Web, some shoppers will visit a store to touch and examine the product. They may then return to the Web for further price comparison. Finally, they may order it online or by phone.

Bringing Shoppers to Store Events

Stores have an advantage over e-mail. In a store, a shopper can use her senses to experience the products firsthand. Store visits also prompt impulse buying. They are ideal for food tastings, cooking demonstrations, instructional workshops, trunk shows, and book signings. For instance, Harry & David held a gourmet grilling sauces tasting event and used e-mail to raise awareness. Home Depot promoted a kids' workshop on how to build a birdhouse through e-mail. Toys 'R' Us used an e-mail to promote a 3D Crayola chalk art event going on in the store. Saks Fifth Avenue e-mails subscribers a monthly listing of flagship-store events. Macy's sent an e-mail promoting its National Wear Red Day for the American Heart Association; if you wore red to a Macy's store on a given day, you received a 15 percent off coupon.

E-mails offer unique ways to create in-store traffic. Walgreens announced that it was giving away free 8 by 10 photos for one day only. All you had to do was upload your photo to its system online and then pick up the print at your local store.

Getting Subscribers to Visit Your Store

The first step in getting e-mail subscribers to visit your store is to capture subscribers' zip code. You can get this on a Web site, in the opt-in e-mail, or in the welcome e-mail. If you don't have the zip code yet, put a box asking for it in every e-mail you send to those who have not yet provided it.

As soon as the subscriber enters his zip code in this box, he should be directed to a landing page showing him the stores nearest to him, complete with name, address, phone number, hours, and a map. If there are several stores near him, get him to click on the store he normally shops at or wants to shop at. *He should never have to enter his zip code again and should never be asked to.* The only exception is if you find that he actually does his shopping at a retail location other than the one nearest his home zip code. If that's the case, change his designated store to the one he uses. Most of your subscribers are probably employed. Their preferred store may be closer to their work than their home, so you have to allow for that. Once you do, from then on, their preferred store should be featured in every e-mail you send them.

The e-mail should come from the manager of the subscriber's local store and include the manager's name and photo. The subscriber shouldn't receive e-mails from some big corporation. Each e-mail is a personal message to Susan from Burton Price, Manager of the Macy's store at 2314 East Sunrise Boulevard. Does having a manager's name and photo on a promotional e-mail make a difference in store visits? This is easy to test. The numbers will answer your question.

How to Use the Store Manager's Name

If the subscriber's local store is within shopping distance of her home, try a personal greeting to her from the store manager above the fold such as:

Susan,

Thanks for subscribing to our e-mails. We'd love to have you shopping in our store.

Next time you are there, look me up, and I will show you around. I have a special gift for you. Ask any of the sales assistants in our store. They know where to find me.

Burton Price, Store Manager

Be sure to keep track of the results. It should be well worth the effort.

Getting the Store Location Correct

A major retailer really missed an opportunity to personalize an e-mail. The e-mail offered a class at "my local store," but nowhere in the e-mail did it tell me where my local store was. I went to the bottom of the e-mail and saw an "enter my zip code" field. I entered my zip code, and the link took me to the general store locator page on the retailer's Web site. I had to enter my zip code again. What a waste of time.

The Relationship between Online and Offline Sales

In 2008, *eMarketer* provided a very useful chart showing the relationship between Web-influenced store sales and retail e-commerce sales. The results of the survey were eye-opening, as shown in Figure 17.1.

Actual walk-in retail traffic purchases as a result of the Web are about four times the volume of online sales. These Web-induced sales can come about in a variety of ways. Consumers can use search engines or banner ads to find Web sites where they do their research before going to the retail store. They can also receive e-mails from stores or Web sites where they have shopped or registered and use the information in these e-mails for suggestions that prompt them to visit the local stores to make a purchase. It is really up to the retailer whether to wait patiently until customers decide to visit the Web site again or to proactively go to subscribers to tell them with e-mails what the store has to offer that may be of interest to them.

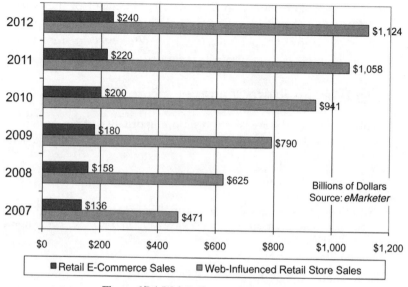

Figure 17.1 Web-Influenced Retail Sales

These are powerful numbers. The relationship between e-mails and offline sales shows that for any retailer who wants to send e-mails to potential customers designed to inform them of what is available in stores, the returns can be phenomenal—even if the retailer does no online business at all.

In 2006, comScore did a study sponsored by Google that found that 25 percent of Web searchers actually bought an item directly related to their Web search. Among these buyers, 63 percent completed their buy offline in some manner, either in a retail store or over the phone. The remainder bought the item on the Web.

The study reported that the highest levels of offline buying were video games and consoles (93 percent), toys and hobbies (88 percent), consumer electronics (84 percent), and music/movies/videos (83 percent). Offline clothing buying reported in the study averaged 65 percent.

Items in Stock in a Retail Store

How annoying to receive an e-mail promoting an interesting product only to find, when you go to the store, that the item isn't in stock. Some retailers have managed to put links in their e-mails that enable readers to check whether an item is in stock at their nearest store. It saves an hour's fruitless trip—and just might represent the secret to creating more offline sales. If some of your stores have special evening events, your e-mails might let your subscribers know about the events at their local store. Banana Republic does an excellent job of previewing shopping events for top customers.

How a Retailer Becomes Web-Savvy

To see just how promotional e-mails can affect overall revenue and lifetime value, let's try what Albert Einstein described as a thought experiment. Imagine a retailer who started with a profitable business with 350,000 customers who visited his stores twice a year, spending an average of $144 per visit. Let's trace this store's possible future based on three scenarios:

- The store has successful retail outlets but no Web site or e-mails.
- The store adds a Web site but doesn't sell on the Web.
- The store adds online sales to its Web site and starts sending e-mails.

Each incremental marketing method has its benefits and costs. Let's first look at the retail-only picture shown in Figure 17.2. The retailer traces the lifetime of 350,000 customers over three years. The 50 percent retention rate in the acquisition year means that half of those who shopped the first year never came back again. This is typical. Marketing

No Web Site Small Retailer		Acquisition Year	Year 2	Year 3
Customers		350,000	175,000	96,250
Retention Rate		50%	55%	60%
Visits per Year		2	3	3
Total Visits		700,000	437,500	288,750
Spending per Visit		$144	$150	$155
Total Revenue		$100,800,000	$65,625,000	$44,756,250
Operating Costs	65%	$65,520,000	$42,656,250	$29,091,563
Customer Acquisition Cost	$40	$14,000,000		
Marketing Costs	$4	$1,400,000	$1,400,000	$1,400,000
Total Costs		$80,920,000	$44,056,250	$30,491,563
Gross Profits		$19,880,000	$21,568,750	$14,264,688
Discount Rate		1	1.1	1.21
Net Present Value Profits		$19,880,000	$19,607,955	$11,788,998
Cumulative NPV Profits		$19,880,000	$39,487,955	$51,276,952
Lifetime Value		$56.80	$112.82	$146.51

Figure 17.2 Retailer with No Web Site

costs include print ads, promotions, and a loyalty card program, which is used to track visits. The retailer used part of the marketing budget to recognize the gold customers and to try to get the lapsed customers to come back.

The Retailer Builds a Web Site

Spending $875,000, the store built a Web site that features its products, sales, corporate history, and management team. The chain doesn't sell from the Web site, but visitors can enter their zip code and find the nearest store location. In addition, there is a search box so shoppers can find a product on the site, with pictures and prices. Occasionally the store offers coupons on the site, which visitors can print out and bring to the store. The site is listed in the search engines, increasing the possibility of visitors finding the site and searching for products. As a result of all this, the retailer has picked up 50,000 new customers (see Figure 17.3).

Web Site No Online Sales Small Retailer		Acquisition Year	Year 2	Year 3
Total Customers		400,000	220,000	132,000
Retention Rate		55%	60%	65%
Visits Per Year		2.2	2.9	3.5
Total Visits		880,000	638,000	462,000
Spending Per Visit		$146	$152	$157
Total Revenue		$128,480,000	$96,976,000	$72,534,000
Operating Costs	65%	$83,512,000	$63,034,400	$47,147,100
Customer Acquisition Cost	$10	$4,000,000		
Marketing Costs	$4	$1,600,000	$1,600,000	$1,600,000
Web Site Costs	$2.50	$1,000,000	$550,000	$330,000
Total Costs		$90,112,000	$65,184,400	$49,077,100
Gross Profits		$38,368,000	$31,791,600	$23,456,900
Discount Rate		1	1.1	1.21
Net Present Value Profits		$38,368,000	$28,901,455	$19,385,868
Cumulative NPV Profits		$38,368,000	$67,269,455	$86,655,322
Lifetime Value		$95.92	$168.17	$216.64

Figure 17.3 Retailer with Non-E-Commerce Web Site

Despite the expensive Web site, the customer lifetime value grew in the first three years, as did revenue.

The Retailer Sends E-mails and Adds Online Shopping

The Web site has been a success. The retailer now takes the next big step. He builds a database of e-mail subscribers who register on the Web site. He offers incentives to store employees to ask customers for their e-mail addresses. The result, after some effort, is that the store has acquired 250,000 e-mail opt-in subscribers plus 100,000 regular shoppers who shopped offline but did not subscribe to e-mails. The retailer begins a weekly series of e-mails to the subscribers, inviting them to come to his store. The e-mails permit shoppers to research, learn of his

Online & Offline Sales Small Retailer		Registration Year	Year 2	Year 3
Non-e-mail Customers		120,000	66,000	39,600
E-mail Customers		280,000	232,400	195,216
Annual Unsubs & Undelivers		17%	16%	15%
End of Year Subscribers		232,400	195,216	165,934
E-mails Delivered	65	18,200,000	15,106,000	12,689,040
Opens	15%	2,730,000	2,265,900	1,903,356
Unique Clicks	19%	518,700	430,521	361,638
Conversions from Clicks	2.20%	11,411	9,471	7,956
Off Line Sales due to E-mails	4.00	45,646	37,886	31,824
Total Sales due to E-mails		57,057	47,357	39,780
Sales from Online and E-mail Induced Retail	$144	$8,216,208	$6,819,453	$5,728,340
Store Sales from Regular Marketing		$128,480,000	$96,976,000	$72,534,000
Total Revenue		$136,696,208	$103,795,453	$78,262,340
Operating Costs	62%	$84,751,649	$64,353,181	$48,522,651
Customer Acquisition Costs	$10	$4,000,000		
Subscriber Acquisition Cost	$2	$560,000		
Marketing Costs	$4	$1,120,000	$1,120,000	$1,120,000
E-mail Costs CPM Incl Creative	$8	$145,600	$120,848	$101,512
Database & Analytics	$4	$1,120,000	$929,600	$780,864
Website Costs with Shopping Cart	$4	$1,120,000	$929,600	$780,864
Total Costs		$92,817,249	$67,453,229	$51,305,891
Gross Profits		$43,878,959	$36,342,224	$26,956,449
Discount Rate		1	1.1	1.21
Net Present Value Profits		$43,878,959	$33,038,385	$22,278,057
Cumulative NPV Profits		$43,878,959	$76,917,344	$99,195,401
Lifetime Value		$109.70	$192.29	$247.99

Figure 17.4 Retailer with On- and Off-line Sales and E-mails

sales, and print coupons to use in his stores. The e-mails are a great success and bring in more revenue.

In addition, our retailer begins to sell his products on the Web. Figure 17.4 shows how his picture has changed.

Changes from various Efforts Small Retailer	52	Registration Year	Year 2	Year 3
Original Lifetime Value		$56.80	$112.82	$146.51
Adding a Web Site — No Online Sales		$95.92	$168.17	$216.64
Online, Offline and E-mails		$109.70	$192.29	$247.99
Gain from Moving to Advanced Marketing		$52.90	$79.47	$101.48
Times 400,000 Base Customers		$21,158,959	$31,788,254	$40,593,170

Figure 17.5 Improved Profits from Adding E-mail and Online Shopping

His first year revenue is now over $118 million, including $5.9 million from online and e-mail-induced sales. We can trace the increase in his sales as he moves up the chain to full online and offline sales with e-mail stimulation in Figure 17.5.

The $40 million in Year 3 shown in Figure 17.5 is pure profit. All the added costs have been included. This example shows how to go about the computation process in moving gradually from offline retailing to full online retailing, supported by e-mail marketing. Use tables like these to begin supporting your e-mail marketing planning. These and all the other charts in this book can be downloaded for free at www.dbmarketing.com.

E-mail Coupons versus Free-Standing Inserts (FSIs)

It is really important to know what members of your audience are doing. Are they buying? Are sales working? Is relationship marketing working? Are the e-mails important? How much do they drive offline purchases? One way to find these things out is to issue e-mail coupons that can be used online or at any of your retail stores.

By e-mail coupons, we aren't talking about the free-standing inserts (FSIs) found in the Sunday newspaper or that arrive every week in the mail. For the past 50 years, manufacturers and retailers have printed and inserted coupons into newspapers. FSIs account for 84 percent of all coupons used by consumers in the United States, but the average response rate is only about 1.2 percent. FSIs usually take about three months from the time they are inserted in a newspaper until they arrive back at the manufacturer, who has to redeem them with some sort of payment to the retailer.[2] These coupons are almost never personalized, and it is seldom possible to know who used them—or even where they got them in the first place.

Yet FSIs are big business. In 2007, 257 billion were distributed with an average face value of $1.26.[3] The top categories were consumer packaged goods (e.g., household cleaning products, pet food, personal products, room deodorizers, snacks, and medicines). The companies involved included Procter & Gamble, General Mills, Johnson & Johnson, Unilever, Nestlé, Kraft Foods, and Kimberley Clark.

Coupons that arrive in e-mails or are downloaded from Web sites are completely different. They can, if used intelligently, permit the advertiser to get instant feedback and to learn a great deal of useful information about the people who use them. The coupons' average response rate is from 5 to 20 percent. Subscribers can print them at home and take them to a store, or they can use them online—with or without printing—with a code entered in the online checkout process.

One advantage of e-mails in driving retail traffic, therefore, is their speed. In its study "Harnessing the Power of E-mail," McKinsey & Company explained why e-mails are so effective at this job. It found that e-mail response rates were 15 percent, compared to 1 percent for direct mail. E-mails cost $0.01 to $0.03 per e-mail, compared to $0.55 for each direct mail piece. And e-mails generate 80 percent of responses within 48 hours.

The Coupon Pass-Along Effect

Once you encourage subscribers to print out coupons at home, they can—and will—pass them along to family members and friends. When someone arrives at your store, ready to buy with a coupon in hand, will your salesclerks turn them down? How you react to this situation depends on how you plan for it. There are two scenarios:

- *The coupon is meant for only one subscriber:* Sally Warren may be a good customer whom you are trying to reward with a special discount or an invitation to Tuesday Night with the Manager. You don't want just any subscriber to have this reward. In this case, place Sally Warren's name

---

[2] According to the Texas Grocery & Convenience Association, the retailer has to "count them, sort them, send them to the right place, then wait ... and wait ... AND WAIT for the reimbursement check!" (http://www.txgca.org/index.php?p=1_32_Coupon-Program).

[3] "FSI Coupons Deliver 257 Billion Offers Worth $320B in Incentives in '07," Marketing Charts(2007), http://www.marketingcharts.com/print/fsi-coupons-deliver-257-billion-offers-worth-320b-in-incentives-in-07-3005/.

prominently on the coupon and, "This coupon is valid only for Sally Warren." You could ask your sales staff to check IDs.

- *The coupon is meant for anyone:* In other cases, the coupon is a traffic-builder—any traffic. You can design the coupon to be passed around. For these coupons, you might say, "For Sally Warren and her close friends" on the coupon and then accept the coupons from whoever presents them. A big advantage here is that if you scan the coupons into your POS system when they are redeemed, you can learn a lot about Sally Warren. She is an advocate who brings traffic into your store. You might send her an e-mail thanking her for doing this. In this situation, when Annette Bricker uses a Sally Warren coupon, you can ask your sales staff to notice this and, while thanking Annette for her purchase, ask her for her e-mail address.

Coach In-Store Pickup System

Coach sends e-mails to its subscribers inviting them to use the e-mail links to research a handbag, footwear, or accessories and pick up selected items at "your chosen Coach store within 2 hours of purchase (during store hours)." Once the subscriber has located an item, she is invited to click the store-pickup button. She enters her zip code. At this point, the Web site provides her with a list of nearby Coach stores that have her desired item in stock. "Once you have completed the checkout process online, you will receive 2 separate e-mails from us. Your order will be ready when the Pickup e-mail has been sent to you." The two e-mails are the order confirmation e-mail and the pickup e-mail.

This system is very convenient for the shopper. It is a lot easier to research a handbag on a Web site than to drive to a store, park, and wander around looking for something. The shopper gets in her car only when she knows that what she wants is waiting for her. But the system is also very convenient for Coach. It brings shoppers into its stores to pick up their purchases, many of whom will walk out with more purchases than just the one they came in for.

Gift Cards: A $26 Billion Business

About 75 percent of consumers bought a gift card at some time in 2008. More than one-half of consumers wanted to receive a gift card as a present. The average consumer spent about 16 percent of his holiday budget on gift cards.

Retailers have found ways to turn gift cards to their advantage. Statistics suggest that many gift card recipients don't use all the cash in their cards. Shoppers will use a $50 gift card to make a $36 purchase, leaving $14 on the card. In such cases, the retailer banks the difference. In other cases, according to *JCK Magazine,* the jewelry industry's leading trade publication, many consumers apply their gift cards toward larger purchases and end up spending more than the amount on the card.

In an article in the *New Yorker,* James Surowiecki describes gift cards as a "socially tolerable version" of giving cash. He explained that gift cards are one of the few ways in which the value of the money spent on a gift equals the receiver's perceived value of it. Gift cards can be purchased on the Web but are usually used offline at a store or restaurant.

In addition, gift cards have two extra benefits. First, with permission, the retailer can go back to the gift-giver and suggest that she give again at the same time next year. Second, the retailer may send e-mails to the gift recipients who can, with their opt-in permission, be offered a chance to send e-mail gift cards themselves.

Gifts.com has signed up several hundred companies for which it provides gift cards, including Barnes and Noble, Bloomingdale's, Macy's, Marriott Hotels, Nike, Dick's Sporting Goods, The Gap, Home Goods, The Sports Authority, Staples, Ticketmaster, and Overstock.com. The system works this way:

- The gift recipient receives an e-mail with the gift card and a redemption code.

- The recipient can then browse through the listed merchants to pick one or several retailers to redeem her gift card with. She can redeem her entire gift amount at one store or split it across multiple stores.

- To redeem her gift, she clicks on the link in the e-mail and enters her claim code on the landing page. She can redeem some of the money now and more later, or spend it all in one shot. (Some merchants send an actual plastic gift card via mail. Others send the card by e-mail.)

The beauty of this system is that the gift-giver doesn't have to decide what to give or pick it out and ship it. He doesn't even have to decide what type of gift to give; it is all up to the recipient.

An E-mail to Profit from a Mistake

An e-mail to subscribers said:

> As a valued Best Buy customer, we want to inform you of an error that will appear in the September 23, 2007, Best Buy ad. On the front cover we mistakenly listed the price of the 50" Panasonic Plasma TV at $1799, before $90 savings. We intended to advertise the 42" Panasonic Plasma TV at $1799, before $90 savings.
>
> Best Buy will not be honoring this price on the aforementioned 50" Panasonic Plasma TV. We apologize for any inconvenience, and we will offer a $100 Instant Rebate on all Plasma Televisions from Sunday, September 23, 2007, through Saturday, September 29, 2007. This Instant Rebate will be deducted from the price you see in the store, including our regular sale prices. Thank you for your understanding. We look forward to seeing you in our store soon.

Here is a wonderful way to take advantage of a mistake to help build a relationship with your customers. You aren't the wizard of Oz behind the curtain, but a real person like the Cowardly Lion who makes mistakes and admits it. Look for opportunities like this, and your subscribers will read your e-mails.

Getting Subscribers to Create Shopping Lists

Target has developed a unique shopping aid called TargetLists, which is featured at the top of its Web site and in its e-mails. Subscribers browsing their e-mails can click on whatever interests them and have it added to their list. The list can be made available to others—spouse, parents, children, friends. TargetLists can be used at home or in the stores. To browse and select items, customers can scan an item's bar code in the store or click on the item they want to add online.

To make sure gift recipients get what they want, the forms are set up so that senders can add specific information about an item in the comments section. They can advise their gift givers about their favorite colors or themes. List makers also can store future gift ideas, track items purchased, find other people's lists, and e-mail their lists to friends and family.

Live Chat Reached through E-mail

One reason for going to a store, rather than a Web site, is that you can ask a question while you are there. Sometimes, though, clerks can be hard to find, and when you find them, they don't always know the answers.

Toll-free numbers have turned most consumers off because they reach a voice-response system that asks them to "listen carefully because our menu has changed." Listening carefully and pushing buttons seldom enables callers to talk to a live person.

The problem can be even worse on the Web when there seems to be no way the customer can reach anyone to talk to. Web customers are very impatient. If they can't find what they want, they simply click their mouse and move on. About three-quarters of Web shopping carts are abandoned by customers who never come back. One solution is a live chat button on the site and in e-mails, providing access to a live operator. Live chat software enables operators to interact with customers by talking to them through instant messaging. Chat software lets operators surf online with consumers through technology called co-browsing.[4] In addition many marketers today send "abandoned cart e-mails" to anyone who puts an item in a shopping cart, but leaves the site without buying it—see below.

Chat operators can converse with several consumers at once, thus increasing efficiency, shortening customer wait times, and allowing more customers to receive help.

Many live support software programs provide a customer survey so that consumers can rate their chat operator once a chat is over. If the consumer is reading the e-mail with a live chat button after hours, it can be set up to let the consumer leave an e-mail message.

When CompUSA set up a live chat system, it found that 68.5 percent of subscribers who ended up making a purchase chatted while browsing their site. About half of them chatted while they were in the shopping cart stage. Overall, about 10 percent of the chat sessions converted to a sale, about 10 times the average Web site conversion rate before it installed the system.[5]

Allurent reported that, "83 percent of online shoppers would make purchases if the sites offered increased interactive elements." And

---

[4] Co-browsing is a software-enabled technique that allows someone in an enterprise contact center to interact with a customer by using the customer's Web browser to show him something. For example, a B2B customer having difficulty placing an order could call a customer service representative, who could then show the customer how to use the ordering pages as though the customer were using his own mouse and keyboard.

[5] Jason Lee Miller, "Study: Live Chat Ups Conversions Tenfold," WebProNews (June 21, 2007), http://www.webpronews.com/topnews/2007/06/21/study-live-chat-ups-conversions-tenfold.

Talisma.com reported that esignal.com, which provides real-time online financial market information, found that by using Talisma chat software, the number of inbound phone calls was reduced by 50 percent and that agents were able to handle more than 5,000 chat interactions per month.

Abandoned Cart E-mails

According to a study by Experian CheetahMail, abandoned cart e-mails produce 20 times the transaction rates and revenue of standard e-mail campaigns. Others also report success with the tactic. For example:

- Diapers.com said that abandoned e-mails approach generated over 10 percent of total e-mail marketing revenue, but accounted for less than 3 percent of its outgoing e-mail volume.

- S&S Worldwide revealed "… a 25 percent conversion rate on personalized transactional messages focused on items left in carts."

- And SeeWhy's Charles Nicholls is quoted as saying that Disney produces "$2 for every remarketing e-mail they send."

Sears Canada Experience

Sears Roebuck put an end to its big catalog in the United States several years ago, but the catalog was still going strong in Canada. It was the largest mail-order catalog in the country. Sears was also a big retailing presence in Canada with 110 retail stores and 1,800 catalog agents. What's more, you could order any Sears Canada product directly off the Web.

The Sears Canada database had been maintained on a mainframe, using 30-year-old software. It took 120 people to do the manual file maintenance. The file was loaded with duplicates. The file was not on line. It could be accessed only through hard copy reports that took a week to produce. Fred Hagerman, list manager for catalog marketing, decided to make a business case for a new database system with modern software and online access to do counts, reports, and selects. He showed that he could pay for the system by just finding and eliminating the estimated 10 percent of duplicate names on the system. Saving of 10 percent of the cost of catalog mailings to an 11 million name database amounted to a lot of money.

He set up a system in which the data from the mainframe could be viewed by a client server through a simple spreadsheet. The new system permitted viewing circulation, media, performance analysis, growth and response rates, and tracking of promotions. The 11 million name database was updated weekly in about two hours and produced all sorts of reports.

Building Active Customers

Before Hagerman arrived, active customers were defined as people who had shopped with Sears in the last 12 months. During the previous decade, the active file had been going down by 3 percent per year. Fred stopped the practice of dropping people who had not bought in 12 months. Each year, Sears was losing valuable data on people who hadn't purchased in a year. It was very difficult to maintain or build any kind of relationship or any kind of long-term learning with customers when you dump their data after a year.

Six Capabilities

The new database system was able to do six new things:

- *Planning:* Planning was aimed at knowing how many customers Sears had, and what they were doing. The company developed an RFM model, based on customers' lifetime value and showing what they spent on catalog items. It created 189 RFM segments. The segments tracked response rate, average order, and dollar per book across all 189 segments for every one of Sears 13 catalogs. All the variable costs of each promotion, whether it was a catalog or a direct mail promotion, could be applied to each of the 189 segments to forecast segment profitability. This told Sears whether it would be profitable or not to mail to each segment. Sears could understand the ramifications of what it was doing for each major promotion. It could accurately forecast what sales it was going to have at the end of the year.

- *Migration analysis:* This enabled Sears marketers to track customer migrations through all the 189 segments on a weekly basis. They were able to learn the level at which the customers came in, how they were moving around in the file, and what their performance was. They were able to forecast an annual file growth on a weekly basis. They were able to know whether they were growing or shrinking and where they needed to worry and replan.

- *Tracking customers:* If a Sears customer had a lifetime value of $2,500 and had made a purchase in the past three months, the customer would be in a specific segment. If there were no purchases in the next three months, the customer would be moved to a lower segment. By using the new system, it was possible to do stimulation activities. Sears could identify customers who left so it could start reactivation programs. In addition to the RFM analysis, it also developed a predictive model.

- *Early warning system:* If business is starting below the marketing plan level, with the new system, Sears could readjust and reallocate marketing expenses to deal with it. Customers were compared not just by RFM segment, but also by media. Do people perform better in a wish book, a sale book, or a spring and summer book? What kind of merchandise do they buy? Do they buy just men's clothing or women's or children's? Do they buy appliances through the catalog?

- *Payment methods:* With the new system, Sears could also look at segment payment methods: Sears credit card, third-party card, and cash and how performance differs among them. It can also look at performance by catalog distribution method; there were eight different methods.

- *Half-life analysis:* By tracking sales in the past, Sears learned that its half-life was 20 days after a catalog was mailed. It was able to track the entire success of a book by sales made during the first 20 days.

What Was the Payoff for the Investment in the Sears Database?

Spending money on building or upgrading a database may be hard to sell. In this Sears case, however, it paid real financial dividends. That is what I am trying to promote in this book: do the numbers and prove your case. Look at what Sears accomplished.

- Customer activity and sales turned up, not down as it had for the previous decade.
- Every single media but one, after the database kicked in, was up.
- The fall and winter catalog had a 10 percent increase in sales.
- The Fall Values catalog had a 7 percent increase in sales.
- The Super Sale catalog sales were up 10 percent.
- The Christmas Wish Book sales increased by 26 percent.
- Sears dropped the size of the Winder Celebration Catalog by 30% but the sales fell by only 2%.

- The Lowest Price catalog sales were up by 37 percent.
- The first reactivation book went out to people who did not receive the regular catalog. The break-even response rate was 3.5 percent. The actual response rate was 4.5 percent. Sears reactivated 12,000 customers and made a profit while doing it.

Later, Sears used the information developed in this database to make a major reorganization of the entire chain combining catalog and retail in a single system.

Supermarket Frequent Shopper Cards

Beginning several years ago, retailers began to issue proprietary cards to frequent shoppers. When these cards were presented at the checkout counter, point of sale equipment permitted the retailer to know what every household was buying and when. Retailers used this data to build databases to study their customer's shopping habits. They discovered, as we have illustrated above, that the top 20 percent of their customers over the course of a year spent about 50 times the amount of their bottom 20 percent. By combining this knowledge with modern POS technology, it became possible for any retailer, according to Brian Woolf, president of the Retail Strategy Center, to "make one offer to a frequent, high spending customer, a completely different offer to a low spending customer, and yet a third offer to a new customer with moderate spending habits."

The Evil of Average Pricing

Trapped in mass marketing, retailers had always had to charge the same price to everyone. When they announced a sale, everyone got the sale price—loyal customers and occasional transaction buyers. By using customer-specific marketing, retail stores could use their proprietary shopping cards to identify who was shopping. They could reward the best customers while they were in the store. The cards then became the basis of the store's customer database. With such a database setup, the stores could adopt two basic principles, as defined by Woolf. The principles are:

- Customers are not equal.
- Behavior follows rewards.

To put these principles to work, retailers had to make sure that different customers received different offers. Occasional, unknown customers paid full price. Loyal, regular customers paid a lower price—on certain merchandise or on all merchandise. Furthermore, the loyalists were made aware that they were the favored ones. They were treated as gold card customers as long as their buying behavior warranted it. Retailers discovered that they could modify customer behavior by the appropriate application of rewards.

Brian Woolf cites some interesting examples of customer-specific marketing:

- A retailer offered a free turkey to those customers who spent an average of at least $50 a week in the two months prior to Thanksgiving. The number of households spending over $50 per week increased by 20 percent over the preceding year.

- A retailer told customers that 1 percent of their spending would be donated to the church of their choice. Result: participating cardholders increased their annual spending by more than 5 percent.

- Senior citizens were given a 10 percent reduction at one chain if they purchased on Mondays. As a result, 67 percent of the seniors' shopping took place on Monday. That was five times the spending level of all other customers on Monday.

New Marketing Focus

"We are no longer trying to take customers away from our major competitor. Our focus is to make money on the customers who are already shopping with us," reported one retail chain executive who used the new system. These customer-specific marketers reduced their advertising costs because through analysis of their databases, they learned about the low profitability and low loyalty of the promiscuous shoppers who were attracted to their stores mainly by heavy advertising. The new customer-specific marketing had three approaches:

- Withdraw low-margin offers to unprofitable customers.
- Offer the best customers aggressive pricing and special benefits.
- Switch from item pricing to total pricing.

This was accomplished by:

- Increased prices for customers with low profitability.
- Decreased prices for high-margin customers.

How could this be done? One retailer's program illustrates the method. It:

- Took a quarter of the items featured in newspaper ads and aggressively priced them—but only for cardholders.
- Converted 1,000 of its 3,000 temporary price reductions to cardholder only specials.

The result was a jump of 6 percent in sales in some of the stores. Overall, gross profits were 1 percent higher because of the new system.

Sweepstakes Can Be Fun

Western Massachusetts spiced up its Express Savings Club with a grand prize sweepstakes of $1 million, plus numerous weekly prizes of $1,000 in cash and $50 gift certificates and state lottery tickets. A cardholder did not know whether she had won one of the fifteen $1,000 weekly cash prizes until she shopped the following week when her card was swiped. If the card carried a winning number, a red light started flashing in the ceiling, and alarm bells sounded in the store. Everyone in the store stopped to see who the lucky winner was.

Noncash Benefits

Neiman-Marcus offered its best customers lunch with the store manager, along with two of the customer's friends, followed by a private fashion show. Caesar's Palace penthouse was available only to those who had at least a $1 million line of credit for gambling at the hotel. Paw Paw Shopping Center in Michigan sent customers, prior to their birthday, a gift certificate for a free decorated birthday cake. As a result, total cake sales increased tenfold in one year. Safeway offered free ice cream on a cardholder's birthday. Tracking showed an average of $10 in increased sales when birthday certificates were redeemed.

At Lees Supermarket in Westport, Massachusetts, when the customer cards were swiped, the computer flashed information to the store clerk that he could use in conversation with the customer: how long had she been a customer? Is she one of the best store customers? How big a check is she authorized to cash without the manager's approval? Mark Dodge of Easy Access in Wisconsin set up a program to activate a store manager's beeper whenever any particularly good customer or group of customers used their card in the store. Albert Lees of Lees Supermarkets thought he knew the identity of his best customers until he set up his database. He was amazed to find that he didn't even recognize his top customer who was spending over $10,000 per year in his store.

Customer Category Management

Cardholder databases permit retailers to group customers not by where they lived, but by how much they spent per week. Research at the Retail Strategy center showed that demographics were not particularly useful as a primary segmentation basis for retailers because there was little correlation to profitability. Instead, by classifying customers by spending, it was possible to determine the lifetime value of customers.

How else was this card-based customer data used? One retailer had a 40-foot aisle devoted to candy. Candy was profitable, but was that the best use of the space? Looking at the customer database, the retailer found that her top customers (top 30 percent who provide 75 percent of the sales) did not buy much candy. What did they buy? Baby products. So he cut his candy counter to 20 feet and added 20 feet of baby products. The reasoning? "We are concentrating on our *top customers* not our *top merchandise*. It is more profitable that way."

Reasons for Failure

Not all attempts at customer-specific marketing have achieved success. There are a number of reasons for the failure. They include:

- *Timidity:* In some cases top management is not committed and does not push the system sufficiently. If you have only 30 percent of your transactions recorded on your cards, there is no obvious profit gain from the system.

- *Puny rewards:* In some stores, the electronic discounts were not meaningful. If the savings are minuscule, the customers will leave their cards at home.

- *Overreliance on vendors:* In some cases, retailers tried to transfer all the costs of markdowns to the vendors. What happened is that the program featured mainly slow moving items that the vendors want to push instead of those items the customers wanted to buy. These programs tended to fail.

- *Information starvation:* To reduce costs, some companies used their system to provide automatic discount without capturing customer purchases. Such practices lose the real value of customer-specific marketing, which lies in the information it can provide.

- *Failure to differentiate:* Where there was insufficient differentiation between the best and the worst customers, the systems did not reward profitable behavior sufficiently to improve the bottom line.

- *Customer-specific marketing was not the core strategy:* If customer-specific marketing did not become the core marketing strategy, the programs usually failed. When the stores continued existing marketing practices unchanged, the new initiatives simply became another promotional program.

- *Internal political problems:* The bigger the chain, the greater the resistance to change. Unless top management was behind it, internal squabbles tended to kill customer-specific marketing before its potential could be realized.

But Does It Pay Off?

What is the payoff from customer-specific marketing when it works?

Daniel Lescoe, vice president of sales and marketing of Big Y Foods in Springfield, Massachusetts, said, "Before we adopted this program, our sales in Western Massachusetts were $272,400,000 which represented about 25% of the market. Two years after adopting the system we moved into the number one position with sales of $364,662,474 and a market share of almost 29%. Every marketing program we develop has one mission: to promote our Express Savings Club. It is a religion for us, not just another promotion."

Roger Morgan, managing director of Morgan's Tuckerbag Supermarkets in Melbourne, Australia, reported on his first full year of customer-specific marketing: "In an industry that has seen average customer transaction values dropping, and customer visits increasing, our stores with this program in place radically went against this trend. We experienced increased customer transaction values with increased customer traffic as well. Some identical weeks experienced 40% sales increases over the previous year. Overall our annual increase over the previous year was in the 20%+ range."

Adding the Non-Cardholders to Your Database

Once you begin to experiment with building a retail marketing database, it will become obvious that there is a definite cash value for every name retained in the database. Profits (from a well-managed database strategy) will be a function of the number of customers (not necessarily credit card-holders) on the database. How can you get at the anonymous majority who pay with cash, check, or non-house credit card?

One method, of course, is to provide such customers with a non-credit "check cashing card" which speeds up the acceptance of checks. Supermarkets use such cards routinely. Department stores can do the same.

Jennifer MacLean reported how one retailer added thousands of customer names to his database in a short space of time. All cash and non-house credit card customers were asked to supply their telephone numbers as a part of the transaction. The numbers were keyed into the POS device. By capturing the information on 304,427 transactions, the retailer discovered that 28 percent were repeat buyers. The unique telephone numbers were sent to a service bureau where the numbers were looked up through an electronic reverse telephone directory system. The names and addresses of 129,623 customers were identified through this process.

The resulting file was checked against the house credit card file. It turned out that 36 percent of these customers were house credit card-holders: two-thirds were active, and one-third were inactive. The remaining 82,869, of course, were new names that were added to the store's marketing database. The fact that many cardholders, previously thought inactive, were actually making purchases at the store came as a pleasant surprise and added to the store's knowledge about its customer base.

Of course, today, one of the best ways to add names is to ask for them on your Web site.

Take-Away Thoughts

E-mails do far more for offline sales than they do for sales within the e-mails.

- Miles Kimball found that sending e-mails announcing a catalog boosted sales by 18 percent.
- Capture the zip code and then show a map of your local store in the e-mails.
- Use the store manager's name.
- Walk-in traffic resulting from e-mails is four times as high as retail e-commerce sales.
- Adding a Web site and e-mails can triple customer LTV for a retailer.
- E-mail coupons can be quite valuable.
- Gift cards sold electronically are big business today.
- E-mails should feature live chat to boost sales.
- Using your database, you can offer different prices to different customers.
- Every name on your database has a value that you can determine.
- Ask for e-mail addresses on your Web site.

A quiz on this chapter and all figures can be found at www.dbmarket ing.com/STM4. Those taking all the quizzes can receive a Successful Completion Certificate from the Database Marketing Institute which can be used in their résumé.

18

Financial Services

Over the past three years, research has taught us several lessons: Nearly half of our customers are unprofitable; almost 20% are very unprofitable. Balances are only loosely correlated with profitability. Demographics are even more poorly correlated with profitability. As a result, every day, over half the new accounts sold will never be profitable. Every day our staff work very hard to retain customers who destroy customer value. ... We have also learned that it is hard, if not impossible, to profitably cross sell our most profitable customers. Most sales to them cannibalize profitable usage. Sales efforts to these good customers should be restricted to retention-aiding devices.

—RANDALL GROSSMAN,
Former Senior Vice President,
Fleet Bank

The need for insurance is usually tied closely to life stage events. Insurance companies should make sustained efforts to gather descriptive family information from their own policyholders through questionnaires, agents, or customer service contacts. Companies can also append purchased data to their policyholder records. ... The objective is to make offers that are relevant to each life stage, rather than offering the same type of coverage to all individuals and families. ... This is an approach that successful agents follow intuitively. Database managers at company headquarters can assist in the process by appending and updating information in their central marketing database so that it is available to agents and marketers throughout the company.

—PIERRE PASSAVANT,
President of Kobs Gregory Passavant

Many US customers use multiple channels when buying financial services products, crossing channels during their path to purchase. Among online adults, 41% of financial product applicants research online but buy offline. Security and a need for hand-holding top the list of reasons for this channel switching. Given that many customers are moving from one channel to another during the buying process, eBusiness and channel strategists need to make sure that channel transitions are as smooth as possible or risk watching prospective customers fall through the crack—or into the arms of competitors.

—EDWARD KOUNTZ AND PETER WANNEMACHER

Financial services offer one of the most profitable applications for database marketing and for e-mail marketing. This is so because financial institutions:

- Usually have a lot of useful information about their customers' demographics and purchase history.
- Can accurately determine the profitability of each customer.
- Are usually important to their customers' lives.
- Have many opportunities to interact with their customers during the average month.

The greatest advance in financial services database marketing has been online banking and the ability to send e-mails to customers concerning their accounts. By 2011, more than 80 percent of consumers who have broadband Internet access in the United States signed up for online banking.

These developments open up a tremendous number of contact opportunities for banks, insurance companies, and other financial institutions to reach out to their customers with financial information that these people want to hear about. For example, Mint.com gives weekly

Your Weekly Summary
A Recommendation for You

Friday, January 14, 2011

Other Mint users are earning 1.30% with a no-fee, high-yield savings account from American Express. Start your new year right.

Your Money $37,282.30

Cash

Checking - 4410
SunTrust Bank (Personal Finance)
Last Updated: 1 days ago

$17,147.74

Savings - 9548
SunTrust Bank (Personal Finance)
Last Updated: 1 days ago

$12,131.10

Checking - 8884
SunTrust Bank (Personal Finance)
Last Updated: 1 days ago

$8,003.46

Credit Cards

Credit Card - 5757
SunTrust Bank (Personal Finance)
Last Updated: 1 days ago

$0.00

4 accounts
last updated today

$37,282.30

Review your accounts to make sure you know where your money is going

Figure 18.1 MINT Weekly Report

information to more than 1 million people about their bank accounts. Look at the example in Figure 18.1.

Any bank customer today can go online and look up his bank balances at any time. But it is a nuisance since you need an account name and password. If are like this account holder, you have to access three different accounts every time. It can be annoying. Here are all of your balances available to you weekly with no work involved. This is from Mint.com which is a free service that makes its money from advertising. Note the reference to an American Express high-yield savings account. Banks should be sending e-mails like these themselves. Why? Because communications like this from a bank to its customers increase retention.

To send such messages, banks need to build a marketing database. The process involves consolidating all their customers' accounts into a single marketing customer information file (MCIF) so that they can understand each household's financial situation. This is not easy. Most banks had their mortgage loans on one computer, checking accounts on another, and credit cards on a third. The records were created by different people in different formats, based on accounts, not on customers. It took most banks several years to realize the importance of an MCIF and to muster the resources to create one. This all came at a time of great turmoil in the banking industry in the 1990s during which almost half U.S. banks were acquired and consolidated with other banks—thus further complicating the MCIF creation problem.

Once the MCIFs were created, however, there was no great rush among banks to do any relationship marketing. Why not? Mainly because banks were then, and still are, organized along product lines. There were separate vice presidents for credit cards, retail banking, home mortgages, automobile loans, trust accounts, and so on. Each vice president was expected to improve sales and profits in her department. The manager of credit cards was not compensated for the number of credit card customers who signed up for a checking account or an auto loan. Nor do the other VPs care much about credit card operations. People do what is in their own economic self-interest.

Sharing of Information

I was approached at a conference by an assistant vice president of a bank who was in charge of selling insurance. He asked me what he could do to sell more insurance to his customers and to improve the retention rate of those that he already had. He explained that he had been sending letters to existing insurance customers, trying to build a relationship with them, but it was not paying off.

"The best way to sell insurance to bank customers," I told him, "is to examine the MCIF to determine which customers are most likely to buy insurance, and market to them. If they don't have insurance now, but since they already have another account with the bank, they should be responsive. For those who now have insurance, the best way to retain them is to sell them another noninsurance bank product. Once they have two or more bank products, their retention rate for insurance should be higher."

"Oh, I couldn't do that. They won't let me have access to the names of other bank customers."

This is the problem.

Many banks today have gotten religion. They understand that customers look at their bank as a single institution, not as a bunch of unrelated products. They understand that to improve sales and retention, they have to become a total financial solution, looking at customers and households, instead of individual product owners. Banks have discovered that there is a clear relationship between the number of bank products owned by a customer and the customer's retention rate. See Figure 18.2.

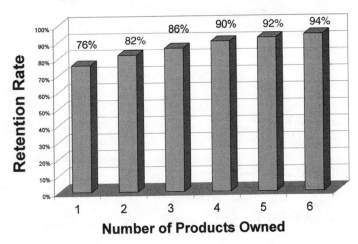

Bank Products vs. Retention Rate

Figure 18.2 Increased Retention Rate Based on Number of Bank Products Owned

Why is this so? Because if you have only a credit card at a bank, you obviously have your checking account somewhere else. You don't think of the card issuer as your bank. If you get an offer for a cheaper card, you might well take it. But if you have your checking account and savings account at a bank, plus the credit card, you will most likely tend to think of the credit card as a part of your total banking experience. You may know the branch personnel. Won't they wonder why you dropped their card?

Communicating with Customers

Fortunately, in the last few years, most banks have set up online banking for their customers. They send the e-mails that provide customers with important data on bill payments on a regular basis, as shown in Figure 18.3.

SUNTRUST	The following Payment has been sent:
Biller:	Helena Hughes
Payment Amount:	$500.00
Date Debited From Your Account:	*Draft
Date Sent to Biller:	1/18/2011
Estimated Date Posted by Biller:	1/21/2011

Figure 18.3 Bill Payer E-mail

It costs the bank nothing to do this after it has been set up. Value to the customer? A very handy e-mail. It lets you know that everything is going well. This would have been impractical in the old direct mail days—too expensive for the bank, and a nuisance for the customer. Just another way to use the database to build a relationship with the customer.

Other Financial E-mail Ideas

E-mail today is playing an increasingly larger role in connecting the customers with their banks. Rather than driving to a branch office to reach the bank, more and more people today are going online. The banks and other financial institutions have to make this easy for their customers, and recognize that this is a profitable method of communicating.

- E-mail subscribers need a preference center where they can choose from a list of preset options concerning which type of e-mails they want and how frequently those messages should come. Since most consumers subscribe to financial services e-mails to be in control of their financial situation, marketers should make sure that subscribers have the control of their e-mails easy to find, rather than having to hunt through the Web site to find them.

- Reward customers for signing-up for e-statements. E-statements can save banks up to $1 to $2 per statement, and they appeal to customers because they greatly decrease the opportunity for identity theft.

- A 2010 report by Fiserv showed that online banking customers were also increasingly likely to maintain other, more profitable accounts with the institution at which they banked online. In 2005, online banking customers were 8 percent more likely to have a savings account at the same bank. In 2010, the report found that this figure had grown to 13 percent.

Unintended Consequences

I had breakfast one day at the National Center for Database Marketing with a marketing officer from a medium-sized bank. Members of its management had come to realize how important it was to customer loyalty to have multiproduct customers. They offered a substantial bonus to all senior branch personnel in those branches that had a high percentage of 5+ customers—meaning customers who were using five or more of the bank's products. The policy was working. Every branch was focused on this objective, but the results were far from what was intended. Many branches were turning down new accounts because they ruined the branch's 5+ percentage.

Benefits to the Customer of Online Banking

Eighty percent of consumers and businesses that have broadband access have signed up for online banking. They use it to:

- Pay bills online
- View their transactions
- Transfer money between accounts

Why do they sign up for online banking and bill paying? According to a Fiserv survey, they do so because:

- *Speed:* Online bill paying is faster than other payment methods.
- *Ease of use:* It's also easier than paying by check.
- *Cost savings:* They like saving money on stamps.
- *Control:* They think that paying bills online gives them more control over the timing of their payments.

- *Convenience and reduction of clutter:* They do not worry about losing bills around their home.
- *Information:* They are better informed about their money.

How Does the Bank Benefit from Online Banking?

Consumers who pay bills online are more likely to continue banking with that bank. According to a 2011 Survey by Comscore:

- 49 percent are less likely to switch banks.
- 67 percent would recommend their bank to a friend.
- 14 percent are more likely to buy an additional product from that bank than from another.
- Many access their bank accounts online several times a week.

Profitability Calculation

Many banks have found a way to organize themselves to take advantage of their MCIFs and create profitable offline and online relationships with their customers. The key to their success is the analysis of profitability. There are three steps:

- Develop an accurate and credible system for determining the profitability of each customer, on a periodic basis, preferably at least monthly, using day-to-day inputs on interest rates and costs.
- Develop segmentation schemes that divide customers into useful and actionable segments based on profitability.
- Based on these segments, develop and implement tactics that are used to modify the behavior of employees and customers to increase sales, improve retention, lower costs, and improve profits.

Profitability calculation is the heart of the system. It is defined as the total profit (less all expenses) earned each month by the products and services owned by a single customer. It is complex, but it is computed automatically by bank software for every product for every customer every month. To understand it, one must understand a few banking terms. It is worth taking the time, because determining profitability is the foundation for a number of very profitable and advanced database marketing segmentation and behavior modification techniques. One of the experts in the use of profitability analysis in banking is Robert James, who was group manager at the Centura Bank. Bob, a graduate of the Database

Marketing Institute had 24 years of banking experience at the time. Here is how he listed the concepts vital to understanding profitability:

- *Cost of funds:* Banks obtain money from depositors and loan it out to borrowers. They make money on the difference in what they pay depositors and what they earn from borrowers. The cost of funds is the amount of interest expense paid for the funds used.
- *Funding credit:* The amount earned by the bank on the deposits that it uses.
- *Margin:* The difference between interest earned and the interest expense.
- *Loan loss provision:* All loans have risk, and some loans never get repaid. The loan loss provision is a pool of dollars reserved by banks to cover expected loan losses.
- *Capital allocation:* Capital is the equity of the company; the difference between assets and liabilities. Capital allocation is the amount of capital set aside for each product to cover unexpected losses and is based on the overall risk profile of the product.
- *Capital charge:* The capital allocated multiplied by the bank's desired rate of return on the capital assigned to the product.
- *Overhead:* The fixed and variable expenses associated with the product. These include origination expense, transaction expense, maintenance expense, and personnel expense. The cost of a customer visiting a branch to cash a check may amount to $1.65 per visit. This is part of overhead.
- *FDIC expense:* The cost of providing deposit insurance through the Federal Deposit Insurance Corporation.

These are banking terms. But the concepts underlying profitability apply to any industry where detailed costs are available, such as insurance, and many service industries.

Using these terms, let's compute the monthly profitability for a typical customer product—an automobile loan. This four-year loan originated two years ago for $15,500 at a rate of 8.5 percent. At this point, the average outstanding balance is $9,806.66. The net profitability of this loan, last month, was $13.74. Figure 18.4 shows how that profitability was calculated. The figure shows that for this product for this customer this last month, the bank made a profit of $13.74 after all costs related to the product were deducted from the revenue.

For comparison, Figure 18.5 shows the profitability calculation for a checking account. In this case, the bank lost $3.49 on this account last

Automobile Loan	
Average Balance	$9,806.66
Capital Allocated	$367.75
Interest Income	$69.46
Less Cost of Funds	$46.50
Margin	$22.96
Fees	$0.00
Gross Profit	**$22.96**
Capital Charge	$4.88
Loan Loss Provision	$3.27
Overhead	$1.07
Total Costs	**$9.22**
Net Product Value	**$13.74**

Figure 18.4 Value of Auto Loan

Non-Interest Bearing Checking Account	
Average Balance	$1,184.84
Capital Allocated	$2.96
Funding Credit	$5.24
Fees (Service Charge)	$6.50
Gross Profit	$11.74
Less:	
Capital Charge	$0.04
FDIC Expense	$0.03
Overhead	$15.17
Total Costs	$15.24
Net Product Value	($3.49)

Figure 18.5 Checking Account Value

month. The gross monthly profit of $11.74 from the average balance of $1,184 was overwhelmed by the high overhead costs of $15.17. The overhead includes the fact that this customer visited the branch several times last month to make deposits or cash checks. At $1.65 expense per visit, the branch visits wiped out the profitability of this particular product. By comparing these two calculations, you will note that the capital allocation for a checking account is significantly less than it is for a loan. This is because, for a bank, loans are more risky than checking accounts.

The same process is repeated each month for every product owned by every customer with the bank. Once completed, a customer's household profitability is computed by summing the net product values for all products owned by the household. See Figure 18.6. This customer's total monthly profit to the bank is $101.51.

Customer J Smith Profitability	Average Balance	Profit
Automobile Loan	$9,806.66	$13.74
Checking Account	$1,184.84	−$3.49
Certificate of Deposit	$15,000.00	$27.05
Credit Card	$2,917.66	$8.11
Home Equity Loan	$20,420.90	$56.10
Total Profit		$101.51

Figure 18.6 Monthly Profitability Calculation

Creating Profitability Segments

After computing all customers' monthly profitability, you group them into customer profitability segments. Figure 18.7 shows an actual example of the way one bank grouped its customers into profitability segments. They created five groups.

Monthly Profit from All Customers				
Segment	Households	% Households	Total Profit	% Profits
5	20,126	5%	$11,180,791	79.67%
4	46,706	11%	$3,483,724	24.82%
3	118,273	28%	$2,221,018	15.83%
2	119,804	28%	$212,669	1.52%
1	118,394	28%	−$3,063,817	−21.83%
Total	423,303	100%	$14,034,385	100%

Figure 18.7 Bank Customers Segmented by Profitability

This can be graphed as a now familiar chart shown in Figure 18.8.

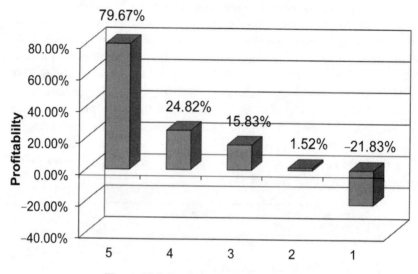

Figure 18.8 Profit by Customer Segment

Every customer in the bank was classified as a 5, 4, 3, 2, or 1, where 5 represented the most profitable customer, and 1 represented the least profitable customers. What Figure 18.8 shows is that the top group, representing only 5 percent of the bank's customers was responsible for almost 80 percent of the bank's total profit. The bottom group, consisting of 28 percent of the bank's customers, was responsible for a loss of almost 22 percent of the bank's profit. This is amazing and insightful information. Until the creation of MCIFs and monthly profitability analysis, no bank in the United States had this kind of information. Some banks still don't have it today.

Once a bank has done this calculation, the profitability segment designation is stored in each customer's database file every month. A personal profile of each bank customer is made available to all customer contact personnel at each point of contact with the customer, including e-mail marketing, teller lines, service desks, or branch managers offices. The profile can include:

- Addresses and phones numbers
- E-mail address
- Birth dates and Social Security numbers
- Home ownership with length of time at present address

- Occupation and employer
- Other financial institutions where the person banks
- The bank officer assigned and the branch
- Whether the customer has filed a financial statement
- All accounts with their current balances, line amounts, and amount owed
- The profitability segment to which the customer belongs
- Suggested next-best product for the customer

Turning Knowledge into Action

Statistical analysts at the bank use this data to build models to predict the lifetime value of each customer, which products a customer is next most likely to need, and which behavior change will improve the customer's profitability. These solutions are shown on the customer's database record screen. Customer contact personnel then utilize the knowledge to improve cross-sell and up-sell opportunities, to make better decisions regarding pricing and fee waivers, and to send e-mails suggesting alternative channels for certain types of transactions.

Each of the five profitability segments has different customer behavior goals:

- For 5s (the gold customers) and 4s, the goal is to retain them, acquire more like them, and expand their purchases of bank products. Since the profit segment 5s and 4s represent only 16 percent of the customer households, but up to 105 percent of the monthly profit, the bank will want to allocate substantial human and marketing resources toward retaining these customers. And since human resources are limited, particularly those resources devoted to sales, the bank should attempt to direct the acquisition activities of its calling officers to prospects who have the potential to be in profit segment 5 or 4. In general, you cannot market profitably to the 5s because they are maxed out. All their money is in your bank. Your goal is retention.
- For 3s the goal is simply to get them to expand their use of your products.
- For 1s and 2s the goals are to reprice their unprofitable products such as loans or certificates of deposit as they mature or are renewed. Concerted efforts are used to migrate these customers' routine transactions to less expensive alternative channels of delivery, such as ATMs and call centers.

Gold Customer Programs

Once you know who the Gold customers are, what can you do to be sure you retain them? Banks are using such tactics as:

- Identifying and assigning personal bankers to them
- Making sure that they get the best service including:
  - Priority problem resolution
  - Priority telephone response
  - Discretionary pricing initiatives
  - E-mails reporting their account balances
- Providing special communications strategies including:
  - Outbound calls from their personal banker
  - Special mailings and product offers
  - Weekly e-mails
  - Annual thank-you mailings
  - Reward programs

One bank has the profitability segment built in to the software that controls its customer service call director. Gold customers' calls are identified before they are answered and are picked up on the first ring. Unprofitable customers may have to wait for five or six rings before anyone answers, and even then, they are likely to reach a voice or touch-tone activated machine.

Analysis of Behavior by Profitability Segment

Beyond identifying profitability segments there is analysis to determine why some customers are so profitable or so unprofitable. For example, one bank divided its entire customer database into 50 segments, from most profitable to least, each representing 2 percent of all customers, and ranked them by the number of bank products they were using. We have already established that the more products customers use, the higher their retention rate is. But how does their profitability vary by product usage? (See Figure 18.9.)

What the bank learned from this analysis was that both the best and the worst customers used a lot of bank products. The average customers used only a few. This suggests that while high product use leads to high retention, it does not necessarily lead to high profits.

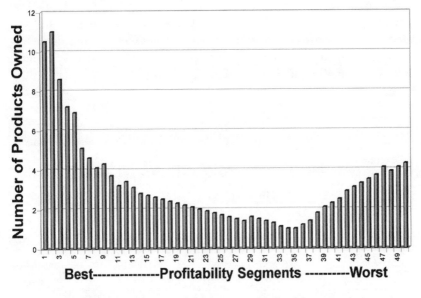

Best--------------Profitability Segments ----------Worst

Figure 18.9 Product Use by Profitability Segment

A similar analysis was done of the same bank customers ranked by the number of times that they visited bank branches. This also showed that both the best and the worst visited bank branches a lot. The average customer used online banking or used an ATM. *Any policy designed to discourage expensive branch visits would seriously affect the bank's very best customers who bring in 80 percent of the bank's profits.*

Computing Lifetime Value and Potential Lifetime Profitability

It is not enough to know the current profitability of a customer. You need to be able to predict the future by making accurate forecasts of each customer's potential lifetime profitability. To forecast the future, you determine for each customer the likelihood of your being able to sell her additional profitable products and the expected net revenue from usage of those products minus the promotional expense involved in the sale of the products. This forecast is added to current profitability to create a reasonably reliable lifetime profitability forecast which can drive bank marketing strategies and tactics.

Fleet developed a bankwide MCIF, which was originally maintained by an external vendor. Once it was up and running, Fleet took its first measure of customer value by simply adding up all nonmortgage deposit and loan balances for each customer. This was a beginning. Next it created the software necessary to determine the net income after deducting the cost of capital (NIACC) for all retail customers. For a typical customer, it looked something like the table in Figure 18.10.

	Check & Savings	Home Equity	Credit Cards	Mutual Funds	Total
Revenue					
Net Interest	$210	$248	−$280	$0	$178
Fees	$18	$18	$396	$1,500	$1,932
Total Revenue	$228	$266	$116	$1,500	$2,110
Expenses					
Amort. Sales Costs	$20	$120	$67	$75	$282
Acc. Maint.	$30	$75	$40	$900	$1,045
Transact Cost	$193	$21	$0	$30	$244
Allocated Overhead	$0	$0	$0	$0	$0
Total Expenses	$243	$216	$107	$1,005	$1,571
Loss Provision	$0	$23	$160	$0	$183
Net Income	−$15	$27	−$151	$495	$356
Taxes	−$6	$11	−$60	$198	$143
NI After Taxes	−$9	$16	−$91	$297	$213
Cost of Capital	$1	$49	$32	$68	$150
NIACC	−$10	−$33	−$123	$229	$63
Annual revenue and costs for typical bank customer having these products					

Figure 18.10 Alternate Method of Profitability Calculation

This is a slightly different method of profitability calculation from that shown earlier. It arrives at the same basic number, however. In this annual calculation for a typical customer, her net profitability is $63, due principally to the fact that she invested in mutual funds. Without this investment, she would have represented a loss of $166 to the bank.

As a second step, Fleet extended this system to its commercial customers. It was using industry benchmark costs for computing profitability. When these processes were working properly, the bank created an in-house data warehouse, which enabled it to keep all of this data current, and to use actual Fleet activity-based costs rather than industry benchmark numbers.

At their PC workstations, power users including both marketing and business analysts accessed the data on each customer, did analytical work and modeling, and developed marketing initiatives. The analysis server, for example, provided for statistical analysis, neural networks, ad hoc query and analysis, and geo-demographic analysis. The data mart provided summarized preformatted data for promotion design, tracking, and analysis, and it enabled the users to do point-and-click drill down analysis. The management reporting server provided on-demand parameterized reports.

Preliminary Lessons Learned

The new system enabled Fleet bank management, for the first time, to really understand its customer profitability and to do something about it. As Randall Grossman, senior vice president and director of customer data management and analysis at Fleet Financial Group explained, the data showed that:

- Half of all customers were unprofitable.
- 20 percent were very unprofitable.
- The balances that people maintained were only loosely correlated with profitability.
- Demographics were even more poorly correlated with profitability.
- Half of the new accounts being currently sold would never be profitable.
- The bank staff was working hard every day to retain customers who would destroy customer value.

Even though half of all customers were considered unprofitable, members of the marketing staff realized that they could not simply walk away from half their customer base. Further analysis showed that:

- It was almost impossible profitably to cross-sell to the most profitable customers. Most of these sales cannibalized existing profitable products. For these gold customers, it was determined that marketing should focus on retention, not cross- or up-selling.
- Some customer profits and losses were temporary, not permanent.
- Some low-profit customers had great potential because their assets were elsewhere, and they were, in fact, gold customers at another bank.

- Some unprofitable customers could be nudged into profitability if they were offered the right products at the right prices.

- There were, however, many customers for whom there was very little potential for profit.

What to Do with the Information?

Faced with these sobering facts, members of the Grossman's marketing staff decided to figure out ways to use the database that they had created to turn the situation around. The key to their strategy was to develop three measures of customer value:

- Lifetime profitability
- Potential profitability
- Potential customer value

Lifetime profitability is the net present value of the expected future stream of net income after the cost of capital, discounted at the corporate hurdle rate. It is calculated based on the products that the customer is now using, including planned repricing. The corporate hurdle rate is the required rate of return in a discounted cash flow analysis above which an investment makes sense and below which it does not. Discounted cash flow is a method of evaluating an investment by estimating future cash flows and taking into consideration the time value of money (the discount rate). As calculated by the bank, customer profitability differed from organizational or product profitability for several reasons:

Many customers' business with the bank cut across business lines, whereas organizational profitability was computed by adding up the profits from each line of business. Some costs in the Fleet system, such as overhead, were not allocated to each customer, since the methods for doing this involved arbitrary decisions which Fleet managers thought might distort the real profitability of the customer.

For those costs that were allocated to the customer, the allocation had, of necessity, to use standard cost factors (such as the cost of a branch visit, telephone call, or product sale) for which it was not cost-effective to determine accurately based on each specific event.

Customer profitability did not "roll up." If two customers shared the same account, the bank gave full credit to both (which one is the decision maker?). For this reason, you could not add up each customer's profitability to get total bank profitability. Organizationally, of course, the account was counted only once, not twice, so product profitability did add up to a bank total.

Given these qualifications, lifetime customer profitability was calculated for each bank customer and stored in the customer's database record each month. Customers were then ranked and segmented. It was possible to pick out the gold customers, those just below gold, the average customers and the unprofitable customers. Each customer's profitability status was flagged in each customer record so that marketers and branch personnel could recognize the customer's value to the bank and develop appropriate strategies and tactics.

Potential Profitability

Potential profitability carried the Fleet analysis one step further. A typical customer had a limited number of bank products. There were usually many other bank products that the customer could be using. The probability of a given customer purchasing an additional product was determined using CHAID analysis (see Chapter 13). For example, if a customer owned a home and had a mortgage of $W, had a checking account with an average balance of $X, a savings account with an average balance of $Y, a monthly credit card usage rate of $Z, an age of 44 years, and 2 children in college, CHAID was used to predict the likelihood of him purchasing more product. See Figure 18.11.

Probability of Purchase	
An Auto Loan	12%
A Home Equity Loan	16%
A Personal Loan	12%
Mutual Funds	21%
A Certificate of Deposit	3%

Figure 18.11 Probability of Purchase

CHAID was also used to predict the average balance that he would maintain on each of the possible additional products. Logistic regressions were then used to determine the expected NIACC that the bank would realize from the possible sale of each of these products to the customer. In each case, an estimate was made of the promotional expense involved in getting him to purchase the product. The potential profitability then was calculated for each product as the:

Probability of purchase × expected NIACC from usage
− promotional expense

The profitability calculation software then added each of the products for this customer with a positive NIACC to get the potential profit.

Potential customer value was then determined for each customer by adding the lifetime profitability (with current products) and the potential profitability (from possible new products). This value was stored in every customer's database record and used to select the most likely candidates for promotion of each product in direct mail or e-mail promotions. It was also used to suggest the next-best product when branch personnel were talking to the customer, or customer service had him on the phone.

Customer Retention Tactics

Knowing who is profitable and who is not is important. But eventually things boil down to tactics. How do you persuade a customer to do what you want her to do? How do you keep customers from defecting? Credit card managers have to deal with defections on a daily basis. They call it "churn." A high percentage of the American public receives competing credit card offers every week. Some of them accept the offers and drop cards, which their banks had spent more than $80 to get them to accept. How can you get customers to keep their cards?

As already explained, the best method is to sell them another product. The more products bank customers have from a particular bank, the less likely they are to drop any particular product. But, ultimately, we will have to do something directly for the credit card customers who are likely to drop their cards. There is, by now, a fairly straightforward method of churn reduction, which combines lifetime value and probability modeling to achieve satisfactory results. Here is the way it works.

Let's consider a typical bank that has 369,502 credit card customers, with an annual churn rate of about 18 percent. If it costs the bank $80 to acquire a credit card customer, the annual loss of the acquisition costs resulting from churn is about $5,320,829—a tidy sum. Something has to be done. Most banks with a large number of credit cardholders allocate an annual retention budget to be spent on projects aimed at getting these defectors to change their minds. Let's suppose that the bank managers have set up a retention budget of $700,000. They want to make the best use of this fund. If they allocate it equally to all cardholders, it will amount to $1.89 per cardholder per year. They are not going to change many minds for $1.89. Either the budget must be increased, or it must be allocated in a much more intelligent way than spending it equally on all cardholders.

The intelligent way to begin is to build a statistical model of all cardholders to determine which customers are most likely to drop their cards. Such a model can be based on experience over the last several years. We know who dropped the card. The model can include such factors as:

- Average amount charged per year
- Average unpaid balance each month
- Number of other bank products owned
- Number of other cards owned
- Income of the cardholder
- Number of years with the bank and with the card
- Balances maintained on other product accounts

A regression model or a neural network can be run, using these and other factors, to develop a score for all cardholders. The score indicates who is most likely to drop the card in the near future. A score of 95 indicates that the cardholder is 95 percent likely to drop the card in the next six months. A very low score predicts that this customer will probably keep his card. Figure 18.12 shows what the model could predict.

To be sure that our retention budget does the most good, we should ignore those loyal customers who are unlikely to drop their card. In this illustration, we concentrate on all customers who have a score of 60 percent or better. There are 276,560 of these. We have safely cut 92,942 customers from our retention program—which gives us more money to spend on the more likely droppers.

Acquisition Ideas

Having a profitable marketing program requires two things: a customer friendly profitable series of communications, and a larger audience for your messages. Financial institutions have to work hard to build up the number of people signed up for online banking and other web based products.

Score	Total Base	Actual Attrition	Percent Attrition	Cumulative Base
95	3,315	1,619	48.84	3,315
90	15,014	3,974	26.47	18,329
85	26,378	4,858	18.42	44,707
80	39,923	7,139	17.88	84,630
75	32,874	5,226	15.90	117,504
70	33,926	6,182	18.22	151,430
65	53,536	6,992	13.06	204,966
60	71,594	9,274	12.95	276,560
55	34,870	2,709	7.77	311,430
50	18,733	907	4.84	330,163
45	12,844	412	3.21	343,007
40	9,833	513	5.22	352,840
35	7,400	223	3.02	360,240
30	6,411	205	3.20	366,651
25	2,355	74	3.16	369,006
20	464	0	0.00	369,470
15	32	0	0.00	369,502
Totals	369,502	56,672	11.28	369,502

Figure 18.12 Selection of Credit Card Customers by Likelihood to Churn

- To help reel-in recent high school graduates, First National Bank utilized a direct mail campaign featuring customized postcards with a scratch-off sticker over a PIN, good for redeeming three free music downloads. Two free movie tickets were also offered upon signing up for an account with the bank.

- With the Hispanic community, one of the fastest growing in the United States, Citibank sought a new way to communicate its credit card offer and show its commitment to understanding this emerging market. Citibank distributed $10 international phone cards in select direct mail pieces. The program has remained a successful and is a staple of the bank's Hispanic acquisition campaign through six reorders and counting.

Lifetime Value

Next, we want to consider lifetime value. We can compute the lifetime value of cardholders based on methods developed throughout this book.

	Acquisition Year	Second Year	Third Year
Card Members	13,433	11,418	10,048
Retention Rate	85.00%	88.00%	92.00%
Annual Profitability	$241	$248	$255
Total Revenue	$3,237,353	$2,831,676	$2,562,210
Acquisition Cost $80	$1,074,640	$0	$0
Marketing Cost $8	$107,464	$91,344	$80,383
Total Cost	$1,182,104	$91,344	$80,383
Profit	$2,055,249	$2,740,332	$2,481,827
Discount Rate	1.00	1.20	1.44
Net Present Value Profit	$2,055,249	$2,283,610	$1,723,491
Cumulative NPV Profit	$2,055,249	$4,338,859	$6,062,350
Lifetime Value	$153.00	$323.00	$451.30

Figure 18.13 Lifetime Value of Credit Card Customers Based on Profitability

Figure 18.13 shows how the bank determined the lifetime value of a group of customers who were using its credit cards. This segment of customers had an annual profitability of $241. It cost $80 to acquire them. Their retention rate was about 85 percent. The bank spent about $8 each year in retention programs. In the third year, the lifetime value of the customers in this segment was about $451. If you compare this lifetime value chart to those in Chapter 3, you will notice that the costs are computed differently. This is because bank profitability includes all costs except acquisition and marketing costs. As you can see, the retention rate of loyal customers goes up, and their profitability goes up as well. The actual computation of lifetime value for bank customers is more complicated than this chart shows because most bank customers tend to have more than one bank product. Their retention rate and lifetime value tends, therefore, to be higher than those who have only one product.

This type of lifetime value is computed for all credit card customers. They are ranked in lifetime value groups for the purpose of allocating the credit card retention budget. The ranking is shown in Figure 18.14. As you look at the figure, you can see that some customers are more valuable than others. What is the point of working to retain customers with a low lifetime value? Once you know their lifetime value, you can spend your retention budget on those who have the highest lifetime value. In this case, the bank decided to make a major effort to retain those 55,323 likely droppers who have a lifetime value of $450 or more. What can we do to retain these people? You can, of course, sell them additional products.

Lifetime Value of 276,560 Cardholders Most Likely To Churn				
A Average Lifetime Value	B Number Members	C Cumulative Members	D Cumulative Percent Members	E Total Lifetime Value
$637.24	17,723	17,723	6.41%	$11,293,800
$550.00	11,334	29,057	10.51%	$5,628,700
$500.00	12,833	41,890	15.15%	$6,416,500
$450.00	13,433	55,323	20.00%	$6,044,850
$400.00	15,534	70,857	25.62%	$6,213,600
$350.00	18,556	89,413	32.33%	$6,494,600
$300.00	20,356	109,769	39.69%	$6,106,800
$250.00	25,543	135,312	48.93%	$6,385,750
$200.00	31,456	166,768	60.30%	$6,291,200
$150.00	35,993	202,761	73.32%	$5,398,950
$100.00	41,789	244,550	88.43%	$4,178,900
$50.00	26,578	271,128	98.04%	$1,328,900
$0.00	5,432	276,560	100.00%	$0

Figure 18.14 Credit Card Customers Arranged by Lifetime Value

That is the first step. A second step would be to provide some inducements. There are many possibilities. Here are seven typical inducements:

- Increase the credit line.
- Upgrade the card to gold status.
- Provide cash advance checks.
- Reduce the interest rate.
- Reduce the annual fee.
- Waive the annual fee.
- Provide air miles for every dollar spent.

Each inducement had a cost to the bank. Each inducement also was more or less effective in reducing attrition. The average attrition was 18 percent per year. Figure 18.15 shows how a budget of about $700,000 could be spent most efficiently in reducing churn among the 55,323 people most likely to drop the card who had an average lifetime value of $450 or more. We are making the assumption here that management has limited us to a budget of $700,000 and has further required that we not include more than 20,000 customers in any one inducement, with a minimum of 2,000 in each inducement as a test of its effectiveness.

Credit Card Retention Budget Calculation Chart								
Inducements Average LTV $531	C Members Selected (Max 20K/ Line)	D Dollars Budgeted (Col C * Col E)	E Dollars Per Member	F Attrition Red. Percent	G Est. Attrition (18% of Col C)	H Est. Red. (Col G * Col F)	I Total LTV Gain (Col H * $531)	J $ Gained/ $ Spent (Col I/ Col D)
Increased Credit Line	20,000	$157,600	$7.88	14.00%	3,600	504	$267,624	$1.70
Upgrade to Gold	2,000	$25,040	$12.52	21.00%	360	76	$40,144	$1.60
Cash Advance Checks	20,000	$70,000	$3.50	6.50%	3,600	234	$124,254	$1.78
Reduce Interest Rate	7,323	$204,971	$27.99	49.00%	1,318	646	$342,967	$1.67
Reduce Annual Fee	2,000	$70,000	$35.00	60.00%	360	216	$114,696	$1.64
Waive Annual Fee	2,000	$80,000	$40.00	69.00%	360	248	$131,900	$1.65
Provide Air Miles	2,000	$90,000	$45.00	72.00%	360	259	$137,635	$1.53
Total	55,323	$697,611			9,958	2,183	$1,159,220	$1.66

Figure 18.15 Calculation of the Ideal Allocation of a Credit Cardholder Retention Budget

What the figure shows is that since the average lifetime value of these 55,323 customers is $531, we can save that amount by preventing the attrition of some of these cardholders. We know that 18 percent of them are going to leave us if we do nothing about it. By using inducements, we can persuade 2,183 cardholders to stay. Their lifetime value is $1,159,220. We have spent $697,611 to keep these cardholders, a return of $1.66 for every $1 spent.

The mathematics of this figure are tricky since we want to stay within the budget, provide some inducement for all 55,323 cardholders, stay within management's arbitrary limitations, and maximize the lifetime value gain. The reader may enjoy working with this chart in the software that is available to readers of this book. The free software is at www.dbmarketing.com.

Prospecting Using E-mails

Kestler Financial Group (KFG) is a national field marketing organization serving over 5,500 independent insurance brokers. KFG specializes in annuities, life insurance, long-term care insurance, and seminars selling systems and securities. When it began, KFG sent plain text e-mails to its brokers asking them to e-mail or call KFG with data on quotes. These e-mails did not contain a way to gather data directly from the e-mail, so response rates were low.

By shifting to a system developed by ExactTarget, KFG increased the impact of its e-mails and made the creation process easier. The surveys let KFG gather information directly from each e-mail, making it easy for agents in different time zones or on tight schedules to contact brokers. They sent bi-monthly e-mails that let a broker request an immediate annuity quote. The new e-mails included sales information, personal incentives, and selling tools. For example, one e-mail included 20 free prospecting letters to send to clients. The system permitted KFG to connect with an agent while he or she was still browsing through the letters.

The return on investment from the new e-mail system proved to be $4,400 for every dollar spent on the ExactTarget software. In a single month, quotes increased by over 12 million, 5.5 million of which were converted to sales. Click-through rates for e-mails were as high as 24 percent, and open rates were about 50 percent. When open rates and click-through rates dropped from time to time, KFG used the system to find out what topics were currently of interest to their agents. This information was included in their next e-communication.

Credit Card Case Study

A bank sought to reduce defections and increase the use of its card. It asked KnowledgeBase Marketing to develop models to identify those highly profitable customers who were most likely to drop their credit cards. These customers were then treated with targeted personalized communications.

To determine profitability, an algorithm was developed that was applied to all the bank's credit card customers:

$$\text{Profitability score} = \text{interchange income} + \\ \text{finance charges} + \\ \text{fees and charges} - \\ \text{cost of funds} - \\ \text{delinquency costs}$$

To determine the likelihood of defection, a series of neural network models was applied to 953 voluntary defectors and 9,520 randomly selected active accounts. After review of the results, the best of four neural networks were chosen along with two regression models.

The models showed the indicators of potential churn presented in Figure 18.16.

Attribute	Tendency
Balance Carried	Defection as revolving balance goes up
Disputes & CS Communications	Retained as contacts go up
Reissue Flag	Retained when not up for reissue
Credit Bureau Score	Defection as score goes up
Trend on Purchase Activity	Retained when increasing

Figure 18.16 Indicators of Potential Churn

Once the bank was able to identify those high-value customers most likely to defect, it began a proactive campaign to communicate with them to prevent them from leaving and to increase their appreciation of and use of their credit cards. After six months, the level of churn in the targeted groups had dropped by 73 percent compared to the controls which did not get the personalized attention. The level of spending by these same groups had increased by 42 percent as compared to the controls.

Age and Income Are Not Enough

A major brokerage firm had been using age- and income-based list selections to target its direct mail to prospective mutual fund buyers. Analysis showed that even though the "over 30 years old, $100,000+ income" segment was more likely than the general population to respond, over 90 percent of its buyers were not coming from this segment. In other words, targeting this group would provide a lift over random selection, but would also exclude the vast majority of likely responders. To understand what was going on, the brokerage built a model using financial and demographic data. The model demonstrated how to select prospects so it could effectively reach over 75 percent of likely buyers instead of 10 percent—a huge improvement over its age and income selection strategy. The model illustrated that buyers of investment products today can no longer be effectively targeted just by age and income. With so many investors in the market, net worth, risk preferences, and attitudes are becoming important in defining customer segments.

In another case, a major mutual fund company marketed a complete line of different funds by direct mail and telemarketing. It was using just age and income to select prospects from compiled lists. It wondered if perhaps it was missing the mark by not selecting different lists based upon prospects' expected tolerances for risk and their fund preferences. A consultant took a sample of the investor files across several of the different funds, overlaid demographic information, and developed segment profiles. It was clear that the company was indeed selling its different funds to markedly different segments; in fact, in several cases, the segments buying conservative funds were mutually exclusive from those investing in aggressive funds. The marketing plan that had tried to target both types of funds with the same lists could not possibly reach both types of buyers and would actually do a poor job of reaching either group. Based upon the model results, the company revamped its entire strategy to target its funds to specific segments.

Loan Application Abandonment

According to ComScore, 54 percent of consumers who start a financial services application online fail to complete it. E-LOAN had similar application abandonment issues. It undertook a three-year effort to target abandoners. The first step was to get a valid e-mail address. To do this, E-LOAN asks for an e-mail address immediately after the applicant's first and last name. Additionally, it asks the applicant to reenter the address to verify it. Thirty minutes after applicants abandon an application on the E-LOAN site, they receive the first of two e-mails asking them to complete their application. If E-LOAN receives no response in a week, it sends a second e-mail to abandoners.

The program converts about 28 percent of the abandoners into successful loan applicants. The cost of the program is about $15,000 to set up, plus the CPM (cost per thousand e-mails delivered) cost per e-mail. Results: 89 percent of abandoners who receive the first e-mail open it. The second e-mail also does well, with 60 percent of abandoners opening it. The first e-mail has a 28 percent lift in completion rate versus a control group of abandoners. The second has a lift of 25 percent over the control group.

Doing Research Online and Buying Offline

Millions of people use Google and other methods to do financial services research. About 40 percent of all online customers who are searching for a financial product end up by buying that product offline—either over the phone or in a branch. Why do they do this?

- Some (about 25 percent) do it because they are hesitant about providing personal information over the Web.

- Mortgage applicants are the most likely to research online but apply offline.

- Another 25 percent did not apply over the Web because they want someone to walk them through the application process either in person or over the phone. The solution to this problem is to provide an online text chat. E*TRADE Financial used proactive online chat by creating a trigger so that only certain online researchers were offered real-time human support. Only seven of the top thirty U.S. financial firms offered online chat on their product pages of their public sites.

- They can't find the help button. Place phone numbers or click to call options on every Web page. This seems like an obvious step, but only three of the top thirty financial Web sites do this.

- Some firms still lack an online application for some products, forcing customers to look elsewhere. Home lending and deposit account applicants are most likely to cite these reasons for choosing to apply offline.

- It is a nuisance to enter the same information over and over again. GEICO phone representatives are able to call up a user's VIN (Vehicle Identification Number) if she begins an application on the Web and then seeks assistance over the phone.

Every financial institution these days has a Web site that explains its products. The clever ones use search engine marketing and pay-per-click to get visitors to their Web sites so they can sell them financial products. Despite years of experience, many financial services providers fail to use the Web properly to get customers. One of the best methods is to get people to sign up for financial e-mails:

- Get to know your customers and develop content that will be valuable to them—such as research, tips for maximizing their investments, and product promotions. E-LOAN varies e-mail content and delivery times to different segments as determined by the recency and frequency of their last interaction. Schwab customers self-segment by selecting which of Schwab's 23 different e-mail products they want to receive.

- Send triggered e-mails in response to a change in market conditions or customer activity, like a drop in interest rates or applying for an account online. Schwab generates trades and contact with investment consultants through e-mails it sends when the value of a customer's portfolio changes.

- Coordinate e-mail with other channels. Integrating e-mail into multi-channel conversations increases customer engagement and decreases customer management costs. American Express Financial Advisors increases response to direct mail efforts when it follows up via e-mail. Schwab uses e-mail to right-channel users of Web features, instead of personal reps, where they can transact, get advice, and self-service their account at a much lower cost to Schwab.

- Use e-mail for acquisition. American Express Financial Advisors finds that e-mail has become one of its most cost-effective acquisition vehicles. It contacts current American Express cardholders and cross-sells them on the opportunity to work with a personal financial advisor.

- Use incentives. American Express Financial Advisors gets a better response to e-mail by including incentives, limiting the number of offers, and acknowledging in the e-mail how it got a prospect's information.

■ Use testing. E-LOAN evaluates subject lines, offers, content, message format, and message timing of its triggered messages. American Express Financial Advisors tests prospect sources, incentives, and creative to optimize its acquisition efforts. Schwab also pilots new programs through e-mail like its New Client Experience e-mail program, which focuses on engaging customers during their first 12 months

About two-thirds of online adults receive financial services e-mails. Why? They say that they want to know what's going on with their money. About one-third of them claim that they never signed up for these e-mails. They may be right. Some financial institutions sign customers up for account alerts and other transactional e-mails without telling their customers what types of e-mail will come to them, when, and why. Many consumers are turned off by e-mail they didn't opt in to receive. Many of them fear that their financial services firm—credit card, bank, or insurance company—will share their personal data with other companies:

■ Some consumers are very interested to learn about new products. Mothers, high-income individuals, and many who rely on advice seek out financial services e-mails for new product information more than average e-mail users. Well-off individuals who are more secure in their financial situation subscribe to more financial-related e-mails than do lower-income consumers. Seventy percent of consumers influenced by "what's hot and what's not" sign up for at least one financial services e-mail, and 18 percent are likely to subscribe to additional e-mails.

■ USAA successfully implemented ratings and reviews on its Web site. The result was almost 16,000 incremental product sales in the first year.

■ "Every 1 percent in retention versus attrition means about $100 million to Wachovia in revenue," said Cece Sutton head of Wachovia's retail bank.

Take-Away Thoughts

■ The greatest advance in database marketing for financial services has been online banking and the ability to send e-mails to customers concerning their accounts.

■ Every bank needs to create and maintain a MCIF (marketing customer information file) that includes information about all types of accounts.

- To promote profits, all information should be shared between product units.

- Eighty percent of consumers and businesses that have broadband have signed up for online banking.

- Profitability calculation by customer is central to financial product marketing success.

- Customers should be grouped into profitability segments with different strategies for each segment.

- For each customer current profitability and potential lifetime profitability should be determined.

- For a large bank half of all customers may be unprofitable.

- Use regressions to determine which customers are most likely to leave. Then develop a plan to deal with the situation.

- Group product owners by LTV and likelihood to churn.

- Prospecting by e-mails today can be very profitable.

- Many online loan applicants abandon the process while filling out the forms. E-LOAN showed that 28 percent of abandoners can be converted by follow up e-mails.

A quiz on this chapter and all figures can be found at www.dbmarket ing.com/STM4. Those taking all the quizzes can receive a Successful Completion Certificate from the Database Marketing Institute which can be used in their résumé.

19

Business-to-Business Database Marketing

Business-to-business e-mail campaigns ... show up looking like long-winded, copy heavy, direct mail solicitations. Some have one giant image with marketing-department–focused jargon. Most seem to miss the mark in understanding what may attract the right buyer and how to deliver real value and relevancy to the inbox. ...

Your tone should be much like it would be in a face-to-face meeting with your prospects: direct, professional, and in a manner that makes your audience want to do business with you. Don't waste your time building up to the pitch—state why you are sending this message and what's in it for the recipient.

The message should clearly articulate the purpose and value to the subscribers while making it easy for them to identify and act on any call to action. Don't bog them down with too many cross-promotional messages or secondary marketing messages. Allow them to scan the e-mail and find out what's in it for them.

Your main measurement analysis should not be based on opens and clicks but on how many leads are generated.

—SIMMS JENKINS
Brightwave Marketing

There are many products and services for which database marketing has limited value. In business-to-business marketing, however, relationship-building activities *always* pay off. Why is the business-to-business area so productive? There are several reasons:

- The sales amounts are usually large. Sales are large enough that there is a significant margin available for relationship-building activities.

- The data on customer purchases is almost always available, since so much of the business is on open accounts. Getting the names of the decision makers, influencers, and ultimate users is often a challenge, however.

- The numbers of customers is usually quite small. In many cases we are dealing with 50,000 customers or less. We can concentrate on these companies and build a complete database of contact history, purchases, and preferences, and use this data to support our relationship-building activities.

- Business customers have problems of their own to solve, including channel conflicts, inventory maintenance, customer acquisition and retention. The supplier is often in a position to help customers solve their problems.

Professor Paul Wang divides business customers into four basic categories as shown in Figure 19.1.

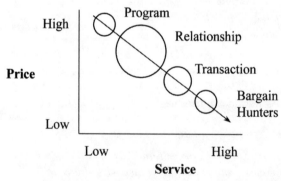

Figure 19.1 Types of Business Customers

There are two axes on this figure: price and service. Some business customers pay a high price and get little service. On the other end, some pay very low prices but get the best service. Let's see why that is.

- *Bargain hunters* are customers that have tremendous market power. Walmart is an example. Here is a customer that demands—and gets—the absolutely lowest prices in the market. Walmart is in a position to make massive purchases at rock bottom prices. At the same time, it can demand—and get—a very high level of service from its suppliers. Walmart often makes its suppliers provide daily shelf restocking. Some goods are placed on Walmart shelves on consignment so Walmart has little investment. In some cases, the suppliers must clean up the sales areas each day. Few other retailers can get such services from their suppliers. For bargain hunters, the supplier has to meet specified requirements in order to sell massive amounts at very low prices. There are many such bargain hunters around. Anyone who sells to Home Depot or Staples knows what it is like to hold a tiger by its tail.

- *Program buyers* are at the other end of the spectrum. Small purchasers of office supplies, for example, do not have the time or the economic incentive to shop around for the best deal. They don't have the market power that comes from volume purchases. Typically, they will buy from a nearby source one month and shift to another source the next month, without any really well-thought-out plan. Many governments, including the federal government, are program buyers. They issue purchasing manuals to their employees which restrict how, what, where, and when purchases can be made. These program buyers have the worst of both worlds. They pay the highest prices and get the lowest level of service. The famous Defense Department purchase of expensive toilet seats is a well-known example. Their purchases are either so small or so specialized that few suppliers find it profitable to do much to attract them. Relationship building may not work here.

- *Transaction buyers*, on the other hand, represent a major segment of any market. These customers try to engage in comparison-shopping for every transaction. They read the ads, consult Google, make phone calls, and get comparative bids. For them, the past has no meaning. They have absolutely no loyalty. Never mind what the supplier did for you in the past; the question is what is your price today? They will shift suppliers of any product for a few pennies difference in price.

Transaction buyers usually get little service. Service is not important to them. Price is everything. There is not much point in trying to win their loyalty, since they have none to give. Database marketing may be ineffective here—only discounting works. They are seldom profitable customers, even though they may buy a lot of product and represent an important segment of any market. The best thing that could happen to these transaction buyers would be for them to shift over to buying from your competition. Give them the competition's catalogs and phone numbers and hope they take the hint. Paul Wang suggests that the only way to make money with transaction buyers is to negotiate annual volume purchase agreements. The buyers get a good deal on price, and you get the volume without having to spend valuable marketing and customer service dollars.

- *Relationship buyers* are the customers for whom database marketing was invented. They are looking for a dependable supplier:
  - Someone who cares about their needs and who looks out for them.
  - Someone who remembers what they bought in the past and gives them special services as a reward.
  - Someone who takes an interest in their business and treats them as individuals.

  Relationship buyers know that they could save a few dollars by shopping around. But they also recognize that if they do switch suppliers, they would lose something that they value very highly— the relationship they have built up with a dependable supplier that recognizes them and takes good care of them. Many of them also realize that there is an emotional and monetary cost to shopping around for every purchase. They want to concentrate on their business success, not on their purchasing prowess.

By classifying your customers into these four segments, you can focus your marketing efforts on the one segment that is really profitable: relationship buyers. Your database is used to record the purchases of these buyers, and to give them personal recognition and special services. You recognize your gold customers. You communicate with them. You partner with them.

Classifying Customers by Segment

How can you classify customers into these four segments? Part of it is easy. You already know who the bargain hunters are. No one who deals with Walmart or Sears or other giant retailers has to be told who they are. Program buyers can almost be ignored. They make small purchases on an occasional basis. They pay full price and seldom respond to sales offers. They, too, are easy to classify.

Your big problem lies in distinguishing transaction buyers from relationship buyers. Here's how one retailer does it. New customers are given a survey form. One question asks, "How important are the following in making your decision about where to buy this product? Rank from 1—most important—to 5—least important:

a. Price

b. Service

c. Reputation of manufacturer

d. Recommendation of a friend

e. Company policy

f. Previous experience

g. Customer service

Those who code *price* as most important are probably transaction buyers. The others may well be relationship buyers. This can be tested later in other ways.

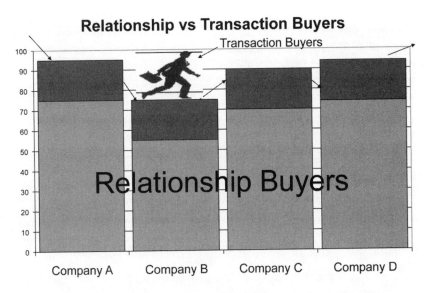

Figure 19.2 Transaction Buyers Shifting from Supplier to Supplier

Your management may insist that most of your customers be transaction buyers. They will point out that when you are on sale, you get more sales. When you are not, the sales decrease. What may be happening, however, is shown in Figure 19.2. Each of the four companies, A, B, C, and D, has a stable base of relationship buyers that stay with them. There is a floating group of transaction buyers that jumps from company to company taking advantage of the sales. They never pay full price for anything. No one makes much money from them. Each company assumes that all their customers are price sensitive, when, in reality, few of their loyal customers are price sensitive at all.

Training Your Customers

How do customers become transaction buyers? They are not necessarily born that way. They become transaction buyers through exposure to their environment and their management. As suppliers, we may feel that we have to take the world as we find it, but this is not necessarily true. We can take customers who are quite prepared to develop a relationship with us and *ruin* them by converting them into transaction buyers. How do we do this? By talking price to them all the time, instead of talking services and relationships. Let's look at how we do it.

You attract customers by offering discounts. Once you have acquired the customer, you hold periodic sales and send out literature extolling your low prices. What a mistake! You are training your customers to think of your product or service as a commodity whose value can be measured only by price. Once you have implanted this idea in their minds, they will learn to shop around. Soon they will find someone who sells something cheaper. Of course, if you are truly an everyday low price dealer like Staples, the focus on price is a valid tactic. But most business-to-business suppliers do not want to be in that league.

What should you do for relationship buyers?

- Describe what your products do, how various businesses are using them, how they are made, and new developments in your field.

- Divide your customers into groups, based on their SIC code: surveyors, architects, builders, and contractors, and send them different messages.

- Create an advisory panel for each group, putting key executives from among your gold customers in each group on the panel.

- Create a newsletter for each group, with the advisory panel on the masthead.

- Sponsor contests in trade associations for the most creative use of your products.

- Learn the birthdays of key people in your customers' companies and send them a card.

- Write thank-you letters periodically for their purchases—not combined with a pitch for more sales—but just a genuine thank you.

At a business-to-business conference, I was asked, "How big a customer base do you have to have so that you can profit from database marketing." It was an interesting question. The answer, it seems to me, is to divide customers into three categories as shown in Figure 19.3.

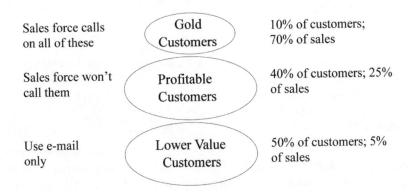

Sales force calls on all of these	**Gold Customers**	10% of customers; 70% of sales
Sales force won't call them	**Profitable Customers**	40% of customers; 25% of sales
Use e-mail only	**Lower Value Customers**	50% of customers; 5% of sales

Figure 19.3 Typical Business to Business Customer Grouping

The top group, in most business-to-business situations, is visited directly by the sales force. The salespeople know these customers by sight and name. You can build a database of these customers, but it may not help the sales force much. If you only have 300 customers in this group and all of them are large enough to justify a sales visit, you don't need a database here. Relationship marketing really works with the middle group. These are profitable customers whose sales do not justify a sales visit. Here, you can organize effective teams to reach these customers by a combination of techniques using the database. The lower-value customers should be served by your Web site and e-mails.

What Is the Proof That Business-to-Business Database Marketing Works?

A manufacturer of lighting products was doing well. It had 45,000 customers—most of them building construction contractors—who purchased lighting products for new buildings from the manufacturer's catalog. A database marketing consultant from Hunter Business Direct persuaded it to try an experiment. He selected 1,200 of the best customers and split them into two exactly equal groups (in terms of annual sales) of 600 each. For the test group, he set up a two-person pilot program consisting of a marketer and a lighting expert. This team determined the top lighting decision makers and made phone calls to these individuals in each of the 600 firms. Over the phone, team members got to know these people. They followed up on bids and quotes, scheduled product training, provided information on new products, and asked about their customer needs. They did not offer discounts. For the other 600, there were no phone calls; only the same excellent service that the company had always given its customers. After six months the team compared the sales to each of these two groups as shown in Figure 19.4.

The test group made 12 percent more orders than they had before, while the control group's orders dropped by 18 percent. The average order size of the test group went up by 14 percent, while the control group's order size fell by 14 percent. In total the revenue gain comparing the two groups was $2.6 million with the test group revenue going up by 27 percent and the control group revenue falling by 30 percent. There could be no better proof than this that customer relationship marketing is highly successful.

Business-to-Business Lifetime Value

Lifetime value tables for business-to-business customers are easy to develop and are highly useful for evaluating strategy. Let's develop the lifetime value of customers of an artificial construct: the Weldon Scientific Company which sells high-tech equipment to factories and laboratories.

This table in Figure 19.5 is similar to those explained in Chapter 3, with some exceptions. Weldon has about 20,000 business customers, including 1,800 independent distributors. The average customer placed

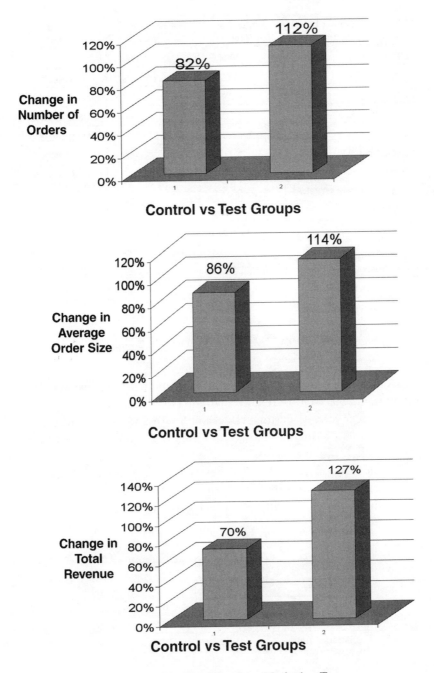

Figure 19.4 Results of Database Marketing Test

Weldon Customer LTV before New Initiatives	Acquisition Year	Second Year	Third Year
Retained Customers	20,000	12,000	7,800
Retention Rate	60.00%	65.00%	70.00%
Orders/Year	1.8	2.6	3.6
Avg. Order Size	$2,980	$5,589	$9,016
Total Revenue	$107,280,000	$174,376,800	$253,169,280
Direct Cost %	70.00%	65.00%	63.00%
Direct Costs	$75,096,000	$113,344,920	$159,496,646
Acquisition Cost $630	$12,600,000	$0	$0
Total Costs	$87,696,000	$113,344,920	$159,496,646
Gross Profit	$19,584,000	$61,031,880	$93,672,634
Discount Rate	1.18	1.33	1.43
Net Present Value Profit	$16,596,610	$45,888,632	$65,505,338
Cumulative NPV Profit	$16,596,610	$62,485,242	$127,990,580
Customer Lifetime Value	$830	$3,124	$6,400

Figure 19.5 LTV of Weldon Scientific Company

an average of 1.8 orders in the year of acquisition, with an average order value of $2,980. Weldon retained 60 percent of its first-year customers into the next year. As customers became more loyal, they placed more orders per year of increasing size, and the retention rate of the remaining customers also increased.

The acquisition cost was $630 per customer. The cost of servicing customers came down substantially after the first year. Most interesting in this figure is the discount rate, which is shown in Figure 19.6.

	Year 1	Year 2	Year 3
Year	0	1	2
Risk Factor	1.8	1.5	1.4
Interest Rate	6.0%	6.0%	6.0%
Acc/Rev. Days	65	85	90
Discount Rate	1.18	1.33	1.43

Figure 19.6 Computation of the Discount Rate

The formula for the discount rate is:

Discount rate $= [(1 + \text{interest rate}) \times (\text{risk factor})]^{\text{year}+\text{AR}/365}$

In the first year, Weldon tries to get new customers to pay upfront and relaxes to a 60-day policy with subsequent orders. For established customers, 90 days for payment is customary. The risk factor drops substantially with long-term customers. The combination of all of these factors gives Weldon a sophisticated discount rate that is responsive to the business situation that it faces.

Relationship-Building Initiatives

Let's suppose that Weldon has decided to experiment with database marketing. It will take the following steps:

- Create a Web site with distributor and direct customer access by means of a PIN. The site will include all of its products, with prices shown based on the customer's volume situation.

- Set up an integrated account management team that contacts all medium-sized and large customers at least six times per year, learning the names of the decision makers, influencers, and actual users of Weldon's products. Annual sales agreements are negotiated with volume discounts.

- Establish an advisory council for each of its six major customer groups, complete with a newsletter, which is published on the Web, and prizes given at professional trade shows for the best use of Weldon's products.

- Design a series of communications to each identified Weldon contact in customer firms. Each new customer receives a welcome e-mail and a link to the Weldon Web site requesting that the customer take a survey. There are thank-you letters for large orders in addition to the e-mails.

What the Web Site and E-mails Do

The savings cost from the Web site and e-mail shopping carts is larger than the time saved would indicate (see Figure 19.7). Because orders are

	Order Processing Time*	Cost Per Order
Phone	28hrs	$27.00
Fax, Mail	42hrs	$18.00
Web Site & E-mail	1.6 minutes	$1.62

*From order receipt until paperwork arrives at factory

Figure 19.7 Order Processing Times and Cost of Various Ordering Systems

processed so much faster and without human intervention, fewer employees are needed in the order-processing department. In addition, by cutting more than a day from each order-processing time, customers get their products faster, which gives Weldon an edge over its competitors. Finally, by getting bills out one day earlier, Weldon's cash flow is improved by a measurable amount. In all, use of the Web site ordering system can cut costs by 3 percent per order. The problem is that in the beginning, only about 10 percent of Weldon's customers would use the Web site to place their orders. To change this, Weldon could give a discount of ½ of 1 percent for all orders placed on the Web site or in e-mails. By the second year, the percentage of customers using the Web site could grow to 60 percent, and by the third year it could be close to 90 percent. The cost savings could look like those shown in Figure 19.8.

	Year 1	Year 2	Year 3
Old Costs	70.00%	65.00%	63.00%
% Using Web Site	10.00%	60.00%	90.00%
Net Saving per Order 2.5%	0.25%	1.50%	2.25%
New Costs	69.75%	63.50%	60.75%

Figure 19.8 Cost Reduction from Use of Web Site for Orders

Let's assume the cost of the first three initiatives is shown in Figure 19.9.

	First Year	Annual Incremental Cost
Electronic Orders	$1,600,000	$300,000
Advisory Councils	$200,000	$150,000
Total	$1,800,000	$450,000

Figure 19.9 Cost of Relationship Building Initiatives

The relationship-building communications to customers, based on their preferences could come to $96 per customer per year.

The result of the initiatives could be a major change in customer lifetime value, as shown in Figure 19.10.

Weldon LTV with New Initiatives	First Year	Second Year	Third Year
Retained Customers	20,000	13,000	9,100
Retention Rate	65.00%	70.00%	75.00%
Orders/Year	1.9	3.4	4.8
Avg. Order Size	$3,078	$6,170	$8,005
Total Revenue	$116,964,000	$272,714,000	$349,658,400
Direct Cost %	69.75%	63.50%	60.75%
Direct Costs	$81,582,390	$173,173,390	$212,417,478
Acquisition Cost $630	$12,600,000	$0	$0
New Initiatives	$2,400,000	$350,000	$350,000
Relationship Building $96	$1,920,000	$1,248,000	$873,600
Total Costs	$98,502,390	$174,771,390	$213,641,078
Gross Profit	$18,461,610	$97,942,610	$136,017,322
Discount Rate	1.18	1.33	1.43
Net Present Value Profit	$15,645,432	$73,641,060	$95,117,008
Cumulative NPV Profit	$15,645,432	$89,286,492	$184,403,501
Customer Lifetime Value	$782	$4,464	$9,220

Figure 19.10 LTV of Weldon Customers after New Initiatives Are in Place

The effect of these new initiatives would be to increase the average customer lifetime value in the third year from about $6,400 to $9,220. What does this mean for Weldon? Assuming that its acquisition program continues to replace lost customers and that Weldon has a steady customer base of 20,000 customers, the program has increased Weldon's profits by $56 million as shown in Figure 19.11.

The first year is costly. Introducing these changes reduces Weldon profits by $1 million. These numbers in Figure 19.11 show, however, that

Boost in LTV	Acquisition Year	Second Year	Third Year
New LTV	$782	$4,464	$9,220
Old LTV	$830	$3,124	$6,400
Difference	($48)	$1,340	$2,821
With 20,000 Customers	($951,178)	$26,801,251	$56,412,921

Figure 19.11 Effect of New Initiatives on Weldon Profits

if Weldon were to institute the relationship-building programs described here, its profits in the third year would increase by over $56 million. Business-to-business relationship building works—and can be shown to work by careful and controlled tests.

Of course, Weldon would probably not apply this program to its entire customer base. Weldon, like all other companies, has some highly profitable customers and some highly unprofitable customers. The relationship-building program will probably work best with the middle group. The top group—Weldon's gold customers—are probably maxed out. They are loyal customers. Many companies have found that they cannot profitably cross-sell or up-sell their best customers. In the same way, Weldon probably cannot have this kind of success with its unprofitable customers. Building a relationship with losers is not a recipe for success. The most profitable group for Weldon's program is the relationship buyers just below the top—people who are profitable, but probably dividing their spending for Weldon type products among a number of different suppliers.

	Customers	Average Sales	Total Sales	Sales Ranking	Lifetime Value	LTV Ranking
Metal Production	254	$339,736	$86,292,944	4	$145,067	2
Light Manufacturing	15,442	$13,851	$213,887,142	1	$5,914	4
Heavy Manufacturing	44	$2,314,189	$101,824,316	3	$988,146	1
High Technology	612	$299,007	$182,992,284	2	$127,676	3
Others	3,613	$2,176	$7,861,888	5	$929	5
Total	19,965	$29,695	$592,858,574		$12,679	

Figure 19.12 Weldon Instruments Corporation Customer Segments

Once Weldon has been able to determine its average customer lifetime value, it can compute the LTV for various segments (see Figure 19.12). The results are often interesting. If you look at Weldon sales, the big money is clearly in light manufacturing, with $213 million in annual sales. But if you look at lifetime value, the 44 heavy manufacturing customers account for almost $1 million apiece. Clearly, any retention strategy should start with heavy manufacturers. You are going to get much more bang for a marketing buck. Next would be metal production, which is low in overall sales, but clearly high in average customer lifetime value.

Figure 19.12 represents the ultimate users of Weldon products. Most of the 15,442 light manufacturing firms and laboratories are served through Weldon's 1,800 independent distributors. This does not mean that Weldon should not cultivate them, but it should not try to sell directly to them. By keeping the distribution channel on the database, Weldon's efforts can be directed at getting these customers to visit or call their authorized distributor.

Finally, let's look at the distribution of Weldon customers by total lifetime value. In Figure 19.13, we have divided Weldon customers into five status groups of approximately equal numbers based on their lifetime value.

	Number of Customers	Lifetime Value	Firm Value Total	Percent LTV
Platinum	3,967	$50,410	$199,976,470	79.0%
Gold	4,004	$9,603	$38,450,412	15.2%
Silver	3,881	$2,903	$11,266,543	4.5%
Bronze	4,210	$1,108	$4,664,680	1.8%
Lead	3,903	($309)	($1,206,027)	−0.5%
Total	19,965	$12,679	$253,152,078	100.00%

Figure 19.13 Weldon Customers Organized by Lifetime Value

The top status level, the platinum, has an average lifetime value of $50,410 and represents about 79 percent of the total customer lifetime value. The bottom group of 3,903 customers includes the true losers, being responsible for a net lifetime value of minus $309. What can we do with this figure? It probably should be combined with the previous figure to determine the direction of Weldon's retention efforts. Why spend money trying to retain customers with a negative lifetime value? Even if they are in a favored group, such as heavy manufacturing or metal production, if they consistently result in a loss of value to Weldon, the retention effort should be reconsidered.

Business-to-Business E-mail Marketing

Customer service is expensive. At a cost of $3 to $8 per call, with thousands of calls per day, companies see a significant drain on the bottom line. Customer lifetime value analysis must be used to determine whether the helpfulness and relationship building is worth the cost. In some cases, companies found that it was not paying its way. Most banks that have done profitability analysis have discovered that about half their customers are unprofitable. A good part of the lack of profits can be traced to the expense of customer service. Federal Express provided a shining example of customer support by having customer reps that could field questions on the exact status of every package shipped at any time. A couple of years later, UPS set up a similar system. But these shining examples came at a significant cost. If every customer called by phone to learn the status of a shipment, all shipments would cost at least $3 more than they do.

B2B E-mail—Contact with Reduced Costs

B2B e-mail marketing is completely different from B2C marketing, mainly because of differences in the audience. Businesspeople are intensely interested in their industry—whether the industry is software, hotels, automotive parts, or insurance. They are seldom interested in some other industry. They feel a community spirit within their industry but are also suspicious that others in the industry are trying to learn their secrets and steal their customers. They are usually keenly anxious to know what their competition is doing, planning, and thinking. They are convinced that the competition knows things that they themselves do not.

Depending on their jobs, businesspeople want to know how products are made and how they are marketed. They want to know the details of new products. They gobble up statistics on their industry. And despite a strong desire not to give up any information on their own companies, they are really interested to know details about their competitors—who their clients are and what their prices are. Case studies are of great interest, then, particularly if they explain how they were done and the results are put in terms of numerical improvements: "20 percent better than the previous method." They will circulate your e-mails with details like this throughout their company.

Your e-mail audience consists of two groups of businesspeople: customers (and prospects) and competitors. You can be certain that your competitors will be reading your e-mails, no matter how hard you try to prevent it. Your job is to define your industry for your customers and prospects and be a trusted source of information for them.

Don't make your e-mails vehicles to push your products or your company. Instead, treat your readers as insiders; give them exclusive inside information on trends that you see: new processes, markets, and products (not necessarily yours). And don't assume that your audience knows everything you do. You can recycle or reprint valid information from the past or provide extensive links to other sources. When you use industry jargon, always provide a link to the term's definition. Because people change jobs so often these days, at least a third of your audience are newcomers who aren't sure what the terms mean. Make it easy for them to find out. Make them want to open your next e-mail to learn more.

Also, make it easy for your readers to e-mail your content to others in their company. The ideal B2B e-mail will have a huge secondary audience of people within any company. Your readers will often gain internal recognition and status from having found your e-mail and passed it around.

Glossaries of terms and statistics in your industry, sent in your e-mails, will be reprinted and saved. They will be the most widely read and circulated e-mails you can send. They establish you and your company as experts in your field.

Your goal is simply to provide to your readers with a source of the most interesting, well-documented information about their and your industry. As a result, your readers will look forward to receiving your e-mails, will print them out, and will forward them to others. They will see you and your company as experts and leaders in their and your field. If you can do this, you don't need to sell your products in your e-mails. Your acceptance and reputation will do that. It is then up to your sales force to move in and take the orders.

The Importance of Personalization

If Volvo Construction Equipment North America sends a customer who is interested in excavators information about pipe-layers, chances are that customer may not jump to open the next e-mail that comes his or her way. Personalization, said John Johnston, e-business marketing manager, is extremely important to the success of the company's e-mail marketing program. "Having the right content is our biggest e-mail demand," he said. "It's something that has to be there."

Each month, the company sends out a newsletter, e-commerce promotions and e-mails tied to specific campaigns. Until 18 months ago, all that personalization happened manually, with someone having to insert newsletter content, for example, by looking at Volvo's CRM system and dropping in the right links, articles, logos and images before sending it out to dealers and end-users. "We grabbed the image, embedded the link and grabbed the right text," Johnston said. "By the time we built it out, it took twice as long as it currently does."

So the company, with help from its ESP, ExactTarget, integrated its CRM system and web site with its e-mail creation and delivery system so customers get not only personalized but also up-to-the-minute content in their messaging. Personalizing e-mails made a huge difference, Johnston said, with open rates increasing 15% to 20% in the past 18 months. "There is an increase in open rates because people see content that is personalized to them," he said.

—Karen J. Bannan

B2B Marketing

By using personalization, Volvo generated a 20 to 30 percent click through rate. The new system boosted the conversion rate.

Administrative Requirements

There are a few requirements for every B2B e-mail. You will need:

- A table of contents, so readers can quickly see and skip to whatever interests them.

- A comprehensive search box, so readers can search for any product or piece of news. Constantly improve what this box can do by monitoring what readers put into it.

- A blog for readers to post comments on—comments that will be read by everyone in the industry.

- A "forward to a friend" function that captures the friend's e-mail address.

- An archive box to permit readers to see an index of all previous e-mails.

- Cookies, so you can greet readers by name in your e-mails.

- A link to your company's history.

- A link to your company's directory, with links to everyone readers may want to get in touch with—including e-mail addresses, phone numbers, and postal addresses.

- A link to product listings, so readers can look up any product.

- A suggestion function, so readers can suggest topics for future e-mails.

- An option for readers for sending shortened text messages to their cell phones.

- A prominent, easy-to-use unsubscribe function.

How You Look in a Preview Pane

B2B marketing subscribers almost all use preview panes when they look at their in boxes. In an E-mailLabs survey, 90 percent of e-mail newsletter subscribers have access to a preview pane, and 69 percent say they frequently or always use it.

After looking at the sender and the subject line, these readers peek at what is in your e-mail. This view can make or break your whole e-mail campaign. Design the top left of every e-mail with that pane in mind. If you have a big colorful ad there, the readers will see nothing of interest.

Writing a B2B Newsletter

A good B2B e-mail newsletter is like the popcorn, peanuts, and TV that go with the drinks at a bar. While you are in the bar talking to your friends, you are munching away and keeping your eye on the TV. When you have eaten, watched, and talked for a while, you will order another drink—which is why the bar provides those free things.

Your newsletter should be filled with articles and information about your industry, not necessarily about your products. Businesspeople like to keep up on what is going on in their industry. That's why they may want to read your e-mail newsletter. If you can provide interesting content once a month, things that people in your industry want to know about, then your company will always be fresh in their minds. They may also be willing to read something about your products and your company, which could lead to an inquiry and an order.

Your job, therefore, is to come up with the interesting content (the peanuts, popcorn, and TV) so your readers will think of your company first when they need products that your company sells. So what should you write about?

Start by signing up for all your competitors' newsletters. You should know what they are saying so you can say something similar, but better. Be sure to go to all the trade shows and mingle with people there to find out what they are saying and thinking about you and your competitors' products. Use Google and Technorati to read what is being posted on relevant blogs. You will get a lot of material for your newsletter from blogs. Create a blog of your own. Talk to your sales reps and your customer service people. They will give you ideas for content. You can exchange news and articles with other newsletters from companies that don't compete with yours.

But the best source of ideas will be your readers. Provide a space in the sign-up form and in every newsletter for them to suggest topics. One interesting idea: when your subscribers are out of the office, which happens a lot in B2B situations, they usually post an automatic notice saying when they will be back. This notice often includes their current title and other useful information. Read all these and add the relevant info to your database record.

Mobile Versions

The percentage of businesspeople who regularly read business e-mails on their mobile devices is more than 60 percent. It is essential that any B2B e-mail message have an option for the stripped-down version.

Create a mobile version of your newsletter optimized for a phone's screen. Include only a small version of your logo. The rest of the content should be easy-to-read text that can be scanned quickly. In the mobile version, include a link to the full edition of your newsletter so readers can check it out on their desktops.

Many executives today use their iPhones and other smartphones to scan and delete e-mails. If you have a weak message, busy execs will delete your messages while attending a meeting. If, however, you have something interesting to say that shows up in the first three sentences, your e-mail may get saved for the executive to read later.

According to MailerMailer, 74 percent of all opens occur within the first 24 hours. Since a few recipients will open your e-mail weeks later, however, make sure your images, links, and landing pages remain accessible.

Topics for your B2B newsletters can include:

- Events of interest: trade shows, new product launch, and so on
- Industry calendars
- Interviews with key executives in the industry
- Tips and best practices
- Surveys and reports on the results
- "Ask the expert"
- Regular columns and features
- Top 10 lists
- Six steps to success
- Industry statistics and benchmarks
- Interactive quizzes
- Reader feedback
- Links to resources and Web sites of interest in the industry
- Best-of-class write-ups of the present and past
- Glossary of terms used in the industry
- Case studies
- Opinions on an industry trend
- Common problems in the industry and how some companies are solving them

Check the clicks on each section of your newsletter to see which are being read and which ones are skipped. Be guided by these clicks.

Creating a Business Blog

A blog can help humanize your company to customers and the outside world. Blogs are a powerful tool for marketing and promotion. Because they are short, they are easy for your customers to read (and you to write), so customers are more likely to come back daily to see what you might have to say.

With a blog, you can show your customers that your company is made up of ordinary people. If you do it right, you can create a blog without becoming too personal or too formal. Company Web sites are often created by a committee. Blogs are just the opposite.

For this reason, you have to be able to assign one person to write for and manage the blog within written guidelines without formal approval of content every day.

Hewlett-Packard uses blogs to show its friendly image to the world. The HP Blogging Code of Conduct is an example of how a large corporation handles blogging. It's worth reading, and perhaps emulating. According to the code:

HP blogs are written by a variety of employees at different levels and positions in the company, so you can expect many viewpoints. You can also expect the following:

- We will strive to have open and honest dialogues with our readers.

- We will correct inaccurate or misleading postings in a timely manner. We will not delete posts unless they violate our policies. Most changes will be made by adding to posts and we will mark any additions clearly.

- We will disclose conflicts of interest.

- Our Standards of Business Conduct will guide what we write about—so there are some topics we won't comment on such as information about financials, HP intellectual property, trade secrets, management changes, lawsuits, shareholder issues, layoffs, and contractual agreements with alliance partners, customers, and suppliers.

- We will provide links to relevant material available on other blogs and Web sites. We will disclose any sources fully through credits, links, and trackbacks unless the source has requested anonymity.

- We understand that respect goes both ways—we will use good judgment in our posts and respond to you in a respectful manner. In return, we ask the same of you.

- We trust you will be mindful of the information you share on our blogs—any personally identifiable information you share on a blog can be seen by anyone with access to the blog.

- We will respect intellectual property rights.

- We will use good judgment in protecting personal and corporate information and in respecting the privacy of individuals who use our blogs.

Comments:

- Comments will be reviewed by bloggers before they are posted on our blogs.

- We will review, post, and respond to comments in a timely manner. We welcome constructive criticism. We can't respond to every comment, but will read all of them.

- We will not post comments that are spam, inappropriate, defamatory, use profanity, or otherwise violate our policies or Terms of Use.

- Because our blogs focus on material of general interest to all our readers, we ask that you direct customer support inquiries through our traditional customer service channels or use our IT resource center forums. Using these channels will allow you to get your issues to experienced HP support representatives in a timely manner.

- Our bloggers will not respond to customer support issues and will not post these comments to their blogs.

Reaching C-Level Executives

C-level executives are the top executives in any company, including such titles as chief operating officer (COO), chief executive officer (CEO), chief marketing officer (CMO), and chief financial officer (CFO). C-level executives make high-level decisions that can affect millions of dollars. It may be useful to survey these executives so you can present a valuable report to the industry. How can you reach them?

Trying to get these busy executives to take 15 minutes to complete a survey presents two problems: much of the information they have is highly confidential, and they aren't usually in a position to accept anything of monetary value as an incentive for participating in a survey. So what can you do?

One of the best methods was outlined by Claire Tinker at ESL Insights, a marketing intelligence firm. She suggests setting up an executive advisory panel. You can begin with a simple e-mail that says, "You are invited to participate in a business study." The invitation has to spell out what executives will get in return for their investment. You can offer a personal incentive or a donation to a charitable organization, and, more important, an executive summary of the research findings. They will be reading information provided by other C-Level executives who work for their competitors.

To get their participation, the invitation has to come from a C-level executive at your own company. It will seem like two senior executives talking to each other, not a researcher asking questions. When the survey is done, send a summary of the results to the respondents with a thank-you note. The results of this survey could be one of the most valuable e-mails you send all year, besides building a close relationship with the C-level executives who participated.

Take-Away Thoughts

- Business to business database marketing always pays off.
- There are four types of business customers: program buyers, transaction buyers, bargain hunters, and relationship buyers.
- Your database is designed to support relationship buyers, who are the most profitable.
- Those interested primarily in price are transaction buyers. You seldom make money from them.
- Create advisory panels for customers based on their SIC codes.
- Create e-mail newsletters for each group.
- Concentrate your newsletters on profitable customers, not gold or lower-value customers.
- B2B LTV is easy to calculate and highly useful in planning your marketing campaigns.
- Electronic marketing today saves millions of dollars.
- Divide your business customers by type of industry. Concentrate on those with the highest LTV.
- Fill your newsletters with information about the industry, not about your products.
- Personalization of e-mail newsletters pays off.

- Mobile versions of your newsletters are particularly useful in B2B.
- Everyone should have a business blog. If it is well done, it will be widely read.
- C-level executives can be reached through surveys and advisory panels.

A quiz on this chapter and all figures can be found at www.dbmarket ing.com/STM4. Those taking all the quizzes can receive a Successful Completion Certificate from the Database Marketing Institute which can be used in their résumé.

20

Why Databases Fail

E-mail "batch and blast" marketing is in distress. It simply no longer performs. Subscriber inboxes are overflowing with permission-based e-mail that is irrelevant. Our research shows that 60% of subscribers just ignore the e-mails, deflating marketer hopes for relationship-building and sales. Worse, half of subscribers unsubscribe or complain to their ISPs, completely severing the relationship and hurting deliverability across the board. Using our old direct marketing friend, data, marketers can finally respond to the fact that response rates have steadily declined year over year and start to provide custom, relevant e-mail experiences for their important subscriber segments. With CRM systems finally providing intelligent and actionable methods for determining a subscriber's place in your sales and product lifecycle, marketers can more easily create relevant subscriber experiences, which is the key to driving response.

—STEPHANIE MILLER,
Vice President of Strategic Services, Return Path Inc.

The mindset of the IT group is very important. Do they value data? Do they understand why the marketing database is so important to the organization? One of my greatest meetings recently was with an IT Director who wondered why his organization wasn't maximizing the opportunities to increase revenue from the existing customer base. I wanted to hug him. Wow, this company can have a successful Database Marketing program because the tech team GETS IT! So the real question is, "Do we have the right skill sets in place to build and manage a marketing database as part of our internal IT infrastructure?"

A successful marketing database is never done. There are always more applications to be built, more models to be refined, more digging into the data. If you have an internal IT team that can embrace that dynamic, then you have the resources to build a Marketing Database internally. If your IT team heads for the hills when they hear the Marketing Department calling, it might be best to consider an outsourced solution.

—EVELYN BARTLETT

Database marketing was invented because of the cost of direct mail postage. The database was used to restrict mailing to those most likely to respond. Gradually the use of a database shifted to learning what customers were interested in and serving them dynamic content based on the data stored about them in the database. In the late 1990s, e-mail arrived and made it possible to send communications to customers at negligible cost. By 2009, led by Apple, millions of consumers bought mobile devices so sophisticated that they could send and receive e-mails in addition to voice and text messages. They could record and play video. Meanwhile, social media such as Facebook and Twitter became very popular on the Web—both on PCs and on smartphones. The customer communication channels that could use the information in a customer marketing database exploded.

Few companies have been able to keep up with these changes. Many of them still have one database for direct mail, a mailing list for e-mail, another database for their catalog operation, and possibly a fourth for their retail stores. To connect most profitably with these people, the databases need to be combined. A combination like this involves internal political problems as well as IT costs. Most companies realize the need to do this, but for budget reasons have put it off into the future.

Database marketing, properly conceived and executed, can bring your company customer loyalty, repeat sales, reduced costs, cross-sales, improved identification of prospects, and a continuing boost to your bottom line. But if you go about it in the wrong way, it will not bring you any of these things, and it could be a costly failure. In this chapter we present the top nine reasons why you may fail.

Mistake 1: Lack of Marketing Strategy

Database and e-mail marketing have at last caught on. There isn't a major corporation that doesn't have a director of database marketing with a customer marketing database of some sort that sends out direct mail and one that sends out e-mail.

A marketing plan using a database aims at building a relationship with each customer: making her feel recognized and special. You become an old friend. You give her things that she wants: recognition, information, and service, and she gives you what you want: loyalty and repeat sales.

But how are you going to do this? To go from a list of names and addresses to building a relationship is a giant leap. Somewhere in your plan there must be a practical program for using the names, which accomplishes a definite objective. You will need:

- Some benefit the customer will gain by being on the database and receiving your e-mails or direct mail.

- A control group that does not get special attention so that you can measure whether your relationship building really pays off.

- An achievable numeric goal which can be translated into profits.

- A series of practical steps that modify customer and company behavior to reach the goal.

- A segmentation system that separates profitable customers from unprofitable customers, and treats each group differently.

- A long-range (three-year) plan with a budget that lasts long enough so that it is possible to show results.

The list of possible steps might include:

- Membership cards with points and credits.
- Newsletters with coupons.
- Surveys and responses.
- A testing program to make sure that what worked before is working well now.
- Personal letters, e-mails, and telephone calls with dynamic content built from information in the database.
- Recognition and special services.

Many, many database and e-mail projects have been undertaken with the goals not being spelled out, without having the budget, or without having worked out what the practical steps should be.

Here is a simple recipe for database marketing strategy:

1. Decide what you want concerning your customers. Do you want to retain them, sell them second products, buy upgrades, provide referrals, or renew their subscriptions or policies?

2. When you have defined the goal, quantify it. By how much and within what time frame? Compare that with what is happening now. If, for example, 43 percent are renewing their policies every year, then set your goal for some other level: 50 percent by the end of next year.

3. Determine how you are going to modify the customer's current behavior. Will you use communications, rewards, or points? Will you use newsletters, e-mails, mobile messages, policy reviews, or sales calls? Will you try to get customers to shift to automatic monthly renewals unless they cancel? Come up with some examples from your experience or industry case studies that show that your method has worked.

4. Figure out how you are going to communicate with your customers including direct mail, e-mail, Web site, or mobile. You will have a lot of internal battles on budget problems.

5. When you have determined the mix of methods, determine how much you are prepared to spend to achieve your goal. This will require building two lifetime value tables that show the current situation and one that shows the achievement of your goal. Put into the table the costs of the behavior modification projects. These tables are very, very helpful. Once you have created them, you may find that your methods may not work or that they are too expensive.

Mistake 2: Failure to Make Communications Interactive

TV ads cannot be a conversation, because the viewer cannot respond. Despite this problem, many of the most successful ads feature a conversation between two people. E-mails, however, can be interactive. They can be filled with links which, when clicked on, will open a new window to something the reader is interested in. E-mails can have reader polls and show the results. Links make messages interesting. Lack of links makes them dull. E-mails can have chat opportunities with a live person.

How often have you received a commercial e-mail saying, "Do not reply to this message"? Sending messages that cannot be answered is probably the worst sin in database marketing. Even when you do not say that, you have the same effect by failing to provide the phone number or e-mail address of the sender in your message. "Who is sending me this message? How can I get in touch with him to ask him a question, or to tell him what I think of his message?" How often has this crossed your mind? Too often. Never let this happen to you.

Your goal is to have the communications to your readers be a way of keeping their interest in your company and its products. You do this by letting them talk to you.

In our condo we have an institution called "Men's Coffee" every Saturday morning at 9:30. At this gathering about a dozen of us gather to talk. We talk on a wide range of subjects. We listen to other people's ideas and opinions. There is one guy, however, who talks nonstop on all subjects. You never can get a word in edgewise. He turns everyone off. He just about ruins the meetings. We all utter a collective sigh of relief when he leaves the meeting early. Don't make your e-mails like this. Give your readers a chance to express themselves, to give their opinions, to get information. Fill your e-mails with interactive links, and you will be successful.

Mistake 3: Focus on Promotion Rather than on Building a Relationship

When database marketing began, the idea was to focus on those who would respond and to send them direct mail. Those less likely to respond would not be mailed in order to save money. After database marketing got going, companies began to use their databases to build relationships with their customers, just as the Old Corner Grocers used to do. They filled their databases with purchase history and demographics so that they could talk to their customers as if they knew them intimately. It worked. You could prove, through testing, that building a relationship with customers pays off. Long-term customers are more valuable than short-term buyers. Discounts may bring in sales, but recognition, perks, loyalty points, and personalization pay long-term dividends.

When e-mail began, no one knew what it would do. One thing was clear. The price of e-mail is one- hundredth the price of direct mail. For this reason you can afford to send e-mails to everyone on your lists as often as you want to—usually more often than your subscribers want to hear from you.

So e-mail is wonderful, but it is also dreadful. Companies have begun sending e-mails all the time. Some retailers send e-mails to their subscribers seven days a week. In-boxes have become overloaded.

What are they putting in these e-mails? Are they using their databases to build relationships? Some are, but most are using the e-mails as promotional vehicles. They feature products on sale, blasting the same content to their entire database.

Part of the responsibility for the debasing of e-mails lies with company managements. They soon discovered that if you increase the frequency of e-mailing, you increase revenue. You may be losing your best customers in the process, but you pick up revenue. Quarterly sales goals replaced customer retention as a goal. When you are blasting content, you really do not have time to do what the corner grocers used to do: to talk to your customers as individuals.

I received a very beautiful e-mail from Land's End –an excellent company that I had purchased from and signed up for their e-mail. It was sent to Arthur Hughes. There is no mention of my name or where I live,

Figure 20.1 Blasted E-mail from a Good Company

or what I like to buy or have bought before. It was a lovely ad with a very good discount, but it is not personal at all. It did not build any kind of a relationship.

On the other hand, here is an e-mail from American Airlines that arrived on the same day as the Land's End e-mail. Look at how they greeted me as shown in Figure 20.2.

Figure 20.2 American Airlines Personalized Offer to Arthur

It starts out with, "Hello Arthur Hughes Advantage Platinum Number D2U0398." Then it describes two great sales from Miami. Why Miami? Because Arthur lives in Fort Lauderdale, 30 minutes away. Arthur frequently flies out of the Miami airport. He has flown recently to Boston, New York, Chicago, London, Moscow, Athens, and Santiago Chile from Miami. American knows that Arthur does these things because it has an extensive record of Arthur's travels in its marketing database. It knows that either of these two destinations would most likely appeal to Arthur.

Land's End also has a database on Arthur. It knows my name, where I live, and what I have bought, but it did not use the data in it in creating the e-mail. To me, it looks as if American Airlines is trying to build a relationship with me, and Land's End is trying to move merchandise. What have I done with the Land's End e-mails? I have classified them as junk mail because I cannot afford to have my in-box filled with e-mails from all the good retailers that I have purchased from.

E-mail blasting is killing database marketing. It kills retention efforts. What you have to do is to decide what your goal in database marketing is. Is it to build a relationship with your customers and retain them, or is it to pick up short-term sales with people interested in discounts?

You don't have to choose one or the other. You can do both. For people who have bought from you several times and are obviously customers that you want to retain, put them on a retention track, and send them e-mails like the one from American Airlines. Don't blast them with promotional material. For the other lesser known people on your database about whom you know very little, blast away.

Mistake 4: Failure to Construct a 360-Degree Database Updated Daily

Some companies today still maintain several different customer marketing databases: one for the catalog, one for retail, one for e-mail, and possibly another for their loyalty program. This is a big mistake. Customers see you as one company. They assume that when they spend a lot of money on your Web site, the staff in your retail stores will know this and recognize them as a gold customer. When they phone in, the customer service rep will say, "Yes, Mr. Hughes. So good of you to call. How is the new washer doing?" But if you do not have a central database that keeps all this information and puts it into the hands of people who have contact with your customers, then what good is it?

The other problem is the update schedule. If your database is maintained internally, your IT department will update it once a month, and you are stuck with that. If you have outsourced it, you can get daily updating—which is what you need if you are going to provide the services that we recommend in this book. Ideally, you should have a datamart that is updated every time something happens, and a database that is updated from the datamart on a daily basis. Your database should be scored so that it will automatically recognize people as silver, gold, and platinum and by LTV and RFM code. It will have the next-best product stored in each customer record. So when you have any customer contact, your staff member will be able to mention the next-best product and recognize whether this is a new or an old customer. Remember, multichannel customers are more valuable than single-channel customers. They spend more. They are more loyal. You have to recognize them and build a relationship with them.

Mistake 5: Failure to Personalize and Segment

Database marketing should be personal. You have spent a lot of money building a database. Now use it to build and maintain a relationship with each subscriber and customer. To begin with, your Web site should use cookies and welcome your returning visitors by name (see Figure 20.3).

Figure 20.3 American Airlines Greeting

I did not have to enter my e-mail, or a password. I just used Google and clicked on aa.com. Every single Web site should do this. What does it cost? Nothing, if you have a database and use cookies. But not only your Web site, your direct mail and e-mails should be personalized. It is not enough to just use the subscriber's name. You should also include dynamic content, if you really want to build a relationship. By dynamic, of course, I mean including something that is relevant to the person you are writing to. What did she click on last? What has she bought? Where does she live? Write a simple waterfall program that finds something in her database record that will help you to personalize your communications before they go out. After all, what are you trying to do with your messages? To sell your products today or to build a lasting relationship? Too many database marketers don't use their database to their advantage. They have all this personal data, but they don't use it in communications.

Think about the Old Corner Grocer. When he talked to a customer, his head filled with associations. He knew her family, where she lives, what she likes to buy, what she does not like, how she felt about the new fire station built next to her house. Your database holds some of these kinds of things. It will never equal the brain of the Old Corner Grocer, but you can try.

Mistake 6: Database Maintenance and E-mail Delivery In-House

Many companies believe that they should build their marketing database in-house on their own mainframe. Some have been successful. Kraft Foods, for example, built its huge customer base on its internal mainframe. The majority of large corporations, however, have outsourced their customer database, and even Kraft finally realized its mistake and turned to outsourcing. Why is this?

- Few company computer systems are designed for marketing. They exist for payroll, inventory, billing, or manufacturing. These operations pay the bills and control the data processing priorities of the company. Marketing must sit in the dugout when these heavy hitters step up to the plate. Marketers find that they cannot get the priority attention that they need to do their job.

- In-house MIS staffs seldom have the specialized software and experience needed to do database marketing or send e-mails. Merge/purge, geocoding, statistical modeling, online access, and ad-hoc counting and selecting are a few of the skills that are needed for database marketing and are seldom available on in-house company computers. E-mail is also very complex.

- Most computer operations, like payroll or inventory, are stable systems that run for years without change. Marketing is dynamic. The software requires constant testing, modification, retesting, and shifts in approach. MIS will not understand having to devote hundreds of hours of program development time on a monthly basis to your marketing database and to send e-mails. "Why can't you guys make up your mind?" is the MIS refrain.

- As a result, it will take you much longer to get your database and e-mail program up and running, *and it will cost you much more* to build your system in-house. Finally: you probably will not be able to do most of the profit-making things recommended in this book.

The solution, of course, is to find an external, experienced service bureau to build your marketing database. If you get the right one, it will have built databases for many others and can bring a wealth of experience to the table. Develop a tight contract that puts you, as the marketer, in control. You will be able to specify and hold your contractor to timetables and quality standards that you could never do with your in-house MIS staff. Do the same thing with an ESP to handle your e-mail. For both functions, consult Forrester for recommendations.

Once your database is successfully built and running and your e-mail program successfully outsourced, they can always be migrated to your in-house computer. But in the crucial formative years, you cannot afford to rely on a part-time pick-up job done by an inexperienced in-house crew. And once they are running right, you will realize what a mistake it would be to change.

The marketing staff of a large telephone company wanted to build a database of its 1 million yellow page advertisers. The plan was to have the database up and running in six months so that it could be used as a lead generating and tracking system for the sales force. The marketing staff received funding approval for a pilot test of the idea. The database was built by an outside service bureau in a three-month period. It enabled the marketers, for the first time, to know who their most profitable customers were and to compare the level of advertising by different industrial classifications. It worked and provided the members of the marketing staff with exactly what they wanted.

The next step was a long-term contract to keep the database updated on a monthly basis using a tape from the MIS billing file as the key input. Seeing a reduction in their key role in the company, members of the in-house MIS group said they could build such a database themselves, and what's more, do it more cheaply. The external contract was canceled.

To build the database in-house, members of the MIS staff had to install new and unfamiliar database software, new merge/purge software, and postal presort software. They had to create a new online access system so that users could work directly with the database. Millions of dollars were spent on acquiring this new software and learning how to use it. The work went slowly because MIS had many other more high-priority projects that took programmer time and funding away from the marketing database. Four years later the database had not been built. The key individuals in the marketing staff who had initiated the program had left the company. The project was canceled.

This experience is not at all unique. Contrast this story with the database experience of companies like Microsoft, Pizza Hut, Western Union, or Nestlé. All of them have large mainframes, yet they have elected to have their *marketing databases* built and maintained at outside database service bureaus. Look at large e-mailers like American Airlines, British Airways, Dell, or Avis. They are big enough to send their own e-mails— but they all outsource them to an experienced ESP.

The biggest problem for database or e-mail marketing in most companies doesn't come from competing media. It comes from IT. In many companies, IT stands in the way of effective e-mail marketing. Here is how it works.

When the Web first came along and no one knew what it was going to be used for, the Internet was regarded in many, if not most, companies as technology. This meant that the building and maintenance of Web sites was assigned to IT. Of course, as you know by now, Web sites and e-mails are primarily brand-building, marketing, and sales tools. Marketing is dynamic. IT, in contrast, is organized and planned. The IT goal is to write programs that run flawlessly for years. Marketing is lucky to create something that lasts for a few months without change.

Eventually, most, but not all, corporate managers have awakened to this situation and moved the Web site and e-mail marketing to the marketing department. In some companies, the battle isn't over yet. The Web site and the e-mail functions are still mixed up in IT.

IT presents another serious problem for e-mail marketing because of central data warehouses. IT typically maintains the central data warehouse. This has presented a problem for direct mail because database marketing often requires scores of data fields (appended demographics, lifetime value, RFM, model scores, etc.), which are essential to segmentation and personalization but aren't related to IT's core functions. Marketing databases need to include prospects and lapsed customers. They need to be updated at least weekly and sometimes daily.

All these functions are constantly changing, unlike regular, periodic functions, like payroll, billing, supply management, order fulfillment, and general ledger. As a result, marketing databases are usually given low priority. For these reasons, the marketing departments have fought to have their marketing databases outsourced to service bureaus, causing IT concern about losing a valuable function.

Even when the marketing database is outsourced to a service bureau, IT usually plays a significant role in central data transfer. Nightly POS data, Web site shopping cart data, and telesales data go through IT before being transmitted to the outsourced marketing database service bureau or anywhere else. This data transfer function doesn't usually represent a problem as long as we are dealing with direct mail to customers. Direct mail typically goes out on a weekly basis. E-mails are another story, however.

To be effective, e-mails have to go out within a matter of seconds after the consumer has made an entry in a Web site or clicked on an e-mail. Daily or weekly updating is just too slow. Consumers want to hear from you while they are still sitting at their PCs or holding their iPhones.

Some IT departments have been reluctant to devote the resources to solving the rapid data transfer problem. In "Maturation of E-mail," JupiterResearch found that 41 percent of the companies studied took three days or longer to respond to service-related e-mail inquiries or simply didn't respond at all:

> *If organizations centralized their e-mail messaging, rules could easily allow for disgruntled customers trying to remedy a service issue to be pulled out of promotional mailings, at least until the clients' issues are resolved. Centralizing e-mail under one infrastructure would also allow confirmation notices to be leveraged for promotional purposes.*

In one company I worked with, when customers signed up for e-mail newsletters, IT needed a week to provide the data needed to send them a welcome e-mail. The beginning of regular promotional e-mails required another week. Outsourced ESPs and outsourced marketing database service bureaus would be waiting to act, but the data wouldn't arrive. Problems like this must be solved if you are to have an effective e-mail marketing program.

Mistake 7: Getting the Economics Wrong

What could you do with a clean list of all the households in the United States that buy Del Monte canned peas? Mail letters to them to sell them more canned vegetables or some similar product? Wrong! This could lose a lot of money. The margin on such products is so pathetically thin that there is no way you could communicate with these households by mail, fax, or phone and have the incremental profit pay for the cost of the communication. The economics just aren't there. That is true of most packaged goods. Who wants to get letters from the people that make our English muffins? Life is just too short to spend it corresponding with the makers of all the products and services that we use every day. There are plenty of situations in which database marketing just isn't going to work. We have to get the economics right.

On the other hand, if you sell automobiles, rental cars, insurance, power tools, vacation cruises, software, or computers, your customer list could be turned into a valuable database.

Big-ticket items, repeat sales items, cross-brand possibilities—these are the lifeblood of marketing databases. Too many companies rush into building a database without thinking about the economics. Say to yourself, "How am I going to make money with these names?" Your answer must be simple and practical—something that you can explain to your mother so she can understand it.

Citicorp, one of the nation's largest banks, became a major entrant into the database marketing field for retailers a while ago. Its idea, called, "Reward America," was to help grocery chains build up a valued customer database, with each customer having a family membership card. When the family came to shop, it would bring the card and present it for scanning while the shopping cart contents were rung up. As a result, the computers in each cash register would have a record of all the purchases made by that family: the date, the time of day, the SKU, the quantity, the price.

The idea caught on fast. Several chains were signed up, and the software was installed. Every night, the cash registers were electronically polled. The data on the day's transactions were fed over telephone lines to each chain's central computer. From there, on a weekly basis, Citicorp retrieved each member household's purchasing data for storage on its mainframe in Connecticut.

With detailed information on the shopping habits of millions of Americans, Citicorp figured it would be able to realize a profit from the sale of this household data to manufacturers, such as Camay, Pampers, Crest, or Del Monte.

It was a great idea. The stores would use the data to learn more about their customers: where they lived, when they shopped, what they bought. They could use the data to pursue customers who stopped buying and to reward loyal customers with daily specials and premiums.

There were many different types of discount arrangements made by the different chains that installed the system. For example, in some systems, members using their cards to purchase goods that were "on special" would receive $2 for buying eight cans of this juice, or $1 for buying three boxes of that cereal. The system would keep track of purchases, so the products did not have to be bought on the same visit. Each month, members could receive a mailing including a purchase summary and a certificate for the amount they had earned so far. In other systems, the reward would be instant—with a discount for special items with each visit, and no retention of credits.

Citicorp made retailers a deal that the supermarkets couldn't refuse: the system was free. It planned to make money at the other end, by selling the purchase data to manufacturers. It hoped to build a database of 40 million households.

Most of the dozen chains that signed up for the system did so because the program was free and offered a way to learn about frequent shopper programs. Unfortunately for Citicorp, many things went wrong.

What Went Wrong?

1. *Rewards must be instant.* The concept of rewarding customers three months down the road for purchases just didn't go over well. If you are going to give grocery shoppers money, they want it now, which explains the success of the instant discounts and electronic coupon programs—such as those run by Catalina marketing. Catalina is the company that makes the systems in supermarkets that generate coupons during the

checkout process. If you bought one brand of yogurt, the Catalina coupon generated might offer you a discount on a rival brand.

2. *The data problems were immense.* Citicorp's central computer choked on the data. The company didn't realize how huge the volume of grocery chain purchase data could be. It did not have adequate software in place. After the program was canceled, it had thousands of tapes stored in its computer center, unprocessed and gathering dust. What can anyone do with the information that on August 3 at 3:40 p.m. Arthur Hughes bought six pounds of potatoes? Nothing profitable! Add to that tens of millions of other transactions that take place every day in American supermarkets, and you will soon bring any computer to its knees.

3. *Few companies wanted the names.* Manufacturers did not jump at the chance to buy the names of their customers, as Citicorp expected they would. The fact is that names and addresses of purchasers of package goods are almost worthless. What can you do with data about someone who has bought frozen spinach? Spam? Clorox? Cool Whip? Think about it. You can't make any money with these name

"But," I can hear you thinking, "that was before the days of e-mails. Perhaps today Citicorp could have made money with e-mail." True, but there is a problem today. You can't buy e-mail addresses the way Citicorp did 10 years ago. Maybe someone will figure out how do Reward America with e-mail and iPhones. The project may not be dead forever, but I have doubts.

4. *Costs exceeded revenues.* The program cost too much to support. Citicorp spent $200 million, and generated about $20 million in revenue. After three years it canceled the program and fired the 174 employees, leaving many retail chains with no way to maintain a system that they had been promoting to their customers.

Looking at the broad picture, what lessons can we draw from the Citicorp experience?

- *Test first.* Before you do something big in the database field, you should test, test, test. Citicorp, a very large and successful bank, approached this project the same way it successfully approached credit cards and other projects: pour in money, and get a national foothold before the competitors know what is going on. It paid off in credit card acquisitions, but it certainly did not work in retailing. If it had been prepared to start on a small scale with one or two chains, experimenting and learning (with just a few employees on the project), it could have gotten the bugs out of the concept at a modest cost—such as $10 million. Then it would have been ready for a successful national rollout in two or three years.

- *Compute the costs.* Don't underestimate the data processing aspects of database marketing. When you compute the data on one household's grocery purchases in a year, you may be talking about 6,000 or more items purchased by a family of four. Multiply that by 40 million households, and you have 240 billion transactions in one year alone. Without really efficient software, the costs and time consumed will bring even the most powerful data center to serious grief and high costs.

- *Work out lifetime value.* Put yourself in the customers' shoes. Successful database marketing is relationship building: one on one with the customer. Some marketers might be thinking, "How can we make money selling data about these rubes?" instead of saying, "Why would anyone want to join a frequent shopper club?" You have to start with the basics. Profits should be created by your having built a relationship with the customer that is satisfying to all concerned.

- *Know your market.* The economics were wrong for the product manufacturers. Few packaged goods manufacturers today know what to do with a database of their own customers. Most of them have millions of names stored in their data centers from previous promotions. They haven't yet figured out how to turn these names into relationships, loyalty, repeat sales, cross-sales, and profits. If this is the case, why would they go out and pay money for more customer names?

If there were a demand for the names because the manufacturers had a way of making money from them, the profits would have solved all of the other problems. But, alas, the demand was not there.

A satisfactory economic solution to database marketing won't come looking for you. You have to find it. And if you can't, maybe it isn't there.

The Reward America fiasco does not invalidate the idea of frequent shopper cards for supermarkets. Since that time, scores of supermarket chains have created their own frequent shopper cards and use them quite successfully. Brian Woolf's excellent books: *Customer Specific Marketing* and *Loyalty Marketing—The Second Act* provide details on how to go about establishing such programs. The benefits of these cards are explained in Chapter 5 of this book.

Mistake 8. Failure to Use Tests and Controls

As pointed out in Chapter 14, it is absolutely essential that you constantly conduct tests to make sure that what you are doing is working properly. You use control groups to measure the success of any database or e-mail marketing strategy. Many new marketing strategies take a long time from the original idea to the actual execution. Once permission and budget is available, there is a rush to get the project out the door before someone changes his or her mind. At that point, the idea of setting up a control group often goes by the board. If the program is a success, it may be that no one notices the control group absence. But if the program does not seem to be a success, the failure to use a control group may cost the marketer his job. It could be that business during that quarter was down everywhere. Those who were exposed to your new strategy might be the only bright spot in an otherwise dismal situation (their purchases went down less). Without a control, you will not know that. Your failure to use tests and controls could doom not only your job but the entire database marketing program.

Many marketers have had difficulties in setting up control groups. It is not difficult to select the customers to be in the group. The difficulty is making sure that their performance is not adulterated by some other marketing program that stimulates them to greater activity. There must be discipline in the organization to ensure that everyone treats the control groups as regular customers, without special programs.

Once you have set up a control group, there are many valuable things that you can learn from it. A case study will show what I mean.

PreVision helped Stride Rite to fill its 135 retail stores with customers in the spring, using a personalized direct mail program to its customer database. It set aside no-contact control groups that matched the audience selection criteria of the households that were mailed to, but did not get any of the communications. The control group proved that their test program gave them a 15.16 percent lift in sales and a 6.12 percent increase in the average basket size.

Mistake 9: Lack of a Forceful Leader

Too many database and e-mail marketing programs fail through the lack of a strong leader to head the project. Leadership is vital. There is much work to be coordinated within the company and with the outside suppliers if a database marketing program is going to produce long-term profit gains. Successful databases usually have outside telemarketers, a service bureau, a creative agency, an ESP and a fulfillment house. Inside they need the coordination of direct and e-mail marketing, market research, sales, billing, customer service, and MIS. Pulling the team together requires a forceful leader. The committee system will never work here. Decisions need to be made on a daily basis to keep the database going, responsive, dynamic, building customer relationships, and making sales.

If you are planning a database in your company, be sure you have found a strong leader and that he or she has been delegated the responsibilities and authority to make it work. Without this, your database will never get off the ground.

How to Do Things Right

What should you do to avoid these mistakes? There are a few simple steps that you can take to be sure that you go about building your database properly:

- *Put yourself in your customers' shoes.* Don't think of what you want to sell, think of what you, as a customer, would want to receive from your company. It may not be a product at all. It may be recognition, attention, information, helpfulness, service, or friendship. If you can deliver on these things, the sales will follow. A database may be the best way to provide these things.

- *Build a database team.* Successful databases have a strong, creative, imaginative leader who has pulled together a team composed of marketing, sales, the service bureau, the creative agency, MIS, customer service, outside telemarketers, brand managers, fulfillment, and billing.

- *Think small and think fast.* Start your database with a small elite group of customers. Start soon. Make every action a test. Conduct your tests, and evaluate your results. Build bigger as you accumulate experience.

- *Keep your eye on the bottom line.* Database and e-mail marketing are supposed to *make money.* Plan your economics. Calculate lifetime value. If you can't quite see how what you're doing will be profitable, then *don't do it!* Rack your brain and find a way to turn your customer relationship into a profitable customer relationship.

Take-Away Thoughts

You can easily go wrong in database marketing. There are nine deadly mistakes enumerated in this chapter:

1. Lack of a marketing strategy.

2. Failure to make communications interactive.

3. Focus on promotions instead of relationships.

4. Failure to have a 360-degree picture of every customer.

5. Failure to personalize your communications.

6. Building a database and sending e-mails in house.

7. Getting the economics wrong.

8. Failure to use tests and controls.

9. Lack of a forceful leader.

To be successful you need to:

- Put yourself in your customers' shoes.

- Build a database team.

- Use your database to support your e-mail program.

- Think small and think fast.

- Keep your eye on the bottom line.

A quiz on this chapter and all figures can be found at www.dbmarketing .com/STM4. Those taking all the quizzes can receive a Successful Completion Certificate from the Database Marketing Institute which can be used in their résumé.

21

Outsourcing

In fact, I'm willing to bet that better than 90 percent of the businesses currently in-sourcing their e-mail can't legitimately justify the practice.

—DAVID BERLIND

A marketing database is extremely different than a transactional or operational database. It's all about the data, getting it right, massaging it, understanding it and making it grow. It starts with messy data provided by us messy consumers. We move all the time and forget to tell you, so you have to run NCOA. We expect you to know who we are, so you have to share data with Call Centers and web sites. We buy things and then stop buying things and don't tell you why. We do things that change our buying habits completely —things like getting married, having babies and retiring.

So the real question is, "Do we have the right skill sets in place to build and manage a marketing database as part of our internal IT infrastructure?"

A successful marketing database is never done. There are always more applications to be built, more models to be refined, more digging into the data. If you have an internal IT team that can embrace that dynamic, then you have the resources to build a Marketing Database internally. If your IT team heads for the hills when they hear the Marketing Department calling, it might be best to consider an outsourced solution.

—EVELYN BARTLETT

If you have been to one of the E-mail Experience Council's E-mail Evolution, the MarketingSherpa, the NCDM (National Center for Database Marketing) or the DMA's (Direct Marketing Association) conferences, you will notice that most of the success stories involve outsourcing to external partners. While anyone can do some form of e-mail or database marketing, those who are most successful seek outside help. What functions can you outsource?

- E-mail delivery
- Designing and building a database
- Customer service and communications
- Telesales
- Building a Web site
- Fulfillment

Why would you want to outsource functions to external partners? There are a number of important reasons:

- *Database experience.* Many service bureaus have designed, built, and maintained databases for other companies in the past. If you get them to help you, you will get the benefit of their experience: the mistakes they have made in the past which they will try not to repeat and the new ideas that others have come up with that you may apply to your own database.

- *E-mail experience.* Creation and delivery of marketing e-mails is one of the most complex functions in the marketing world. It is new and constantly changing. No one company can possibly keep up with the developments. Therefore, it makes sense to outsource your e-mail marketing to a company that is managing e-mail marketing for a hundred or more large, sophisticated companies. This way you can get the benefit of the latest concepts in this fast-moving world.

- *Expertise.* Some companies have achieved unique knowledge of particular fields such as financial services, pharmaceutical direct to consumer, business to business, loyalty programs, direct response TV, or Web advertising that you simply could not replicate in-house in a short time.

- *Speed.* If you are going to set up a database, a Web site, e-mail marketing, or a teleservices operation inside your company, it will take a lot longer to do it internally than if you go to an outside experienced provider. Internally, you will have to hire skilled people and train them. This takes time and money. Outsourced functions can usually get started in half the time.

- *Economy.* If you compare the cost of performing these functions inside with doing them at an outside source, you will find that in most cases, you can save money. To do database marketing, there is a lot of software to be purchased and people to be trained to use it. This is expensive. Ditto for e-mail marketing.

- *Entrepreneurship.* Building inside usually involves full-time people. They may not all work for the marketing department. Typically, your MIS department may want to build the Web site, maintain the database, or send the e-mails. When you need something done now, and not a month from now, your MIS director may say, "I have two programmers out sick, and a four-month backlog of regular work. You will just have to wait." And she is probably right. But, if you tell your external ESP or service bureau partner to undertake a new project, she is likely to say, "Great! When do I start?" Why the difference? For the service bureau, this is money. She is maintaining a dozen other databases or 100 other e-mail marketing programs right now. She can divert other people or take on additional contract programmers to meet your needs. That is not easy to do in-house. It is easy to throw your weight around with an ESP or a contract service bureau. It is not as easy to do that inside your company.

Why Do Large E-mailers Outsource Their E-mails?

Most marketers outsource the entire e-mail creation and sending process to an ESP, giving the provider instructions (usually digitally) as to who is the audience for the e-mails, what the content of each e-mail should be, what triggers will be used, and so on. Other firms develop the content but outsource e-mail sending, using an ESP's software.

Why would you outsource these functions? First, e-mail delivery is a highly specialized function, which requires special software and staff training. Even after a dozen years, the ESP function is still new and changes every year going in new directions that are hard to predict. Today, more than 50 U.S. ESPs specialize in e-mail delivery for clients, and at least 12 of them are large companies that have attracted corporations with more than $1 billion in annual sales as clients. Experienced ESPs, with 100 or more clients, have developed considerable experience they use to advise and support each client. This experience isn't available to a company that does its e-mail delivery internally.

What Services Do ESPs Provide to Their Clients?

All of the 200 test companies for which we provide data on in this book use an e-mail service provider (ESP) to deliver their e-mails—as do virtually all the large corporations in the United States. For this reason, we need to explain what these ESPs do for their clients. They provide:

- Strategic guidance on strategies and tactics that have proved to work elsewhere and could be adapted for use with a client's e-mail marketing program.
- IP warming.
- Deliverability monitoring, showing daily real-time results.
- The ability to provide information on industry trends and best practices stemming from the ESP's experience with many other clients.
- The ability to deliver triggered e-mails, which have much higher ROI than regular e-mails but often require complex software.
- Sophisticated analytics support.
- The ability to integrate data from multiple channels.
- Specialized software, typically some sort of campaign builder or campaign insight software.

What an ESP Usually Does for You

E-mail service providers are really essential for any company sending commercial e-mails to their subscribers. Few companies, from large to small should take on the delivery of e-mails themselves.

- A typical major ESP sends e-mails for 100 or more different clients, so an experienced staff is important. ESPs have made mistakes in the past (everyone does) and have learned from them. They know what they are doing. This may not be true of an individual company's e-mail marketing staff. In-house staff has to learn to use highly specialized e-mail marketing software. The training takes time and resources.
- Any company doing its own e-mail delivery will also have only a small trained group that knows how to send mass e-mails. If someone is out

sick, on vacation, at a conference, or gets a promotion, the company may not have enough staff to get out the day's promotion. An experienced ESP, on the other hand, servicing 100 or more clients, has a sufficiently large staff that it can always move people around to get out today's jobs.

■ The ESP should be able to keep up with constant innovation, as well. In the e-mail world, scores of new ideas are being tried all the time. Some work well. Some don't. But overall, e-mail marketers are learning more about viral marketing, mobile devices, links, interactivity, subject lines, deliverability, microsites, JavaScript, HTML techniques, and so on. The e-mail marketing industry just doesn't stand still. A typical ESP that manages e-mails for a large number of clients finds that some of these clients have e-mails on the cutting edge of technology. In the course of creating these e-mails, members of the ESP staff learn how they work. They will be able to suggest some of these advanced ideas to other clients. Since they have built these new techniques, they will know how to apply them. A small in-house staff, unfortunately, will not be exposed to these new ideas. Result: their e-mail techniques may fall behind the industry.

Get Organized Internally

Before you outsource a function, you need to get your internal house in order. Too many companies have divided responsibilities for functions like e-mail or database marketing. This problem becomes even worse when e-mail is outsourced. Consider some of the problems.

The Competing Media Problem

Many corporate managers are unaware of many of e-mail's functions. As a result, their e-mail programs' effectiveness is less than it could be. Even worse, e-mail marketing is seen as competition by various media silos within a corporation. In many companies, e-mails are sent independently by several different groups. These groups send e-mails to the same subscribers without coordination. It is an internal competitive race. Figure 21.1 illustrates the problems.

In addition to these many units sending promotional and transactional e-mails to the same subscribers, the internal media divisions are often uncoordinated. This situation frequently leads to over-mailing to

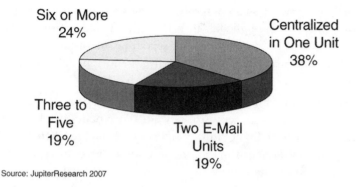

Six or More
24%

Centralized
in One Unit
38%

Three to
Five
19%

Two E-Mail
Units
19%

Source: JupiterResearch 2007

Figure 21.1 Units Responsible for e-mail

subscribers and to messages that lack a consistent branding and style. In some cases, multiple e-mail units lead to delivery problems, as incorrect mailing practices by one department taints the reputation of the whole company. Decentralization becomes more of a problem as e-mails become central to the company's multichannel strategy.

How to Outsource

To outsource a function, you have to find someone to do business with, and that is where you need a request for proposals, or an RFP. In this chapter, we give you some suggestions on how to write such a document. However, you might want to consider outsourcing the RFP function as well.

Outsourcing the RFP Function

There are consultants who write RFPs for other companies. Using such consultants can save you many weeks of one-time-only learning. Using the skills and resources of someone who has done the same function two or three times for other companies can save you time and money.

Creating an RFP Committee

Any significant RFP will require some sort of internal committee to prepare it and to select the winners. Typically, a committee will consist of people from marketing, e-mail marketing, MIS, sales, customer service, contracting, and, if available, your direct agency. Marketing should chair the committee to keep it focused on the marketing goals.

Qualifying the Participants

Your first job is to decide whom to send the RFP to. You can solve this problem by calling people you know in the industry and asking them. Attend the DMA, the MarketingSherpa Conference, the E-mail Evolution Conference, or the National Center for Database Marketing where you can meet with a dozen companies over a couple of days. It is important to prequalify the participants so as not to waste your time and those of unqualified firms. You might consider sending out a one-page e-mail or letter survey form which would ask some key questions to determine if the recipient companies have the skills to handle and the interest in your project. For those who respond positively, you might follow up with the confidentiality agreement, getting this signed before you send out the RFP. Don Hinman of Acxiom suggests that this letter should contain a précis of your situation and ask respondents to provide a two-page description of how they would handle your requirements. This would not be a statement of how wonderful they think they are, but how they would go about solving your problems.

Here, in alphabetical order, is a list of the top 15 ESPs rated by Forrester Research in 2010:

- Acxiom
- Alterian
- BlueHornet
- Experian Marketing Services
- ClickSquared
- Datran Media
- e-Dialog
- E-mailvision
- Epsilon
- ExactTarget
- Lyris
- Responsys
- Silverpop
- Yesmail
- Zeta Interactive

There are many others. Serious marketers should consult Forrester before selecting an ESP.

And here are the Forrester top-rated database marketing service bureaus as of 2011:

- Acxiom
- Allant
- Epsilon
- Harte-Hanks
- KBM Group
- Merkle
- Quaero
- Targetbase

Don't send out too many RFPs. Four is plenty. What is wrong with sending out ten or fifteen or more? Two things. You will be wasting the time of scores of people in answering your RFP. And you will be wasting possibly weeks of time of your committee members reviewing thick responses from far too many companies. Trim the project down to size before you send anything out. Do your homework in advance, not after the fact.

Writing the Scope of Work

The first step in an RFP is a definition of the work to be done. A well-developed scope of work will guide your thinking and actions, and it will help your prospective partners understand what is required. There are several parts to a scope of work:

- *Background.* You need to describe your company, its products, and its customers. Start a few years back and tell how you got to where you are today. Explain whether you are in a growth phase or a mature phase. Talk about how products are sold. Is there a channel of distributors and retailers? Are there independent or company-owned dealers or agents? How are you organized to sell? Describe the marketing staff and the sales staff. If there is a database already, describe it. How big is it? What data is in it? How is it updated and maintained? Who uses it and what for? What is the culture of your company, and where is it going? Do you sell in your e-mails or Web site? What are the e-mails supposed to accomplish?

- *The problem.* You would not be writing this RFP today if there were not some problem to be solved. How did the problem come about? Is it caused by external competition? By a change in the market? What steps have already been made to solve this problem, and why did they not work out?

- *The solution.* Describe how you think the problem can be solved by using external resources. What do you think outsiders can do to help? Explain what changes in the database, or the Web site, or customer service, or inside sales, or sales force automation you think would lead to a satisfactory solution to the problem. Give your ideal answer.

- *The goal.* You need a one-paragraph statement of the goal of your database marketing program. Examples:

  - Reducing attrition by 5 percent within the next year.

  - Increasing customer lifetime value by 10 percent in the next year.

  - Increasing our customer or subscriber base by 20 percent per year for the next three years.

This goal should give a meaning and purpose to your entire scope of work.

- *Your strategy.* To support your goal, the scope of work must spell out an overall strategy, outlining how you are going to get from here to there. The specific project for which you are seeking assistance may be as mundane as producing thank-you letters or responding to DRTV ads. The strategy indicates how this particular activity is aimed at achieving the specified goal. Without this strategy statement, your outsource partners may not see the real purpose in what they are doing. You may miss your objective because the implementers don't have the full picture. There is a second reason why this strategy statement is important. By putting it in writing, you may realize that what you are asking the outsourcers to do cannot achieve the goals you have set. You may have to change the scope of work before you issue the RFP.

- *The customers.* Provide a description of your customers and subscribers. What are they like? What problems have they had in working with your company? What do they want from your company that they are not getting? Why are the defectors leaving? What would you like to do in the way of communications with customers that would be better than what you are doing right now?

- *The size of the work.* How big a solution are you looking for right now? Some companies make the mistake of thinking too big. They look for some huge comprehensive solution that will take several years to implement and that could pose great funding difficulties. You are much better off coming up with a master design that begins with only one small step for mankind. Database marketing and e-mail marketing are best accomplished by a series of small successes, rather than massive reorganizations. Lay out a series of small improvements that you think that an outside firm can undertake within a few months and that will demonstrate to your management that real progress is being made. In the course of implementing these small improvements, you will undoubtedly see new projects that should be carried out. These could be amendments to the original contract.

- *Break the job down into phases.* If the project is very large, it is better to break it down into phases. You can scope out Phase 1 in great detail, and list what will happen in Phases 2 and 3 in less detail, since you will get separate bids on them later. The winner of Phase 1 will probably get Phases 2 and 3 as well, but that is off in the future. If the winner of Phase 1 does not work out, you can bid out the other phases. It gives you much more flexibility than bidding the whole thing out at once. Once you get started on database or e-mail projects, you will be learning a lot and changing your strategy and direction, based on what you learn. So the phase idea may make very good business sense.

- *Quantitative measures.* You have to give your prospective partners some idea of the numbers they are dealing with. If you are thinking of a call center, estimate the number of calls per day, per week, per year. If it is a database, tell how many records are in the database now and how many will be added each month. For e-mails, tell them how many and of what type you plan to send out. Provide a sample of the e-mails, or the data, on a CD which you provide to the bidders so that they can get a feel for what you are talking about.

- *Organizational location.* Who is going to use the data? Describe the divisions of your company and how each division will use the data. Will one unit be responsible for the e-mails, or will you have several different units sending e-mails independently of each other? If possible, provide a flow chart that explains where the data comes from, who works on it, and where it goes. Explain the mission of each group: "Inquiries go to the telemarketers who qualify them and set up appointments for the sales force. They enter data into the database which is used by the fulfillment staff to send out brochures. The data generates an automatic e-mail or fax that thanks the inquirer for the call and reminds him of the appointment."

- *The timing.* When do you plan to begin the project, and when do you expect to see the first results? Lay out a time line that covers the first year of the project so that the bidders can see what resources they have to commit and when.

- *The pricing scheme.* This is a most difficult requirement. You will be getting bids from several possible partners. You want to be able to compare apples to apples. It would be helpful, therefore, for you to give them some sort of numerical measurements to price out. You might ask the bidders how they prefer to submit the prices: answer your questions, submit their own price section, or to fill in a spreadsheet or table. To be sure that the prices are comparable, each bidder should submit one table that shows the total amount to be spent in years 1 and 2. This will help you to understand what each is suggesting.

  Examples of individual price comparisons might be:

  - Database updating based on the number of records involved.
  - Web site creation and maintenance.
  - Fulfillment costs per piece.
  - Modeling costs per hour.

- *The budget.* You probably should not announce this in the RFP, but you have to have agreement from management of the amount of money that is budgeted for this project before you send anything out. If there is no budget, do not send out the RFP. The size of the budget will affect the scope of work. You simply cannot create a practical RFP without a budget. If asked by the bidders, it is helpful to tell them a range. "We expect to spend between $300,000 and $500,000 on this project during this next year." If you say that, you will eliminate bids in the $1+ million range, which are far beyond your budget. It will also encourage some bidders to think of creative ways to end up in the low end of your range.

- *Competition is a good idea.* If the project involves cleaning your records and providing access to them using the bidder's system, you might create a file of 25,000 of your customers (complete with all the messiness and duplications that currently exist) and give the same file to the bidders, asking them to show you what they can do with your actual data. A competition like this can really separate the sheep from the goats.

- *Evaluation criteria.* Tell the bidders how you will go about evaluating their responses, including any weighting that you want to include:

"Innovation 40 percent, experience 30 percent, price 30 percent," and so on. Tell them how long you will take to review their RFP and when you expect to announce who will get the contract.

- A *confidentiality requirement.* Your project is likely to contain proprietary information about your company. Before the bidders are allowed to see it, they should sign a confidentiality agreement. Your RFP should refer to this agreement.

Rules of the RFP

By this time, there are many unwritten rules of the RFP process. Bidders on your work will expect you to be fair, to be honest, and to give everyone a chance to ask questions. Doing a good job of following rules for your RFP will establish your relationship with your potential partners. Here are some of the unwritten rules:

- *Due date.* Specify exactly when the responses are due including date and time of day. Be sure to give bidders at least 30 days from the date you send out the RFP. This is important. Never make the time less than 30 days. You will get slipshod responses if you do.

- *Questions.* Announce when you send out the RFP whether questions will be permitted (you should permit them), how bidders can ask the questions and of whom, and whether they may be in writing, at a meeting, or by phone. Unless your project is very large (and we do not recommend large projects—see below), you should entertain telephone or e-mail questions, with a cutoff date. By that date, you should send out an e-mail message to all the bidders with a summary of the questions and the answers. It is important that you be fair to everyone and that you appear to be fair. You will want to do business with these people in the future.

- *Digital submission.* In the old days, responses to RFPs arrived at the last minute by Fedex, with 10 or more copies. That was before the days of the Internet. Today, companies accept proposals by e-mail or through a Web response device. We are getting very digital these days. The advantage in a digital submission is that you can easily put several proposals on a spreadsheet to compare them. We are database marketers. Let's be up to date. You may want to have the responses in two separate reports: the work proposal, and the pricing. Sometimes it is useful to decide on the proposal without being influenced by the prices.

- *Where to send.* If you do insist on hard copy proposals (which is very old-fashioned), tell bidders where to send the proposal, providing a Fed-Ex compatible address (not a post office box), since many of the proposals will come in at the last minute.

- *Extensions.* Provide in the rules whether time extensions will be permitted and how to go about getting an extension. You may not think that this is important, but it almost always comes up, so think it through in advance.

- *Bidders list.* Decide whether you will release a list of the bidders to the bidders. I think this is a good idea and could help in the bidding process. I would issue the list early enough so that all bidders can know what they are up against before they bid. It will help you to get relevant and comparable offers.

Your Partners

If you are going to accomplish the objectives spelled out in the scope of work, you will need your contractors to become your partners. Too many inexperienced marketers look on their outside help as "vendors." They tell them as little as possible about the overall project, saying, in effect, "Don't ask too many questions. Just do what I tell you, and shut up."

You won't get their hearts and minds involved in your database project if you treat them as vendors. Without their hearts and minds, you may miss some vital ideas about improving your customer relationships, which may make your project less effective than it could be. It could even get you into real trouble.

> *Partner example:* A partner maintained the database for a Fortune 500 company that was doing DRTV. The program got 1 million responses in the first six months, for which the partner did the fulfillment. It was great business and highly profitable. There was only one problem. The people answering the ads were the wrong people. They were not buying the product. No one at the company asked the partner about this. The partner's dilemma: Should we tell the company about it? The partner decided that it had to. Some of the company's marketing staff were thankful for the information. But others thought that the partner had exceeded its charter, which was to do the fulfillment and shut up. What do you think?

> *Vendor example:* Another company asked its vendor to select a group of preferred customers who were to receive special recognition and benefits. The vendor was not asked to set up a control group. It was not told what was to be done with the

preferred customers, but it thought the absence of a control group was bad database practice. On the other hand, pointing this out might anger the agency that had set up the program and considered the partner a mere vendor. The vendor decided to keep quiet. Later the agency was fired when the absence of a control group was proven to undermine the validity of the results. What should the vendor have done?

Your objective in the RFP, therefore, is to find a partner who feels as involved in the success of your e-mail marketing, database marketing, or Web site project as you do. How can you do that? The psychology of management tells us that your effectiveness as a manager is determined by the extent to which you allow your employees to influence you. If you listen to what your employees say and use your influence to carry out the good suggestions that they make they will feel that they are an important part of the company. They will put their hearts and minds into the work. You will be successful as a supervisor. The same principles apply to outsourcing functions. Treat these companies as partners, and you will reap significant benefits.

Key Questions

How can you find out if the people bidding on your job have the imagination, drive, resources, skills, and chemistry necessary to become your partners? There is a simple answer: treat them as professionals. Ask them these questions:

- *Company history.* Who are they? What have they done in the past? What is their company philosophy? Ask them to provide references.

- *Their solution to the problem.* Have them describe in their own words how they propose to go about carrying out the scope of work.

- *The training involved.* Most database or Internet projects involve training in the new system for company employees. Ask about training. The response should describe this training and provide the pricing for it.

- *Who owns the software?* Since there is usually proprietary software involved, the response should indicate what that software is and who owns it. The proposal should spell out how the updates to the software will be provided and who is supporting the software.

- *Innovative ideas.* Ask them to describe some innovative ideas that they have for your project or that they have developed in working with other clients.

- *Biographies of the leaders.* Have them tell you about one or two of the key people whom you will be working with and what their background is. There is a caution here. If you have a big project, the partner will have to hire additional workers. Few firms have enough employees sitting around doing nothing waiting to see if they win a contract with you. Don't insist, therefore, that you know, in advance, all the people who will be working on your job. If they are able to tell you, it would probably be a lie.

- *References.* You absolutely must have a list of names and telephone numbers from companies that have used your prospective partner's services in the past. Call these people and ask them what it is like working with this partner.

- *Executive summary.* Tell them to write a one-page summary listing the key benefits of the system they propose.

- *Project costs.* They should use the scheme that you have laid out for the project. However, by all means, if they request it, permit them to give you their pricing in addition on some other basis they feel more comfortable with.

What Not to Do

RFPs can become deadly bores for everyone involved. In 32 years of direct marketing, I have seen some really horrible examples. Here is what to avoid:

- *Too many questions.* Many RFPs are designed by a committee. Twenty people throw in anything that they can think of. The questions go on for 10 pages or more. To get good results on an RFP, keep the questions to a minimum—one page or less.

- *Too many pages.* Many RFPs are up to 100 pages in length. They include all sorts of legal restrictions such as antidiscrimination environmental protection issues. A good solution to this problem is to have your legal team draft a separate document containing all the legal restrictions. Ask the bidders to sign this document. Then put a clause in the RFP referring to the fact that the document is signed and covers the work to be done under this RFP.

- *Cover too much in one document.* As I already pointed out, successful database marketing consists of a number of small successes, which lead to a great overall success. If you make the project too big and comprehensive at the beginning, you may have trouble getting the money for it or finding one external supplier who can do everything that is required. You should divide the work into phases.

- *Not enough time to fill it out.* Many RFPs require that the responses come in within two weeks. This is not enough time. For a good RFP you should allow at least 30 days. You will then have solid, well-thought-through responses. Some companies just don't bid on RFPs where the time line is too short. They might have ended up being your best partners.

- *Boring.* Database marketing and e-mail marketing should be fun for the marketer and for the customer. We want to use the e-mails and the data in our database to delight the customer with unexpected recognition and relationships. Our employees will be happy with the system because they will feel the goodwill coming to them from the delighted customers. Your RFP should reflect the joy and enthusiasm that comes from successful e-mail and database marketing. If your document is boring and puts people to sleep, your partners may get the wrong idea about your company or your project. If your RFP is boring, rewrite it before it goes anywhere.

- *No money.* Some companies make the mistake of issuing an RFP before there is an approved budget for the activities to be covered in the RFP. This is a terrible waste of time for your company and for the partners who bid on your project. Some marketers think, apparently, that the RFP process will jump-start their marketing program. The winning partner will be so impressive that management will cough up the money. This seldom happens. Why? Because RFPs that have no budget, soon get out of control. People on the committee put anything into it that they can dream up. Since there is no budget, there is little reason for leaving anything out. The final monstrosity looks exciting to outside partners, but it is all a sham. It will hurt the reputation of your company in the e-mail and database marketing community and make it more difficult later to get good partners to pay attention to you.

- *Scam RFP.* Sometimes companies decide to build their database inside with MIS. To be sure that the project is well designed and cost effective, they issue an RFP, getting outside prospective partners to bid, hoping that they can come up with some innovative ideas. The marketing staff has no intention of awarding the project to anyone outside, since it is already "wired" for MIS. This is a fraud and a deception. If you are a self-respecting database or e-mail marketer, you should have nothing to do with such a deceitful scheme.

- *Gullibility.* The RFP process can generate lies and exaggerations. Take everything you are told with a pound or two of salt. Question the references closely and get to the bottom of any claim. If it sounds too good to be true, it probably is.

Evaluating the Results

If you have drafted a long, boring RFP with too many questions and legal paragraphs, now is the time you will pay for it. You will have to review six or eight thick and boring responses. Every member of your committee will have to read through hundreds of pages of boring responses. You will have to use a spreadsheet to compare the results. This may take you a couple of weeks if your documents are voluminous. Finally, you get your committee together and select the finalists.

Try to stick to your schedule. Most companies fail to do this. They get the responses in by October 15, announcing that they will make a decision by November 1. In fact, the evaluation process is much more complicated than they thought. There is no decision until late in January. By this time, they have missed the schedule for the early spring launch. The wining bidder will have to race to get going, skipping several important steps. The project will be in trouble from the start.

How Important Is Price for E-mail Marketing?

When outsourcing database marketing, we are looking for a company that is responsive to our needs and does a rapid and accurate job of maintaining our data and making it available to all our employees over the Web. It is fairly easy to describe these functions. Once they are described, the cost becomes a relevant evaluation factor.

With e-mail marketing the picture is quite different. E-mail marketing is highly creative. It changes from day to day. You are looking for an ESP that not only gets the e-mails out rapidly with zero errors but that is constantly coming up with new ideas. What kind of ideas are we talking about?

- How to get subscribers to open their e-mails.
- How to make each e-mail an adventure for the readers.
- How to reduce unsubscribes.
- How to do viral marketing.
- How to make e-mails work on mobile devices.

- How to boost the number of subscribers.
- How to find creative ways to do transactions and triggers.
- How to write compelling e-mails.
- How to do testing to improve your marketing.
- How to build retail store traffic.
- How to create powerful subject lines.
- And so on.

These are the things that you should be looking for in an ESP partner, not price. Why not price? Because even the highest-priced ESP can deliver an outstanding return on investment if it is good at these things. E-mail marketing is so inexpensive compared to direct mail that price considerations should be last on your list of criteria for selecting a partner.

To illustrate the unimportance of price, let's consider two ESPs, one of which is only one point higher in several of the above factors, but *three times* higher in price, than a low cost ESP competitor. See Figure 21.2.

Compare this with a highly effective ESP that charges three times as much for its services as shown in Figure 21.3.

Low Cost ESP		This Year	Second Year	Third Year
Subscribers		500,000	375,000	281,250
Unsubscribes	15%	75,000	56,250	42,188
Undelivers	10%	50,000	37,500	28,125
Delivered E-mails	104	52,000,000	39,000,000	29,250,000
Opens	12%	6,240,000	4,680,000	3,510,000
Unique Clicks	20%	1,248,000	936,000	702,000
Conversions	3.00%	37,440	28,080	21,060
Revenue	$102.45	$3,835,728	$2,876,796	$2,157,597
Costs	40%	$1,534,291	$1,150,718	$863,039
Cost of Acquisition	$0.30	$150,000		
ESP Cost per 1000	$2.00	$104,000	$78,000	$58,500
E-mail Creation	$5.00	$260,000	$195,000	$146,250
Total Costs		$2,048,291	$1,423,718	$1,067,789
Gross Profit		$1,787,437	$1,453,078	$1,089,808
Discount Rate		1	1.1	1.21
Net Present Value		$1,787,437	$1,320,980	$900,668
Cumulative NPV		$1,787,437	$3,108,416	$4,009,084
Lifetime Value		$3.57	$6.22	$8.02

Figure 21.2 Low Cost ESP

High-Performance ESP		This Year	Second Year	Third Year
Subscribers		500,000	385,000	296,450
Unsubscribes	14%	70,000	53,900	41,503
Undelivers	9%	45,000	34,650	26,681
Delivered E-mails	104	52,000,000	40,040,000	30,830,800
Opens	13%	6,760,000	5,205,200	4,008,004
Unique Clicks	21%	1,419,600	1,093,092	841,681
Conversions	3.50%	49,686	38,258	29,459
Revenue	$102.45	$5,090,331	$3,919,555	$3,018,057
Costs	40%	$2,036,132	$1,567,822	$1,207,223
Cost of Acquisition	$0.30	$150,000		
ESP Cost per 1000	$6.00	$312,000	$240,240	$184,985
E-mail Creation	$5.00	$260,000	$200,200	$154,154
Total Costs		$2,758,132	$2,008,262	$1,546,362
Gross Profit		$2,332,198	$1,911,293	$1,471,695
Discount Rate		1	1.1	1.21
Net Present Value		$2,332,198	$1,737,539	$1,216,277
Cumulative NPV		$2,332,198	$4,069,737	$5,286,015
Lifetime Value		$4.66	$8.14	$10.57

Figure 21.3 High Performance High Cost ESP

The high-performance ESP puts more people on the job and brings its broad experience to bear. As a result:

- Unsubscribes go down from 15 percent in low cost to 14 percent in high performance.
- Undelivers go from 10 to 9 percent.
- Opens go from 12 to 15 percent.
- Unique clicks from 20 to 21 percent.
- Conversions from 3 to 3.5 percent.
- Third year LTV goes from $8.02 to $10.57.
- Cost of the high performance ESP goes up from $2 per thousand to $6 per thousand.

We gain more than $1.2 million (see Figure 21.4) in profit after paying three times more for the high performance ESP. Conclusion: in searching for an ESP, price is relatively unimportant.

Comparison LTV	This Year	Second Year	Third Year
Low-Cost ESP Sub LTV	$3.57	$6.22	$8.02
High-Performance ESP	$4.66	$8.14	$10.57
Gain	$1.09	$1.92	$2.55
Times 500,000 Subscribers	$544,762	$961,321	$1,276,930
Extra Cost High Performance	$208,000	$162,240	$126,485
Return on Investment	$2.62	$5.93	$10.10

Figure 21.4 Comparison of Low Cost vs. High Performance ESP

Meeting with the Finalists

The last step is a half-day session with each of the finalists. Before these sessions, your committee members should agree on a simple list of evaluation criteria, based on what they have seen in the RFP responses. Don't pay the expenses of the bidders who come to your meeting. Let them get there on their own. The atmosphere should be cheerful, not formal. After all, these may be your partners for years to come. See how you relate to them. See how interesting and innovative they are. Let them do any kind of presentation they want. Have a nice long question-and-answer session after their presentation.

Before the meeting, let everyone know how much time is available for the meeting. The time should be the same for all bidders. Let them know what you want them to do at the meeting (one hour presentation, one hour of questions). Let them know what is available for them to use such as a PC projector or monitor, or an outside telephone line.

When the last presentation is over, have your committee meeting right away. If possible have the interviews during the first part of a week and the committee meeting during the last part of the same week when everything is fresh in everyone's mind. Make a decision. Announce it. Get started.

The Contract

Selecting a partner is not the end of the process. It is the beginning of a process. You need to draw up a contract that incorporates all the concepts of the winning partner's proposal. This may take some time. It is a good idea to begin work immediately based on a purchase order from your company so that valuable time is not lost while the lawyers fight over detailed provisions. Time is of the essence. You are not building relationships with your customers while you haggle over contract wording.

The Transition Team

To hit the ground running, you need a single point of contact in both companies. It should be someone who has authority to make decisions and to get answers. One of the first problems will be to get MIS to provide the essential data: the customer database, and the definitions of the fields. Sometimes that takes *months!* Knowing that you will have this problem, you should begin to plan for the transition long before you have finally selected a partner. MIS may drag its feet because it wanted the project in the first place and is unwilling to help the partner. You may have to go to a higher level to get this problem resolved.

In the early weeks, you will be inundated with detailed questions:

"What is the format for the product codes?"

"How can you tell which region a customer is in?"

"The format for the customer data changed last year. Where is the format for the old data?"

These questions have never come up before. You don't know the answers, *and nobody else does.* Your business partner will have to get these answers, or the project will never get off the ground. Be prepared for the questions and figure out a way to get rapid answers.

Take-Away Thoughts

- Database and e-mail marketing are so specialized that outsourcing is a must for any large company.

- By outsourcing, you gain experience, expertise, speed, economy, and entrepreneurship.

- ESPs provide their clients with strategic guidance, specialized software, deliverability monitoring, and IP warming.

- Many companies have several internal units sending e-mails to the same subscribers. This may hurt the company's multichannel strategy.

- Internal IT may represent the biggest obstacle to success and to outsourcing.

- To outsource, you need to issue an RFP. This function can also be outsourced.

- Go to conferences and consult Forrester to learn whom to send the RFP to.

- Do not send RFPs to more than four companies.

- Your RFP should provide a scope of work, your company background, the problem to be solved, your marketing goal, your strategy, and the size of the job.

- Having bidders compete may be a good idea.

- Treat those whom you work with as partners rather than vendors. You will get better service.

- Don't ask too many questions.

- Give bidders at least a month to write their proposal.

- Invite the top two to come in for a formal presentation.

- For e-mail marketing, quality of service is much more important than price.

A quiz on this chapter and all figures can be found at www.dbmarket ing.com/STM4. Those taking all the quizzes can receive a Successful Completion Certificate from the Database Marketing Institute which can be used in their résumé.

22

The Future of Database Marketing

*We're still the same human beings we always were.
Consumers still act like consumers; people still search
for love and friendship. But the Internet has freed us
from the boundaries of distance and many of the risks
of embarrassment in social interactions. ... But just as
I have no desire to give up cars, trains and planes to
return to the hay-eating, vet-needing, poop-generating,
one-horsepower horse, I don't want to go back to pre-
Google research, pre-Amazon shopping, pre-blog news
media, or the loneliness of villages limited by
geography.*

—Orson Scott Card

*The hardest thing to do in marketing is to talk with
relevance directly and personally to the people who pay
your salaries (your customers) and get them to do what
you want them to do. In other words the hardest thing
to do in marketing is direct marketing. Yet senior
management delegates direct marketing, such as e-mail
messages to juniors and wonder why the results aren't
what they want. ... Recognize and accept that e-mail
marketing is not a cheap alternative to other marketing
media—treat it with respect. Why quibble over the cost
to send messages that you can track, to people you
know, when you don't question paying enormous costs
for messages in mass media you can't track?*

—Malcolm-Auld

To understand the future, we must first understand the past. As you know by now, database marketing grew out of direct marketing. The main goal was to build a customer database to figure out who was most likely to respond—using, among other methods, RFM, demographics, and modeling, so that you could save postage by not mailing to unlikely responders.

After the databases were built, smart marketers figured out that there was a second use for the database: learn more about your customers so you could create segments and personalize your message to each segment. This was where the real profits from database marketing came in. You could boost customer retention by building a real relationship with each customer—send birthday cards, thank them for their purchases, remind them of anniversaries, create loyalty programs, and suggest relevant additional purchases. Database marketing enabled large corporations to build relationships similar to those between the Old Corner Grocers and their customers. Database marketing became very profitable. The profits could be measured by lifetime value.

Then, out in left field, Web sites were born. At first they were just brand advertisements, like print or TV ads. Late in the 1990s, Web shopping carts were discovered. Gradually customers began to trust corporations with their credit cards. Some Web sites, like AOL, became shopping centers or malls where you could find dozens of different companies selling products. At the same time, broadband began to reach the average American home. Google was invented as a wonderful indexing system so you could ask any question and get answers. You could look up any product, and Google would lead you to hundreds—no thousands—of Web sites where these products were on display and for sale. Google killed off the shopping center idea. Broadband killed off AOL which had been based on dial-up service.

When e-mail marketing began, around 1998, it proved to be so inexpensive (compared to direct mail) that many marketers said to themselves, "We don't need a database. We just need a list. We can afford to e-mail everyone on that list." The more they mailed, the more they made. So the batch and blast database promotion system was born.

For the next 10 years, thousands of large corporations did just that. The result was that consumer in-boxes overflowed with e-mails from legitimate corporations. A relevant e-mail sent too often becomes irrelevant. This is where we are today—too many e-mails in consumers' in-boxes. Many consumers consider many of the e-mails from reputable companies to be spam because the volume is so overwhelming. What was okay a couple of times a month became unwelcome when it arrived several times a week.

Meanwhile, in 1995 Amazon began with a different idea. Build a marketing database, and use it to understand potential customers. Let them tell you what they want. Amazon took all the concepts in this book and built three massive marketing databases: one for customers, one for products and a third for their one million merchant partners. It turned the retailer's marketing ideas upside down. For years, the central concept of retailing was to figure out what most people want and stock those things in your stores, advertising periodic sales to get people to come in and buy these popular items. There really was no room in traditional stores for unpopular or seldom-purchased items. How could such obscure products be sold? Google provided the answer. Enter any crazy product name into Google, and Google will list hundreds of merchants selling these little-known items.

Amazon began by assembling information about these millions of obscure products and making deals with their merchants—deals that were profitable for both the merchant and for Amazon. What Amazon brought to the table was a database of customers who had listed their names, addresses, e-mails, and credit cards with Amazon so that they could "buy with 1 click"—no need to enter all this information each time they shopped.

The three databases that are central to the Amazon process enable Amazon to do unique things that most retailers cannot do. When an Amazon customer buys a book by Richard Rhodes, the database remembers it. Three years later when Rhodes comes out with a new book, Amazon can send an e-mail to all those who bought his other books. For a few dollars Amazon realizes hundreds of dollars of sales to these folks. Today, Amazon sells more lesser-known products than well-known products. It has built a big part of its business on the long tail.

At the same time, Amazon's product database became almost unique in the industry. Not only did Amazon sell new products but it made it possible for individuals and merchants to sell both new and used products through Amazon. How about product ratings and reviews? Amazon set up a system so that there are customer reviews of almost any product it sells. For each product sold on Amazon—new or used—Amazon signed up a dozen or more merchants who sell that same product. Amazon displays them with their prices and shipping costs so you can buy what you want from almost anyone. Amazon provides ratings and reviews of the *merchants* as well as of the products.

One product ad on Amazon for blenders lists 37 merchants selling brand new identical blenders and 4 merchants who sell used versions of this particular 54615 blender. There are 103 customer reviews of this model blender. Think of the size of the product marketing database that

Amazon maintains! The data about this particular blender is probably larger than the database maintained by most companies on any of their products—and Amazon has 29 million other products like this.

Another page shows the 37 merchants that sell this same blender for Amazon. You can read information about many different sellers of this blender, both new and used. These 37 sellers of blenders can read what you are reading. They can change their price. Note that seller J&R has 558,910 product sales ratings. This information is from the third database. Where else can you get this kind of information?

Customer Reviews

You can read any or all of the 103 customer reviews of this blender.

By clicking, you can read positive and negative reviews. There is enough information here that you could spend half a day reading information before you spend your $20 on a blender. Once you buy it, you can write your own review. There is nothing hidden here.

Only a very few companies such as Walmart have such a wealth of information about products for sale. It is expensive to collect and store it.

Walmart has similar information on this same blender on its Web site priced identically to the blenders at Amazon. It has 75 customer ratings and reviews. The differences are that there is only one seller (Walmart) on the Web site and no used products on sale. Buy.com lists eight sellers of this blender, all at significantly higher prices. Amazon has set the standard that other merchants struggle to emulate.

If you were Target, could you equal this information? Unlikely. That is why in 2001 Target became for the next 10 years an Amazon partner. In 2011 Target decided to go it alone, just as Toys "R" Us and Borders—former Amazon partners—did previously. What happened to Borders after leaving Amazon was not good news:

> In retrospect, the "partnership" with Amazon.com seems like anything but. Amazon did everything for Borders—inventory management, content development, back-end fulfillment and customer service—and grew its business into the juggernaut it is today. The wealth of intellectual capital and hard-earned lessons that Amazon realized over the years from selling to Borders' online customers stayed inside Amazon's Seattle headquarters. All Borders got out of the deal was a percentage of sales. Target will now have to spend

*millions (if not billions) to build out its new
e-commerce infrastructure during the next two years—
integrating the various ERP, customer relationship,
retail analytics and supply chain systems. And,
of course, one of its chief competitors—besides
Wal-Mart—will be Amazon.com, which continues
to dominate all comers online.*

—THOMAS WAILGUM in CIO 2009

So Amazon took the marketing database idea and ran with it.
Walmart and others have copied it. Most other marketers, however, have
taken the batch and blast e-mail idea (which does not require a database) and ran with that. So what does the future of database marketing
hold? Is database marketing in the future dead or alive?

1. *Database marketing is still essential for direct mail.* Direct mail is alive
   and well. A medium that gets a consistent 2.67 percent response
   rate with database marketing guiding it will be around for the fore-
   seeable future. Consumers who buy by mail still have their mail-
   boxes filled with profitable direct mail despite the massive volume
   of e-mail. Where direct mail beats other media is in its shelf life.
   A paper catalog can continue producing sales for six months or
   more after delivery. An e-mail or a text message is seldom good for
   more than 48 hours.

2. *Database marketing is essential to support loyalty programs.* Loyalty programs work. Millions of Americans collect and treasure their miles.
   Loyalty builds retention and repeat business. All loyalty program
   members' data is stored on a database. Database marketing is an
   essential tool of any loyalty program.

3. *Database marketing is at the heart of business-to-business marketing.* Business
   purchases can be predicted. Database marketing is used to determine
   which businesses to target and for what.

4. *Financial services of all types will use database marketing for a long time.*
   Financial services are lucky that in their operations they collect a lot
   of data about their customers. They can use this data to identify who
   will buy what and when using database marketing. They will use both
   physical and electronic communications to reach out to their customers, guided by reliable databases.

5. *Triggered e-mails and direct mail work together.* You cannot send birthday,
   deadline, and reminder messages without a database. These messages

are opened and read and will generate profits far into the future. You need a database for triggered messages.

6. *Customers like to express their preferences.* Whether it is product reviews, frequency preferences, blogs, or mobile marketing, people like to tell their suppliers what they think. Profitable suppliers will listen and put customer views in databases so that they can honor them.

7. *Profitable Web sites greet returning customers and provide dynamic content.* You cannot do these things without a database.

Direct Mail and E-mail Working Together

This is a book about database marketing: using a database to build relationships with your customers who are contacted, in general, through direct mail, e-mail, text mail, or phone. In Chapter 3, we learn about a definitive test relating these direct mail and e-mail with online and offline purchasing channels. It shows something profound and fundamental that holds promise for those looking to build profitable relationships with their subscribers and customers.

Grand Total	Count	Response Rate	Average Order Value	Dollars per Name Mailed	Increase from Control	% Sales in Store	% Sales Online
Direct Mail and E-mail	35,000	25%	$71.71	$17.67	$3.35	79%	21%
Direct Mail Only	35,000	24%	$68.62	$16.39	$2.07	83%	17%
E-mail Only	35,000	23%	$67.82	$15.71	$1.40	79%	21%

Figure 22.1 Test of Three Groups Using Direct Mail and E-mail

Figure 22.1 shows that both media working together are better than either one alone—and even more important—that e-mail produces 3.76 offline sales for every 1 online sale.

A Practical Database Marketing Example

Albert Einstein developed his theories using thought experiments. He thought, "What would happen if ..." Let's use that method with a large retailer that is sending millions of e-mails and does not use dynamic content. It blasts 123.6 million e-mails a year to 1.4 million subscribers. Everyone gets the same e-mails. For the retailer to create four or five segments and create personalized dynamic content for each segment would require creating a modern database. The retailer would then have to use that database with a much larger creative staff to send really relevant content. If it were to do this, however, its subscribers would undoubtedly respond with higher open, click and conversion rates. The unsubscribe rates would go down. But to do this the retailer would have to spend $3 million per year more than it does now on its e-mail program. Would the retailer do this? Would it work? Let's look at the numbers.

Figure 22.2 shows the LTV table of this actual retailer that had more than 450 large stores throughout the United States in 2011. It has a Web site that features its products, and it sends 123 million e-mails a year. Its non-e-mail sales resulting from the e-mails delivered each year are five times the sales within the e-mails. Figure 22.2 shows the actual situation as of 2011.

You will note that we have included the cost of replacing the subscribers lost through unsubscribing in the cost section of this figure (line 16).

Current Situation – Batch and Blast		This Year	Next Year	Third Year
1 Subscribers		1,443,409	858,540	510,659
2 Unsub	33.93%	489,749	291,303	173,267
3 Undeliver	6.59%	95,121	56,578	33,652
4 Next Year		858,540	510,659	303,740
5 Delivered	7.14	123,671,283	73,559,679	43,753,297
6 Open	13.69%	16,933,799	10,072,224	5,990,959
7 Unique Click	11.80%	1,998,789	1,188,880	707,146
8 Conversion	1.38%	27,530	16,375	9,740
9 Non-e-mail	5.00	137,652	81,876	48,700
10 Total Sales Resulting from E-mails		165,183	98,251	58,440
11 Revenue	$97.32	$16,075,102	$9,561,471	$5,687,163
12 Cost	40%	$6,430,041	$3,824,588	$2,274,865
13 Acquisition	$0.10	$144,341		
14 Sending	$2.00	$247,343	$147,119	$87,507
15 Create 876 E-mail Campaigns	$300.00	$262,800	$262,800	$262,800
16 Replace Unsubs	$8.46	$4,143,274	$2,464,419	$1,465,837
17 Total Costs of E-mail Program		$11,227,798	$4,234,508	$2,625,172
18 Profit		$4,847,304	$5,326,963	$3,061,991
19 Discount Rate		1	1.1	1.21
20 NPV Profit		$4,847,304	$4,842,694	$2,530,571
21 Cum NPV Profit		$4,847,304	$9,689,998	$12,220,569
22 LTV		$3.36	$6.71	$8.47

Figure 22.2 LTV of Large Retailer with Batch and Blast

This is a large, successful retailer that wants to keep the business going. The company bought the concept of LTV and knows that if the subscribers are worth $8.47 each, that the retailer will be losing $8.47 in profits every time one of these valuable people defects for whatever reason. So they are built into the LTV table as a cost when they leave.

You will also note (line 3) that there is a high unsubscribe rate. Why? Probably because the retailer is sending 58 e-mails per year per subscriber with no segmentation and no personalization. If we look at typical unsubscribe rates for our 80 standard retailers, we see this picture shown in Figure 22.3.

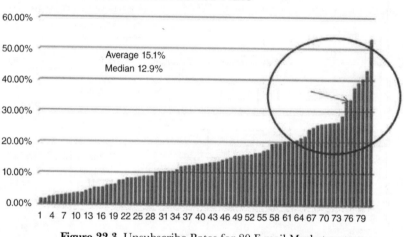

Figure 22.3 Unsubscribe Rates for 80 E-mail Marketers

Our retailer is on the high end with an unsubscribe rate of 33.93 percent, but it is not alone. Those with high unsubscribe rates are all batch and blast retailers that send identical content on a frequent basis to their subscribers. What we know for sure is that the subscribers it is losing are more valuable than the subscribers it is keeping. This is shown in Figure 22.4. This data is the result of an actual case study in 2008 in which the spending of those customers who left two large women's clothing store chains was compared with the spending of those who did not leave the stores. In both cases the dollars per buyer for those customers who left were higher than the dollars per buyer for those who did not leave.

What is this retailer saying in these e-mails? It is featuring low prices (rather than building a relationship or concentrating on the quality of goods or service) (see Figure 22.5).

Company A	Unsubs and Undels		
Number of Purchases	Buyers	Revenue	$/Buyer
1	3,654	$528,140	$144.54
2	551	$181,528	$329.45
3	146	$79,704	$545.92
4+	156	$168,071	$1,077.38
Total	4,351	$957,443	**$220.05**
Not Leaving	58,556	$10,373,267	**$177.15**

Company B	Unsubs and Undels		
Number of Purchases	Buyers	Revenue	$/Buyer
1	4,054	$386,847	$95.42
2	753	$159,822	$212.25
3	262	$81,355	$310.52
4+	292	$207,911	$712.02
Total	5,361	$835,936	**$155.93**
Not Leaving	95,036	$10,954,319	**$115.26**

Figure 22.4 Value of Subscribers Staying and Leaving Due to Batch and Blast E-mails

$599.99 ~~List Price: $1199.99*~~
YOU SAVE $600.00 (50%)

Figure 22.5 What Our Retailer's E-mails Look Like

Figure 22.5 represents a perfectly profitable way to sell products, but it is not database marketing. The retailer may have acquired the e-mail subscribers by building a relationship with them (it is a great brand name) but it is ruining the relationship with these subscribers by telling them (after they sign up) how cheap the company really is.

What's wrong with that? In today's world, everyone knows about Amazon and Google. People know that with a couple of clicks they can probably find the same item from another retailer for less than $599.99. So why should they buy this item from this retailer? Because it has a great brand with a great reputation that cares about Gene Williams and his physical fitness goals. It can recommend this product to Gene because Gene has listed his goals in the retailer's preference center, and he has bought other fitness products there. Why not say, "Gene, this is probably the best product for you to use in reaching your fitness goal," rather than stressing the price and the saving.

As you know, there are two types of consumer buyers: relationship buyers and transaction buyers. Relationship buyers buy from you because they like you and trust you to advise them and sell them products that they need and that fit in with their overall goals. Transaction buyers don't care about these things. They care only about price. You can ruin your relationship with relationship buyers after you acquire them by sending them a continuing stream of direct and e-mail messages that stress only your low prices.

Are you Walmart or Amazon? No. So learn who your subscribers are, and you build a relationship with them so that they will not care if your products may be a little more expensive than someone else's. That someone else does not care about them the way that you do. That someone else does not send them personal database marketing messages that build personal relationships. You know Gene Williams. That is your ace in the hole. Build on it. Use it. Don't ruin Gene by talking to him only about price—an area in which you will probably lose.

So let's see what would happen if our retailer were to use database marketing. Let's compare the numbers in Figure 22.2 with those in Figure 22.6. In Figure 22.6 we have modified the retailer's current numbers to show what would happen if it were to adopt relationship marketing principles as recommended throughout this book.

Some notes: We are using relationship marketing. We are sending different personal messages to each of our subscribers. To do this, our creation costs (Line 15 in both charts) have gone up from $262,800 per year to $1,314.000 per year—a big jump—but it is the only way to do database marketing properly. At the same time in Line 16 we have created a database (rather than a mailing list) that costs us $1 per subscriber per year—again, more than $1 million per year in increased costs. Our subscriber acquisition costs have gone up because we are appending demographics of about $0.40 to each name acquired.

What have we gained from these additional expenses? Quite a lot. We have reduced our unsubscribe rate to the median amount of 12.9 percent (see Figure 22.3). Creating a database and dynamic content has made quite a difference. We are assuming that because of building relationships with our subscribers, our open, click, and conversion rates (lines 6, 7, and 8 in Figure 22.6) will go up by 20 percent as will the off-e-mail multiplier. We have compensated for the loss of e-mail subscribers (Line 17). This $4.2 million will be used to replace the lost subscribers by active programs to generate new ones.

Using Database Marketing		This Year	Next Year	Third Year
1 Subscribers		1,443,409	1,162,089	935,598
2 Unsub Using Median Number	12.90%	186,200	149,909	120,692
3 Undeliver	6.59%	95,121	76,582	61,656
4 Next Year		1,162,089	935,598	753,250
5 Delivered	7.14	123,671,283	99,567,750.04	80,161,995.56
6 Open (20% Higher)	16.43%	20,320,559	16,360,082	13,171,502
7 Unique Click (20% Higher)	14.16%	2,878,256	2,317,284	1,865,645
8 Conversion (20% Higher)	1.65%	47,573	38,301	30,836
9 Non-e-mail (20% Higher)	6.00	285,436	229,804	185,016
10 Total Sales Resulting from E-mails		333,009	268,105	215,851
11 Revenue (Same AOV)	$97.32	$32,407,406	$26,091,203	$21,006,027
12 Cost	40%	$12,962,963	$10,436,481	$8,402,411
13 Acquisition (Higher)	$0.50	$721,705		
14 Sending	$2.00	$247,343	$199,136	$160,324
15 Creation of 1,314 Campaigns	$1,000	$1,314,000	$1,314,000	$1,314,000
16 Database (New Function)	$1.00	$1,443,409	$1,162,089	$935,598
17 Replce Unsubs	$22.98	$4,278,871	$3,444,919	$2,773,504
18 Total Costs of E-mail Program		$20,968,289	$16,556,624	$5,183,426
19 Profit		$11,439,117	$9,534,579	$15,822,602
20 Discount Rate		1	1.1	1.21
21 NPV Profit		$11,439,117	$8,667,799	$13,076,530
22 Cum NPV Profit		$11,439,117	$20,106,916	$33,183,447
23 LTV		$7.93	$13.93	$22.99

Figure 22.6 LTV after Database Marketing

Overall, our LTV (Line 22 in Figure 22.2, and Line 23 in Figure 22.6) has gone up from $8.47 in Figure 22.2 to $22.99 in Figure 22.6—a dramatic increase. This change has increased our profits from e-mail marketing by more than $20 million as shown in Figure 22.7.

Figure 22.7 shows that the Return on Investment from your database marketing is $10.55 in the third year for every dollar invested. Would management risk spending $9 million per year more than it does now, to get these profits? I am not sure that it would. For managers to do this, they would need a really smart CMO who understands database and e-mail marketing and LTV. The numbers are there, and they do not lie. It would take real leadership, but that is what database marketing is all about.

Gains from DBM	This Year	Next Year	Third Year
Batch and Blast LTV	$3.36	$6.71	$8.47
LTV with Database Marketing	$7.93	$13.93	$22.99
Gain	$4.57	$7.22	$14.52
With 1,443,409 Subscribers	$6,591,813	$10,416,918	$20,962,878
Return on Investment	$2.15	$4.71	$10.55

Figure 22.7 Results of Database Marketing

Prediction

As the future unfolds, I predict that people will get tired of overloaded in-boxes with constant non-personalized batch and blast e-mails from reputable companies. Companies will have two choices: turn to relationship marketing using databases, as shown in this book, or give up and become an Amazon partner (which would still be profitable). Going it alone as a batch and blast marketer will not be an option for the long run.

Companies using database marketing will do the analysis it takes to determine that using database marketing, instead of batch and blast, will be profitable for them. They will let their customers know that they will not receive more mail than they want to receive, and they will personalize the mail with content designed for the subscribers. It will cost them more to do this, but, as in the example above, it will pay dividends. They will lose fewer customers and gain more friends and sales.

Unfortunately, many companies will not do this. The current trend (was it ever different?) is to say that each quarter's sales have to reach some given number, regardless of how you get there. Worries about losing valuable customers, giving customers what they want, looking at the long run will all take a back seat to next quarter's numbers. The profits from database marketing will be impossible for these—and all—companies that seek only quarterly revenue projections and ways to cut costs. Furthermore, the customers they will lose through unsubscribes will be more valuable than the transaction buyers they keep.

Conclusion

There will probably always be some companies that rely on massive frequent non-personalized e-mails delivered to lists of consumers without building or maintaining a database. This method has been successful for many companies. You do not need a database if you find that you are making a profit from frequent e-mails to PCs or to iPhones. But you will suffer in the long run. What you will be doing is gradually losing your best customers and converting the rest of them into transaction buyers. If companies are going to maximize their profits over the long run, they will need a marketing database now and forever.

Take-Away Thoughts

- Database marketing grew out of direct marketing. The first use was to save money on postage.

- The second use was to find out what people were interested in (from the database) and create dynamic content in direct mail.

- Then e-mail came along and drastically reduced the cost of communication.

- But the cost became so low that everyone began to send e-mails. In-boxes were overloaded with messages.

- Billions of promotional e-mails are sent today that do not use the information in a marketing database.

- Amazon came along with a different idea: build a massive customer database and a massive product database. Enlist a million suppliers to sell new and used products through the Amazon Web site.

- Amazon sells more hard-to-find products than mainstream products—while being the largest e-commerce seller in the world.

- Customer ratings and reviews are the most widely read part of any e-mail or Web site. To succeed, you must have them, and you must get customers to provide them.

- For 10 years, Borders was an Amazon partner. Then it decided to go it alone. Result: Borders is facing bankruptcy.

- Database marketing is still essential for direct mail, which is still alive and well.

- It is essential to support loyalty programs, business-to-business marketing, and financial services.

- Profitable Web sites and e-mails greet returning customers—an essential part of their success. You cannot do this without a database.

A quiz on this chapter and all figures can be found at www.dbmarketing.com. Those taking all the quizzes can receive a Successful Completion Certificate from the Database Marketing Institute which can be used in their résumé.

23

A Farewell to the Reader

We are back where we started. Database marketing is a long-range strategy for building lasting relationships with people whom we get to know intimately, who look on our companies and our employees as friends. On the other hand we have some companies pursuing short-term marketing strategies that involve sending massive communications that shout to unknown people about their companies' low prices. Both strategies work in generating profits: one over the long run and the other for next quarter's results. The problem with the second strategy is that we may be losing our most valuable customers. "Who cares," say the batch and blast advocates. "The purpose of business is to make a profit for the stockholders. They don't ask for long-run profits. They ask for high returns right now."

Amazon is based on database marketing. Amazon is succeeding. Its business model is a long-range strategy. Massive e-mail marketers who fill up our in-boxes every day are also succeeding. The contest between the two approaches resembles the "Tragedy of the Commons."

The *tragedy of the commons* is a dilemma arising from a situation in which multiple individuals, acting independently and rationally, focusing on their own self-interest, will ultimately deplete a shared limited resource even when it is clear that it is not in anyone's long-term interest for this to happen.

In medieval Europe herders often shared a common parcel of land on which they were each entitled to let their cows graze. Each farmer's self-interest was to put as many cows as he could on the land, even though the quality of the commons is temporarily or permanently damaged from overgrazing. The herder receives all the benefits from the additional cows, while the damage to the commons is shared by the entire group. If all herders make this individually rational economic decision, the commons will be depleted or even destroyed to the detriment of all.

The commons today, of course, are the in-boxes of millions of Internet users. We may rationally send a couple of messages a month so as not to overburden our customers. These two messages are drowned out in shared in-box space with thousands of other companies that do not show similar restraint.

Price versus Quality and Service

Another way of looking at the difference between database marketers and batch and blast practitioners is in their idea of the importance of price. Generally speaking, if you look at what the batch and blast advocates are doing, it tends to be sending millions of e-mails saying that their products are on sale. Effective database marketers' messages say that they have wonderful products and superb customer service. They stress high technology, high fashion, and high levels of service. They use their subscribers' names and include dynamic content in their direct mail and e-mail messages.

The question to answer is this: is price the only difference that people care about? Clearly, that is not the case. There are people who really value high quality and service and are willing to pay more to get them. What the batch and blast advocates seem to be saying is that, "Yes, there is a segment of the market that wants high quality and service, but most people are shopping based on their desire for low prices." They haven't the time or resources to differentiate the two groups, so they operate on the assumption that the price conscious folks are the vast majority. They go with the largest group and ignore the rest in their marketing program.

My feeling is that the quality seeking proportion of the U.S. population has been vastly ignored in the rush to make quick profits from e-mail marketing. I think that many marketers will eventually realize that there are several different buying groups out there and that it is worthwhile and profitable to learn more about your customers and, using database marketing, send them dynamic content based on what we can learn of their interests.

What will happen in the future? Who knows? In this book we have laid out the case for the database marketing approach. We believe in it. The ultimate solution will occur through the interplay of many companies operating in a free economy.

The way to estimate the possibilities of proposed database marketing strategies, and to evaluate the effectiveness of existing ones, is to create test and control groups and calculate the lifetime value of both groups. Lifetime value is the *net present value of future profits to be received from the average customer.*

In free market transactions, both the buyer and the seller *always* make a profit. The way to increase your sales, therefore, is to find a way for the buyer to make a profit. In today's situation, what the buyer sees as a profit may not necessarily be a low price. It may be recognition, helpfulness, service, information, convenience, and an opportunity to identify with a friendly and reliable organization—your company. Database marketing may be the ideal way to provide those things at the least cost.

Conclusion

Let us end with the words we started with in Chapter 1: Database marketing is not just a way to increase profits by reducing costs and selling more products and services, although that is, and must be, one of its results. It provides tools that provide management with customer information. That information is used in various ways to increase customer retention and acquisition rates—the essence of business strategy. The database provides both the raw information you need and a measurement device essential for the evaluation of strategy.

Looked at from the customers' point of view, database marketing is a way of making customers happy; of providing them with recognition, service, friendship, and information for which, in return, they will reward you with loyalty, reduction in attrition, and increased sales. Genuine customer satisfaction is the goal and hallmark of satisfactory customized database marketing. If you are doing things right, your customers will be *glad* that you have a database that includes them. They will appreciate the things that you do for them. If you can develop and carry out strategies that bring this situation about, you are a master marketer. You will keep your customers for life, and be happy in your work. You will have made the world a better place to live in.

Glossary

1:1 marketing   A marketing system in which each customer gets marketing messages specifically tailored for her, based on information about her preferences and purchases contained in her database record.

A/B split   Dividing a list of subscribers into two parts, with A getting one version of the e-mail or direct marketing piece and B getting the other.

acquisition   Most companies are set up to acquire new customers rather than to retain existing customers. Acquisition of additional e-mail subscribers is a major profit making opportunity today.

acquisition cost   The cost of acquiring an opt-in subscriber's e-mail address.

ad hoc query   Modern database marketing access tools permit you to ask questions like, "How may women over age 60 have bought more than $200 from us in the last 4 months?" Such a question is an ad hoc query.

administration center   Standard area of an e-mail or a Web site where users can always find important links, such as unsubscribe functionality, e-mail to a friend, and a search box.

affinity groups   Customer or product groups. Customer groups would include parents of new babies, sports enthusiasts, people who like to travel. Product groups would include categories such as financial service products, women's clothing, automotive.

algorithm   a mathematical formula resulting from predictive modeling. The algorithm is used to score a subscriber database to predict who will open, unsubscribe or convert to a sale.

animation video   Avatars, games, and other interactive links in e-mails.

appended data   Demographic data, such as age, income, and children, that can be appended to any file that contains a name and postal address.

attrition rate   The opposite of retention rate. The percentage of customers this year who will no longer be buying next year.

authentication   A way of equipping e-mails with verifiable information so recipients know it is from a genuine source.

autocad   Computer-aided design programs used by surveyors and others.

avatar   The graphic representation of a user in an e-mail that often moves with the user's mouse.

average pricing   A system in which all customers in a retail store pay the same price regardless of the amount of their purchases.

back end   As in the phrase "back end analysis." Refers to the results of actions with people who have responded to your initial offer.

banner ads   Small advertisements inserted on Web sites. If a viewer clicks on a banner, he is transported to the Web site of the advertiser paying for the banner. There he can register and purchase products. Banner advertising is becoming one of the most successful ways of reaching new customers.

behavioral data   Customer responses, purchases, store visits, and so on. Behavior is usually more powerful in predicting response than are demographics.

bits   These are electronic on/off signals. E-mails are broken into bytes (such as numbers or letters). Each byte contains eight bits. A bit is a digit in the hyperlink binary number system "http://cplus.about.com/od/introductiontoprogram ming/g/binarydefn. htm" binary number system. It can have two values, 0 or 1. In computer memory, a bit is a small electrical switch which is either on (value 1) or off (value 0).

blog (short for Web log)   Combines text, images, links, and other media related to its topic. Also used as another name for a Web site. Readers can leave comments. Most blogs are primarily text but may contain images and video. They are maintained by an individual or a company.

blogger   An individual who maintains a blog.

bounce   Undelivered. E-mails that aren't delivered and for some reason bounce back. The sending server tries several times more before the bounce is considered permanent.

brand loyalty   Loyalty to a brand which is valuable both to the brand and the customer. The advertiser spends a lot of money to build up a brand image in the minds of millions of people. This helps to acquire and retain customers. The customers benefit because they enjoy shopping for well-known name products.

break even (verb); breakeven (noun and adjective)   An RFM cell breaks even on a test or a rollout if the net profits from sales to the cell exactly equals the cost of mailing to or telephoning to the cell. The formula for the breakeven rate is: BE = (cost per piece) $\div$ (net profit from the average sale).

bytes   Electronic representation of a letter or number. A byte contains eight bits.

C-level executives   Top-level executives, such as a COO, CMO, or CFO.

call-me button   A button on a Web site that, when clicked, will initiate a text chat or a live phone call between the customer and an agent at the Web site. Call-me buttons are becoming more and more popular as more people use the Web.

caller ID   A feature of telephone systems in which the call receiver knows the number of the calling party before she picks up the phone. Used by commercial customer services to get the customer's database record on the screen before the call is taken. It is very helpful and friendly for the customer.

campaign   A situation in which promotional e-mails are sent. Campaigns are measured by opens, clicks, and conversions. Most database and e-mail marketing is conducted by campaigns.

CAN-SPAM Act of 2003   Established the U.S. national standards for commercial e-mail. Requires the Federal Trade Commission (FTC) to enforce its provisions.

cardholders   People who own and use plastic cards issued by a retail store. Use of this card permits the retailer to know who is shopping and what that customer is buying. A powerful marketing tool.

CASS   See *coding accuracy support system.*

cell code   After completing RFM analysis or traditional merge-purge for a mailing, every customer is assigned a cell code which identifies recency, frequency, and monetary level of buying (or the list from which the customer's name was selected). RFM cell codes typically vary from 555 (Most recent, frequent and highest monetary) down to 111 (least of all of these).

CHAID (chi-square automatic interaction detection)   CHAID is a classification tree technique in modeling that displays the modeling results in an easy-to-interpret tree diagram going from top down instead of from the bottom up.

channel   A method of purchasing online, retail stores, catalogs, phone, and so on.

churn   Customers may switch to a different service provider (of phone service, credit cards, etc.) because of a better price, quality of service, quality of customer care, equipment and technology, billing issues, or simply more effective marketing campaigns. The percentage of customers who churn in a particular time period is defined as the churn rate.

click   An e-mail reader uses his mouse to click on a link to open it or see a new page.

click-through rates   Number of clicks divided by number of opens in an e-mail campaign.

clickstream analysis   Analysis of a series of packets from e-mail users that indicate opens, downloads, clicks, or conversions.

client   A computer application, such as a Web browser, that runs on a user's local computer or workstation and connects to the Internet. Microsoft Outlook is an e-mail client.

Cluster Codes   A code that can be applied to a household to indicate the lifestyle of the inhabitants. In PRIZM NE, each ZIP Code is assigned one or several of sixty-six clusters, based on the shared socioeconomic characteristics of the area. The clusters each have snappy names and short one-line descriptions encompassing the key demographic for the cluster.

coding accuracy support system (CASS)   A U.S. Postal Service certified system that improves the accuracy of delivery point codes, zip+4 codes, 5-digit zip codes, and carrier route codes on mail pieces. CASS provides a common platform for measuring the quality of address-matching software and diagnosing and correcting software problems. It appends address quality and type codes to each record.

collaborative filtering   A method of making automatic predictions (filtering) about the user's interests by collecting taste information from many users (collaborating). The underlying assumption of collaborative filtering is that those whose tastes or views agreed in the past will agree in the future. Examples: opinions on a book or a movie.

continuity   Products or services bought as a series of small purchases rather than all at one time. An example would be the Book of the Month Club or other products shipped on a regular schedule.

control group   A group of customers or subscribers that does not get a promotion that is sent to another group that is being tested. The success of the promotion is measured by the difference in response of the group promoted to compared to that of the control group (after subtracting the cost of the promotion).

conversion   The desired action the marketer wishes the e-mail subscriber to take, such as to purchase a product or request more information.

conversion rate   The percentage of responders who become customers.

cookie   Information stored by a company on a user's PC that enables a sending server to know that this user has visited the Web site or read an e-mail. It enables Web sites to say, "Welcome back, Arthur."

copy   The text of your direct mail or e-mail piece.

co-registration   A system whereby one company, such as an airline, signs up its subscribers for another company's (such as rental car company) e-mail subscribers.

CPI   (cost per inquiry) Total cost of a lead generation system divided by the number of leads generated.

CPM   (cost per thousand) Rental names are usually purchased on a CPM basis. E-mail delivery is usually billed based on CPM.

cross-selling   Encouraging customers to buy products from other departments in the company or categories of products.

CTR   CTR for an ad is defined as the number of clicks on an ad divided by the number of times the ad is shown (impressions), expressed as a percentage.

cyber Monday   The Monday after Thanksgiving. A great day for e-mail sales.

dashboard A custom and useful arrangement of clickstream data from a campaign.

database The place where data about subscribers is stored. Used to create personalized direct mail and e-mail content.

database marketing The system of using stored customer or subscriber data in a database to personalize direct and e-mail communications.

DCOA (dynamic change of address) Over 30 percent of people who move never submit a change of address with the U.S. Postal Service. The DCOA file retains records of address changes for more than seven years, including multiple moves and forwarding addresses.

de dupe Identification and consolidation of duplicate names usually done in a merge-purge operation.

deciles Groups of tens utilized in a method of dividing customers based on their spending or response. Very common in marketing research. Too numerous for RFM.

deliverability The percentage of e-mails that reaches its destination.

deliverables The number of e-mails that are delivered.

demographic data Information about customers or prospects, such as age, income, presence of children, home value, own vs. rent, and so on. Demographic data can be purchased and appended to a customer database or mailing file from such companies as Experian, KnowledgeBase Marketing, or Equifax. See *behavioral data* for contrast.

descriptive modeling Modeling that describes the demographics and behavior of subscribers. See *predictive modeling* for comparison.

direct marketing The practice of delivering promotional messages directly to potential customers on an individual basis as opposed to through a mass medium. Direct marketing can use mail, phone, or the Internet.

direct mail Advertising circulars or other printed matter sent directly through the mail to prospective customers or contributors.

discount rate In lifetime value calculation, it is necessary to determine the net present value of future revenue or profits. The discount rate is divided into future dollar amounts to calculate the net present value. The formula for the discount rate is $D = (1 + i)^n$ where i = the rate of interest including risk, and n = the number of years you have to wait to receive the money.

discounts A deduction from the usual cost of something, typically given for prompt or advance payment or to a special category of buyersIf database marketing is done properly, it is not necessary to give discounts to customers, since they value the relationship with their supplier more than the discount. Discounts reduce the perceived value of the product and the relationship, and erode margin. If you have to give something, give points or premium, not discounts.

double opt-in method   Preferred method of signing up e-mail subscribers. When people sign up for your e-mails, you send an e-mail to them, asking them to confirm the subscription. These people are not added to your database until they have confirmed that they want to receive your e-mails.

download   A white paper or other document subscribers can get from your site; usually offered in an e-mail or a website.

DPV (delivery point validation)   DPV is software that contains all delivery point addresses serviced by the U.S. Postal Service. The software confirms that an address actually exists, allowing users of this service to avoid mailing to an invalid address.

drill down analysis   Analytic tools that permit users to view the details behind any query. For example, "Which customers bought more than $1,200 this year broken down by product categories."

DSF² (delivery sequence file)—second generation   An address hygiene tool that provides additional address information about a DPV-verified address to minimize address delivery errors that are not detected by NCOALINK or CASS-certified processing. DSF processing further classifies an address as business, residential, vacant, seasonal, or throwback (i.e., rerouted), and it also identifies the mail delivery method—curbside delivery, door slot, neighborhood delivery, and collection box unit, or central delivery.

e-mail   Electronic mail that is fast becoming the most popular method of communication between customers and suppliers. It is rapidly replacing fax and regular postal mail.

e-mail service provider (ESP)   A service company that sends and sometimes creates e-mail messages for clients.

employee loyalty   Employee loyalty can be defined as employees being committed to the success of the organization and believing that working for this organization is their best option. Not only do they plan to remain with the organization, but they do not actively search for alternative employment and are not responsive to offers. Frederich Reichheld in *The Loyalty Effect* pointed out that the best way to ensure customer loyalty is to have loyal employees, since many customers build relationships with the sales and customer service personnel.

enhancement   Appending demographic or lifestyle data to a database or a list.

entrepreneurship   To be successful in marketing, it is useful to outsource as much as you can to specialists who are entrepreneurs. Entrepreneurs have the freedom to be creative and the financial incentive to be successful. The opposite of an entrepreneur is an employee working for a regular salary.

ESP   See *e-mail service provider.*

event-driven programs   Database programs that are triggered by events to produce output (usually communications), such as a birthday letter, anniversary letter, thank-you letter, and so forth.

extranet A system in which your best customers are given their own private page on your Web site which they reach through a password (PIN) or cookie. There they see messages, products, services, and prices just for them. Extranets build customer loyalty.

file fatigue Sending too many unwelcome messages to your customers produces file fatigue at which point they cease to read or be interested in your communications.

focus groups Groups of consumers asked to discuss their reactions to a proposed product or ad.

format The way data (name, address, and other fields) is organized on a disk or tape. There is no standard format. Every company has its own.

frequency How often e-mails are sent to subscribers; also how often subscribers open a message, click on a link, or buy a product. Also the number of times that a customer has made a purchase from you, such as orders per month, phone calls per month, checks and deposits per month, items per month. A part of *RFM analysis*, frequent buyers respond better than infrequent buyers.

frequency programs Programs designed to increase the frequency of purchases made by customers by rewarding them in some way. Frequency programs often work quite well.

frequent shopper cards Cards that are issued to customers by supermarkets to give them special benefits when they shop using the cards. The cards enable the supermarket to know who is buying what and when, and to reward desired shopping behavior. These cards are scanned at point-of-sale terminals when shoppers go through the checkout lines.

FSI (free-standing insert) A coupon that falls out of a newspaper or magazine.

fulfillment The process of sending goods or literature to a prospect or customer. Fast fulfillment is essential to successful database marketing.

funnel The route a prospect takes to reach the marketer's goal, such as buying a product.

Gains chart The segments in a CHAID tree diagram that show how "deep" into a file one must go to select prospects that have the results you are looking for in terms of dollar value or response rate.

geocoding A system for assigning a census code to any name and address. Once a file is geocoded, you can append census data (income, race, etc.) to the records and assign cluster codes.

geodemographics Ways in which customers can be grouped, such as by zip code, age, income, presence of children, type of home, and so one. In some cases geodemographics are useful in segmenting prospects and customers. In many cases, they don't work at all.

gift certificate   A voucher given as a present that is exchangeable for a specified cash value of goods or services from a particular place of business.

gift registry   Preferred gifts listed by customers with a retailer.

gold customers   A very small percentage of all customers is always responsible for a very large percentage of revenue and profits. They may be called Gold, Silver, Platinum. etc. The top group contains the gold customers. Special programs are developed to reward and retain these valuable customers. In some cases, it is not possible to market to them, because they are already giving you all their purchases in your category. You give them super services.

goodmail certification   A system used by some ISPs as part of their e-mail filtering services.

GUI   (graphical user interface) Software that permits users to access their data by manipulating a mouse.

half life   When you send out an offer or catalog, it may take months until the last sale has been made from the offer. On one day, half of the dollars or responses will have come in. This is your half life day. Once you know what that day is, you multiply by two, and you will know the eventual success of the offer. Half life permits rapid tests. Free software is available at www.dbmarketing.com.

hardware   Computers and disks, tape drives, printers, and other gear that are plugged into computers.

householding   A process in which all people and their accounts are grouped by the house that they live in so that they get only one letter per house in a promotion.

HTML (hypertext markup language)   Computer language used to create e-mails and Web sites.

impression   A measure of Web advertising. Every time a viewer opens or clicks on a Web site that includes your banner ad is an impression. You pay the Web site $X per thousand impressions. See also *CPM*.

inactives   Subscribers or customers who have not opened their e-mails or purchased in some time.

integrated account management   A system in which a central telemarketer supervises a customer account team including customer service and a field sales force.

interactive e-mails   E-mails filled with links to interesting content.

Internet   A modern system that links computers all over the world including e-mail and access to Web sites. The Internet has a lookup system so that you can find and view any Web site if you know it's name (URL).

ISP (Internet service provider)   a company that provides individuals and other companies access to the Internet. Examples: AOL, Yahoo.

JavaScript   A scripting language used for Web development.

KPI (key performance indicator) Quantifiable measurements, agreed to beforehand, that reflect the critical success factors of an organization. Example: e-mails opened, or clicks.

LACS (locatable address conversion system) LACS enables companies to update their mailing lists when addresses have been converted by local authorities from rural to city style address.

lead In business-to-business situations, a prospect that has expressed interest in your product and has supplied the company's name and address is considered a lead.

lead tracking The process of keeping up with what has happened to a lead (a prospect who has expressed an interest in your product or service). Lead tracking is very difficult because salespeople prefer not to report on the status of leads.

lettershop An independent company that handles all the details of printing and mailing letters. Also called a *mail shop*.

lifecycle The position of the subscriber is in relation to the marketer: opener, buyer, repeat buyer, advocate, lapsed buyer.

lifestyle A combination of age, income, housing type, and so on that defines how the subscriber lives. Each consumer has his or her own unique lifestyle, which may resemble that of millions of others. A wealthy senior citizen may have a very different lifestyle from a young unmarried hospital nurse. Each may be interested in buying different products and services. Once you understand their lifestyle, you can market differently to them.

lifetime value The net present value of the profit to be realized on the average new customer during a given number (usually three) years. Lifetime value is used to measure the success of various marketing strategies including retention, referrals, acquisition, reactivation, and the like.

lift The improvement in response from a mailing resulting from modeling, segmentation, or some other change in the mailing preparation. Divide the response from a segment by the overall response, subtract 1 and multiply by 100.

link HTML code that, when clicked on, leads to a specified URL.

list broker A service that brings list owners and prospective list renters (users) together.

list maintenance Keeping a mailing list current through correcting and updating the addresses and other data.

list rental The process of renting (for one time use, or other periods) a list of names of customers owned by some organization for an agreed-upon cost per thousand.

losers Customers who cost you more in expenses than they deliver in profits. Every company has losers, but few have figured out what to do about them.

loyalty Customer loyalty is usually measured by the retention, renewal, or repurchase rate. Loyalty can be increased or decreased by things that you do for customers. Loyalty is easier to achieve if you recruit loyal customers to begin with. Loyalty is seldom increased by discounts.

loyalty programs Programs designed to increase customer loyalty. The term also applies to points programs in which customers earn credits for purchases.

LTV See *lifetime value.*

marginal utility The extra value you get by acquiring one more unit of a product or service. Typically, marginal utility decreases with each additional unit acquired.

market rate of interest The interest rate paid for waiting to receive future sums of money.

market research A scientific method of determining what products and services people want and are willing to pay for. Market research uses surveys, focus groups, and modeling. Differs from database marketing, which is designed to build relationships with customers.

marketing database The repository in which all the data about subscribers, customers, prospects, and lapsed customers is stored.

mass marketing A highly successful method of reaching millions of people to tell them about available products and services. Uses TV, radio, print ads, and the Internet.

MCIF (marketing customer information file) A system used by banks to view all the bank services used by a household. MCIF is an essential first step for banks wishing to do database marketing.

merge-purge A software system used to merge many different input tapes or files in differing formats and put them into a common format for a mailing. Merge-purge detects duplicates.

message transfer agent A computer program or software agent that transfers e-mail messages from one computer to another.

microsite A small Web site, typically created for a specific campaign.

migration Customers can be encouraged to migrate from standard to deluxe products, from a few products to many products, from small balances to large balances. Customer migration is a valid marketing technique.

minimum test cell size The formula that determines the least number of people that can be included in a test within a larger test and still achieve valid results. The formula is: Minimum test cell size = 4 ÷ (breakeven rate).

MIS (management information systems) The central data processing staff of a company. Often called IT (information technology) or DP (data processing).

modeling Statistical procedures using multiple regressions or CHAID that are used to predict what subscribers or customers will do based on what similar people did in the past. Market research uses models to predict customer behavior based on past behavior plus demographics. Models usually require appending demographic data. They are often costly to run. In some cases they can accurately predict churn or identify customer segments that are most likely to purchase a product.

monetary In RFM analysis, the total amount that the subscriber has spent for products.

monetary analysis Part of RFM analysis. Monetary analysis involves categorizing all customers by the total amount that they have purchased (per month, year, etc.) and sorting all customers by that amount. The resulting file is divided into quintiles. The top quintile (highest spenders) usually has a higher response rate than lower quiintiles.

MTA (message transfer agent) Software that transfers e-mail messages from one computer to another. An MTA is responsible for the core tasks involved with delivering of e-mail, including: queuing, scheduling, connection management, data transfer, processing of deferrals, bounce generation, and tracking of delivery status.

multibuyer A person who crops up on two or more independent rented lists. Multibuyers usually respond better to a direct offer than other buyers do.

multichannel customer A subscriber who has bought from more than one channel.

multiple regression A statistical technique that predicts values of one variable on the basis of two or more other variables.

NCDM (National Center for Database Marketing) A convention held twice a year by the Direct Marketing Association.

NCOALINK (National Change of Address) A U.S. Postal Service system under which about 20 service bureaus nationwide have exclusive use of the change of address forms filed by persons or businesses that are moving. These forms are keypunched, and can be used by the service bureau to update your file of prospects or customers to obtain their correct current address. A worthwhile service for database marketers.

negative option A system in which products or services come automatically, charged to a credit card, unless the customer specifically requests that it be stopped.

net names The actual names used in a mailing, after removing the duplicates and matches to your customer list. In some cases, you can rent names on a net-name basis.

net present value (NPV) The present value of money to be received in the future. It is equal to the future money divided by the discount rate.

next-best product (NBP) The results of an analysis of many customer purchase behaviors plus demographics that selects for each customer the next-best cross-sell product for each customer based on profit to the company, needs of the customer, likelihood of sale, cost of marketing, and so on. The NBP is put into each customer record on the database.

NIACC (net income after capital charges) A banking term used in determining customer profitability.

nixies A U.S. Postal Service that provides footnotes as to why an address match could not be found. This service is very useful in correcting bad addresses.

NPV See *net present value.*

Nth A system in which a small test group is selected from a large database. Using an Nth, the test group is an exact statistical replica of the larger database. To get an Nth, divide the desired size of the test group into the size of the database. For example, if there are 40,000 in a test group and 400,000 in the database, the result is 10. An Nth would be the result from putting every tenth record into the test group.

one-click ordering A technique used by Amazon that permits subscribers to buy any product with only one click.

one-to-one marketing See *1:1 marketing.*

open rate The percentage of delivered e-mails that were opened by the recipients.

operational database The opposite of a marketing database. The billing database that keeps track of who bought what.

opt-in e-mail address An e-mail address of a subscriber who has given permission to be sent promotional e-mails.

outlier In modeling, someone who have bought much more or much less than the average and who should not be used in the model.

outsource The process of hiring expert companies and consultants to perform marketing functions such as building databases, telesales, fulfillment, and market research. Outsourcing is usually more cost-effective and efficient than using in-house staff.

overlaid data For any consumer or business-to-business file, it is possible to find data providers who will overlay data to enrich your knowledge of your customers or prospects. Overlaid data can include SIC codes, income, age, presence of children, and so on. Only use overlaid data if it improves your marketing success.

package The envelope, container, or look of an outgoing direct mail piece.

packaged goods Products sold in retail stores. Database marketing seldom works with packaged goods because you cannot tell who is buying your products, and the margin on each sale is too small to finance the relationship building involved.

packet   Electronic forms that transfer data from one computer to another.

PDF (portable document format)   An Adobe PostScript standard file format that preserves the graphic look of a document.

penetration   Your customers as a percentage of the universe that defines your customers' type of household or business. "We had a penetration ratio in that zip code of 8 percent."

permission-based e-mail address   An opt-in e-mail address.

personalization   The process of including personal references in an outgoing mail piece, such as, "Thank you for your order of Feb. 23 for six boxes of hard candy, Mrs. Williams." With a database, personalization can be achieved very inexpensively. The lift is usually enough to pay the extra cost.

personalized e-mail   E-mail that uses the recipient's name or other personal data in the text.

phishing   Illegal attempts to secure information from Internet users via false premises.

points programs   A method of rewarding customers for their purchases and thereby helping them to build up equity in the relationship. Airline miles programs are the most successful points programs. There are other similar successful programs in both consumer and business-to-business marketing.

POS system (point of sale system)   A system in which goods are bar-coded and scanned at the time of checkout. In some cases, consumers have frequent shopper cards which can be scanned at the same time so that the retailer can learn what each customer is buying. POS systems are a major breakthrough in database marketing in retail situations.

postal presort   Sorting outgoing letters in a special way to take advantage of postal discounts.

predictive model   An analytical technique that ranks all customers or prospects by their likelihood to do something (respond, buy, cancel service, etc.). It is useful in acquisition and in reducing churn.

preference form   A form that subscribers fill out to tell the company what they would like in terms of products, frequency, and so on.

premiums   What you give customers in lieu of discounts. Premiums are better than discounts because they do not appear to reduce your price point or margin. They build loyalty, whereas discounts do not.

present discounted value (PDV)   A financial process for calculating the present value of an amount of money to be received or paid in the future. The formula is $PDV = V \div (1 + i)^n$ where V = future value, i = market rate of interest, n = time in years.

president's club A marketing technique in which certain of the best customers are designated as being in the President's club. They receive benefits not available to other customers. It helps to keep them for a lifetime.

preview pane A function in Outlook that allows users to see a part of an e-mail before they open it. Also called *reading pane*.

prizm cluster A segment of U.S. consumers created by Nielsen using catch names like Pools and Patios or Shotguns and Pickups.

profiling A method of understanding large groups of customers by segmenting them into groups with similar lifestyles and purchasing habits.

profitability Banks have developed a system using their MCIF in which the profitability of each household is measured every month. Customers are segmented into profitability groups. The profitability of a household is determined by adding all revenue received during the month and subtracting all costs and interest paid.

program buyers Types of business-to-business buyers for whom their purchasing manual or buying schedule is more important than price or marketing messages. Many government agencies are program buyers.

proof of permission Proof that you have adhered to the CAN-SPAM Act in acquiring subscribers' permission to send them e-mails.

query A question designed to retrieve information from a database. The result can be a count, a cross tab, or a report. See *ad hoc query*.

quintiles A division of customers into five equal groups based on spending or response. Quintiles are more useful for RFM than deciles, which are used in marketing research.

random select Selecting subscribers for an e-mail by an arbitrary method.

reactivation A program that encourages lapsed customers or subscribers to start buying again.

recency The most powerful single factor affecting customer repurchases. The customer most likely to buy from you again is the customer who bought from you most recently. A basic factor in RFM analysis.

reference accounts A business account that may not be profitable in itself but that may bring in a lot of other business because the account is prestigious or well known.

referral programs Programs designed to foster referrals by rewarding those who refer people who become customers. Can be more cost-effective than almost any other database marketing program.

referrals A referral is a customer who came to you as a result of the recommendation of another existing customer. Referred customers have a higher retention rate and spending rate then the average newly acquired customers.

For this reason, it is vital that you keep track of both referred people and those who refer them in your database.

reformatting Changing the format of a rented list to a new record format that matches a desired arrangement. This is done in traditional merge-purge. It is not a complicated process.

regression analysis A statistical method used in modeling. Regression analysis includes any techniques for modeling and analyzing several variables, when the focus is on the relationship between a dependent variable and one or more independent variables. Using a regression, the influence of various variable factors is assigned a weight in their ability to predict an outcome, such as a purchase or a response.

relational database A relational database is what is needed for database marketing. Such a database is kept on disk and consists of related files (name and address, orders) that are related to each other by ID numbers and accessed by indexes.

relationship buyers People who want to do business with you because they like your products, your employees, or your brand. The opposite is *transaction buyers* who are interested only in price.

relationship marketing The process of building a relationship with customers that results in the customers becoming more loyal, buying more, and remaining customers. Another word for *database marketing*.

relevance The process of creating e-mails that subscribers want to open, read, and act on. You find such e-mails that you find profitable. Relevant e-mails make subscribers happy. They open them and read them.

renewal rate The percentage of current subscribers or customers who sign up for service when their current contract expires.

repurchase rate The percentage of current customers who will buy your brand again when they make their next purchase in your category. For U.S. automobiles, the satisfaction rate is about 90 percent. The repurchase rate is about 35 percent.

response The people who respond to your ads or direct marketing appeals. On the Internet, a response is someone who has clicked on your banner ad.

response device A form, post card or envelope that is returned to a sender for the purpose of completing a donation or purchase. A response device is important because it always contains the prospect number and a source code that identifies the offer, package, list, segment, and the like.

response rate The percentage of people who received your direct marketing offer who responded to it with a further inquiry or a sale. On the Internet, it is the percentage of impressions that resulted in a response.

retention rate   The percentage of customers who made a purchase from you last year and who have made a purchase from you this year. This is the most important single number in a customer lifetime value table.

return on investment (ROI)   A key measure of the success of any direct marketing action. The dollars in profit gained from each dollar invested.

rewards   Something that you give customers in addition to the product or service to thank them for their patronage. Rewards can be premiums or points or status symbols. An important database marketing tool.

RFM (recency, frequency, and monetary) analysis   An old, powerful, and highly predictive way of determining who will respond and buy. A method of coding existing customers. Used to predict response, average order size, and other factors.

RFP (request for proposals)   a request for proposal is issued at an early stage in a procurement process, where an invitation is presented for suppliers, often through a bidding process, to submit a business proposal on a specific commodity or service. The RFP process brings structure to the procurement decision and is meant to allow the risks and benefits to be identified clearly upfront.

risk revenue matrix   A simple matrix with the likelihood of churn on one axis and lifetime value or revenue on the other. The matrix is used to focus attention on those customers who have the highest lifetime value and the highest likelihood of leaving. You save your retention program dollars by concentrating on these rather than on all customers.

ROI   See *return on investment.*

rollout   After a successful test in direct marketing, you expose a much larger group to your offer. This called a rollout.

RON (run of network)   An Internet advertising term. Advertisers who place a RON ad with a large number of sites simultaneously get instant feedback as to which sites are giving them the best response. RON is the cheapest form of Internet advertising and may be the best.

router   A computer on the Internet that sends packets to their destinations.

RSS (really simple syndication)   A Web feed used to send subscribers frequently updated content.

saturated market   A situation in which everyone has the product, and the market is essentially a replacement market. For example, tires, batteries, PCs, and televisions.

search engine marketing   Using meta-tag words or pay-per-click search engines such as Google bring customers to your website.

seeds   People (often your employees) to whom you send all e-mails so that you will know how they are received.

segments Groups of customers whom you have identified as having similar purchase patterns. Creating and using segments is essential to successful database marketing.

sender field The place in an e-mail where the sender's name and address appear.

shopping cart Online purchase system.

SIC code or NAICS Coding system designed by the U.S. Department of Commerce for classifying the products and services produced by companies. The Department of Commerce has a list of all the businesses in America. It has assigned eight digit codes to each business. Using these codes, or just the first three numbers it is possible to classify every type of business such as a restaurant, law firm, or a plastics manufacturer.

SKU (stock-keeping unit) A warehouse term for the products that a company produces. Each different product has its own SKU number.

source codes Codes of letters or numbers used to identify a particular offer on a particular date. The codes are stored in the customer's database record so you have a promotion history.

spam E-mail sent to Internet users who didn't ask for or want the e-mails. Spam is illegal in the United States and most countries, but it is hard to prosecute. More than 80 percent of all e-mails are spam.

spending rate The amount that a customer spends with you in a month or a year.

SQL (Structured Query Language) A query language used with the IBM software DB2. Often pronounced "sequal."

status levels Levels in a loyalty program.

straddle pricing A retail pricing method in which prices for occasional shoppers are set higher than the competition's prices, whereas prices for regular customers are set lower than the prices of the competition.

strategy development Marketing strategy is a process that can allow an organization to concentrate its limited resources on the greatest opportunities to increase sales and achieve a sustainable competitive advantage Database marketing is successful only if it is accompanied by a winning marketing strategy. No one system works universally. Strategies are always being upset by the market competition.

subject line The place in an e-mail where the sender puts the subject of the e-mail.

suppression files Using names on one file (a customer file) to suppress or drop names from another tape (a prospect file). Examples: the DNC (do not call) file, the DMA do not mail file, or a deceased or prison file.

surrogate measurements   Estimating one outcome which is difficult to measure by measuring another outcome that is easier to measure. In marketing, the success of an offer is often measured indirectly by awareness, focus groups, Neilson ratings, and so on. In direct marketing and Internet marketing, success is measured directly by responses and sales.

sweepstakes   An offer promising a randomly drawn prize to all respondents, regardless of whether they buy your product or not. Those who do not buy, but still respond to the sweepstakes may be valuable names to rent out or for other offers. In comparison to buyers, sweepstakes respondents are generally much less valuable.

targeting   The system in which a specific group of prospects is selected for marketing based on assumptions about their interest in the product or ability to purchase.

teaser rates   Introductory, very low, credit card interest rates that are then raised to normal levels after the introductory period of a few months has passed.

telesales   Salespeople who talk on the telephone to prospects and customers. In business-to-business transactions, telesales is preferred by many customers over sales force visits. In consumer situations, outbound telesales is often resented. Inbound telesales (where customers call a toll free number) is preferred.

ten-day rule   If a subscriber makes a purchase within 10 days of receiving a promotional e-mail, you can credit the e-mail with the sale.

test groups   Groups of customers selected by an Nth who are made asked to test the validity of an offer. If the response is good, the marketer will go to a rollout.

testimonials   Consumer product reviews that can be read by others.

text chat   A box on an e-mail where viewers can converse with an agent live about the purchase process.

text e-mail   E-mails that have no HTML coding.

third-class mail   Over 85 percent of all mail carrying advertising or promotion is sent by third class (bulk rate). It is much less costly than first class. It usually requires postal presort. If it is not delivered for some reason (bad address, person no longer there) this mail is thrown into the trash by the U.S. Postal Service, and the sender will not know it.

touches   A customer contact through personal visit, phone, letter, e-mail, or fax. Customers like to hear from their suppliers. Touches should be planned in advance.

trade deficit   The difference between what we sell to foreigners and what they buy from us in a year. A high trade deficit is not necessarily bad for U.S. consumers or businesses.

transaction buyers   Customers who are only interested in price, not quality or service. They have no loyalty and will leave you for a better offer at any time. It is hard to make money from transaction buyers.

transactional e-mail   E-mail related to a purchase, such as thanking the subscriber for a purchase.

triggered e-mail   An e-mail based on something that has happened to the receiver, such as a birthday, anniversary, and the like.

two-step offer   A promotion system in which you get responders to call in for a brochure, catalog, or salesperson's visit, which then makes the sale.

undeliver   An e-mail subscriber whose e-mail didn't get delivered for some reason.

unsubscriber   A subscriber who has requested to no longer receive your e-mails.

up-selling   Prompting customers to buy upgraded products when they had intended to buy something of lower cost.

update   To modify a database record to insert new information into it, or to delete it. Updating is done either in batch mode (fast and cheap) or online (slow and costly). Usually done once a month. Some companies can do this several times a day.

URL (uniform resource locator)   The Web address of a picture or text.

validation group   In modeling you create two groups of customers. You develop an algorithm that predicts the response of one group to certain stimulae. To test your algorithm, you apply it to the validation group. If it is a good algorithm it will correctly pick the actual responders in the validation group.

viral marketing   Marketing that encourages subscribers to forward e-mails to their friends.

virtual distributors   Distributors that have warehouses and stock a limited number of products. Virtual distributors have a Web site and may have no warehouse at all. They arrange shipment to customers directly from the manufacturers.

Web advertising   Banner ads on Web sites have become a universally successful method of reaching new customers. A good response rate to a Web ad is usually less than 1 percent. Web advertising is paid for by CPM (cost per thousand impressions).

Web analytics   The study of Web site visitor behavior, including Web traffic, e-mail opens, clicks, and conversions.

Web beacon   An object embedded in an e-mail, invisible to the user, that allows the marketer to see if the recipient has viewed the e-mail.

Web site   A set of interconnected webpages, usually including a homepage, generally located on the same server, and prepared and maintained as a collection of information by a person, group, or organization. Every company in the world today has its own Web site on the Internet, advertising its products and services. An increasing percentage of businesses, particularly business-to-business commerce takes place through Web sites. Best customers are given personal pages on company Web sites.

weight   In a model, the significance of a variable in the outcome. A high weight means that the variable affects the outcome in a strong way.

welcome e-mail   The e-mail sent to subscribers after they have signed up to receive your e-mails.

white mail   Mail received from a buyer or donor who has not included the response device, so you cannot determine the source code of the offer which promoted the purchase or gift.

white-listing   The process in which subscribers add your sending address to their address book.

widget   Small pieces of software that can be embedded in a Web site or placed on a user's computer.

World Wide Web (www)   Another name for the Internet. Company Web sites names (URLs) usually begin with www.

Index

About the Author

 **Arthur Middleton Hughes** has been work-ing in direct, database marketing service bureaus and ESPs since 1978. He began as a programmer, writing direct mail and data-base conversion software for such clients as Compaq, Nestle, and Western Union. In 1991 he wrote the first of nine books on data-base and e-mail marketing. From 1993 to 2000, as vice president of The Database Marketing Institute, he and Paul Wang gave 28 two-day seminars in Database Marketing to 1,400 database marketing professionals. Since 2000, Arthur has developed LTV, RFM, Subscriber Acquisition and marketing strategies for such companies as BMW, American Airlines, British Airways, Dell, and Universal Music while working for SourceLink, DoubleClick, KnowledgeBase Marketing and e-Dialog.

Arthur has been a key speaker in marketing conferences in the U.S., Canada, U.K., Japan, Taiwan, Australia, New Zealand, Brazil, Venezuela, Columbia, Malaysia, Thailand, Portugal, and Greece. His Web sites are www.dbmarketing.com and www.AdamSmithToday.com.

Arthur lives with his wife Helena in Fort Lauderdale, FL.